# ELIZABETH I
# AND HER PARLIAMENTS
## 1559-1581

*By the same author*

QUEEN ELIZABETH I
THE AGE OF CATHERINE DE MEDICI
THE ELIZABETHAN
HOUSE OF COMMONS

ELIZABETH I

From the Mildmay Charter,
Emmanuel College, Cambridge

# ELIZABETH I
## AND HER PARLIAMENTS
### 1559-1581

by

## J. E. NEALE

*Astor Professor of English History
in the University of London*

## ST. MARTIN'S PRESS · NEW YORK

1958

PRINTED IN THE UNITED STATES OF AMERICA

# CONTENTS

7

# CONTENTS

## PART FIVE

# THE PARLIAMENT OF 1572

## PART SIX

# THE PARLIAMENT OF 1576

## PART SEVEN

# THE PARLIAMENT OF 1581

# ILLUSTRATIONS

# PREFACE

THIS volume is the first of two in which I hope to fulfil the promise made in my *Elizabethan House of Commons* to write a parliamentary history of Elizabeth I's reign. Though my approach to the subject is implicit in the title, some explanation will not be amiss. I have focused the narrative on the relations between the Crown and Parliament: partly because the story would have been formless and unreadable if I had attempted to discuss all the business that came before Parliament; and partly because my purpose is to reveal the significance of the Elizabethan period in the constitutional evolution of England, and, more specifically, to banish the old illusion that early-Stuart Parliaments had few roots in the sixteenth century. While this central intention has usually determined the themes selected in each Parliament, I have also had in mind the need to recreate the personalities and the daily life of the Elizabethan House of Commons, and have written on the assumption that nothing human is outside our interest, provided it has relevance.

The leisurely scale of the work must find its justification in the inherent interest of the story; and of that I am doubtless a prejudiced judge. But here, again, I have had certain considerations in mind. The narrative is constructed very largely from manuscript sources, many of which have not been printed or even used by historians, and some of which — as, for example, the new diaries of 1572 — are of superlative interest. No evidence exists on which to construct a similar story for an earlier period; and it has therefore seemed to me an excusable ambition, if not a paramount duty, to write worthily of England's Parliament, when first this can be done.

I have treated the Queen's own speeches as sacrosanct, and have quoted them in full: a concession made to no one else. They are few, but are involved and difficult. They may halt the reader and send him to *The Oxford English Dictionary*, or he may feel inclined to skip them. But they are curiosities of history, and in their own way are as distinctive, as personal, and as inimitable as Mr. Winston Churchill's great speeches in our own time. I hope that my judgment on this point, where I have deliberately sacrificed lucidity, will not be pronounced wrong.

In the Preface to my previous book I tried to indicate the rich help and service I have received from very many persons during a lifetime of historical research. To renew my thanks in general does not mean that I forget individual debts. I hope that owners of manuscripts will see some reward for their invariable courtesy to me in the contribution their treasures have made to the story. To my research students, now a goodly company in this and other countries — America in particular — my thanks blend with pride in their work. As an act of pious memory, I would mention the late Edna Bibby of Manchester. She was a gifted researcher, and, had not illness incapacitated her, she would have given us the history of the Puritan Classical Movement we so much need. Her father generously handed over to me her papers, and I have drawn on some of them in this volume.

I owe a special debt to Miss Helen Miller, who has been assisting me in editing the parliamentary diaries and other material for Elizabeth's reign. Her work, concurrent with my writing of this volume, has been invaluable. And here I may appropriately explain to scholars that the rarity of references in my footnotes to Simonds D'Ewes's *Journals* is owing to the fact that I have drawn my information from the original manuscripts which lie behind that seventeenth-century collection of parliamentary documents. I am also indebted to my colleague and former student, Mr. J. Hurstfield, for the care with which he read this book in typescript, and to Mr. H. S. Bennett of Emmanuel College, Cambridge, and Mr. D. T. Piper of the National Portrait Gallery for their assistance over the illustrations. My debt to my wife remains, as always, beyond evaluation. In a subordinate way — and Jonathan Cape will not mind the subordination — so does my debt to a publisher who has become my very good friend.

Had dedication been a habit of mine, I should have been prompted to offer this volume to my College, which released me from most of my duties last session in order that I might be free from the multifarious distractions of academic life. I hope that I have properly discharged that obligation; but the debt I owe to a community which has given me so many years of deep happiness in its service can never be discharged. How long it will take to complete my narrative, now that I am back in harness, I would not like to prophesy.

J. E. NEALE

University College,
London

# INTRODUCTION

AT the close of the fifteenth century, when the Venetian ambassador to England wrote a descriptive account of this country, he said nothing about Parliament. His silence may not be of great significance, but certainly no foreign visitor, half a century later, setting out to discourse on how England was ruled and governed, would have been guilty of such an omission.[1]

At that time the general tendency on the continent was for representative assemblies to decay. It was the age of the New Monarchy, and of the Reception of the Roman Civil Law, with its central doctrine that what pleased the Prince had the force of law. But in England the Common Law, organized and taught in those unique institutions, the Inns of Court, stood as a bastion which not even a Tudor monarch had either the need or the power to destroy. The Common Law being secure, so necessarily was Parliament, for the inevitable amendments and extensions of this law — other than in judicial interpretations — could only be effected by statute. Thus the need for parliamentary legislation made our representative assembly an indestructible organ of the constitution. So did taxation. While the Crown was supposed to live of its own — that is to say, to pay its ordinary expenditure from its own ordinary and permanent revenues — it could call on the country for additional money, by way of taxes, to meet extraordinary burdens; and by an established principle of the constitution, which there was little serious risk of the monarch being able to reverse, taxation had to be granted by the attorneys or representatives of the community in Parliament.

Legislation and taxation: these were the two functions which guaranteed that the English Parliament would survive when the trend of the age was hostile. But in those days neither was a continuous process. They called for only occasional meetings. Moreover, Parliament's judicial function as the High Court of the Realm, which in the Middle Ages had demanded annual or even more frequent assemblies, had atrophied and was no

[1] *Italian Relation*, ed. C. A. Sneyd (Camden Soc.).

15

longer a reason for calling it. As for what we might term its political role, relating to policy and administration — a role which, along with the constant need for legislation and taxation, makes the Parliament of today a normal part of our constitutional machinery — there was as yet no theoretical or assured scope for that. In the sixteenth century the system of government was personal monarchy. Questions of policy and the direction of the administration were the Crown's preserve, entrenched in its prerogative. A meeting of Parliament might offer an occasion for the expression of grievances, but it was not the sole or even the normal channel of complaint. Politically speaking, Parliament was little more than a convenient safety-valve.

At the opening of the sixteenth century Parliament was essentially a legislative and taxing body, its meetings intermittent. Even at the end of the century the same description might be formally applied to it; but in the meanwhile it had become a political force with which the Crown and government had to reckon. The change was brought about by developments in the power, position, and prestige of the House of Commons. The century started with Parliament a unitary institution, truly bi-cameral only in prospect.[1] It had merely one operative or executive centre: that was in the Lords. The Commons did not control their own discipline, or defend their own privileges. They could not arrest or imprison anyone. Their Speaker could issue no warrant. Members were supposed, in an uncertain sort of way, to enjoy free speech; but this had not yet been converted into a formal privilege, craved by the Speaker at the opening of each Parliament.

The transformation began in the reign of Henry VIII. In 1515 an Act of Parliament, which we may assume to have originated with the government, gave Speaker and Commons control over the attendance of Members, who thereafter had to obtain a licence from them if they wanted to leave before the close of the session. Of little contemporary significance, its object was obviously to secure better attendance, not to diminish the Crown's control of discipline. But it meant that

---

[1] A. F. POLLARD, *Evolution of Parliament*, p. 117. For the argument of these pages, and appropriate references, see my essay, 'The Commons' Privilege of Free Speech in Parliament', *Tudor Studies*, ed. R. W. Seton-Watson, pp. 257 seqq.

for the first time the House was exercising independent executive authority. From such humble beginnings came greater things.

By 1543 the Commons were ready for a new step forward, this time on their own initiative. Instead of turning, as in the past, to the King or Chancellor or Lords for defence of their privilege of freedom from arrest, they decided to enforce it on their own authority. This was in the famous Ferrers' case — the first precedent of its kind known either to sixteenth-century or later commentators — when the House sent its Serjeant-at-Arms to release an imprisoned Member. He returned with a broken mace and without the prisoner: the result one might expect from a novel assertion of power. Thereupon the Commons rose as a body and went up to the Lords. Fortified by the sympathy of their superiors, they renewed their action, after rejecting, with sound instinct, the offer of the Lord Chancellor to help. At their second attempt they were successful; and the unlucky officials who had previously refused to release Ferrers were themselves imprisoned by order of the House. In thus arrogating to themselves a right to imprison offenders, they had successfully brought off a double usurpation of power. Ferrers happened to be a servant of the King. When Henry VIII heard of the incident he assembled a parliamentary audience and delivered himself of an eloquent speech, wholeheartedly and learnedly supporting the Commons; but had this royal 'architect of Parliament' been able to see into the future, he might well have had misgivings about the precedent he was condoning.[1]

It was in this reign, also, that the formal privilege of freedom of speech appeared. We can be reasonably certain that no medieval Speaker asked for such a privilege, and, so far as we know, Sir Thomas More was the first to do so, in 1523. His was the type of mind, intelligent, imaginative, and courageous, to conceive the idea of turning a dangerously vague prescriptive right into a formal concession.

In these days we hardly need reminding that freedom is a subjective notion, varying in content with person, country, and century. From the point of view of some parliamentarians

---

[1] Hall's Chronicle, in Ed. Hall, *Henry VIII*, ed. C. Whibley, ii. 315; HOLINSHED'S *Chronicle* (1587), iii. 955-6; PRYNNE, *Parliamentary Writs*, iv. 779, 851 seqq.

barely fifty years later, the freedom for which More asked was
a limited one. His petition, set in a lengthy argument, was as
follows: 'It may therefore like your most abundant Grace . . .
to give to all your Commons here assembled your most gracious
licence and pardon freely, without doubt of your dreadful displeasure, every man to discharge his conscience, and boldly in
everything incident among [us] to declare his advice; and
whatsoever happen any man to say, [that] it may like your
noble Majesty, of your inestimable goodness, to take all in good
part, interpreting every man's words, how uncunningly soever
they be couched, to proceed yet of good zeal towards the profit
of your realm and honour of your royal person.'[1]
    As we embark on our study of Elizabethan parliamentary
history, it behoves us to be clear about More's meaning. He
was asking, in effect, two things: that Members should be free
to oppose any bill that was before the House; and that a favourable construction should be placed on what they said. There
can be little doubt that he had in mind what we should describe
as government bills, opposition to which must have put Members in jeopardy of the King's displeasure. These bills were a
relatively recent development. They were a device of great
significance in the modernization of the institution: quite unknown, for example, to the French Estates General, which
remained medieval, and became moribund in consequence.
It was the emergence of a government legislative programme
at meetings of Parliament that created the need for a formal
privilege of free speech, and explains its appearance at this
time.
    On the negative side, More's description did not suggest that
freedom extended to the introduction, by those we would call
private Members, of a bill or motion on any subject. In other
words, it did not include a right of initiative: a matter with
which we shall be very much concerned in the Elizabethan
period. The agenda of the House of Commons was not involved
in the privilege. Nor did More fail to recognize, by implication,
that there was such a thing as licentious speech, and that the
King might punish Members who gave offence. There was —
there could be — no hint that the House of Commons had any
jurisdiction at all in this disciplinary matter.

¹ Roper's *Life of More*, ed. E. V. Hitchcock (E.E.T.S.), p. 16.

Though our evidence records only two subsequent claims for the privilege before the accession of Queen Elizabeth, all or most of More's successors probably followed his example. However, instead of the lengthy expository passage in which this pioneer necessarily placed his initial request, repetition and the formalizing effect of time reduced it to a brief demand for freedom of speech. In this way it lost the definition given it in 1523, and at the accession of Queen Elizabeth there was merely the vague phrase 'freedom of speech', into which the pioneers of a new generation could read — as the Queen caustically said — whatever seemed meetest 'to their idle brains'.

Thus, between 1515 and 1558 the House of Commons had acquired the right — not the exclusive right — to control the attendance of its Members; it had created for itself the right to enforce its privilege of freedom from arrest; it had invented a power to imprison offenders against its privileges and its dignity; it had converted an uncertain prescriptive enjoyment of free speech into a formal privilege possessing revolutionary possibilities; it had even established precedents for punishing licentious speech by Members, thus covertly encroaching on the jurisdiction of the Crown, though on each occasion it took care to recognize that discipline in such matters belonged to the Sovereign. In brief, it had arrogated to itself the functions of a court. Elizabethans took to referring to it as such, and at length the greatest lawyer of that age, Sir Edward Coke, set the seal of his formidable authority on the term. Arthur Hall, an irascible Elizabethan M.P., whose story will be told in due course, scornfully alluded to the Lower House as a new person in the Trinity. He was a better historian than he or his fellows realized. In place of the simple medieval conception of a High Court of Parliament, these men were formulating a mystical creed, which might be expressed as follows: The House of Lords is a court; the House of Commons is a court; and yet there are not two courts but one court, the High Court of Parliament.

We have been moving too much at the rarefied heights of constitutional theory. Let us come to earth, for it is there, among the Members of Parliament, that we must tarry if we are to know the true value of theory. If we ask how far the Commons in Henry VIII's reign were allowed to enjoy the degree of free speech for which Sir Thomas More asked, the answer cannot be as clear as might be wished. In the Parliament of 1523, when More made his claim, Cardinal Wolsey was rather truculent. The Commons were obstinate. But this was over a very heavy tax demand, when, if ever, the House could be difficult. When the next Parliament met in 1529 the atmosphere changed. This was the long Reformation Parliament, which lasted till 1536 and held eight sessions: an unprecedented duration for a single Parliament. It must have taught Members, as nothing else could, to work together, and one imagines that the development of parliamentary tradition went on apace. Moreover, the King needed the Lower House as the spearpoint of his attack on the Church. Bishops and abbots being entrenched in the House of Lords, he went into partnership with the Commons. The great government bills were introduced there: a significant departure in procedure, which hastened the day of parity between the two Houses.

Henry VIII wooed the Commons and built up their strength. Incidents reveal him exercising extraordinary restraint for so masterful a ruler. When a conservative Member, Sir George Throckmorton, opposed one of the main anti-papal bills, the King sent for him and had a heart-to-heart talk: if an occasion when one heart was surely palpitating can be described as such. Henry, we are told, loved to 'confound them all with his learning'; and though argument must have been one-sided in an age familiar with the saying that the wrath of the Prince is death, it seems as if free speech was permitted. However, the story of Thomas Broke, a representative of Calais, whose religious affinities were at the opposite extreme to those of Throckmorton, suggests that we should be cautious. In 1539 he spoke in the Commons against the sacrament, and was answered by a royal official and others, who, as a correspondent wrote, 'taunted him so that I think he will have little mind to reason the matter again'. Stephen Gardiner, discussing the incident, declared that, 'being a burgess', Broke 'might well declare his mind and opinion'. All the same, he was called to account for his action. 'Before his departure out of the city,' Gardiner added, 'he shall be otherwise after a more due and straight fashion examined than he have been yet . . . , as well touching his said motion as of such as should cause him to move the same.' Broke's views were heretical. His speech might therefore be regarded as licentious and so liable to disciplinary action.[1]

The Imperial ambassador had a poor opinion of the freedom permitted in Parliament: 'No man there', he wrote, 'dare open his mouth against the will of the King and Council.' It was a biased and erroneous statement. On the other hand, Gardiner was perhaps more facetious than sound when, in 1547, apologizing for the length of a letter, he remarked, 'I am like one of the Commons' House that, when I am in my tale, think I should have liberty to make an end'. Perhaps it would be wiser to reflect on Sir George Throckmorton's opinion that 'the Common House was much advertised by my Lord Privy Seal [Thomas Cromwell], and that few men there would displease him'. Formal tolerance there may have been, but also informal coercion; and nuisances were not suffered lightly. These were early days for free speech.[2]

However, the Reformation forced people to think critically on issues of transcendent importance to their consciences. In such a situation individuals, though they might be few, were bound to probe the limits of freedom of speech. This tendency, coupled with the political necessity for Henry VIII to carry with him the popular will as expressed in Parliament — even, indeed, to give the impression of following it — inevitably added to the stature of the Lower House of Parliament. Moreover, it was about this time that there began the great sixteenth-century invasion of parliamentary borough-seats by the country gentry, which in the course of the next half-century was to transform the House of Commons into an assembly mainly of gentlemen, most of whom were there because they ardently desired to be: men of character, education, and wealth, who, given the occasion, were likely to display independence of mind and to exploit the opportunities opened by Henry VIII's indulgent policy.

Though brief, Mary Tudor's reign marked a stage in this apprenticeship to future greatness. With a woman ruler there would in any case have been a subtle psychological change in

---

[1] *Tudor Studies*, pp. 269-70 and references; *L. & P. Hen. VIII*, xiv (i). 1108.
[2] FOXE, *Acts & Monuments*, ed. Pratt & Stoughton, vi. 33; S.P. Hen. VIII, cxxv. fol. 246.

the nature of authority. Parliament might pass an act to declare that 'the regal power of this realm is in the Queen's Majesty as fully and absolutely as ever it was in any of her most noble progenitors, kings of this realm'.[1] Though a legal fact, it remained an anomaly. To men like John Knox it was something worse, being repugnant to nature and contumely to God. How could a Queen hope to inspire the same awe as a King? It was a situation to release the critical, combative instincts of sixteenth-century mankind. To make matters worse, the Queen's policy was unpopular with many of the politically articulate gentry. It was especially unpopular in the city of London: a fact of vital importance, for here public opinion was moulded during the gathering of litigants and sightseers from the provinces four times a year, during the legal terms. If Mary's political sense had been stronger than her religious fervour, if she had been content to restore the Church to its state at the end of her father's reign, and if she had approached the offer of marriage with Philip of Spain dispassionately instead of emotionally, her reign, it is true, would still have been uneasy, but the atmosphere would have been very different.

Her first Parliament revealed how independent Members of the Lower House could now be. A fortnight after its start the Imperial ambassador reported that things were not going well. There was difficulty about religion. The owners of monastic and other Church property 'would rather get themselves massacred than let go'; and a majority were adamant about Papal authority, which, he added in a later dispatch, 'the English loathe more than ever'. According to the French ambassador, there was 'marvellous dispute' over the main government measure repealing the Church legislation of Edward VI's reign, and a number of the Commons — our two estimates varying from one-quarter to one-third of those present — had the courage to vote against it. When the Speaker made the inevitable request to the Queen to marry, he urged her to choose an Englishman; which she regarded as a piece of unprecedented impertinence and told him and his colleagues so.[2]

In the next two Parliaments the Commons seem to have been

---

[1] Title of 1 Mary, st. 3, c. 1.

[2] *Spanish Cal. 1553*, pp. 305, 323, 349, 363 seqq.; *Ambassades de Noailles*, ed. Vertot (1763), ii. 227, 247, 256, 269-70.

more pliable. No doubt, defeat of Wyatt's rebellion and the flight of the more ardent Protestants into exile abroad temporarily stilled or diminished the critical tone so evident in 1553. The Queen's marriage with Philip was peacefully effected, and events marched steadily to reconciliation with Rome, though at no time did the Lords and Commons waver in defence of their monastic properties. Then came a change. By the time Mary's fourth parliament met in the autumn of 1555 the religious persecution was running strong; hope for the continuity of the régime had received a mortal wound in the Queen's false pregnancy; discontent was astir again.

In the elections to her third Parliament the Queen had had recourse to circular letters addressed to sheriffs and others, in the hope of securing a Catholic assembly and preventing the intrusion of the gentry into borough seats, obviously because too many critics were finding their way into Parliament. In 1555, under instructions from King Philip, similar steps were taken to procure a tractable assembly. They failed miserably. The Venetian ambassador reported: 'Whether by accident or from design' — 'a thing not seen for many years in any Parliament' — the House of Commons 'is quite full of gentry and nobility, for the most part suspected in the matter of religion, and therefore more daring and licentious than former Houses, which consisted of burgesses and plebeians'. While we must wait for a biographical study of these Parliaments to reduce the statement to its justifiable proportions, the bare events make it clear that a majority of the House of Commons was ready to join in open opposition to the government.[1]

There was, indeed, a degree of organization about the parliamentary opposition in 1555, which, though in some ways a flash in the pan, marks a significant stage in the evolution of the House of Commons. Perhaps already conversations had been going on which in the spring of 1556 were to result in what is known as the Dudley conspiracy, involving possibly a dozen M.P.s. They included Sir Anthony Kingston, son of Henry VIII's Comptroller of the Royal Household: a Protestant and a west-country gentleman of wealth, renown, and many followers. In one of the confessions that followed the Conspiracy we are told of seven M.P.s — the majority representing

<hr />

[1] My *Elizabethan House of Commons*, pp. 286-8; *Venetian Cal.* VI. i. 227, 251.

west-country boroughs — who, 'with such other young heads', were accustomed during this Parliament to meet at Arundel's tavern in Poultney Lane. Here, in their table-talk, they expressed their dislike of the Queen's Catholic proceedings, and 'with great wilfulness' arranged 'to resist such matters as should be spoken of in the Parliament, other than liked them'. It foreshadows the development of tavern-politics. We know that Sir George Throckmorton had already indulged in the pastime in Henry VIII's reign, and it may well have been fairly common at eating houses where M.P.s gathered for the midday dinner; although parliamentary business was deemed to be secret and it was a misdemeanour to discuss such matters outside the Chamber. A novelty in 1555, if novelty it was — and of that we can only judge by the inconclusive absence of earlier evidence — lay in the planning of opposition tactics.[1]

Some further light on the methods of this group comes from Queen Elizabeth's great statesman, Sir William Cecil, who was drawn into their web and narrowly escaped punishment in consequence. In this Parliament, runs an entry in his diary, 'I spoke my mind freely, whereby I incurred dislike'. 'But it was better to obey God than man', he sententiously adds. A member of his household, writing after his death, expands the story. He tells us that 'there was a matter in question, for something the Queen would have pass' — almost certainly one or other of two bills, which will be mentioned later — 'wherein Sir Anthony Kingston, Sir William Courtney, Sir John Pollard, and many others of value, especially western men, were opposite'. Cecil spoke on their side, and, 'having that day told a good tale for them, when the House rose they came to him and said they would dine with him that day': at Arundel's, perhaps, for that is where this group dined. Cecil answered, 'they should be welcome, so they did not speak of any matters of Parliament'. Needless to say, they did not keep off the forbidden topic, and in consequence Cecil found himself in trouble with the Privy Council.[2]

Such were the factious gentlemen with whom the government had to cope in this Parliament of 1555. A critical spirit

<hr/>

[1] E. H. HARBISON, *Rival Ambassadors at the Court of Q. Mary*, pp. 273, 280; S.P. Dom. Mary, viii. fol. 58.
[2] PECK, *Desiderata Curiosa* (1779), i. 9.

was early engendered over the subsidy bill: an easy subject on which to provoke strife. But the Queen herself got over that difficulty by waiving a part of the grant. It was a different story with two other principal measures, even though the government took the precaution of introducing them first in the Higher House, thus lending them momentum before they encountered the worst opposition. One was a bill to renounce the Queen's rights to the clerical First Fruits and Tenths, which had been transferred from the Papacy to the Crown by the Henrician Reformation, and which Mary's conscience, as she explained in a passionate plea to a substantial delegation from Lords and Commons, would not allow her to keep. To laymen the bill was obnoxious because of its implied criticism of their ecclesiastical holdings and because their own pockets were likely to suffer from any impoverishment of the Crown. After a chequered passage through the Lords, it made very heavy weather in the Commons. The debate on the second reading stretched over into another day, with long arguments. It looked as if the bill would be lost. However, the third reading was put off for six days, and meanwhile the opposition was apparently reduced by private persuasion, so that the measure at last passed on a division by 193 votes to 126. Even this success was only achieved by keeping everyone behind closed doors on empty stomachs and at other inconvenience until 3 p.m.: a demoralizing experience, as we know from a Member who suffered it in 1597.[1]

The second bill was directed against the religious refugees on the continent. When it came to its third reading, the leaders of the opposition were determined that they should not be again overreached by the manœuvres of the Speaker and government party. To gain time and the chance of getting at the 'Noes' in private, supporters of the bill wanted to adjourn the debate; and with the aid of the Speaker they might have had their way. But, culling a leaf from the tactics earlier adopted by the Court party, Sir Anthony Kingston, with the backing of his friends, took the keys of the Chamber from the Serjeant-at-Arms and locked the doors. Standing there, he insisted on an immediate division, declaring in a loud voice

---

[1] *Venetian Cal.* VI. i. 228-38, 251, 256-7, 270; *Commons Journals* (hereafter cited as *C.J.*), i. 46.

that he did not choose to have this bill treated like the last, 'which was carried against the consciences of many Members by means of delay'. We are reminded of the famous occasion in 1629 when the Speaker was forcibly prevented from adjourning the House. As then, so now, the House condoned an outrage; and, stirred by the courage of their leaders, the majority rejected the bill. When the Parliament ended, Kingston was summoned before the Privy Council and sent to the Tower, from which, however, he was released, on his humble submission, after only a fortnight's imprisonment.[1]

We know too little about this interesting Parliament, but, if we can believe a dispatch from the usually reliable Venetian ambassador — and though difficult to square with entries in the *Commons Journal*, the story cannot be dismissed as impossible — there was another occasion when the opposition group displayed a tactical precocity more in line with the maturer days of Elizabeth. In its desire to reduce the number of gentry in Parliament and so thin out the opposition, the government, we are told, introduced a bill compelling the boroughs to observe the law about electing residents as their representatives. The opposition — most of whose leaders sat for boroughs — countered by tacking on to the measure a place-bill prohibiting the election of 'any stipendiary, pensioner, or official, or of any person deriving profit in any other way from the King and the royal Council'. Their move effectively put an end to any further progress with the original bill.[2]

The Parliament of 1555 ended on December 9th, and in the following March the Dudley Conspiracy, in which Sir Anthony Kingston and his friends were involved, was betrayed. It is therefore not surprising that the last Parliament of the reign seems to have proceeded on a subdued note, though the subsidy bill had a prolonged and evidently difficult passage through the Commons. This Parliament met again on November 5th, 1558. On the 17th it ended abruptly when the Commons were summoned to the Upper House to hear 'that God had taken the Queen to his mercy, and had furnished us with another sovereign Lady, my Lady Elizabeth. . .' The

---

[1] *Venetian Cal.* VI. i. 275, 283; DASENT, *Acts of Privy Council*, v. 202-3, 208; HARBISON, op. cit. pp. 273 seqq.
[2] *Venetian Cal.* VI. i. 251.

Clerk closed his *Journal* with the words: 'I pray God save her Grace long to reign over us, to the glory of God. Amen.'[1]

A new age had dawned, as full of hope for many Englishmen as the old had been of despondency. Not an easy age — revolutionary times never are; and certainly not easy for a young Queen of twenty-five. Parliament was to prove both the bane and the triumph of her reign. In the swift traverse that we have taken over half a century of its history, we have seen where time and policy and the courage of the individual had brought the House of Commons by November 1558. Clearly, Sir Thomas More's ideal of 1523, when he made the first formal request for freedom of speech, had been realized. The right to speak and vote against any measure — the right of opposition — had been won: indeed, certain Members had ventured beyond freedom into licence. Three factors had been mainly responsible; the presence of many gentlemen in the House of Commons, the clash over religion, and the rule of a woman.

All three factors were present — the first in an intensified form — in Queen Elizabeth's reign. There was, however, a profound difference. The opposition in Mary's reign had been Protestant, or inclined, for political and other reasons, to sympathize with Protestants. A Protestant programme being out of the question, its role was that of mere opposition: to modify or defeat government measures. Hence both its need and its inclination were to exploit freedom of speech within the limits of Sir Thomas More's definition of the privilege. In doing this it learnt parliamentary tactics; and continuity in the membership of successive Parliaments ensured that the memory of them would endure.

For any significant advance a different situation was needed. The new reign provided this. In contrast with Mary Tudor, Queen Elizabeth was popular. True, there were some doubtful moments in the early years, but as time went by her hold on the affection of the people surpassed all measure. In contrast also with the previous reign, her Parliaments were not split over the main religious issue of Catholic *versus* Protestant. After the statute of 1563 came into operation, imposing the Oath of Supremacy on Members of Parliament, the Lower House contained no avowed Catholics: not, be it added, that any appre-

[1] *C.J.* i. 52.

ciable difference can be perceived in the Parliaments of 1559 and 1563, which were free from the oath. United in the Protestant faith and in loyalty to their Protestant Queen, Members were strongly affected by the ceaseless peril to the régime, both from abroad and at home. It lent revolutionary excitement to the age. Protestant England, dependent on the slender thread of a single woman's life, became personified in the Queen.

It is not surprising that in these circumstances the House of Commons was militantly Protestant, ready nearly always to sympathize with its zealous and vociferous left wing of Puritans. These men were devoted to their Queen. She was their Deborah, their Judith. She was also their affliction. They were doctrinaire and fanatical: she was *politique*. Her Protestantism differed from theirs, and she was opposed to them on other vital questions of policy. They wanted to advance beyond the Anglican Church Settlement: she was determined to progress no further. They wanted to settle the succession to the throne as guarantee against a future relapse to Catholicism: she saw the present danger of that policy and preferred to do nothing. Invariably they wanted action: too often for their liking, she was resolved on inaction. It was the perennial conflict of radicalism and conservatism.

Puritan Members of the House of Commons became what Protestants had been in Mary Tudor's reign: an opposition. But it was an opposition in a significantly new sense: one with a positive programme which was not hostile to the régime, but professed to aim at the fulfilment of its Protestant destiny. Sir Thomas More's definition of freedom of speech, adequate for simple obstruction, was not capacious enough for their need. They wanted to initiate: to introduce bills and motions of their own, to frame the agenda of Parliament. Having little historical sense and a convenient memory for precedents, they read into the vague phrase, 'freedom of speech', a meaning that was bound, if it prevailed, to lead to the destruction of personal monarchy as the Tudors knew it, and to the evolution of parliamentary government as the modern world has known it.

Henry VIII had effected a marriage of convenience between the Commons and the Crown. He had enhanced their power because his will and their will had been broadly the same. In

Elizabeth's reign the will of the Crown and the will of Parliament — the will, that is to say, of the gentry of England, politically articulate in the House of Commons — were often at variance. But the contest went on in a kind of romance that excluded any thought of divorce.

# ELIZABETH I
# AND HER PARLIAMENTS
## 1559-1581

# PART ONE

# THE PARLIAMENT OF 1559

---

CHAPTER I

## INTRODUCTORY

IN Tudor as in earlier and later times, the death of the Sovereign automatically cancelled the authority by which officials of the Crown held office. There was a momentary vacuum in administration, and to fill this — to appoint Privy Councillors and reconstitute the administrative machine — was one of the tasks confronting Elizabeth at her accession on November 17th, 1558. Though a vital and delicate business, it was routine. Problems of an extraordinary nature also required attention. One was to bring to a formal end the war with France, upon which Mary Tudor had entered as the bemused ally of her husband, Philip II: it had cost England Calais, a loss humiliating to the nation's pride. Religion was another matter; and here Elizabeth inherited a divided country. It was certain that she would not continue her sister's policy, and consequently, she had to consider what form of religious settlement to make. There was a third problem of hardly less importance, though it lacked the immediacy of the others. This was her marriage. A Virgin Queen — a woman who ruled without the aid and comfort of a husband — was a phenomenon as yet beyond the imagination of sixteenth-century mankind.

Inevitably, public policy had to take account of the formal state of war with France. Already, before Mary Tudor died, the fighting had ceased and peace negotiations were under way. Since the authority of the English commissioners lapsed with the death of their Sovereign, it had to be renewed, and Elizabeth saw to this on November 23rd.[1] In the impoverished and powerless state of the country, the need for peace was as urgent

---

[1] FORBES, *Transactions in the Reign of Q. Elizabeth,* i. 1.

33

as before, but the new Queen was in some respects less favourably placed than her predecessor to bargain over it. Her ally and companion in the negotiations, Philip II, was no longer King of England. More disturbing, the enemy, France, possessed in Mary Queen of Scots, the Dauphin's wife, a potential claimant to the English throne and a menace to policy. It seemed as if all the authority and power of European Catholicism might be mustered on her behalf, should any move be made against the faith by the new English government. Elizabeth was the offspring of a marriage which the Catholic Church regarded as invalid; and even in England there was a statute of her father's declaring her illegitimate. Mary Tudor — understandably — had left this section of the act unrepealed; and in fact it remained unrepealed, on the constitutional ground that the crown covered all such flaws.[1]

Elizabeth's position appeared far from strong. During the peace negotiations the Queen of Scots' claim was flaunted by quartering the arms of England with those of France and Scotland. True, a union of England with France and Scotland would have been disastrous for Spain, and Philip II was therefore compelled to act as Elizabeth's protector: a situation that the wily young Queen and her able advisers knew how to exploit. But to assume that peace appeared as attainable in prospect as it seems in retrospect would be wrong. One of the English commissioners, writing to Cecil on January 9th was very gloomy. He feared that the French, knowing the weakness of England, would deceive Elizabeth, separate Spain by craft, and conquer the country for Mary Queen of Scots.[2]

Dr. Wotton, the writer of the letter, also referred to conditions at home: 'the most dangerous divisions in religion among ourselves, which either must make Christ to be a liar, or else will go nigh to subvert the realm'.[3] His fears were dupes, but that was far from apparent at the time. The new Queen was dedicated by her parentage and education, by her role during Mary's reign, by the religious and political affinities of her household and circle of intimates, and by the rapturous Protestant welcome of the citizens of London — dedicated, indeed, by all the hopes centred upon her during the last five

---

[1] 28 Hen. VIII, c. 7; cf. CAMDEN's *Elizabeth* (1688), p. 18.
[2] FORBES, op. cit. i. 18 seqq.      [3] Ibid. p. 19.

years — to carry out a religious revolution. It was difficult to estimate the dangers of such a course; difficult therefore to be sure of the pace at which the revolution could be prudently accomplished.

Death had been helpful by removing the most distinguished Catholic leader, Cardinal Pole, on the same day that Mary Tudor died. Moreover, 'that accursed cardinal' — as the Spanish ambassador called him because of the omission — had left five bishoprics unfilled, and another four were vacated through death before the end of the year: ten sees in all out of twenty-six.[1] The Catholic citadel was undermanned. Nor was that all. Bonner, its most obstinate defender, placed in the strategic see of London, was more or less disarmed by the infamy which the persecutions of Mary's reign had brought upon him; Nicholas Heath, Archbishop of York and Mary's Lord Chancellor, was a moderate man, who had served Henry VIII, was loyal to Elizabeth and on the most friendly terms with her;[2] while the venerable Tunstall, Bishop of Durham, was another Henrician on whose moderation the new Queen could count. Nevertheless, the government of the Church was in Catholic hands; and with the international situation apparently so favourable, resolute men in such a position might have proved formidable. Though the accession of Elizabeth had opened the floodgates of Protestantism, and though, in London especially, the revolutionary spirit was vociferous and confident, it must have been a question with the Queen and her advisers whether change could be brought about otherwise than in stages and with subtlety.

Sir Nicholas Throckmorton, notorious in the old reign and eminent in the new, had written to Elizabeth to tender his advice the moment he heard of Mary Tudor's death: indeed, before he had confirmation of the brave, the heartening news. No one could suspect such a zealot of timidity or lukewarmness, and yet the burden of his advice was caution: 'to succeed happily through a discreet beginning'. Concerning religion, he urged her 'to have a good eye that there be no innovations, no tumults or breach of orders'.[3] Within a week or two the Queen

---

[1] Cf. BIRT, *Elizabethan Religious Settlement*, p. 44.
[2] Cf. Heath's remarkable letter in B.M. Cotton MS. Vespasian, F. xiii. no. 229.
[3] Printed by me in *Eng. Hist. Rev.* lxv. 91-8.

was probably considering when to summon her first Parliament and therefore giving serious thought to the most difficult and important problem of all — the religious settlement. In all likelihood advice was tendered or sought from a number of people. Of the documents which may once have existed, three have come down to us, all written by Protestants. It says much for the perplexities of the time that they differed seriously in their counsel.[1]

The most cautious came from an eminent lawyer, Richard Goodrich, a man well qualified to offer advice on ecclesiastical matters. Of his hostility to the Papacy, to Catholicism, and to the more extreme of Mary's bishops — whom he would have committed to the Tower — his paper leaves no doubt at all. But in his opinion it was no less perilous to take half-measures against the Pope than to abolish his authority altogether. Consequently, he advised a policy of dissimulation until Parliament met; hoodwinking the Papacy — as in fact Elizabeth did — by retaining the English agent at Rome and promising to send a great embassy there; dragging out the deception through most of the summer of 1559, while the religious revolution was effected. To destroy Catholicism required time; and therefore if the first Parliament of the reign was to meet 'before or in March' his advice was to attempt no Reformation in that session. In such an event — and Parliament in fact met in January — both the supremacy of the Pope over the English Church and the Catholic order of its service should be retained. The only parliamentary measure which he felt disposed to advocate at so early a time was repeal of the fifteenth-century heresy laws, by virtue of which Mary had carried out her religious persecution. The bishops would thus be disarmed and quiet persons might live safely, while certain mild modifications in worship could be carried out without parliamentary sanction, and 'learned and discreet' Protestant priests encouraged. This ultra-cautious advice, coming as it did from a man whom the Privy Council placed on a committee to consider the government's parliamentary legislation, deserves careful thought.

The second of our three documents has attached to it the name of Armagil Waad, a man with an official and diplomatic background, who had served both Henry VIII and Edward VI.

---

[1] They are printed in GEE, *Elizabethan Prayer-Book*, pp. 195-215.

Its title, 'The distresses of the Commonwealth, with the means to remedy them', indicates its wider range. The author was impressed with the weak position in which the government found itself: 'the Queen poor; the realm exhausted; ... division among ourselves; wars with France and Scotland; the French King bestriding the realm, having one foot in Calais and the other in Scotland; steadfast enmity but no steadfast friendship abroad'. It required great cunning and circumspection, he declared, to reform religion and maintain concord and unity among the people. 'I wish that you would proceed to the reformation having respect to quiet at home, the affairs you have in hand with foreign princes, the greatness of the Pope, and how dangerous it is to make alteration in religion, specially in the beginning of a prince's reign. Glasses with small necks, if you pour into them any liquor suddenly or violently, will not be so filled, but refuse to receive that same that you would pour into them. Howbeit, if you instil water into them by a little and little, they are soon replenished.'

Little by little: reformation by stages. This counsel, along with the even less adventurous advice of Richard Goodrich, is well worth pondering as we turn to the third and famous paper known as 'The device for alteration of religion in the first year of Queen Elizabeth'. Its anonymous author begins abruptly with the recommendation that the alteration of religion should take place in the first Parliament of the reign. It was to be revolution at a blow — a national Church, complete with Protestant Prayer Book: no gradual approach here. Though clearly not an extremist in his religious views, he was as mystical in his main argument as any zealot. The sole justification for his policy of 'thorough' is to be found in the remark: 'The sooner that religion is restored, God is the more glorified, and ... will be more merciful to us and better save and defend her Highness from all dangers.' True, there were dangers to be foreseen and remedies provided. He analysed the former almost as realistically as Goodrich and Waad. He also outlined the remedies: they are no match for his perils. Except as an act of faith, his argument is unconvincing; and if the course of our story shows that it failed to convince the Queen — supposing indeed that she saw it — we need not be surprised. The author goes on to suggest how the revision of the Book of Common Prayer should be accomplished; and the precise nature of his proposals, along with the illusion that they fit into the subsequent course of events, has led historians to regard the document as the basic official programme for the Elizabethan religious settlement. Indeed, it was no more than a Rejected Address.

Goodrich evidently contemplated the possibility of not holding a Parliament before April 1559; but in a similar though less complicated situation Mary Tudor had sent out the writs for her first Parliament within a month of her accession to the throne. Elizabeth did the same. The writs were dated December 5th, 1558, summoning Parliament for January 23rd, 1559.[1] In preparation, the Privy Council, on December 23rd, appointed a committee to consider 'all things necessary for the Parliament', on which they placed Sir Thomas Smith and our lawyer Richard Goodrich, neither of whom was a Privy Councillor though both were equipped to give advice on the technical aspects of ecclesiastical legislation.[2] How far this committee discussed the nature of the religious settlement, it is impossible to say. Probably not at all. Even the Privy Council was not at liberty to frame its own agenda, and in matters of high policy could only discuss what the Sovereign authorized it to discuss. The author of 'The Device', for example, contemplated a period of secrecy during which the preparatory steps he advocated would be known only to an inner circle; and he suggested that among the nobility four only — the Marquis of Northampton, the Earl of Bedford, the Earl of Pembroke, and the Lord John Grey — should 'be made privy to these proceedings, before it be opened to the whole Council'. Most likely, the Queen sounded her Councillors and others personally at Court, while Sir William Cecil gathered advice, drawing up in his customary way the *pros* and *cons*, before a policy was framed and the Council as a body allowed to discuss it. The Council's committee — as its composition suggests — may simply have been concerned with drafting the legislation.

The elections to Elizabeth's first Parliament were conducted without recourse to circular letters, such as Mary Tudor had employed in a vain effort to keep Protestants out of her House of Commons: at least, no such letters are known, and the

---

[1] D'EWES, *Journals of Parliaments of Elizabeth*, p. 2.
[2] DASENT, *Acts of Privy Council*, vii. 28.

balance of probability is strongly against them. As a result of the elections, there were many changes in the county representation: more, it would seem, than usual, though change was a normal feature in county elections at this period. The probable explanation is that the Marian government's instructions to elect Catholics had exerted most influence in the counties, where the sheriffs and responsible magnates were susceptible to official advice. This pressure was now gone. Everyone was aware that there was a new régime of a different religious complexion, and in counties where there was any keen or substantial division among the gentry along religious lines the new political climate probably had the effect of depressing the spirits, prestige, and electioneering powers of staunch Catholics. After all, as we know from the Rutland election of 1601, by late Elizabethan days it was accounted an impertinence for Catholic recusants even to vote at an election. If county elections tended to reflect the character of the government in power, there is nothing mysterious or sinister in that.[1]

As for the boroughs, the Marian government had failed dismally in its repeated efforts to stop them from electing gentlemen instead of resident burgesses; and the history of such a Parliament as that of 1555 shows that they could not be prevented from sending to Westminster a substantial number of critics of the régime. Stop such efforts, and what was likely to happen? Few Englishmen at the end of 1558 can have felt any pride in a government that had lost them Calais. Doubtless there were many sincere and devoted Catholics left in the new England; doubtless, also, there were some Catholics in Elizabeth's first House of Commons — though the story of that parliamentary session would seem to indicate that the number cannot have been large. Nevertheless, most if not all factors combined to place leadership in the hands of Protestant enthusiasts and to exalt their spirits. If there was a revolutionary character about this House of Commons; if Catholic opinion, though not altogether voiceless, was negligible; if counsels of moderation were ineffective and the overwhelming majority were swept along by religious zealots, whose psychological moment this was: is it surprising? The old legend which made this a packed Parliament was not only needless: it was bad

[1] Cf. my *Elizabethan House of Commons*, pp. 135, 286 seqq.

psychology. Having long ago been demolished factually, it should be regarded as doubly defunct.[1]

In the House of Lords there was a potential attendance of sixteen bishops, ten sees being vacant: to which should be added, in order to obtain the full ecclesiastical element, the Abbot of Westminster and the Prior of St. John. Some, however, were licensed to be absent and name their proxies: not, indeed, that there is any evidence of proxies, either spiritual or temporal, being used in the voting. The maximum attendance of spiritual peers was eleven, the general attendance before the crucial break at Easter fluctuating between eight and ten. Of temporal peers there were sixty-one, excluding the Lord Keeper, Sir Nicholas Bacon;[2] and of these, three only were newly created and two restored to their peerages, no attempt being made to modify appreciably the political or religious complexion of the lay element. Their attendance also fluctuated, touching a peak of thirty-nine at the beginning of the session, but sinking to twenty or so even on days when there was business to do. Half the temporal peers executed letters of proxy, but this action did not necessarily imply absence from all sittings. The House of Lords was therefore a small working assembly, approximating to fifty at its strongest and less than thirty at its weakest. It had at its service judges and other legal officials who received writs of assistance and were used for the technical scrutiny of bills or, if minor officials, as messengers between the two Houses.

We know little about the method of working of the Upper House, except for what can be deduced from the formal and laconic *Journal* kept by the Clerk. If this official also had rough notes or 'scribbled books' in which he jotted down brief epitomes of the speeches and proceedings, as Bowyer and Elsing had in early Stuart days — and it seems most unlikely — no trace of their existence has survived. No Lord that we know of kept a private diary of proceedings, nor were the proceedings interesting enough to excite much comment from foreign ambassadors or from letter-writers. Though far surpassing the Lower House in prestige, the Upper House did not emulate it

---

[1] Cf. C. G. Bayne, 'The First House of Commons of Q. Elizabeth', *Eng. Hist. Rev.* xxiii. 455, 643.
[2] Cf. list in *Lords Journals* (hereafter cited as *L.J.*), i. 544-5.

in independence. The lay peers were too intimately attached to Crown and Court to be persistent critics of the Sovereign. For most of them a government bill which was known to have the backing of the Sovereign was tantamount to a royal command. Of course, the bishops were sensitive to a higher loyalty; but even some of Mary's bishops were so imbued with the tradition of serving the Crown that they were uneasy when their consciences led them into opposition. When, for example, Bishop Scot of Chester spoke against the Supremacy bill he declared that one of the considerations which 'pulled him back from speaking anything in this matter' was the knowledge that 'the Queen's Highness . . . is, as it were, a party therein, unto whom I do acknowledge that I owe obedience'.[1] Though the spiritual peers, to a man, voted against every ecclesiastical bill in the Parliament of 1559, their action ought perhaps to be regarded as an exercise of conscience and of the privilege of free speech, rather than an effort to defeat the government. Nor must we be too modern in our interpretation of the intentions of lay peers who voted against government bills. It is well to remember that the function of a Tudor House of Lords was less to impede the Crown than to assist it in controlling the Commons.

The Parliament of 1559 was summoned to meet on Monday January 23rd, but when the whole assembly of Lords and Commons gathered in the Parliament Chamber that day, Sir Nicholas Bacon, occupying the office of Lord Chancellor, though with the lesser rank, and salary, of Lord Keeper of the Great Seal, announced that the Queen, owing to bodily indisposition — the weather, too, was bad — had postponed the ceremonial procession and opening of Parliament for two days. Thereupon the Clerk of the Parliaments read the letters patent, required by even so brief a prorogation.[2]

On the Wednesday, January 25th, after the Court had dined early — about 10 a.m. if the Spanish ambassador has the time right — the royal procession moved off. As the Queen passed by, the people in the street knelt, crying 'God save and maintain thee!', to which Elizabeth, turning first to one side and then to the other, answered 'Grammercy, good people!', 'smiling most sweetly on all of them'. At Westminster Abbey there was

---

[1] STRYPE, *Annals*, I. ii. 408.          [2] *L.J.* i. 542; *Venetian Cal.* vii. 22.

another of those little touches by which she had already indicated that the religious climate was changing; for, being met
by the Abbot, robed pontifically, with all his monks carrying
lighted torches, she exclaimed, 'Away with those torches, for
we see very well.' Nor was this the only sign. The man chosen
to preach the sermon was Dr. Cox, a married priest, once Dean
of Westminster and soon to be made a bishop, who was one of
the returned Marian exiles: one of those 'ministers of Lucifer'
whom the Spanish ambassador rightly feared. According to
the Mantuan agent in London, Il Schifanoya — whose dispatches are a precious and fairly reliable source of information
at this time — Cox inveighed against the monks as the impious
authors of the Marian persecution, and praised the Queen
whose divine mission it was to end such iniquities, destroy the
monasteries and all images, and purify the Church. The sermon, according to this writer, lasted an hour and a half. If it
was as outspoken and provocative as he suggests, it can hardly
have won royal approval.[1]

The opening speech in Parliament was made by Sir Nicholas
Bacon, whose duty was to expound the reasons for its meeting.
Unlike the modern King's Speech, these speeches were orations.
They were not necessarily intended to outline the government's
legislative programme. It was almost by convention that
Bacon constructed his speech in three sections: the Church or
religion, the Commonwealth or secular welfare, and taxation.
Consequently, we must not read too much into the words with
which he summarized the first section: 'the well making of laws
for . . . uniting of the people of this realm into an uniform order
of religion, to the honour and glory of God, the establishment
of His Church, and tranquility of the realm'. Nor can we derive
any precise knowledge of the government's intentions from the
generalities into which he expanded this initial summary.
Though Protestant in tone, he was far from echoing Dr. Cox:
rather, he bade his audience banish from their mouths 'all
contentious, contumelious, or opprobrious words, as heretic,
schismatic, Papist, and such like names and nurses of seditions,
factions, and sects'. In the course of a felicitous passage in
praise of the new Queen, he drew a contrast in guarded though
unmistakable words between the late Queen — whose personal

[1] *Venetian Cal.* vii. 22-3; *Spanish Cal. Eliz.* i. 25.

SIR NICHOLAS BACON

Lord Keeper of the Great Seal

policy had led to discontent at home and to the disastrous subordination of England's foreign policy to the interests of Spain — and a princess such as they now had, 'to whom nothing — what nothing? — no, no worldly thing under the sun is so dear as the hearty love and goodwill of her nobles and subjects'. Money was needed; but, as the Queen, 'even from her own mouth', had bade him say: 'Were it not for the preservation of yourselves and the surety of the State, her Highness would have sooner adventured her life (which our Lord long preserve) than she would have adventured to trouble her loving subjects with any offensive matter, or that should be burdenous or displeasant unto them.' There was a further command of the Queen's: 'Her Majesty's will and pleasure is that nothing shall be demanded or required of her loving subjects but that which they of their own free will and liberality be well contented readily, gladly, frankly, and freely to offer. So great is the trust and confidence that she reposeth in them.' On this astute note, which — for all but the few to whom the Catholic way of life meant everything — was a heartening promise of new times and an inspiring leader, the sitting ended.[1]

The whole Parliament assembled again on the Saturday for the presentation of the Speaker. The Commons had elected for this office Sir Thomas Gargrave, 'one of the honourable Council in the North Parts, and learned in the laws of this realm', as the Clerk described him: a Yorkshireman in his early sixties, who had attained the rank of a royal official after service in the household of the Earl of Shrewsbury, and had retained his membership of the Council in the North through all the religious changes since Henry VIII's reign. He had sat in four previous Parliaments and though described as a 'favourer of religion' — that is, of Protestantism — in 1564, his faith probably sat as lightly on him as did that of the Vicar of Bray. The selection of such a man by the government — for theirs was the initial, though informal choice — is not without significance. It hardly suggests an intention to give extremists in the Commons their head.[2]

Gargrave duly presented himself to the Queen as the elect

[1] B.M. Harleian MS. 5176, fols. 105b seqq.
[2] *C.J.* i. 53; *D.N.B.* sub Gargrave, Thos.; REID, *King's Council in the North*, passim.

of the Lower House, disabling himself, as custom required, in
'comely and modest manner'. He was 'enabled' in a pleasing
reply from the Lord Keeper. Thereupon he began what the
Clerk of the House of Commons described as 'a notable
oration, touching partly the decays of this realm, with some
remedies for the same; and also made certain petitions for the
ancient liberties'. What he said we do not know; nor was the
reply of the Lord Keeper — which we possess — long enough
to reveal whether the oration had been inspired by conscious-
ness of a revolutionary occasion. Perhaps not. The ancient
liberties for which the Speaker petitioned were four: access to
the Queen and her nobles for his reports and conference; permission to amend any slips he might make in reporting the
decisions of the House; 'liberty of speech for the well debating
of matters propounded'; and 'freedom from all manner of suits'
— the privilege generally known as freedom from arrest — for
Members and their servants.

The privileges were granted with the normal cautionary
words. As yet the Crown felt no need to define freedom of
speech. Members were granted this liberty with the sole proviso that 'they be neither unmindful nor uncareful of their
duties, reverence, and obedience to their Sovereign'. With a
final injunction to the Speaker to prefer public business before
private bills and so reduce the duration of the Parliament, Sir
Nicholas Bacon brought these preliminary proceedings to an
end.[1] While the Lords adjourned, the Commons returned to
their Chamber to read the usual single bill giving the Speaker
seisin of his chair.

The government, at this first Parliament, had a number of
important measures to pass. One recognized Elizabeth's title
to the throne. Though statutorily clear enough, since it rested
on an act of her father's in 1544, her title might be regarded as
soiled by a previous and still unrepealed act declaring her
illegitimate: soiled also by a Marian act of 1553.[2] Her sister
had been in a similar position on her accession to the throne;
and never was the contrast between the two Queens more
strikingly displayed than in their several solutions of this same
problem. The statute Mary devised opened with an exordium

---

[1] B.M. Harleian MS. 5176, fols. 108b, 109b.
[2] 35 Hen. VIII, c. 1; 28 Hen. VIII, c. 7; 1 Mary, st. 2, c. 1.

on the theme 'Great is Truth and it shall prevail'. It then
moved on through a long review and refutation of Henry VIII's
divorce of her mother, pronounced the divorce void, and repealed the statutory declarations of her own illegitimacy, while
leaving her sister a bastard.[1] The *dévote* spoke here. Elizabeth's
bill was a simple recognition of her title to the succession under
the act of 1544, rescinding in purely general words everything
repugnant to the same. No abstractions on this occasion; no
complex about the past; no aspersions on her father; nor even
on her sister. In another very brief bill she was concerned to
restore her legal position as her mother's heir; and once more
the text was confined to herself and the present, ignoring her
mother's reputation, which was inseparable from her father's.
What shrewd, hard sense, devoid of passion! The past was left
dead and buried.[2] In addition to these two bills there were
others, dealing with treason and kindred problems. Together
they constituted the secular side of the Elizabethan establishment. They were introduced into the Lords, where they
encountered no hostile vote and probably no opposition at all.

Bridging, as it were, the secular and ecclesiastical establish-
ments was a bill to restore to the Crown the clerical First Fruits
and Tenths which had first been annexed from the Papacy
by Henry VIII and then renounced by Mary in the face of
substantial opposition from the Commons. The preamble contained some biting comment on the political folly of Mary's
action, but this was in contrast to the prevailing note of
moderation which kept allusions to the late Queen studiously
correct. The bill began its passage in the Lords, where it was
the first measure to be read. The government must have been
deliberate about introducing it there instead of in the Commons,
perhaps regarding it as a test — in the result of which they were
confident — of where the Lords stood on such a matter. It
made rapid progress and was not even committed. All the
temporal peers — even Viscount Montague, the most obdurate
Catholic — voted for it. The spiritual peers, however, all voted
against it: which can hardly have failed to disappoint the
Queen.[3]

---

[1] 1 Mary, st. 2, c. 1 (*Statutes of Realm*, IV. i. 200-1).
[2] 1 Eliz. caps. 3, 23 (*Statutes of Realm*, IV. i. 358-9, 397).
[3] 1 Eliz. c. 4; *L.J.* i. 544-6.

In this bill the first blow for the new Reformation had been struck, and in its passage through the Lords the pattern of the story had been set. Clearly, if the bishops were voting unanimously against a semi-political bill, they were certain to oppose all ecclesiastical measures, thus destroying any hope the Queen may have had of compromise. On the other hand, the lay peers had shown themselves Henrician in their support of Crown policy and their preference of national to ideological interests. In this connection the Count de Feria, Philip II's special ambassador, made a comment, which, though not to be taken too seriously, is a useful pointer as we move into the mysteries of this Parliament. 'The Queen', he wrote, 'has entire disposal of the Upper Chamber in a way never seen before in previous Parliaments.' His comparison with the past was of course little more than a *façon de parler*: after all, Mary's peers had passed the very opposite measure without fuss in 1555, while the Commons — in whose assembly prejudice flourished and *noblesse oblige* was not a duty — jibbed vigorously.[1]

In the Commons, the only official business before the House on its first full morning was a motion for supply; and ten days were to elapse before the government revealed its ecclesiastical policy. To Protestant zealots, who had come to Parliament to overthrow the Papacy and Catholicism, silence was unendurable. When supply was discussed, someone or other hit on the bright idea of questioning whether or not this was a valid Parliament. Elizabeth had followed a precedent set by Mary Tudor, who, before she was able to restore Papal supremacy by repealing Henry VIII's Reformation statutes, for conscience' sake dropped the title 'Supreme Head of the Church' and replaced it by an enigmatic and innocuous '&c'. In reverse — and how ironic this contrast in the guise of imitation — Queen Elizabeth, lacking statutory claim to the title but considering it, as her father had done, an inalienable prerogative right, had revived the device of etceterating herself. It meant — it could only mean — 'Supreme Head of the Church' when an Act of Supremacy should publicly proclaim the title.

In the writs summoning Parliament *&c* had been used and not *supremum caput*. It was this which gave the House the excuse

[1] *Spanish Cal. Eliz.* i. 32.

and procedural opening to start up a propaganda debate at the very outset of the session. 'There was great talk about giving the title of Supreme Head of the Anglican Church to the Queen', wrote Il Schifanoya, 'much being said against the Church [of Rome].' After debate, the question whether the Parliament was valid, notwithstanding the omission of *supremum caput* from the writs, was referred to the large committee appointed for the subsidy, and presumably there was occasion in committee for more radical talk. Needless to say, in due time the committee reported favourably. One can only express admiration for the tactical abilities of Protestant leaders who had so quickly perceived, created, and seized this opportunity for airing their views.[1]

This over, and before the government came along with its Supremacy bill, the Commons started another hare. 'Arguments that a request may be made to the Queen's Highness for marriage', noted the Clerk in his *Journal* on February 4th; and Members seem to have roamed in this delectable field most of the morning. In the afternoon of February 6th the Speaker, Privy-Councillor Members, and thirty others were granted audience by the Queen, when the Speaker made 'request to her Highness for marriage'. During the debate in the House, Members may well have urged, as a Letter from London in the *Venetian Calendar* suggests,[2] that the Queen be asked to marry within the realm: that is, to marry an Englishman. A body of men in emotional reaction from the previous reign would instinctively have thought this way, and the Queen's reply seems to imply that there had been talk of the kind. But the Speaker and his immediate advisers were discreet men, and the speech in which he 'solemnly and eloquently set forth the message' was, as Elizabeth herself remarked, 'simple and contained no limitation of place or person'. After a little pause — so Richard Grafton, the printer and chronicler, tells us — the Queen made her answer.[3] Perhaps the Speaker was instructed

---

[1] *C.J.* i. 53; *Venetian Cal.* vii. 26, 28; F. W. MAITLAND, *Collected Papers*, iii. 159; POLLARD, *Political Hist. of England, 1547-1603*, p. 195.

[2] Vol. VII, p. 28. Cf. STRYPE's *Smith*, p. 247.

[3] Grafton was perhaps present, and certainly seems from his comment (cf. his *Abridgement of the Chronicles*) to have been a Member of this Parliament. Camden (*Elizabeth*, pp. 25-6) gives an epitome of the petition, but I know of no text from which he could have made it, and it does not correspond with the Queen's description. I have therefore ignored it.

not to report it to the House until he had received the authentic text: at any rate, it was four days later that he announced 'the Queen's Majesty's answer to the message; which (written) was read to the House by Mr. Mason, to the great honour of the Queen and the contentation of this House'.[1]

It was the first of several royal utterances to which her faithful Commons were to listen: doubtless much too euphuistic for modern taste (though not inappropriate for Tudor utterance); involved, often studiously and wisely obscure; but magnetic, always distinctive and distinguished, and never failing in emotional effect.

'As I have good cause' — the Queen began — 'so do I give you all my hearty thanks for the good zeal and loving care you seem to have, as well towards me as to the whole state of your country. Your petition, I perceive, consisteth of three parts, and mine answer to the same shall depend of two.

'And to the first part, I may say unto you that from my years of understanding, sith I first had consideration of myself to be born a servitor of Almighty God, I happily chose this kind of life in which I yet live, which I assure you for mine own part hath hitherto best contented myself and I trust hath been most acceptable to God. From the which, if either ambition of high estate offered to me in marriage by the pleasure and appointment of my prince — whereof I have some records in this presence, as you our Lord Treasurer well know; or if the eschewing of the danger of mine enemies or the avoiding of the peril of death, whose messenger or rather continual watchman, the prince's indignation, was not little time daily before mine eyes — by whose means, although I know or justly may suspect, yet I will not now utter; or if the whole cause were in my sister herself, I will not now burthen her therewith, because I will not charge the dead: if any of these, I say, could have drawn or dissuaded me from this kind of life, I had not now remained in this estate wherein you see me. But so constant have I always continued in this determination — although my youth and words may seem to some hardly to agree together — yet is it most true that at this day I stand free from any other meaning that either I have had in times past or have at this present. With which trade of life I am so throughly acquainted that I trust

[1] *C.J.* i. 54.

God, who hath hitherto therein preserved and led me by the hand, will not now of His goodness suffer me to go alone.

'For the other part, the manner of your petition I do well like of and take in good part, because that it is simple and containeth no limitation of place or person. If it had been otherwise, I must needs have misliked it very much and thought it in you a very great presumption, being unfitting and altogether unmeet for you to require them that may command, or those to appoint whose parts are to desire, or such to bind and limit whose duties are to obey, or to take upon you to draw my love to your liking or frame my will to your fantasies; for a guerdon constrained and a gift freely given can never agree together. Nevertheless — if any of you be in suspect — whensoever it may please God to incline my heart to another kind of life, ye may well assure yourselves my meaning is not to do or determine anything wherewith the realm may or shall have just cause to be discontented. And therefore put that clean out of your heads. For I assure you — what credit my assurance may have with you I cannot tell, but what credit it shall deserve to have the sequence shall declare — I will never in that matter conclude anything that shall be prejudicial to the realm, for the weal, good, and safety whereof I will never shun to spend my life. And whomsoever my chance shall be to light upon, I trust he shall be as careful for the realm and you — I will not say as myself, because I cannot so certainly determine of any other; but at the least ways, by my good will and desire he shall be such as shall be as careful for the preservation of the realm and you as myself.

'And albeit it might please Almighty God to continue me still in this mind to live out of the state of marriage, yet it is not to be feared but He will so work in my heart and in your wisdoms as good provision by His help may be made in convenient time, whereby the realm shall not remain destitute of an heir that may be a fit governor, and peradventure more beneficial to the realm than such offspring as may come of me. For, although I be never so careful of your well doings and mind ever so to be, yet may my issue grow out of kind and become perhaps ungracious. And in the end, this shall be for me sufficient, that a marble stone shall declare that a Queen, having reigned such a time, lived and died a virgin.

'And here I end, and take your coming unto me in good part, and give unto you all eftsoons my hearty thanks, more yet for your zeal and good meaning than for your petition.'[1]

These speeches, as we can tell from the style and from the specimens we still possess in Elizabeth's own hand, were always composed and written by herself. She played with their wording in the manner of a precious stylist, improving here, inverting phrases there. Her anxiety on this occasion to assure the Commons that there would be no repetition of her sister's blunder — no Spanish marriage — is very clear; and so is her intimation that she was not blind to the problem of the succession to the throne.

Beguiled though they seem to have been by the Queen's evasive speech, the Commons were not content to rest and be thankful. Perhaps they thought that if they acted on the assumption that there would be a marriage, they might help to bring that desirable event to pass; perhaps they were merely anxious, after their recent experience of a King Consort and a foreign marriage, to make sure that national and religious interests would be more diligently safeguarded than they had been at the marriage of Mary Tudor and Philip of Spain. At any rate, five days after the Queen's answer had been read in the House, they chose thirty of their number to meet twelve of the Upper House, who had been appointed at their request to discuss 'the authority of that person whom it shall please the Queen to take to husband'. Unfortunately, this entry in the Commons Journal is all we know of the incident. Apparently, nothing came of the move. Elizabeth must have frowned on it. Perhaps, when the conference took place, the Commons were told that the time was not ripe for a marriage treaty. It was not. As we know, it was never to be.[2]

---

[1] B.M. Lansdowne MS. 94, fol. 29; D'EWES, Journals, p. 46. The speech appears to have been printed (cf. D'EWES, p. 47a), though I know of no such copy surviving. If publication was immediate, it suggests a propaganda purpose. Grafton printed a version of his own, 'as near as I could bear the same away', in his Abridgement of the Chronicles, 1563, from which Holinshed took his text. Camden gives a version differing from both D'Ewes and Grafton.

[2] C.J. i. 54.

## CHAPTER II

# THE RELIGIOUS SETTLEMENT:
## BEFORE EASTER

THOUGH one of the principal themes in English history, the Elizabethan religious settlement is shrouded in mystery. We know of course that the Parliament of 1559 enacted two famous statutes: the Act of Supremacy, which finally severed this country from Rome by substituting royal for Papal supremacy in the Church; and the Act of Uniformity, which gave the Anglican Church its Prayer Book and made England a Protestant country. It is a tribute to the enduring qualities of the settlement that in looking back it has seemed natural and inevitable: as though from the beginning there could have been no other policy than that of the middle-way — the *via media* of tradition. But when and how this policy was shaped, or even what happened in Parliament, has been a matter of guesswork, based on the most meagre and baffling evidence. Meagre and baffling the evidence remains. Its scrutiny therefore has to be close — on occasions perhaps even forbiddingly close — if we are to force it, as we can, to yield its dramatic secret.[1]

By way of preface, let us remind ourselves of those three early papers offering counsel on religious policy. One — that by Goodrich — was opposed to any significant legislative action in a Parliament meeting so soon as this. At the other extreme, the paper known as 'The Device' advocated an immediate and complete Protestant policy. The third, by Armagil Waad, with its theme of little by little, may be said to have adopted a middle position. In the light of what ultimately happened it might appear that the counsel of 'The Device' prevailed; and so in fact historians have assumed. But what we have to bear in mind is that in December 1558 or January-February 1559 its argument would have seemed to any dispassionate and cautious statesman the least cogent of the three, and that if events had

---

[1] The interpretation adopted here was first advanced in my article, 'The Elizabethan Acts of Supremacy & Uniformity', in *Eng. Hist. Rev.* lxv. 304-32 (July 1950), which contains further detail, though occasionally the treatment is fuller in this narrative.

not worked out in its favour we should have had no difficulty in understanding why it was rejected.

And so to our story. It begins when on February 9th the Clerk of the House of Commons entered in his *Journal* the first reading of a 'Bill to restore the supremacy of the Church of England &c. to the Crown of the realm'. It was a government bill: of that there need not be the slightest doubt, though it was phrased, like so many others, as a petition from Lords and Commons. Tactics determined its introduction into the Lower rather than the Higher House, just as tactics in 1554-55 had led Mary's government to introduce their crucial second Act of Repeal, restoring Papal supremacy, into the Higher House. In the House of Lords were the Marian bishops, who had already shown a united front against the bill for First Fruits and Tenths, and who, as the Protestant divine, Jewel, some-what dolefully remarked, 'reign as sole monarchs in the midst of ignorant and weak men, and easily overreach our little party, either by their numbers, or their reputation for learning'. It was better publicity — if that word may be used — to meet episcopal opposition with the Commons as well as the Crown behind the measure.[1]

This Supremacy bill was the first of three that were before the Parliament of 1559. No text survives, but by a process of argument which seems sound enough we can deduce that it was substantially the same as the final bill which became a statute, except for employing the Henrician title of Supreme Head of the Church. We can be reasonably confident that, like our statute, it contained a brief section reviving an act passed in the first Parliament of Edward VI, the purpose of which was to have Communion administered in both kinds: that is to say, for the laity to partake of the wine as well as the bread, instead of confining the wine to the priest as in Catholic practice.[2]

This provision for Communion in both kinds — one brief section, embedded like a fossil in a very long act — deserves to be famous. It is the vital clue which enables us to penetrate our centuries-old mystery and to reconstruct the story of the 1559 Parliament. In the first place, it seems a glaring anomaly.

---

[1] *C.J.* i. 54; *Zurich Letters* (Parker Soc.), i. 10.
[2] Cf. *Eng. Hist. Rev.* lxv. 308-9.

Why insert a clause dealing with the Church service in an act concerned with the government of the Church? Nor is that all. In addition, it appears to be redundant. What was its purpose, if from the start the government intended to have an Act of Uniformity, imposing on the country a Protestant Prayer Book, in which of course there was also provision for Communion in both kinds? We can be sure that the Elizabethan government was quite aware of such arguments, for when some months later, in October 1559, they prepared corresponding legislation for the Irish Parliament, the section about Communion in both kinds was omitted from the Irish Act of Supremacy.[1] Why, then, was it included in the English Supremacy bill?

The explanation is obvious. When the Supremacy bill was first drafted there cannot have been any intention to proceed with a parallel bill of Uniformity. Royal Supremacy, yes; but no Protestant Prayer Book. In other words, Reformation was to be accomplished by stages. It was Armagil Waad's policy of little by little; and it was not new. Henry VIII had proceeded step by step in his break from Rome, and Mary Tudor had restored Catholicism in two stages, separated by a Parliament and by rather more than a year. Even closer was the Edwardian parallel: so close that the Elizabethan government would seem to have copied it. Edward VI's doctrinal Reformation began with this very provision for Communion in both kinds. It was enacted in his first Parliament and was to serve as an *interim* until his first Act of Uniformity and Prayer Book were passed in the second parliamentary session, a year or so later. We must suppose that in the same way the Elizabethan government had in mind to produce a Prayer Book and a bill of Uniformity in their second Parliament. In the meanwhile the old Catholic order of service was to continue, modified by Communion in both kinds — a sop to Protestants, and an innovation not necessarily obnoxious to Catholic minds.

There was a great deal to be said for such a policy: all those arguments, foreign and domestic, which Goodrich and Waad had used in their memoranda two to three months before. Government policy, in fact, had proved more daring than that of Goodrich and more cautious than 'The Device'. In all probability the Queen herself was largely responsible. She was an

[1] *Statutes at Large, Ireland* (1765), i. 275 seqq.

admirer of her father. She told the Spanish ambassador, Feria, that she was 'resolved to restore religion as her father left it';[1] and, save for the small item of Communion in both kinds, that was what she was doing — temporarily, at any rate. She may also have hoped to emulate Henry VIII by carrying at least the more moderate and nationally-minded of the Marian bishops with her: Nicholas Heath and Cuthbert Tunstall, for example, and others. If she had in mind as her ultimate aim — and there is reason to think that she had — a conservative Protestant settlement, the retention of some of the Marian bishops would have saved her from too great dependence on the Protestant divines, men who had been in exile under her sister and had become infected, in varying degree, with the revolutionary spirit of the *dévot*.

As armchair strategy it was superb. Had the *interim* settlement embodied in this hybrid bill of Supremacy prevailed, then between the first and second Parliaments of the reign the oath of supremacy which the bill contained would have been used to get rid of recalcitrant bishops and other influential clergymen; these would have been replaced by Protestants; and so, when the second Parliament met (which at the earliest would have been in the autumn of 1559) the parallel representative assembly of the Church, known as Convocation — both its Higher House, in which the bishops sat, and its Lower House, consisting of the clerical proctors — would have been Protestant: not, as it was in January 1559, Catholic. Consequently, the Protestant Prayer Book, before being considered by Parliament, could first have been passed through Convocation, the legislative organ of the Church, as was proper with matters of doctrine: a procedure impossible in the conditions of January-May 1559. In Parliament itself, instead of meeting with the unanimous dissent of the spiritual peers it would have had their unanimous approval. Constitutional procedure would have been possible, in place of the revolutionary methods by which the Settlement was in fact carried. The failure of this strategy meant the creation of a precedent which, as we shall see, dogged Elizabeth throughout her reign in her parliamentary struggle with Protestant extremists.

But when all is said and done, politics remain the art of the

[1] *Spanish Cal. Eliz.* i. 37.

possible. Caution may have been the watchword in official circles, but 'Haste! post haste! haste for life!' was the mood of the Protestant zealots, who had speeded back from exile on hearing 'the joyful tidings of God's favour and grace restored unto us by the preferment of the most virtuous and gracious Queen Elizabeth'. During Mary's reign close on five hundred religious or political refugees had fled to the continent: a number raised by wives, children, and servants to approximately eight hundred. They were drawn from various classes of society, the largest being the gentry. The divines also were numerous, and many of them eminent. If those who later became ministers are included, the clerical element probably approximated to one-third. A small number in relation to the population of England: but leadership counts more than numbers, and these people had that singleness of purpose which leads men to sacrifice home and fortune for their faith.[1]

Abroad, most of them had lived as communities in Switzerland or in the free towns of Germany, in contact with what they termed 'the best-reformed churches': that is to say, churches of Swiss pattern. The second, more advanced Edwardian Prayer Book of 1552, with its conception of Holy Communion as a commemorative act, had stood as an unbridgeable gulf between them and Lutherans. Even before exile faced them, some had become infected with Calvinism, the most extreme of respectable Protestant faiths. It is not surprising that while abroad the general tendency was towards the left. At Frankfort there was serious trouble between early arrivals on the one side, who with the Scot, John Knox, as their minister adopted a Calvinistic service and 'discipline'; and, on the other side, later arrivals led by Dr. Richard Cox — whom we have met as the preacher on the opening day of Elizabeth's first Parliament — supported by equally distinguished divines, who were intent on preserving 'the face of an English church' and wanted the Edwardian Prayer Book. By means which were far from creditable Knox was driven out of Frankfort to Geneva; but in spite of this victory — and the fact is of deep significance — the Anglican party at Frankfort adopted a simplified version of the 1552

Prayer Book, which, in the interests of harmony, laid aside certain practices 'in their own nature indifferent'.[1]

Not only had the men at Frankfort devised a more radical Prayer Book: at Zurich, and at Strassburg as well, the distinguished English divines, on whom Elizabeth might have to rely for her Protestant church, had become accustomed to greater simplicity. Geneva itself — City of God to hundreds of sixteenth-century Protestant refugees and to thousands besides — had been attracting more and more Englishmen. An English church had been established there. Numbering 47 persons at the start, a further 139 were added later, and perhaps even more. It has been calculated — though we must remember that contact did not necessarily mean conversion — that something like a quarter of the total number of English exiles came under Genevan influence. Thus by November 1558, so far as the *émigrés* were concerned, the second Edwardian Prayer Book had ceased to be 'most godly'. The New Jerusalem they were anxious to build required better foundations.[2]

These Englishmen had not only been concerned with living and worshipping and bickering. They had been writing, publishing, and showering on the homeland books and pamphlets. Propaganda had become an instinct of theirs and they were expert in the art. In spite of their differences they were united by a common fate. And among the leaders in the various centres of exile there was this measure of agreement: that the conservative first Edwardian Prayer Book of 1549 was intolerable, and even the second — that of 1552 — contained remnants of Popery of which it needed to be purged. How far this placed them from Queen Elizabeth we are already in a position to surmise and we shall see more clearly as the story progresses.

When the news of Mary Tudor's death reached Geneva, the prominent men there, with that superlative instinct for organized politics that was characteristic of Calvinism, sent a messenger to the English congregations at 'Aarau, Bâle, Strassburg, Worms, Frankfort, etc.', urging that though there had been jars among them over the Book of Common Prayer and ceremonies, they should now forget their differences, embrace

---

[1] Cf. C. H. GARRETT, *The Marian Exiles*; M. M. KNAPPEN, *Tudor Puritanism*, pp. 118 seqq.
[2] KNAPPEN, p. 148.

one another, and consult together. 'If we (whose sufferance and persecutions are certain signs of our sound doctrine) hold fast together, it is most certain', they wrote, 'that the enemies shall have less power; offences shall sooner be taken away; and religion best proceed and flourish.' It was the united front, on the initiative of the revolutionary left. How well our own time knows it! The men of Aarau fell for it. Those at Frankfort were more cautious. Though they trusted 'that both true religion shall be restored and that we shall not be burdened with unprofitable ceremonies' — significant words these — it was, they pointed out, for the authorities and for Parliament to decide such matters.[1]

In any case, the Genevans moved too late. When their messenger arrived with the proposal, many of the exiles were *en route* for home. As White, Bishop of Winchester, said when he preached Mary's funeral sermon on December 14th: 'The wolves be coming out of Geneva and other places of Germany and have sent their books before, full of pestilent doctrines, blasphemy, and heresy to infect the people.'[2]

'The wolves' found a House of Commons much to their taste. Some day we shall know more about the composition of this Parliament, though never, alas, as much as we might like to know. But already this can be said. There was a vital core of at least twelve and probably sixteen returned exiles in the House: possibly more. It included two men of exceptional importance and influence: Sir Anthony Cooke, father-in-law of Sir William Cecil and Sir Nicholas Bacon, a man whom Sir Nicholas Throckmorton had suggested to Queen Elizabeth as a possible Lord Chancellor; and Sir Francis Knollys, whose wife was the Queen's cousin, who had been appointed Vice-Chamberlain and Privy Councillor on January 14th, and who throughout his career — as we shall have occasion to note — proved a godly, outspoken Puritan. Each was the type of man impatient of playing mere politics over religious causes.

To keep them in this mind they had their spiritual leaders who had been in exile with them: Cox, Grindal, Horne, Jewel, Sandys, Scory — to mention some only, who became bishops early in the new reign. Many of these divines seem to have remained in London during the Parliament. Jewel, who arrived

---

[1] *Troubles at Frankfort*, pp. 223-7.       [2] STRYPE, *Annals*, I. i. 154.

a little late, though in time enough to take a prominent part in events, wrote to his continental host and friend, Peter Martyr, on April 14th saying that 'Sandys, Grindal, Sampson, Scory (and why should I particularize these?) all of us remain still in London'.[1] It is a safe guess that these men kept in touch with those of their flock who were in Parliament, as well as with other Members and with sympathizers at Court, endeavouring to realize that complete religious establishment according to 'the best-reformed churches', which, awake and asleep, had been their inspiration while in exile. They constituted, as it were, an unofficial Convocation attached to Parliament, the pressure group of a revolutionary party; and one is reminded of the national synods which, later in the reign, Puritan ministers held in London in Parliament-time in their efforts to presbyterianize the Church of England.

In addition to the vital core of *émigrés* in the House of Commons, there were at least sixty-four other Members who had sat in Mary's obstreperous Parliament of 1555, most of whom might, with due caution, be reckoned along with the radical core. The tale is not yet fully told. Rather more than a quarter of the names of Members are unknown, and informed guesswork would certainly add some of these missing Members to our Protestant nucleus. One hundred out of a total membership of 404 seems a reasonable, perhaps an over-cautious estimate of the number whose sympathies would have been wholeheartedly with the yearnings of the *émigrés*.

'As for the rest, they be at devotion;
And when they be pressed, they cry "A good motion!" '

So wrote a satirist of Elizabeth's second Parliament.[2] His point — that in a large assembly a resolute minority, knowing its own mind and how to lead, can carry the day — is sound enough, provided the majority is not antipathetic. And a House of Commons elected in the opening months of Elizabeth's reign was not likely to be that. If our evidence suggests that the House went full-cry after its radical leaders, sweeping aside any feeble Catholic opposition or the cautious promptings of moderate or official opinion, there seems to be nothing inherently impossible or even improbable in that. It simply means

[1] *Zurich Letters*, i. 18.    [2] Cf. my *Elizabethan House of Commons*, p. 283.

that the 1559 Parliament was like every other Elizabethan
Parliament; or, indeed, like the 1555 Parliament as we might
imagine it in an Elizabethan setting.

No wonder, then, that on its first working day the House of
Commons had found an excuse for starting up a debate on the
Church. It was upon such an assembly and against such a
background that the government launched its hybrid Supremacy
bill on February 9th. A cold douche for ardent zealots! Beyond
the Clerk's laconic entry of the first reading we know nothing
of what happened. The bill was a long one. Reading the text
must have absorbed much time, but as there was only one other
bill read that morning — an unimportant and presumably short
private bill, read first thing while latecomers were assembling —
there was time for debate. We can guess its tone from the addition of Sir Anthony Cooke's name against the Clerk's entry.
He was entrusted with the bill — or so we may interpret the
Clerk's shorthand — commissioned to take it away, master the
text, and probably 'article' it (that is, divide it into epitomized
sections) in preparation for the second-reading debate. That
the House chose for this task their most eminent independent
*émigré*-Member is surely eloquent testimony to its mood.

The second reading came on February 13th. Most of this
morning and practically the whole of the next were spent on
the debate: an unusual duration for debate in those days.
Early on the 15th the bill was committed, in all likelihood to a
substantial number of Members. The Clerk entered only two
names, possibly signifying that for the better conduct of business
the bill was divided into two and each entrusted with half.
These two names — well may we mark them — were Sir
Francis Knollys and Sir Anthony Cooke. The 'exiles', it would
seem, were in control of the House.[1]

And now we are confronted with two puzzling entries in the
*Commons Journal*. On February 15th, after the committing of
the Supremacy bill and the reading of another bill, the Clerk
noted the first reading of 'The bill for order of service and
ministers in the church'. The next day his initial entry was a
first reading of 'The book for common prayer and ministration
of sacraments'. It is not likely that either involved much, if
any, debate; nor do they reappear in the *Journal*. They clearly

[1] *C.J.* i. 54.

reflect an independent move by the House or by some of its members, but what its character was we can only guess. Two explanations are possible. The 'exiles' may have been ready with a programme of their own — a radical bill and Prayer Book — which they persuaded the House to have read. This is the more extreme solution of the problem: not incredible, though perhaps unlikely. Prudence might suggest a more moderate explanation. As we shall see, there is good reason to believe that the Commons, bitterly disappointed with the timidity and limitations of government policy, decided during their prolonged debate on the Supremacy bill to extend its scope so as to secure the minimum settlement that radically-minded Protestants would willingly accept and the maximum that they could hope to secure. This was a restoration of the religious situation at the death of Edward VI. It involved reviving the second Edwardian Act of Uniformity and its accompanying Prayer Book of 1552. In these circumstances the House may have decided to remind themselves of those measures by having them read, in part or whole. As we have remarked, the two entries do not recur, and we can resume the main course of our narrative without worrying further about them.[1]

In committee the government's Supremacy bill was so drastically amended that it re-emerged as a new bill, read for the first time on February 21st. It is vital to our story to discover what it now contained: that is to say, what alterations the committee had made. The text has not survived, but there are contemporary comments which help to solve the problem.[2] One fact is certain: the committee had extended the bill to include a Protestant service, thus in effect converting it into a measure both of Supremacy and Uniformity. It also seems that they once more made marriage of the clergy permissible, as it had been in Edward VI's reign: a matter of intimate concern to *émigré* ministers, many of whom were married.

Now these two points give us our clue to what had happened. We must revert to Mary Tudor's reign to understand it. Mary had carried out her Counter-Reformation through two parliamentary Acts of Repeal: the first, in 1553, repealed the statutes

---

[1] Cf. my article, *Eng. Hist. Rev.* lxv. 313.
[2] Cf. ibid. pp. 314 seqq., where the evidence is discussed.

of Edward VI's reign, thus abolishing the doctrinal reformation; the second, in 1555, repealed Henry VIII's Reformation statutes, which had nationalized the Church but left its doctrine Catholic. The Supremacy bill which the Elizabethan government had drafted concentrated on nullifying Mary's second Act of Repeal, thus restoring the Church to its character at the death of Henry VIII. It studiously refrained from mentioning the first Act of Repeal, though some reference might have been expected because of the clause about Communion in both kinds. As likely as not, the government was afraid of directing attention to the subject of doctrinal reform.

Doctrine, however, was the subject that the Commons were most set on discussing. Their leaders were astute men. They must surely have seen that far and away the simplest and most promising way of obtaining the complete Protestant Reformation which they desired was to insert in the government's Supremacy bill a clause nullifying Mary Tudor's first Act of Repeal and reviving those Edwardian acts that suited them. If this is what they did — and it squares with our evidence — then we must conclude that they revived Edward VI's second Act of Uniformity, along with the 1552 Prayer Book; and also revived the Edwardian act permitting the clergy to marry.

Such action would not, of course, satisfy the Genevans. It would also fall a little short of the purity and simplicity of worship to which the exiles at Frankfort and elsewhere had grown accustomed. But would the latter — would, for example, Sir Francis Knollys who was in touch with Privy Council, Court, and Queen, or would Sir Anthony Cooke, in close acquaintance with Cecil and Bacon — have courted certain failure for the sake of the difference between the 1552 Prayer Book and the modified version of it used at Frankfort? One imagines not.

Both argument and evidence lead to the conclusion that the new bill — the second Supremacy bill this session — revived the 1552 Prayer Book and re-established the religious structure as it was at the death of Edward VI. It had the seductive merit of seeming to be conservative policy: though, as we shall later see, it had no chance of winning the Queen's approval. There was another feature of the government's bill with which the

Commons were dissatisfied: the moderation shown to Catholics who refused its oath of supremacy. They stiffened the penalties. Perhaps this was done by making a second refusal of the oath treason.

Except for the usual trifling private bill, read to pass the time before the House filled, a whole morning was spent on the second reading of this new Supremacy bill. 'Some', we are told, 'spoke in favour of moderation'; others, no doubt, deplored with Calvin the infirmity which would not suffer them 'to ascend an higher step'. As for the Privy-Councillor Members, some of them, conscious of their responsibilities, were probably embarrassed: though not Sir Francis Knollys, who was a godly man first and an official thereafter. What the Queen's Secretary, Sir William Cecil, thought of it all, remains a mystery. If an obscure remark from the Spanish ambassador can be trusted — and if it can, the Queen's personal control of policy becomes more evident — he abetted this Protestant move in a tortuous way.[1]

Perhaps an odd Catholic voice made itself heard. Perhaps it was on this occasion that Dr. Story — a scholar-lawyer who in Mary Tudor's reign had assisted the hated Bonner in his persecutions, and whose chequered career ended in a traitor's death, a Protestant tract and ballads, and eventual beatification at Rome — uttered his courageous if sinister comment on the lack of foresight shown by Catholics when power was theirs. 'I did often times in Queen Mary's time say to the bishops that they were too busy with *pecora campi* (for so it pleased him to term the poor commons of England), chopping at twigs. But I wished to have chopped at the root, which if they had done, this gear had not come now in question.' 'Story had his wanton words', said William Fleetwood, recounting this episode in the Parliament of 1572, 'and passed without punishment.'[2]

The House was obviously satisfied with the new bill as devised by its committee, for it was not committed after the second reading. It was read a third time on February 25th and went up to the Lords.

[1] Birt, *Elizabethan Religious Settlement*, p. 75; *Troubles at Frankfort*, p. 51; *Eng. Hist. Rev.* lxv. 318-19.
[2] *D.N.B.* sub Story, John; *Old English Ballads, 1553-1625*, ed. Rollins, p. xviii; 'A Declaration of the Life & Death of John Story', in *Harleian Miscellany* (ed. 1753), iii. 100; Thos. Cromwell's MS. Diary of the 1572 Parliament.

But the Commons did not stop at this fundamental attack on government policy. They started another, an almost equally revealing move, to pick up the threads as they had been left at the death of Edward VI. This they did by introducing a bill, read a first time on February 27th — two days after they had disposed of their Supremacy bill — 'for making of ecclesiastical laws by thirty-two persons'. Their object is not obscure: it was to revive the commission — first appointed under Henry VIII, then continued through Edward VI's reign, under Cranmer's leadership and including a number of men still on the scene in 1559 — whose function had been to draw up a reformed body of church law to replace the Catholic Canon Law. Cranmer's commissioners had done their work, and it survived and still survives in a famous book or document known as the *Reformatio Legum*.[1] But the authority of the commission had run out and the document had been left without proper sanction: understandably, since radical opinion, frustrated in the 1552 Prayer Book, had here found its expression. To cite one instance: the 1552 Prayer Book had stipulated that communicants should receive the bread and wine kneeling — an injunction so obnoxious to the Puritans of the time that they had obtained the last-minute insertion in the printed Book of the so-called 'Black Rubric' to explain that neither adoration nor any real presence of Christ's natural flesh and blood were implied. In the *Reformatio Legum* the radicals had completed their victory. It contained the astonishing clause: 'The Eucharist is a sacrament in which they who sit as guests at the Lord's holy table receive food from the bread, and drink from the wine.' What had proved 'both too liberal and too drastic' for the Duke of Northumberland, our Elizabethan House of Commons in 1559 was evidently intent on at last establishing by reviving the commission-procedure of Edward VI's reign.[2]

It is quite inconceivable that this bill could have originated with the government. It was utterly at variance with the Queen's policy at this juncture, and hateful to her at any time. Moreover, while the bill passed the Commons readily enough, without even the scrutiny of a committee, it got no further than

[1] Ed. E. Cardwell, 1850.
[2] *C.J.* i. 55; C. H. SMYTH, *Cranmer & the Reformation*, p. 259; POLLARD'S *Cranmer*, pp. 281-4.

a first reading in the Lords; and we need have little hesitation in attributing its dismal fate to instructions from the Court. Significantly, the next time this reform of the ecclesiastical laws was mentioned in connection with Parliament was as an item in the radical programme presented to the Lower House of Convocation in 1563; and it came up again in 1571 when it was printed by John Foxe, the Puritan ex-exile and martyrologist, and brought to the attention of the Commons in the course of a Puritan attack on the Elizabethan Prayer Book. In brief, this episode in 1559 fits into — one might almost say, demands — our thesis of an organized movement operating through the House of Commons, the object of which was to force upon Elizabeth and her government a complete Protestant programme, at least as radical as that achieved by the close of Edward VI's reign.

But to return to the Supremacy bill, now before the Upper House. A fortnight elapsed between the first and second readings, during which, presumably, the Queen had to decide on her attitude to the Commons' amendments. It looks very much as if a tussle was going on at Court between radical, moderate, and conservative opinion. The Protestant divines, who for lack of any practicable alternative were drawn on for the Lent sermons — the great occasions of public preaching in the year — exploited their opportunity, uttering before Queen and people, as Il Schifanoya tells us, 'the most base and abominable things that were ever heard against the Apostolic See'.[1] Then, on March 13th the Supremacy bill was given a second reading in the House of Lords, debated, and committed to thirteen temporal peers and two bishops. Had the government wished to treat the Commons' amendments sympathetically, doubtless its influential members in the Upper House could have secured a majority on the committee to carry out its will. In fact, while the committee was, numerically speaking, overwhelmingly safe on the subject of royal supremacy, in matters of doctrine it contained a bare majority of conservatives — men who ultimately voted against the Act of Uniformity.[2]

[1] *Venetian Cal.* vii. 46; *Machyn's Diary* (Camden Soc.), pp. 189-90; *Zurich Letters*, i. 27.
[2] *L.J.* i. 555, 563; *Eng. Hist. Rev.* xxviii. 537.

In committee the Commons' amendments were evidently deleted and the bill restored to its original form, perhaps with the addition of an escape clause permitting the Queen, if she wished, to renounce the title of Supreme Head of the Church: a title unpalatable to radicals and conservatives alike on account of her sex, and one which she was telling the Spanish ambassador at this very time that she would not take. No doubt the committee had acted on direct or indirect instructions from the Court.[1]

It was at this juncture — presumably on March 17th, when the House of Lords was dealing with the amendments made in committee — that Bishop Scot of Chester delivered a long speech, the text of which has come down to us. Containing about 7000 words, it must have occupied the major part of the sitting. His main argument was concerned with the transfer of supremacy from the Pope to the Queen, and was opposed to it; but in the opening section he referred with thankfulness to the committee's amendments, as a result of which the Catholic service of the Church was retained and the extreme penalties of the bill mitigated.[2]

The bill, thus amended, was read a third time on March 18th and passed, with twelve dissentients — two temporal, and all the spiritual, peers — out of an attendance of forty-five. Nicholas Heath, Archbishop of York, appears to have stated the Catholic case on this occasion, in a dignified speech, delivered, as he declared, 'for the discharge of his conscience'. It was appreciably shorter than Bishop Scot's and paid a tribute to the new Queen which was surely genuine. 'We may assure ourselves', he said, 'to have of her Highness as humble, as virtuous, and as godly a mistress to reign over us as ever had English people here in this realm, if that her Highness is not by our flattery and dissimulation seduced and beguiled.' His criticism was directed against the title 'Supreme Head of the Church of England, immediate and next unto God'. Parliament, he declared, had no right to grant spiritual government to her. Moreover, as a woman she was incapable of fulfilling Christ's injunction to Peter to feed his flock. He quoted St. Paul on the obligation of women to be silent in the church and

---

[1] Cf. my article, *Eng. Hist. Rev.* lxv. 321.
[2] STRYPE, *Annals*, I. ii. 408-23.

not to lord it over men: in this speaking with the same voice as John Knox and the general run of sixteenth-century mankind. As we know, the widespread prejudice on the point was ultimately to have its effect.[1]

Meanwhile, Members of the House of Commons were presumably aware that the Lords were stripping the Supremacy bill of their additions; and their leaders at any rate must have realized that when it came back to them they would be faced with the choice of accepting the Lords' amendments and losing a Protestant Prayer Book, or rejecting the bill and retaining the supremacy of the Pope. The latter alternative could not be contemplated. Parliament, moreover, was thought to be near its end.[2] The subsidy and the main government bills, with the exception of this one, were through; and Easter — which fell this year on Sunday, March 26th — was close at hand. If they were capable of a counter-attack, speed was essential.

On March 17th, without waiting for the amended Supremacy bill to pass the Lords, the Commons introduced a bill, to which the Clerk in his *Journal* gave the descriptive title 'that no persons shall be punished for using the religion used in King Edward's last year'. It was read twice that morning and ordered to be ingrossed, and the following morning was given a third reading and passed. There was no commitment: indeed, judging by the amount of other business transacted on both days, there was probably no debate. The procedure proclaims their desperate urgency. If there was any opposition it must have been rudely brushed aside by a House overwhelmingly set on passing the measure in the minimum of time.

Should any doubts linger about the temper and outlook of this body of men, they must now vanish; for this cannot have been a government bill. It was flatly contradictory of the Queen's policy. It must have been introduced by the leaders of the Protestant party, who, as Il Schifanoya tells us, were angry and in revolt against the action of the Lords. Their intention is clear. If they were to be denied uniformity on the basis of Edward VI's second Prayer Book, they would demand nonconformity on the same basis. One may doubt whether

---

[1] *L.J.* i. 565; STRYPE, *Annals*, I. ii. 399-407.
[2] Cf. *Venetian Cal.* vii. 46.

the leaders really hoped to get the bill through the Lords. To accomplish this by Easter, they would have needed the indulgence of speedy procedure, as well as the informal support of the government. No: the bill was a propaganda demonstration, meant to proclaim the determination and defiance of the Commons of England and coerce the conservative party at Court. The tactics were those of revolution.[1]

The Supremacy bill, restored broadly speaking to the form first given it by the government, came back to the Commons, was agreed to by them, and was ready for the royal assent by March 22nd.[2] Fortunately, at this critical point our evidence becomes clear and decisive.

The Queen intended to give her consent to the bill. Of that we can be certain; for on March 22nd, the very date on which the bill finally passed the Lords, she issued a proclamation which announced the making, among other statutes, of the Act of Supremacy 'in the present last session of Parliament' — words which anticipated the imminent prorogation or dissolution of Parliament. The proclamation further declared that as Easter was at hand and the Supremacy Act too long to be printed and published in time, and as no other form of Communion Service could as yet be legally established, the statute of Edward VI for Communion in both kinds (restored in the new Act of Supremacy) was revived and in force. On this great Feast Day, when all communicated who could, the people were to have their Communion in both kinds, either at their own parish church, or elsewhere if the priest proved obstinate. 'Great numbers, not only of the nobility and gentlemen but also of the common people' — announced the proclamation — were unwilling to receive the sacrament except in this form, 'according to the first institution and to the common use both of the Apostles and the Primitive Church'.[3]

These last words must have given pleasure to radicals: Protestant propaganda had not been without its effect. But how far from their aspirations all this was. 'I see that the heretics are very downcast in the last few days', wrote the Spanish

---

[1] *C.J.* i. 58; *Venetian Cal.* vii. 52-3.

[2] *C.J.* i. 58; *L.J.* i. 568.

[3] GEE, *Elizabethan Prayer-Book*, pp. 255-7; STEELE, *Tudor & Stuart Proclamations*, i. 53, no. 502.

ambassador on March 24th. And no wonder! Unless a miracle happened, their great Parliamentary campaign was lost.[1]

[1] *Spanish Cal. Eliz.* i. 44.

## CHAPTER III

# THE RELIGIOUS SETTLEMENT:
## AFTER EASTER

THE miracle did happen. The Queen changed her mind. This surely must be one of the significant moments in English history; and fortunately we can date it with remarkable precision. On March 22nd, the date of the proclamation, Elizabeth undoubtedly intended to end Parliament. During the evening of the 23rd she sent to the Spanish ambassador to arrange an audience for 9 a.m. on the following day; but — he tells us — as he was about to set out for the interview he received a message cancelling it, since she was very busy. 'She had resolved', he added, 'to go to Parliament today — March 24th — at 1 o'clock, after dinner', to give the royal assent to bills.[1]

From this evidence we may assume that on March 23rd Elizabeth was still intending to end Parliament before Easter; and, indeed, she was hardly likely to have proposed seeing the ambassador had her policy been changed. Her message on the morning of the 24th, can either be taken at its face value, or be more subtly — and perhaps erroneously — interpreted as putting off the audience at an embarrassing moment when she had yielded to Protestant agitation. And so we must conclude that either in the night watches of March 23rd-24th — at a time when, as we know from other critical incidents in her reign, Elizabeth, in common with other human beings, felt misgivings most acutely — or between 9 a.m. and 1 p.m. on Good Friday, March 24th, the Queen changed her mind. Instead of going to Parliament to end the session, she had it adjourned over Easter to April 3rd, and, in so doing, altered the pattern of the Elizabethan religious settlement. If this had not happened, England would have had to wait for its Protestant Prayer Book till another Parliament; and how the conflict of religions would have worked out in the meanwhile or what the character of the ultimate settlement would have been are questions that might well be added to the enthralling game of historical might-have-beens.

[1] *Spanish Cal. Eliz.* i. 44.

What had led the Queen to change her mind? On the domestic front the policy of little by little had obviously broken down. Historical situations do not repeat themselves; and certainly the situation which confronted her was different from her sister's, or her brother's, or her father's. The Catholic bishops had voted unanimously against all change. Elizabeth might — in fact, her actions were to reveal that she did — still hope to prevail on some of them to stand by her. But their united front had made her dependent for the reconstruction of the Anglican Church on the Protestant divines who had been on the continent: critically dependent, as the ecclesiastical appointments of the next year or so were to show. These divines had in turn displayed a united front. And this perhaps was the more unexpected happening. On the domestic front it was the decisive factor. Their operations through the House of Commons (assuming that they supplied advice as well as spiritual exhortation) or the tactics of the leaders in the Lower House (if we attribute the planning to them) had been superb, even astounding. At Court they had their supporters among the Privy Councillors, who must have played upon the Queen's mind: Knollys we can be sure about, and in all probability the powerful and Puritan-minded Earl of Bedford; probably also Sir William Cecil, Sir Nicholas Bacon, and the Queen's old Welsh servant, now her Treasurer of the Household, Sir Thomas Parry; doubtless others.

But decisive as were the tactics of the House of Commons, they would scarcely have prevailed if there had not been a change in the foreign situation. The principal reason for the new policy — of this there seems little doubt — was the news, which reached England on Palm Sunday, March 19th, that the commissioners had concluded peace with the French at Câteau Cambrésis. Elizabeth could now feel secure enough on her throne to take the second step in her religious settlement. The policy of caution had lost its last, imperative justification; and perhaps it was at this moment that William Cecil, whose post as Secretary and qualities of mind and character gave him great influence with his mistress, came over unhesitatingly to the new policy. Two months later, one of the Protestant divines, Edmund Grindal, who was soon to become Bishop of London and later Archbishop of Canterbury, writing to a continental friend, summed up the situation as he had watched it develop in London: 'We were indeed urgent from the very first that a general reformation should take place. But the Parliament long delayed the matter and made no change whatever until a peace had been concluded between the Sovereigns, Philip, the French king, and ourselves.'[1]

With the change of policy the government continued to follow the precedents of Edward VI's reign. His first Uniformity bill had been preceded by a disputation of the bishops, held in the Parliament House, with the Commons going in as on-lookers.[2] A similar overture was to precede the Elizabethan Act of Uniformity. From a letter of Jewel's we know that this had been decided upon by March 20th. The first discussion, he wrote, was to take place on March 31st, when nine Catholic leaders were to confront nine Protestant — Scory, Cox, White-head, Sandys, Grindal, Horne, Aylmer, Guest and Jewel himself. With the exception of Guest, all the Protestant protagonists had been in exile during Mary's reign, and all, with the exception of Whitehead, were to become bishops: striking proof of the government's dependence upon them, and therefore of their latent power.[3]

Such disputations were becoming a sixteenth-century habit, and Catherine de Medici was to attempt to solve her religious difficulties at the famous Colloquy of Poissy two years later. Catherine, it has been said, did not know what the word dogma meant: her Colloquy was a fiasco and a political blunder. Elizabeth had been brought up on Melanchthon's *Loci Com-munes*: she was no stranger to theology. Her colloquy was also a fiasco, but it was not a political blunder. Its object, Jewel wrote, was to deprive the Catholic bishops of any excuse that they had been put down only by the power and authority of the law. In other words, it was to serve as propaganda on which to launch the religious settlement: revolutionary technique with which in these days we also are familiar. That it was planned as the forerunner of liturgical and doctrinal reform seems obvious from the three subjects of debate, as Jewel stated them on March 20th: the use of the vulgar tongue in church

[1] *Spanish Cal. Eliz.* i. 42; *Zurich Letters*, ii. 19.
[2] GASQUET and BISHOP, *Edward VI & the Book of Common Prayer*, pp. 397 seqq.; *Original Letters* (Parker Soc.), i. 322-3, ii. 469.
[3] *Zurich Letters*, i. 10-11.

services; the right of every provincial church to establish its own liturgy; the lack of scriptural justification for the propitiatory sacrifice in the Mass.

But this raises a question. Why did Elizabeth commit herself to the disputation, with its clear implications, on or before March 20th, and yet on March 22nd, or even as late as the morning of the 24th be resolved to end Parliament without a Protestant Prayer Book and Act of Uniformity? The answer is inherent in personal monarchy and in the character of the monarch. The disputation, we may assume, was the policy of the Protestant divines and their party, who clearly foresaw and passionately desired its logical outcome. The Queen, under pressure, conceded them the means, without necessarily willing the end — or rather, the immediate fulfilment of their policy. She was fighting a battle of retreat. We shall watch the continuation of this contest, with its profound effect upon the Anglican Church and upon the quality of English life through the centuries to come.

The disputation duly began, before Privy Councillors and peers, in the choir of Westminster Abbey on March 31st. As might have been anticipated, the proceedings did not go smoothly; and at the next meeting, on April 3rd, the refusal of the bishops to agree on procedure brought the debate to an abrupt end. Their obstinacy — or the official account of it, which was disseminated in print — was at least as good propaganda for the new, doctrinal phase of the Elizabethan settlement as a Protestant victory in argument would have been. The day of this final fiasco was the day to which Parliament stood adjourned; and that morning the Clerk of the House of Commons made only a single entry in his *Journal*, noting that the Speaker and a few of the House met, read part of a bill, and then adjourned to hear the disputation between the bishops and — as he put it — 'Mr. Horne, Mr. Cox, and other Englishmen that came from Geneva'. The Englishmen from Geneva! As a matter of fact, none came from that city. But 'Geneva' was a meaningful word: a bogy to some, an inspiration to others.[1]

When parliamentary business got under way again, the

---

[1] FOXE, *Acts & Monuments*, ed. Pratt and Stoughton, viii. 679-93, 798 (and cf. H. G. DUGDALE's *Life of Geste*); *C. J.* i. 59.

Commons pressed forward with a bill which can hardly have
been sponsored by the government but very much concerned
the *émigrés* and their friends. They had introduced it a month
earlier, on March 8th, when the Clerk described it as a bill 'to
restore spiritual persons that were deprived [in the time of
Mary] for marriage or heresies . . .' Presumably the bill did
restore them: high-handed action, indeed, to originate in a
House of Parliament. They now took the measure up again,
but in committee made it seem more palatable by recasting
it into a form which permitted the Queen to do the restoration.
Their second thoughts were only less objectionable than their
first, for they were threatening the royal prerogative by proposing to use parliamentary authority to sanction what the
Queen herself could do as Supreme Governor of the Church;
and no doubt it was with Elizabeth's concurrence, if not at her
suggestion, that the Lords rejected the bill on its third reading
in their House.[1]

At the same time the Commons were busy with a bill to
restore to the Crown any colleges and chantries revived under
Mary. This may have been a government measure, but at the
committee stage the Commons substituted for it a new bill extending its scope to include the dissolution of those monasteries,
etc., which Mary had restored. Their hand can be traced in
the preamble, which, in contrast to the studied restraint of
government bills, made a full-blooded attack on the Catholicism
of Mary's reign: alluding to the reduction of the realm 'rather
to darkness and superstition than to the true knowledge and
honouring of Almighty God'; and to the 'rules, ordinances,
rites and ceremonies in their services and common prayers,
repugnant to the usage of the holy Catholic and Apostolic
Church of Christ'. It was the language of 'the Englishmen from
Geneva'. The bill ultimately passed the Lords, with the
spiritual peers dissenting, and for lay company, Viscount
Montague.[2]

The most interesting feature about this bill is that for the
time being there would have been no such measure if Elizabeth
had ended the Parliament on March 24th. Mary's monasteries
and chantries would have remained legally valid, though of

[1] *C.J.* i. 57, 59, 61; *Eng. Hist. Rev.* xxviii. 541.
[2] *C.J.* i. 59, 60, 61; *Statutes of Realm*, IV. i. 397-8; *Eng. Hist. Rev.* xxviii. 541.

course the oath of supremacy might have wrought havoc on monks, nuns, or priests. Theoretically, however, there might still have been an Abbot of Westminster when Elizabeth's second Parliament met. If this strikes us as strange, it is tribute to the revolutionary agitation of the Protestant exiles and their supporters in the House of Commons. It certainly would not have seemed strange in the previous November, when Richard Goodrich and Armagil Waad were writing their advice on religious policy.

While the Commons were dealing with these bills, the government was using the House of Lords for another measure that they would not have ventured to bring forward while their policy was one of caution and compromise. This was the notorious bill to strengthen the finances of the Crown at the expense of the bishops: giving Elizabeth power during vacancies — of which there were already many, and soon to be more — to exchange parsonages impropriate and tenths held by the Crown for an equivalent value of the temporal possessions of archbishoprics and bishoprics. A bad bargain it was for the Church; and Elizabeth did not shrink from using its powers.[1] But there is more to be said for it than used to be thought; and in any case, the forcible redistribution of wealth in society is no novelty today, nor was it in the sixteenth century. Cecil may have been responsible for the policy: he was to advise a Scottish statesman that the way to reduce the political power of the Church was to diminish its wealth. However, what most interests us in this narrative of ours is the tactics of the government in bringing the bill first into the Lords. They preferred to incur at once the hostile vote of all the spiritual peers rather than start the measure in the Commons; for the latter course would have involved facing the Lower House without the additional impetus of support from the temporal peers, and then facing the Upper House after strong initial hostility from the religious zealots below. When the bill came to the Lower House, sure enough it was taken to a division after the third reading and passed with ninety negative votes in a House reduced through absentees to 224. We probably have here an indication of the irreducible Puritan core in this Parliament of 1559: godly men who joyously

[1] Cf. *Cal. Patent Rolls, Eliz.* ii. 191, 224, 285, 306, 309-10, 323.

harried the Papists, but would not betray the Church in the
interest of the State.[1]

All these bills, however, are of secondary interest. They
deserve attention mainly for the consistency of their stories
with our general interpretation of the Parliament. The two
principal measures in these post-Easter sittings were the bills
of Supremacy and Uniformity. Though the former had passed
both Houses before Easter, a new — the third — bill of Supremacy had to be drafted, because Elizabeth had now finally
decided to drop the title of Supreme Head of the Church and
adopt that of Supreme Governor. The Spanish ambassador
took credit for her scruples: the *émigrés* attributed them to one
of themselves, Mr. Lever. The fact is that both conservatives
and radicals were relieved; though, if the Spanish ambassador
can be believed, Cecil had to face criticism in the Commons at
all this chopping and changing.[2]

The bill had a rapid passage through the Commons, without
a committee. In the Lords it was committed; and, having now
before them the prospect of Protestant doctrine in the Church,
the conservatives took care to add a schedule ensuring, among
other safeguards, that the ecclesiastical commissioners provided
for in the bill — who might well be drawn from the dominant
radical party — should not define heresy in a novel form. To
this, when the bill came back to them for concurrence, the
Commons retorted by an amendment limiting heresy in a
manner suitable to themselves. The Commons also devised an
additional proviso which declared that nothing done by this
Parliament should hereafter be judged heresy or schism: they
were thinking of a possible counter-reformation in the future.
Much good their proviso would have done if that calamity had
happened! The Lords acquiesced. On its third reading they
had passed the bill with only one temporal peer — the faithful
Viscount Montague — joining all the spiritual peers in their
dissent.[3]

This third Supremacy bill, which became our statute, still
contained the clause about Communion in both kinds that had

[1] *L.J.* i. 570-1; *C.J.* i. 59-60.
[2] *Spanish Cal. Eliz.* i. 52; *Parker Correspondence* (Parker Soc.) p. 66; *Zurich Letters*,
i. 24.
[3] MAITLAND, *Collected Papers*, iii. 191-2 (cf. my additional comment in *Eng. Hist.
Rev.* lxv. 330, n. 5); *Eng. Hist. Rev.* xxviii. 537-9.

been in the first and second bills. And once more this invaluable piece of evidence — the key to the whole story of the Elizabethan settlement — emerges as a vital clue. When the government, in the following October, sent over the bills for the first Irish Parliament of the reign, they took this clause, as we have noticed, out of the Irish Supremacy act; but they made a separate bill of it and sent it over, along with the bills of Supremacy and Uniformity. They had obviously prepared alternative policies: the Uniformity bill and the Elizabethan Prayer Book, if the Irish Parliament could be brought to agree; Communion in both kinds as a *pis aller*, if the larger policy failed. In fact, the Uniformity bill passed and the other was not needed.[1]

In this Irish parallel lies our clue, for the most plausible explanation for the retention of the clause in the English Supremacy bill would be a similar predicament: a fear on the part of the government that they might not secure agreement over the Prayer Book. But agreement between whom? There can be practically no doubt that the contestants were the Queen and the Protestant divines.

As we have seen, the Queen changed her policy when she decided to adjourn Parliament on March 24th and when she consented to the disputation at Westminster. This was the time — about the end of March — when action must have been taken to prepare a revised Prayer Book; and the men who were designated for the task by the events at Westminster and stood out as the leaders of the victorious Protestant party were the nine divines who had disputed with the Catholic bishops — eight *émigrés*, into whose company, somehow or other, one stay-at-home, Edmund Guest, had been intruded. Now it looks as if Guest, as the most conservative among them and the most likely, therefore, to be acceptable to the Queen, was saddled with the task of revision. We can perhaps afford a guess that Cecil was responsible for this attempt to fuse the infusible. At any rate, our sole evidence at this juncture is to be found in an anonymous and undated letter, which Cecil appears to have ascribed to Guest and which fits into our story. He came across it in 1566 when searching for another document

---

[1] *Cal. Patent Rolls, Eliz.* i. 29; *Statutes at Large, Ireland*, i. 275 seqq.; DUDLEY EDWARDS, *Church & State in Tudor Ireland*, p. 177.

to send to Archbishop Parker. There seems little risk in assuming that it was originally addressed to him.[1]

From this letter, which is concerned with explaining and justifying certain features of a new Prayer Book, it would appear that if the work of revision was the result of instructions from Cecil — and the author's expectation or even assumption that his revised Book would go before Parliament seems to support this theory — then those instructions had been to base the revision on the conservative first Edwardian Prayer Book of 1549. If, on the other hand, the revision was made on the initiative of the reformers, then Cecil had obviously been alarmed at its radicalism and was demanding justification for departures from the 1549 Book.

In fact, the 'service' which the author had sent to Cecil, expecting it to become the Anglican Prayer Book, had been based on the more radical of the two former Books: the 1552 or last Edwardian Prayer Book. But it had advanced further, like the revised book of Frankfort in Mary's days. It was the type of revision to be expected from the divines who had been at Frankfort or Strassburg or elsewhere, but not at Geneva; and while no certain proof can be offered for the inference that the Westminster disputants were its sponsors, the weight of circumstantial evidence points that way.[2]

[1] The letter is printed in GEE, op. cit. pp. 215-24 (cf. my comments in *Eng. Hist. Rev.* lxv. 326-9). The manuscript text of the letter, among the Parker MSS. at Cambridge, is a copy, lacking the ending and signature. It has always been regarded as the document sent to Parker by Cecil on December 21st, 1566. If it was – and I have based my narrative on this assumption – then we must, I think, accept Cecil's statement that it was written by Guest. Presumably the original was signed, and Parker had this copy of the text, omitting the formal ending and signature, made before returning it to Cecil (cf. his letter in *Parker Corres.* pp. 290-1, where he promises to return the document he wanted – the letter to which Cecil's of December 21st was probably the reply). However, we should note that the identification of this anonymous document with the one mentioned by Cecil reposes solely on its position next to Cecil's letter among Parker's MSS.: far from convincing evidence. Professor E. C. Ratcliff of Cambridge, in a valuable interchange of letters I had with him and Professor Norman Sykes, questions the ascription to Guest on the ground of Guest's belief in a real presence in the eucharist. If – but only if – this is not the document that Cecil sent to Parker on December 21st, then the argument is cogent. Personally, I shall not be surprised if someday the missing evidence turns up, and we are able to identify the writer as one of the exiles, say Jewel. Such a discovery would add strength to my main argument; but in the present state of our knowledge I have thought it wiser to be conservative.

[2] A Puritan reminiscence, twenty-seven years later, reads: 'In the beginning of her Majesty's reign a number of worthy men . . . desired such a book and such order for the discipline of the Church as they had seen in the best-reformed Churches

As we know, this radical revision did not become the Prayer Book of England. Instead, it led to a crucial struggle at Court. The situation might be summed up in the following way. From her initial and purely political predilection for the Church as her father left it, the Queen had been driven by events as far as the first Edwardian Prayer Book, where both theological and political reasoning would probably have stayed her: political reasoning, because the 1549 Book, which Stephen Gardiner had once said 'he could with his conscience keep', offered, with its implication of a real presence in the Communion, the prospect of compromise with conservatives at home and alliance with Lutherans abroad.[1] Now, however, after Easter, it was a question whether pressure from the left could drive the Queen on another stage or more. In this contest we may see an explanation of the delay which occurred in introducing the bill of Uniformity into Parliament. We may also see why the government retained the clause about Communion in both kinds in its new Supremacy bill. No one could be certain of the outcome: deadlock — and therefore no Act of Uniformity and no Prayer Book — was not impossible.

In the end, compromise came in the form of the Elizabethan Prayer Book. It reflected political realities. Elizabeth could not construct her Protestant Church without *émigré* support: she therefore surrendered most. The Prayer Book was that of 1552, the minimum these divines would accept. But the imprint of the Queen is on it. For example, in those double sentences with which the bread and wine are administered in the Communion service: 'The body of our Lord Jesus Christ, which was given for thee, preserve thy body and soul into everlasting life: and take and eat this in remembrance that Christ died for thee, and feed on him in thine heart by faith, with thanksgiving.' The first half was the formula of the 1549 Book, implying a real presence; the second was that of 1552, and was Swiss doctrine. In this strange amalgam, now sanctified by the usage of centuries, we can see where the Queen stood fast, and the divines stood fast. The 'Black Rubric' — last minute

---

[1] Cf. *Eng. Hist. Rev.* lxv. 318, 328.

abroad' (*A Seconde Parte of a Register*, ed. A. Peel, ii. 84). In my article (*Eng. Hist. Rev.* lxv. 313) I used this quotation at an earlier stage of the story. Perhaps it is more appropriate here.

victory of the Puritans in 1552 — was removed, as was the
prayer to be delivered 'from the tyranny of the bishop of Rome,
and all his detestable enormities', which had been in the
Litany of both Edward VI's Prayer Books. And, crucially
important, the Queen had a conservative proviso inserted in the
Uniformity bill, which produced the much-discussed Ornaments Rubric and led to the great Vestiarian Controversy with
Elizabethan Puritans. The Church, if Elizabeth could manage
it, was at any rate to look old-fashioned and decorous.[1]

It had been a stubborn struggle. Can one doubt that? Talking to the Spanish ambassador on the day that the Uniformity
bill finally passed in the Lords, Elizabeth said 'that she wished
the Augustanean confession' — the Lutheran confession of
Augsburg, a phrase which we may take to correspond with the
1549 Prayer Book — 'to be maintained in her realm'. And then
she added that 'it would not be the Augustanean confession,
but something else like it, and that she differed very little from
us as she believed that God was in the sacrament of the
Eucharist, and only dissented from three or four things in the
Mass'. Far from being diplomatic prevarication, it was a *cri
de cœur*.[2]

The Uniformity bill, but not the Prayer Book — this was
merely described in the bill — was introduced into the Commons on April 18th, read a second time and evidently debated
but not committed on the 19th, passing the following day.
Quick work! Neither the divines nor their supporters in the
Lower House can have attached vital importance to the proviso about ornaments, with its repulsive corollary on vestments.
Indeed, we know they did not. Sandys, one of the Westminster
disputants, writing to Parker on April 30th, commented: 'Our
gloss upon this text is that we shall not be forced to use' the
ornaments. As for Elizabeth: Parker, in later years, recalled
that, talking to him once or twice on a certain point, she had
told him that she 'would not have agreed to divers orders' of
the Prayer Book, had it not been for this proviso about orna-

---

[1] Grindal's dimmed memory of the struggle, seven years later, was expressed in
a letter to Bullinger: 'We . . . contended long and earnestly for the removal of
those things that have occasioned the present dispute; but as we were unable to
prevail, either with the Queen or the Parliament, we judged it best, after a consultation on the subject, not to desert our churches for the sake of a few ceremonies'
(*Zurich Letters*, i. 169).

[2] *Spanish Cal. Eliz.* i. 61-2.

ments. As with many another compromise, each party was reading its own meaning into it.[1]

In the Lords the bill had as rapid a passage. Exercising their privilege of freedom of speech, Bishops Scot and Thirlby and the Abbot of Westminster spoke against it, and at the passing eighteen peers — nine spiritual and nine temporal — dissented. The Spanish ambassador reported that it was carried by only three votes, which is quite credible, though there is no means of verifying the statement. But this does not mean that the bill was in any real danger, nor do those nine hostile lay votes — two from Privy Councillors — signify Catholicism. Viscount Montague was the only lay peer who can be classified with the Catholic bishops.[2]

The fact is that there was a last-minute effort to persuade the Queen to veto the bill. Sandys mentioned this in his letter to Parker. It was a subtle attack, directed against a point in the Communion service and based upon the Gospel account. Sandys attributed the leadership in this Court intrigue to Dr. Boxall, Dean of Peterborough, formerly Privy Councillor and Secretary to Mary Tudor, who, he said, got hold of the Spanish ambassador and 'the Treasurer': no doubt meaning the Marquis of Winchester, Lord Treasurer, who, significantly enough, voted against the bill. Others were involved. 'I trust they cannot prevail', added Sandys. He was evidently not too sure, though Cecil was 'earnest with the book', and the Protestant divines had dealt with Boxall's point.[3]

For us the interest of this evidence is that it squares with our interpretation of the Queen's predilections. What hope could such intrigue have had, what danger could it have presented to the radical Protestant party, unless Elizabeth at heart preferred the 1549 Prayer Book? Moreover, it probably explains why there were nine lay votes, in place of one, against the bill in the Upper House: these noblemen presumably knew and shared the Queen's personal views, felt that she had been coerced and outmanœuvred by the radicals, and voted as they did in order to strengthen the final, conservative move over the veto.

Parliament met for the closing ceremonies of the session at

[1] *Parker Correspondence*, pp. 65, 375.
[2] Cf. *Eng. Hist. Rev.* lxv. 331.
[3] *Parker Correspondence*, pp. 65-6.

2 p.m. on Monday, May 8th, when, with 'the Queen's Majesty sitting in her royal seat, the Lords and Commons attendant, Mr. Speaker — as the Clerk of the Lower House wrote — made a learned oration, and, exhibiting the bill for the subsidy and the bill of tonnage and poundage, required the Queen's assent might be given to such bills [as had been] passed by both the Houses'.[1]  Mr. Speaker's speech has not survived, but the answer of the Lord Keeper, Sir Nicholas Bacon — in length about 3000 words — found a place in the several collections of this statesman's orations, made for the edification of his generation and the next.

The great issues of the session were not overlooked. Speaking in the name of the Queen, Bacon remarked that when Her Majesty considered how in their discussions they had 'banished all sudden, rash, and swift proceedings, dangerous enemies to all good counsells'; when also she considered what freedom of speech had been used and permitted for the plain declaration of every man's knowledge and conscience; how learnedly and cunningly the disputable matters of moment had been argued and reasoned and how advisedly resolved; and lastly, 'with what well-nigh an universal consent and agreement' they had been enacted: she not only commended their wisdom and diligence, but trusted that as no private man could infringe the decisions of Parliament, so none would by word impugn or gainsay them, being thus made at leisure and with liberty. A section of the speech dealt specifically with uniformity in religion. Watch, declared Bacon, would be kept on hinderers, especially on those that subtly by indirect means sought the contrary of what had been so deliberately established in Parliament; on 'those that be too swift, as those that be too slow', extremists of the left as well as the right. There cannot be good governance where obedience faileth. Great heed would be taken of factions and sects, 'the very mothers and nurses to all seditions and tumults': 'founded for the more part either upon will or upon the glory of men's wits', they should be sufficiently repressed and bridled.

Here spoke the statesman, not the *dévot*. And it was for the Queen that he spoke; perhaps even on her brief. Certainly the speech accords with her policy as we have interpreted it; and

[1] *C.J.* i. 61.

the value she attached to a moderate settlement, excluding religious innovations of any kind, can be seen in one of the Lord Keeper's arguments. 'No man in obeying the laws made at this session . . . should thereby be forced any otherwise to do than either himself hath by law already done' — that is, in Edward VI's reign — 'or else others have before this time done, whom both for wisdom, virtue, and learning it shall not be unseeming any man here (without offence be it spoken) to follow and take example of.'

In thanking both Lords and Commons for their grants of taxes, Bacon conveyed 'certain noble and princely observations' of the Queen. It was only too evident that the money proceeded 'not of your superfluities but rather of your necessities'; from subjects who had in the past been 'continuously charged and burdened with these things to the universal impoverishing of the whole realm'; and — what was worse — in 'no ways to the strengthening, amending, or honouring of the same'. Their readiness in making the grants sprang from their benevolence and affection to Her Majesty, which she 'accepteth and taketh for the greatest benefit and most precious jewel that a subject can present to his Sovereign'. 'She findeth herself earnestly disposed, if your sureties and the State's would so suffer, as freely to remit these grants as you did gladly grant them.'[1]

When the Lord Keeper had ended, the royal assent was given to bills. The Queen did presumably veto one bill — 'for admitting and consecrating of archbishops and bishops' — which had passed both Houses before Easter.[2] But the Court intrigue to persuade her to veto the bill of Uniformity failed. The Parliament was dissolved.

The main structure of the Elizabethan religious settlement was now determined. In giving way to the Protestant divines Elizabeth had been wise. Thereby she obtained as conservative and comprehensive a Church as was possible. It may seem strange to say that this was the most propitious occasion for compromise: the beginning of the reign, which brought the exiles home from the continent, exalted by the miraculous ways of God — 'The Lord has caused a new star to arise': 'Now is the time for the walls of Jerusalem to be built again in that king-

---

[1] B.M. Harleian MS. 5176, fol. 110.
[2] It finally passed the Lords on March 23rd (cf. B.M. Stowe MS. 357, fol. 50b).

dom, that the blood of so many martyrs, so largely shed, may not be in vain';[1] an occasion, moreover, that witnessed a similar upsurge in the country and in the Lower House of Parliament. But future events at home and abroad were to intensify, not diminish the revolutionary, crusading spirit. No subsequent Elizabethan House of Commons would have agreed to the Prayer Book of 1559 — without, indeed, the most bitter struggle and a degree of coercion fatal to harmony; while to have delayed a settlement would in itself have made comprehension so difficult as to be practically unattainable. The Puritan movement might have developed as a Separatist movement.

The compromise of 1559 of course created its own difficulties: they will scarcely ever be absent from our parliamentary story. The Queen did not forget her defeat. Her vigorous action in the Vestiarian controversy that was to disturb and distress the Anglican Church suggests more than statecraft: it suggests a passionate resolve to have the pound of flesh provided for in her bond. Doubtless she detested Puritanism the more for having wrested so much from her in this Parliament. For their part, the *émigré* divines, who had hoped and worked for a simpler, purer form of service, divided in their reactions to the compromise. Writing to Peter Martyr when all was over, the gentle, scholarly, and lovable Jewel revealed himself a disillusioned man. 'As far as I can perceive at present, there is not the same alacrity among our friends, as there lately was among the Papists. So miserably is it ordered, that falsehood is armed, while truth is not only unarmed, but also frequently offensive. The scenic apparatus of divine worship is now under agitation; and those very things which you and I have so often laughed at, are now seriously and solemnly entertained by certain persons (for *we* are not consulted) as if the Christian religion could not exist without something tawdry. Our minds indeed are not sufficiently disengaged to make these fooleries of much importance. Others are seeking after a golden, or as it rather seems to me, a leaden mediocrity; and are crying out that the half is better than the whole.' It is not surprising that the first phase of the Elizabethan Puritan movement was a struggle over vestments: it was the aftermath of the 1559 Parliament.[2]

[1] *Zurich Letters*, ii. 4; STRYPE, *Memorials*, III. ii. 163.    [2] *Zurich Letters*, i. 23.

The fascinating element in this story is that the criticism, the anger, the bitterness of the radicals were not focused on the Queen: 'This woman, excellent as she is and earnest in the cause of true religion', as Jewel wrote on April 14th. And a fortnight after Parliament ended, his sentiment was unchanged: 'We have a wise and religious Queen and one too who is favourably and propitiously disposed towards us.' They fought the forces of darkness about her at Court, but she was to them a child of light.[1] To read their praise of Elizabeth, when we know that she was their main obstacle, is both surprising and pathetic. There had been no such immunity for her sister. It is the supreme paradox of Elizabeth's reign: partly resolved by the lack of a rising sun for the critics to worship, a successor on whom to pin their hopes; but surely also by the art with which she concealed or offset the less popular features of her rule.

[1] *Zurich Letters*, i. 18, 33. Even Thomas Sampson held this view (cf. ibid. p. 64).

# PART TWO

# THE PARLIAMENT OF 1563

---

## CHAPTER I

## INTRODUCTORY

THE change of policy at Easter 1559 had enabled the political and religious settlement of the country to be carried through at a single Parliament: at any rate, whatever radicals thought, that was the Queen's point of view. Consequently Parliament could assume its role as a merely occasional piece in the Tudor constitution. Four years were allowed to pass before a new assembly was summoned; and the timing of this had one main reason, money.

In normal times the Crown was expected to 'live of its own'. Its ordinary revenue, excluding taxation though including customs duties, should have sufficed for ordinary expenditure; and in the careful hands of the new Queen this was possible. Times, however, had not been normal. The revolt of the Scots in 1559 — inspired alike by the fiery eloquence of John Knox and by native revulsion against the French 'occupation' of Court and government under the Queen Mother, Mary of Guise — had compelled Elizabeth, at the turn of the year, to intervene in support of the Protestant Congregation. It was a sound stroke of policy. It drove the French out of Scotland, turned that country to Protestantism and dependence on Elizabeth, and closed the postern gate of England to the hereditary enemy and the forces of Catholicism. Sound policy, but expensive, swallowing more than the whole yield of the taxes voted in the Parliament of 1559: which in any case had been granted to liquidate past debts. And now, in the autumn to winter of 1562, when the writs for her second Parliament were issued, Elizabeth was involved in another military adventure, intervening in the first of the French Religious Wars in order to bolster up the Huguenot cause, weaken her Catholic enemies, the Guise family, and incidentally recover Calais or acquire any other titbit for England. From 1558 to 1563 — our financial historian tells us[1] — military expenses alone cost more than £750,000: this when 'ordinary revenue' amounted to about £200,000 per annum, and the yield of a parliamentary subsidy with its accompanying fifteenths and tenths was just under £200,000, or — expressed as an annual income from taxation over the first thirty years of the reign — about £50,000 per annum.

Clearly there had to be taxation, and consequently a Parliament. From the official point of view there was little other occasion for the assembly. Cecil expected it to be of short duration. 'The matters of moment like to pass', he told a colleague in France, 'are not many: reviving of some old laws . . . and the grant of a subsidy.'[2]

But, as the previous Parliament had shown, in this new dynamic age the initiative in public policy was no longer being left to Crown and government. The gentlemen of the House of Commons wanted to be up and doing when they felt strongly on some subject. And at this particular juncture there was one subject on which anyone with a little public sense was likely to have very strong views. It was the succession to the throne.

Though wooed from abroad by kings, princes, and dukes, with some of her own subjects aspiring to Europe's most glittering prize, Elizabeth still remained unmarried. She was the last of the Tudors, and there was utter confusion about the identity of her rightful successor, were she to die childless. If mere seniority of descent from the Tudor line was reckoned, Mary Queen of Scots had the strongest claim. But she was an alien, and as such — so the argument ran — was excluded by the Common Law of England, while Henry VIII's will, which had statutory sanction behind it, was also against her. Needless to say, English Protestants, with the preservation of their religion at stake, regarded these bars to Mary's claim as effective. In the same line of descent from Henry VII's elder daughter, but free from the disqualification of alien birth, was Lord Darnley, whom Mary was to marry in 1565, thus appa-

---

[1] F. C. DIETZ, *English Public Finance, 1558-1641*, p. 16.
[2] T. WRIGHT, *Q. Elizabeth & Her Times*, i. 121.

rently increasing her menace to England's Protestant future. There were arguments also against Darnley's right to the succession. Henry VIII's will had given preference to the Suffolk line, descended from Henry VII's younger daughter; and here two women represented the elder descent — Lady Catherine and Lady Mary Grey, sisters of the unfortunate Lady Jane Grey, the nine-days' Queen — while by a younger descent another woman, Lady Margaret Strange, came into the debate. In 1561, much to Elizabeth's anger and disgust, Lady Catherine had made a clandestine marriage with Protector Somerset's son, and produced a son. It encouraged supporters of the Suffolk claim, but exacerbated the succession question. In turn there were arguments against the rights of the Suffolk line, and the names of other claimants were drawn into the dispute, prominent among them being the Earl of Huntingdon, an earnest Puritan and attractive for that reason to a vigorous section of the community. Obviously, the succession was a complicated and thorny subject, calculated to split the nation into factions. In the course of time, though it became increasingly dangerous to indulge in any activity concerning the matter, quite a pamphlet literature appeared, mostly in manuscript.

In 1559, when the Commons asked Elizabeth to marry, their object had been to clarify this problem by the most natural solution of marriage and a child. The emphasis had been on marriage. But this was bound to change as the years went by and the imperial votaress continued her way, 'in maiden meditation, fancy free'. In October 1562 Court and country were sharply reminded that in an age of plague, epidemic, and sudden death, the bliss of the new England depended on the precarious thread of a single life. Elizabeth fell victim to smallpox, which had been particularly rife in the circle of ladies of rank, and, among others, had killed the Countess of Bedford. On the day that the disease reached its crisis, the Queen lay unconscious and was thought to be dying. Cecil had been hastily summoned from London to Hampton Court where she was staying, and the Council anxiously discussed the succession, failing to reach agreement. Some — including, in all probability, Cecil — were for Lady Catherine Grey, some for the Earl of Huntingdon: in other words, a Protestant succession.

To those in authority — and to others as the news reached them — the country must have seemed very close to civil war on that day.[1]

After Elizabeth's recovery the question of her marriage was more urgent than before, but the emphasis had shifted abruptly to the succession. As we shall see, the Queen was opposed — and throughout her life remained opposed — to naming a successor. She must have anticipated trouble with Parliament; and no doubt the Spanish ambassador was broadly right when at the end of October he reported that she would have been glad, for this reason, to avoid summoning a Parliament, if only she could have raised money in another way. A month later — after the writs had gone out — he reported that some gentlemen, on the excuse of dining together, were holding meetings at which, as he understood, they were discussing the succession to the throne. One remembers the meetings at Arundel's tavern in Mary Tudor's reign; and perhaps it was at this same eating house that they were meeting now. Organized politics, if only in a rudimentary form as yet, were making their way into English life. Later still, the ambassador reported that there had been a meeting of gentlemen at the Earl of Arundel's house with the Duke of Norfolk and Lord Howard of Effingham, the Lord Chamberlain, present, which lasted until 2 a.m. They had discussed the succession, and were seemingly partisans of the Suffolk line. The Queen, he wrote, 'wept with rage' when she learnt of the meeting, and had a stormy interview with the Earl, in which — if our informant can be credited — the hectoring was not one-sided.

Cecil sensed what was in the wind. In his letter from which we have already quoted, written two days after the opening of the Parliament, he added: 'I think somewhat will be attempted to ascertain the realm of a successor to the crown, but I fear the unwillingness of her Majesty to have such a person known, will stay the matter.'[2]

In addition to the succession question, there was religion. The Settlement of 1559 had left the *émigrés*, and those who sympathized with them, dissatisfied with the ornaments proviso in the Act of Uniformity and the rubric in the Prayer Book

---

[1] *Foreign Cal. 1562*, pp. 269, 444, 458; *Spanish Cal. Eliz.* i. 262-3.
[2] *Spanish Cal. Eliz.* i. 265, 271, 273; WRIGHT, op. cit. i. 121.

derived from it; dissatisfied with the cross and candles kept in the Royal Chapel, which were a constant reminder of the rubric, and an offence to conscience; dissatisfied also with the vestments — surplice and cope — as well as the out-of-door garb that the Queen could insist on the clergy wearing. Something like a compromise kept the peace between 1559 and 1563. Along perhaps with the memory of piecemeal reform in the past, it seems to have inspired these men, or some of them, with the hope that the Settlement had been in the nature of an *interim*, pointing to the fulfilment of their godly prospectus in the second Parliament of the reign. At any rate, the radical party among the clergy were set on reform: on establishing articles of doctrine for the Church; on purifying the Prayer Book, especially over rites and vestments; on reviving that parliamentary bill about the Canons of the Church — the *Reformatio Legum* — which they had vainly tried to pass in 1559; and on other matters. Emerging, as we can now see that they do, from the frustration of 1559, their proposals acquire a new significance.[1]

Whereas in 1559 the synod of the Church, known as Convocation, had been in the hands of the Catholics, and the Protestant divines had in consequence been forced to work through the House of Commons, these men were now in strength — though, as it turned out, insufficient strength — in Convocation; and naturally it was through this organ of ecclesiastical legislation that they attempted to work. In the Lower House of the 1563 assembly a slightly modified version of the radical programme was put to the vote after a heated debate, was supported by an appreciable majority of those present, but was defeated by one vote — fifty-nine to fifty-eight — after proxies had been invoked.[2]

The result of concentrating their effort on Convocation was that the Parliament of 1563, which, if the radical divines had so planned it, might well have witnessed a troublesome Puritan agitation over the Church, was strangely free from that type of conflict. But having failed to mould their own assembly to their wishes and thus exploit the proper constitutional machinery, the left-wing of the clergy was driven back, for future occasions,

---

[1] STRYPE, *Annals*, I. i. 473 seqq.
[2] CARDWELL, *History of Conferences*, pp. 117-20; STRYPE, *Annals*, I. i. 502-6.

on the irregular expedient of 1559 — on organizing its agitation through the House of Commons. In consequence, not only the quality of Elizabethan parliamentary history — that, indeed, we shall see — but the whole future of English constitutional development was profoundly affected.

The writs for the Parliament of 1563 went out in early November 1562, summoning the meeting for January 11th. There were 420 members of the House of Commons to be elected, 90 from the counties, the rest from the cities and boroughs. Of those chosen, probably rather more than 150 had sat in the previous Parliament. A few Catholics were returned: if we exclude 8 whose religious views were at one time or another questionable but who took the oath of supremacy, the number appears to have been 27. An impotent few in such a large assembly: and they were almost counterbalanced in number, and far exceeded in influence, by the Marian exiles, of whom there were 24.[1]

Sir Anthony Cooke was there, with his eldest son, who had also been in the previous Parliament; Sir Francis Knollys; with a brother and a son; Francis Walsingham, Elizabeth's future Secretary; John Hales, Clerk of the Hanaper and reputed author of the *Discourse of the Commonweal* — economist, social-reformer, friend of scholars, an impetuous man, it would seem, for a fellow-member dubbed him 'Hales the hottest', and indeed he was to get into very hot water over a tract on the succession. There was Henry Kingsmill, who left his mother and his sisters in his will each a 'Geneva Bible in English of the great print', inscribed 'The life of man is short and subject to many displeasures'. He was one of two brothers in this Parliament, both of whom possibly obtained their seats through the patronage of the Bishop of Winchester, a Marian exile; and they had another brother, friend of the two eminent Puritan leaders Dean Sampson and Dr. Laurence Humphrey, a Fellow of All Souls College at this time, a 'phoenix among lawyers, and a rare example of godliness among gentlemen', who turned to divinity and went abroad to Geneva and Lausanne. Truly a Puritan family. There were also Dr. Thomas Wilson, author of *The Arte of Rhetorique* and *A Discourse on Usurye*, and Sir

[1] These figures are taken from a London M.A. thesis on the personnel of this Parliament by a student of mine, Miss Norah Fuidge. I have revised them.

Thomas and Robert Wroth, father and son — 'Wroth the aspirer', as our satirist wrote, though whether of the father or the son (the latter probably) is not clear. These were some, some only, of the Marian exiles.[1]

We possess a manuscript entitled 'A lewd pasquil set forth by certain of the parliament men', which lampooned forty-three of this company of gentlemen in the second and rebellious session of theirs in 1566.[2] 'Here rests us our choir', wrote the scribe at the end of his list. Among them are names which even 400 mouldering years have not reduced to the skeleton biographies of the genealogist; men who, for the moment maybe or for longer, will live again as our story unfolds. There was Paul Wentworth — 'Wentworth the wrangler', the lampoon calls him, 'the controversialist' as we may charitably interpret it — a Buckinghamshire gentleman 'of a good house and of good breeding', whose father, Sir Nicholas, had been Chief Porter of Calais under Henry VIII and Edward VI. Entering Parliament for the first time, he was, like his elder and more famous brother, Peter, who was to follow his parliamentary example later, in 1571, a strong Puritan and courageous leader. The Queen had her fill of these two brothers. Another of their kind was the Member for Scarborough, a Yorkshire gentleman, who had sat for the same constituency in 1559: 'Strickland the stinger' — the sharp-tongued. There was Thomas Norton — 'Norton the scold': 'act, insist, speak, read, write, in season and out' — joint author of *Gorboduc*, translator of Calvin and Peter Martyr, hammer of Catholics: a man who deserves a prominent niche among English parliamentarians. Another was the lawyer James Dalton, expelled from Lincoln's Inn for heresy in Mary's reign, who was to run into trouble over the succession question in the next session: 'Dalton the denier': 'Not I, Lord' — a jest on an episode of 1566. Then there was our witty and loquacious friend, the future Recorder of London, William Fleetwood — 'Fleetwood the pleader'; and two other lawyers of a Puritan cast of mind and of great ability, who were to attain to the Speakership and the Bench — Robert Bell and Christopher Yelverton. 'Bell the

---

[1] Miss Fuidge's thesis; *D.N.B.* sub Kingsmill, Andrew.
[2] Cambridge Univ. Library MS. Ff. v. 14, half in Latin, half in English. A copy of the English half is in B.M. Stowe MS. 354, fol. 18.

orator', 'Yelverton the poet': and judging from the prose of Yelverton's speeches the word 'poet' was not inapt. 'Seckerston the merry', pride of Liverpool, their Alderman-Member, and 'Goodere the glorious', the Warwickshire gentleman who was the poet Drayton's patron: we can believe that the descriptions were appropriate. But why, apart from a prevailing love for alliteration, was Warnecombe 'the weary', why 'Grice the backbiter', or 'Newdigate the crier'?

The great majority — at least thirty-five — of this 'choir' of effectives were from the borough seats, those breeding places of parliamentary nuisances. Mary Tudor had tried to keep such men out of Parliament: Queen Elizabeth spoke winged words to them, but appreciated their part in her emotional drama. The lampoonist — whoever he was, and no doubt he was a gentleman-'burgess' — dismissed the rest of the House as a parrot-like chorus. Perhaps it was the disdain of the young for the old, of the back- for the front-bencher. If not a joke, it was to some extent calumniation. As for the 'choir', they sang, not in unison but at least with a predominantly Puritan voice. That we can detect; and it is instructive.

On Monday, January 11th, 1563, when the session was due to start, the weather was foul and the Queen 'somewhat sick of a stitch'.[1] The Parliament was therefore formally prorogued until the following day, when, about 11 a.m. the resplendent procession made its way to Westminster Abbey, there to attend the customary service before crossing to the Parliament Chamber. The sermon on this occasion was preached by the Dean of St. Paul's, Dr. Alexander Nowell, a Marian exile, whose radical views and abhorrence of Popish ceremony had not been tempered by the sweets of office. He was the unfortunate man who, two years later, preaching a Lenten sermon before Elizabeth and a large congregation at Court, inveighed against a recent Catholic book dedicated to the Queen, and then went on, with obvious reference to the crucifix kept by her in the royal chapel, to attack images and idolatry. Elizabeth, whose patience with these precisionists had reached breaking point, and who perhaps — as the parliamentary sermon of 1563 might suggest — had been tried long enough by this particular preacher, interrupted the sermon with the cry, 'Do not talk

---

[1] B.M. Cotton MS. Titus F. 1, fol. 59; *C.J.* i. 62.

about that!' Not hearing her, Nowell went on, whereupon she
raised her voice still louder: 'Leave that, it has nothing to do
with your subject, and the matter is now threadbare.' For
pure pity, Archbishop Parker took the Dean home to dinner
with him: 'he was utterly dismayed'.[1]

On our parliamentary occasion, in 1563, Nowell started off
his sermon on conventional lines; and dull reading it makes
for us moderns at this stage. Then he began to be topical and
political, giving his views on the questions that he thought
Parliament should deal with. The House of Commons, we may
recollect, had been dissatisfied in the last Parliament with the
leniency shown to Catholics in the government's Supremacy
bill, and had tried to sharpen the penalties. Had not their
friends and their saints been burnt at the stake under Mary
Tudor? The tables were now turned. They had failed in their
purpose in 1559, but the mood remained: with the Commons,
as we shall see, and with the *émigré* divines, as Nowell's sermon
shows. The Queen's clemency, he declared, ought now to be
changed to justice. Those Catholics who have not hitherto
reformed but remain obstinate and do not comprehend
clemency or courtesy should be used otherwise. 'Some will
say, "Oh bloody man! that calleth this the house of right, and
now would have it made a house of blood." But the scripture
teacheth us that divers faults ought to be punished by death.
And, therefore, following God's precepts, it cannot be accounted
cruel.' He would not punish anyone keeping his opinions to
himself; but if opened abroad, they do harm, and he should
be cut off. 'By the scriptures, murderers, breakers of the holy
day, and maintainers of false religion ought to die by the
sword', after the clergy had first tried to win them from their
errors by the sword of the spirit. We might say of Dean
Nowell, as of zealots in general: he had little sense of humour.
What but his own argument had justified the Catholic burnings?

Nowell wanted a law for observance of the Lord's Day, and
sharper laws for adultery and murder, commending the distinction in France of the halter for felony and the wheel for
murder. He was a whole-hearted supporter of the Queen's
foreign policy: her intervention in Scotland in 1560 and her

---

[1] DIXON, *History of the Church of England*, vi. 86-7; *Parker Correspondence*, p. 235;
STRYPE, *Parker*, iii. 94.

present intervention in France. Give liberally of your money, he adjured his audience; and he promised this on behalf of the bishops and clergy. He only wished that when the abbeys were being dissolved, two in each shire had been set aside: the one for the reward of the soldier, the other of the scholar. He had a few words to say on depopulation through the expansion of pasture. There were good laws for the maintenance of tillage, but they were not executed. Also, he desired provision to be made against vagabonds. Indeed, one rather suspects that Cecil or someone had arranged for a little advance-publicity on the government's legislative programme this session.

Perhaps it was Nowell's technique to administer his doses of sharp medicine at the end. He now launched out on the succession question; and if the celebrated story of 'To your text, Master Dean' had arisen from this sermon instead of two years later, the Queen might have won a little sympathy. 'All the Queen's most noble ancestors', ran Nowell's words, 'have commonly had some issue to succeed them, but her Majesty yet none; which want is for our sins to be a plague unto us. For as the marriage of Queen Mary was a terrible plague to all England, and like in continuance to have proved greater, so now' — addressing himself to Elizabeth — 'the want of your marriage and issue is like to prove as great a plague . . . If your parents had been of your mind, where had you been then? Or what had become of us now? When your Majesty was troubled with sickness, then I heard continual voices and lamentations, saying: "Alas! what trouble shall we be in? Even as great or greater than France. For the succession is so uncertain and such division for religion! Alack! what shall become of us?" ' As a man is much troubled in his conscience before he hath made his will, so no doubt is the Queen's Majesty much troubled for the succession of this crown.

All this was tactless enough, but the god-fearing Dean plunged in deeper. 'Of late, as I chanced to walk up and down here in this church, I espied a ruinous monument or tomb of one of your ancestors, the longest reign that ever was; and yet his crown in the dust. And passing a little further, [I] espied another like monument of one other of them, who reigned not half so long and yet twice more noble; and his crown in like manner. . . A little off, [I] saw the funeral place of that most virtuous imp, your most noble brother of famous memory, King Edward the Sixth, and your sister Queen Mary. And now of later times, for your and our better example, the end and death of the Lady Jane, your almoner, and other, even near or here about your Court; which be worthy monuments and admonitions for us to remember the same, being the most certain thing that can be. And again, the uncertainty when the hour shall be or how soon; which I for my part, weighing and foreseeing in my judgment the ruin of this my most natural country to be at hand, thought to take to my meditation . . . When I heard of the calling of this Parliament, I was thereby encouraged, hoping and not doubting but there should be such order taken and good laws established which should again erect up the decay of the same.'[1]

'Here rests us our choir': what an incitement the reports of this sermon must have been to our troublesome forty-three — to 'Wentworth the wrangler', to Norton — 'act, insist, speak' — and many of the others! 'I see', said Elizabeth much later in life, when another preacher dwelt on mortality and let his godly zeal for frankness outrun discretion, 'the greatest clerks are not the wisest men.'[2]

When, after the Abbey service, Queen and Lords and Commons had assembled themselves in the Parliament Chamber, the Lord Keeper, Sir Nicholas Bacon, began his opening oration. First protesting his inability for the task — though encouraged by the experience of the Queen's great benignity and gentleness and the patience of his audience — he divided his main discourse into two parts: one touching religion, the other policy.

God's law being perfect, any imperfections, Bacon argued, must spring from themselves: from both the clergy and the laity. As regards the dearth of ministers and the unfitness of some, the Queen did not doubt that the bishops would diligently do all that was possible in face of so great a scarcity of fit men. Divergence of doctrine was not to be tolerated — here he was tilting at Catholics; nor was neglect of the rites and ceremonies agreed upon by common consent — here it was the Puritans.

---

[1] Cotton MS. Titus F. 1, fols. 61-4. Printed in *Nowell's Catechism* (Parker Soc.), pp. 223-9.
[2] JOHN HARINGTON, *Nugae Antique*, ed. Park (1804), ii. 216 seqq.

Discipline was needed. For lack of it, and despite the Act of Uniformity, 'the common people in the country universally come so seldom to Common Prayer'. Since doctrine and discipline were matters which chiefly concerned the bishops, the Queen looked to them, now they were assembled in Parliament, to confer together, and, if they found need for any temporal enactment, to exhibit it here in Parliament: a comment we shall do well to note, for it enunciated the Queen's principle that the initiative in ecclesiastical legislation should come from the clergy, not the laity. What friction that principle was to cause!

From the topic of religion, on which he dwelt long enough to show that Queen and government were seriously concerned about the shortcomings in the Church, Bacon turned to matters of 'policy', first domestic and then foreign. On domestic policy he spoke in general terms: about laws being either too sharp and burdensome or too loose and soft, questions that he enjoined Parliament to inquire into; and about the slothfulness or corruption of temporal officials whose duty was to see to their execution. On this latter point he threw out an idea of his own: that there should be a triennial or biennial visitation of the realm, on the pattern of ecclesiastical visitations, to see that the laws were being duly executed and to punish faulty officials.

On foreign policy, his 'last and greatest' theme, he was concerned with 'defence against the foreign enemy abroad, and his confederates bred and brought up here amongst ourselves'. His object was to justify further taxation. He reviewed the condition in which Elizabeth had found the country at her accession: 'ragged and torn'; in war with a mighty enemy; Calais 'the chief fortress' lost, to the great dishonour and weakening of the realm; frontier towns insufficiently fortified; Crown revenue greatly spoiled and the realm greatly indebted; munitions consumed; the navy in bad state. The Queen had in consequence been compelled to make peace on unsatisfactory terms. Since then, certain old cankered enemies of the realm had attempted to subject the Scots to the government of France, and if the Queen had not intervened, ere this they might have troubled us not only at Berwick but at the walls of York. In like manner she had intervened in France. These tasks had cost her Majesty as much as two of the greatest subsidies: an impossible burden for the ordinary revenue of the Crown. The Queen, he declared, employs her own treasure, yea and her lands and credit, not in glorious triumphs or superfluous and sumptuous buildings of delight, nor in any other matters of will and pleasure, but in the service and defence of her people. 'Relieving of the realm's necessity is become the Prince's delight. A good change: God continue it.' The Queen from her own mouth had commanded him to declare how loth she was to summon this Parliament and burden her loving subjects with a request for aid.

After briefly summarizing the points of his speech, the Lord Keeper ended with an order to the Commons to choose a Speaker.[1]

The man whom the government had arranged to nominate was a west-country lawyer, Thomas Williams, aged forty-eight or forty-nine, a member of the Inner Temple. He had sat in three previous Parliaments and was now representing Exeter. Little is known about him: indeed, his likening of himself, in his disabling speech, to 'one among the Romans chosen from the plough to a place of estimation, and after went to the plough again', may not have been quite so fantastic as the occasion suggests. Perhaps he was connected with the Earl of Bedford, though he does not appear to have owed his parliamentary seat to this influential Councillor. His epitaph states:

> The Common peace he studied to preserve
> And true religion ever to maintain.

There is a Puritan smack about the second line; but Mary Tudor's reign does not seem to have jeopardized his career. It was Sir Edward Rogers, the Comptroller of the Queen's Household, the senior Privy Councillor present, who nominated him as 'being grave, learned, and wise' and 'very meet to that office'; 'whereupon the whole House with one entire voice cried, "Mr. Williams! Mr. Williams!" ' 'Reverently disabling himself', he was answered by Secretary Cecil and was led to the chair by Mr. Comptroller.[2]

[1] B.M. Harleian MS. 5176, fols. 89-92. A lengthy report is in Cotton MS. Titus F. 1, fols. 66 seqq.
[2] D.N.B.; Miss Fuidge's thesis; C.J. i. 62.

On Friday, January 15th, he presented himself to the Queen in full ceremonial assembly, most humbly disabled himself in a charming, short speech, was appropriately answered by the Lord Keeper, and then embarked on his 'excellent' — and carefully prepared — oration: an 'epistle' he deprecatingly called it. Excellent it probably was, though the admirable narrator who preserved for us a very long report of it may have improved its felicity and clarity, as we can see that he did with the Lord Keeper's speech on the previous Tuesday.

Time past, time present, and time to come were his themes. Time past was concerned with the manifold benefits bestowed upon them by the Queen. 'When God planted your Highness in this place, you found it not so furnished with treasure as other your predecessors have . . .; which notwithstanding, you did not take the extremity of penal statutes and other forfeits due to you . . .' You 'purged this Church of all ill service and placed therein service to God's honour'. The great plague and dearth these twenty years past, due to debased coinage, have been remedied in one year, with little loss to your subjects. By intervention in Scotland and France, peril and loss to your Crown and subjects have been prevented. Good laws have been made; great charge borne by your Majesty. 'And for the last part and principal point of all other, your Highness hath brought and restored again God's doctrine into this realm, for which your humble subjects most heartily give thanks to God and you, by the mouth of me their appointed Speaker.'

'Time present' led him to the popular and hackneyed comparison of the community to the human body, with its moral of co-operation. 'I find in divers histories great commodities grow to princes by searching out . . . not only the wants of their subjects but knowledge of their talk, whereby the better they both understand their own faults and the flatterers which they have about them. Which order the wise and prudent Marcus Aurelius used and long time reigned honourably. The noble conqueror Alexander, in the beginning of his reign, used the same; but leaving that order and having no regard to his living, was destroyed. Which like example was seen by that notable and valiant warrior, Julius Caesar.'

These examples emboldened him to speak of three abuses in this realm, 'all three notable monsters: necessity, ignorance,

AN DNI 1567  ÆTATIS SVÆ 69

Rogers Contoller
to Quen Elizabeth.

SIR EDWARD ROGERS

Vice-Chamberlain 1558-59
Comptroller of the Household 1559-67

and error'. 'Necessity is grown amongst ourselves so that no man
is contented with his degree, though he hath never so much.'
On the dearth of schools: 'I dare say a hundred schools want in
England, which afore this time hath been. And if in every
school there had been but a hundred scholars, yet that had been
ten thousand. I doubt whether there be so many learned men
in England' as this number now lacking. Want of schools,
scholars, and good schoolmasters brings ignorance, the second
monster. The occasion of these two monsters is want of church
livings and preferments. 'Covetousness hath gotten the livings':
for example, by impropriations. 'The universities are decayed,
and great market towns and others without either school or
preacher,' because 'the poor vicar hath but only £20, and the
rest, being no small sum, is impropriate.' Many a Puritan voice
was to raise the same cry as Speaker Williams.

Error was the third monster, 'a serpent with many heads':
'Pelagians, Libertines, Papists, and such other, leaving God's
commandment to follow their own traditions, affections and
minds.' Like Tantalus who had apples even hanging at his
mouth, 'so are we plagued, for, having God's word and His
name even in our mouths, yet we live as infidels'.

'Time to come' brought in Cato and Hannibal and an adjura-
tion to the Queen to build a strong fort for the surety of the
realm, 'set upon firm ground and steadfast, having two gates,
one commonly open, the other as a postern, with two watchmen
at either of them, one governor, one lieutenant, four soldiers,
and no good thing there wanting. The same to be named the
fear of God; the governor thereof to be God, your Majesty the
lieutenant, the stones the hearts of faithful people; the two
watchmen at the open gate to be called knowledge and virtue,
the other two at the postern called mercy and truth; all being
spiritual ministers. This fort is invincible if every man will
fear God.'

Some further elaboration upon this conceit of a fort — a gem
of oratory his listeners probably thought it — and Speaker
Williams came abruptly to earth with his official petitions:
access for himself to the Queen, as also to the Lords, if matters
of importance arose requiring their opinion; liberty to correct
any report he made to Queen or Lords on behalf of the Commons, should he misreport their meaning; freedom of speech;

and 'the old privilege' of freedom from arrest for Members and their servants. The petitions were in that order, and the crucial third was worded: 'That the assembly of the said Lower House may have frank and free liberty of speech to speak their minds without any controlment, blame, grudge, menaces or displeasures, according to the old ancient order.' 'Old and ancient!' As we know, it was in all likelihood the fortieth birthday of the privilege. How swift is oblivion! With a modest apology for his 'tedious' speech, 'void of eloquence', and offering his heart and good will to the Queen and his prayer for her 'long to reign over us', Mr. Speaker Williams ended.

The Lord Keeper replied with a brief summary of the speech and short favourable comment in the name of the Queen, and then answered the petitions. 'For the first, being for free access to her person,' the Queen 'granteth it, not doubting your discretion' in the use of it; 'for the second . . . this also she granteth, although . . . she trusteth you will not offend therein; and for the third, to have free speech, she granteth also, so that it be reverently used; and to the last [freedom from arrest] . . . she is pleased therewith, howbeit great regard should be therein had not thereby to avoid or delay their creditors' — an allusion to the common use of this privilege to evade arrest for debt. This was the second, and it was the last, occasion upon which Elizabeth could grant the privilege of free speech without thought for the peril latent in its vagueness.

With an injunction to make their laws as few and plain as possible, to proceed with great and weighty matters first, and to use speed so that the Parliament might soon be ended, the Lord Keeper brought the sitting to an end.[1] Business was now before them.

---

[1] Cotton MS. Titus F. 1, fols. 69 seqq.

## CHAPTER II

# THE SUCCESSION QUESTION

GREAT and weighty matters first: to independent Members with an aptitude for leadership this injunction had meant a radical Protestant settlement of the Church in 1559. In 1563 it meant the settlement of the succession question, the sole way, they thought, of preventing civil war at the death of a childless Queen and of assuring the maintenance of Protestantism in England.

In 1559 they had started their agitation on the first full day of Parliament. In 1563 they did the same. 'A motion made by a burgess at length for the succession': possibly one of our 'choir'. So runs the entry made by the Clerk of the House of Commons in his *Journal* on January 16th, coming after the first reading of two unimportant bills. Three hours or so were probably spent on the discussion; and the next day too, after getting through the first reading of five more bills, there were 'arguments by divers wise personages for motion to be made for the Queen's marriage, and succession of the crown'. The call of dinner must have put an end to what was perhaps a long sitting; and it was not until the third morning, when they returned to the subject as the second and main item of business, that they concluded the debate by appointing a committee, consisting of the Speaker, Privy Councillors, and twenty-four others, charged with drawing up articles for a petition to the Queen.[1]

Unfortunately, we are still in the period when the *Commons Journal* is too jejune to be informative, when the *Lords Journal*, in spite of its impressive appearance, is even less informative and can be more misleading, when Members' diaries do not exist, and even correspondence, both official and private, is singularly unhelpful. What went on during this prolonged discussion — whether the speakers were sufficiently reckless to air their opinions on the rival claims to the succession — we cannot say with any certainty.

From the Queen's point of view it was harmful to have any

[1] *C.J.* i. 62-3.

open debate of the problem, dangerous to attempt the naming of a successor. Apart from the general consideration that this would inflame instead of allaying faction and that neither claimants nor their supporters were likely to submit meekly to their rights being overriden, even by act of Parliament, there was the particular problem of Mary Queen of Scots. English Protestants might be of a single mind in their opposition to her claim, but unless nobility and people could unite in favour of one alternative claimant, what chance, in the event of Elizabeth's death, would any rival stand against the power of Scotland, supported by continental help? The succession to the throne was not in the nature of a gift, at the disposal of Sovereign or Parliament. It was a right, inherent in someone by virtue of heredity and the law. The law might be obscure; but were Mary and her people likely to acquiesce peaceably in a parliamentary definition of it that was hostile to their interests?

It behoved Elizabeth, for the sake of what might happen at her death as well as during her life, to find a basis of agreement with Mary: an agreement which would guarantee English interests and Protestantism. Mary's marriage was the crux of the problem. As yet she was free. If she could be induced to take a husband at Elizabeth's hands, who in himself seemed adequate surety for English interests and would ween her from Catholicism, then indeed it might be sensible to name a successor to the English crown — name Mary. On her throne in Scotland she could be less of a danger or nuisance during Elizabeth's lifetime than Lady Catherine Grey or another English claimant.

It was during this Parliament of 1563 — in March — that Elizabeth, in conversation with the Scottish Secretary, Maitland of Lethington, first broached the idea of marrying her beloved Robert Dudley to Mary. To posterity it has seemed fantastic, grotesque, bewildering: anything except intelligent and genuine. The circumstances have hardly been appreciated. No one was more acutely aware than Elizabeth herself how near she had been to death in the previous October and how near the country had been to a war of the succession. She appreciated the concern of Parliament and was sensitive to the relentless pressure from all sides, but found few to agree with her policy. Sir John Mason, one of her Councillors, thought that in her caution she showed 'a better judgment' than many who were so earnest in the matter: his, however, seems to have been a minority, almost a lone, point of view. Cecil, who in all probability favoured Lady Catherine Grey's cause — though, as he himself said, he was too circumspect to do anything that might cause offence — was clearly in favour of an established succession, as he was of the Queen marrying. He prayed for 'some common order' by which 'we poor subjects may know where to lean and adventure our lives with contentation of our consciences'. If, caught in this desperate dilemma and left almost in isolation, the Queen conceived an essentially personal plan — a startling but not unimaginative way out of her difficulty — it is not surprising. Certainly, it indicates that the pressure of Parliament was not without effect.[1]

To let Parliament name a successor at this juncture, when the decision would undoubtedly have been hostile to Mary, would have ruined Elizabeth's Scottish policy. Indeed, it was most desirable to prevent any indiscretions occurring in debate. In normal circumstances her strong sense of discipline would probably have prompted her to attempt this; but in January 1563 neither she, nor her Councillors, nor others had recovered from the fright of the previous October, and discipline may have been out of the question. There were many in the House of Commons — some with memories of 1559 when they had been allowed a great deal of latitude — who were too ardent to be discreet; and the odds are that in the debate on those three mornings they threw discretion, if not to the four winds, at least to one or two.

We know that the various claims to the succession were discussed at this time. When, a year later, Lord John Grey, Catherine Grey's uncle, was being examined by Councillors on the subject, he declared that 'many communed thereupon in the Parliament, some in favour of the Scottish Queen, some of the Lady Margaret Lennox — Darnley's mother — some of the Lady Catherine, some of the Lady Margaret Strange, some of the Earl of Huntingdon'. While the statement does not necessarily imply that the discussions took place in parliamentary debate, or even within parliamentary precincts, we may perhaps conclude that some did. John Hales — 'Hales the

---

[1] *Spanish Cal. Eliz.* i. 313; WRIGHT, *Elizabeth & Her Times*, i. 130, 173, 180.

hottest', one of our 'choir' of forty-three — wrote a notorious tract on the succession during this Parliament, in which he defended the Suffolk line against all others and pronounced for Lady Catherine Grey as the rightful heir apparent. Though couched in the form of a parliamentary speech, it was clearly not delivered as such. On the other hand, he may well have aired his views in the debate. We learn that he showed his pamphlet to Fleetwood and Foster — two of our 'choir'. Without a doubt, these M.P.s, whether in private or in public — and probably both — were canvassing actual claims: not unnaturally, because their policy was to get the order of succession to the throne precisely and legally stated.[1]

There has come down to us a parliamentary speech written by Sir Ralph Sadler, an eminent public servant and keen Protestant, who had served Henry VIII, been a member of Edward VI's Privy Council, and though not of the Council at this time was to rejoin it in 1566. The speech is undated, but must have been written in 1563 or 1566, and more likely in 1563. Though we cannot be sure that it was delivered, the odds are that it was.

'I am not fit to speak in so great a matter as this is,' he began, '. . . but because I have heard some speech uttered here touching the title of the Queen of Scots . . . wherein it seemeth that she hath some fautors and favourers in this House, I am the rather moved to utter mine affection in that part.' I cannot say who hath the best title to succeed the Queen's Majesty, 'but being a mere natural Englishman, I do find in myself a great misliking to be subject to a foreign prince . . . And for the Queen of Scots, though she were indeed next heir in blood to the Queen's Majesty, yet being a stranger by the laws of the realm, as I understand, she cannot inherit in England, which is a good argument to me that the nature of Englishmen hath always so much detested the regiment of strangers that they have made laws to bar all titles which any stranger may claim of inheritance within the realm'. The Scots, he declared, were equally averse to an English ruler; and he told a story to illustrate his argument. When in 1543 he was engaged in the negotiations for the treaty of Greenwich, which provided for the marriage of Prince Edward of England and the present

[1] HAYNES, *Burghley Papers*, pp. 412, 414.

Queen of Scots, and was arguing the merits of the marriage with Sir Adam Otterburne, a Scot, the latter retorted: ' "If", quod he, "your lad were a lass and our lass were a lad, would you then . . . be content that our lad should marry your lass and so be King of England? . . . I assure you," quod he, "that our nation, being a stout nation, will never agree to have an Englishman to be King of Scotland. And though the whole nobility of the realm would consent unto it, yet our common people and the stones in the street would rise and rebel against it." '

'Now if these proud, beggarly Scots', continued Sadler, 'did so much disdain to yield to the superiority of England . . . why should we for any respect yield to their Scottish superiority or consent to establish a Scot in succession to the crown of this realm? . . . And I fear lest I may say with the Scot, that though we do all agree unto it, yet our common people and the stones in the street would rebel against it.' This was not the sort of speech, cutting as it did across her diplomacy, that Elizabeth would have tolerated in silence if she had been in control of the scene.[1]

By January 26th the committee appointed by the Commons had the petition to the Queen drafted, and it was read to the House. The reader was not the Comptroller of the Royal Household, whose name alone of the members of the committee had been entered by the Clerk in his *Journal*, indicating what we might term the convener: the person to whom he gave the names of the committee, with the time and place of meeting. It was Thomas Norton — 'Norton the scold' — one of the most conspicuous of our 'choir'. Apparently — and the phrasing of the petition confirms the conjecture — the independents had dominated the committee, though Cecil and other Councillors were on it. The Councillors in the House were now instructed to seek permission for the Speaker and whole House to exhibit their petition to the Queen; and later that morning, when sending a bill to the Higher House, request was made that the Lords would further their action: 'which', notes the Clerk, 'was well allowed of the Lords'.[2]

---

[1] B.M. Additional MS. 33593, fols. 3-4. Printed in *Sadler Papers*, ed. Sir Walter Scott, ii. 557-61.
[2] *C.J.* i. 63-4.

The audience took place in the gallery at Whitehall on the afternoon of January 28th. Speaker Williams read the petition. Time and again, with what the Councillors at any rate must have regarded as calculated naivety, it assumed that the Parliament, coming so soon after the 'great terror and dreadful warning' of the Queen's illness, had been summoned principally to deal with the succession. 'They cannot . . . but acknowledge how your Majesty hath most graciously considered the great dangers, the unspeakable miseries of civil wars, the perilous intermeddlings of foreign princes with seditious, ambitious, and factious subjects at home, the waste of noble houses, the slaughter of people, subversion of towns, intermission of all things pertaining to the maintenance of the realm, unsurety of all men's possessions, lives, and estates, daily interchange of attainders and treasons' if you should die without a known heir. After a palpable allusion to the peace negotiations at the beginning of the reign, when the French pretended that Mary Queen of Scots was the rightful Queen of England, the Commons continued, in words surely penned by our zealots: 'We fear a faction of heretics in your realm, contentious and malicious Papists, lest they most unnaturally against their country, most madly against their own safety, and most traitorously against your Highness, not only hope of the woeful day of your death, but also lay in wait to advance some title under which they may renew their late unspeakable cruelty, to the destruction of goods, possessions, and bodies, and thraldom of the souls and consciences of your faithful and Christian subjects. We see nothing to withstand their desire but only your life. Their unkindness and cruelty we have tasted. We fear much to what attempt the hope of such opportunity — nothing withstanding them but your life — will move them.'

The argument was reinforced by historical parallels from English, French, Scottish and Ancient history: 'from the Conquest to this present day the realm was never left as now it is without a certain heir, living and known'. As politeness and tact — hope also — demanded, there was a humble request to Elizabeth to marry. It was brief, and quite subordinated to the main theme of the succession. This they wanted settled at once, during the Parliament; and they promised in return to 'employ their whole endeavours, wits, and powers' to devise the strongest laws for the preservation and surety of her and her issue, 'and the most penal, sharp, and terrible statutes to all that shall but once practise . . . against your safety'.[1]

The Queen, noted the Clerk in his *Journal*, 'thankfully accepted' the petition, 'with an excellent oration deferring the answer to further time'. According to the jaundiced tittle-tattle of the Spanish ambassador — a very dubious authority at this time — she 'told them that the matter required further consideration, and with that turned her back on them and entered her own apartment'.[2] We should take our colour from the former statement, not the latter. We possess the text of the Queen's speech.

'Williams', she began, 'I have heard by you the common request of my Commons, which I may well term (me thinketh) the whole realm, because they give, as I have heard, in all these matters of Parliament their common consent to such as be here assembled.

'The weight and greatness of this matter might cause in me, being a woman wanting both wit and memory, some fear to speak and bashfulness besides, a thing appropriate to my sex. But yet, the princely seat and kingly throne wherein God (though unworthy) hath constituted me, maketh these two causes to seem little in mine eyes, though grievous perhaps to your ears, and boldeneth me to say somewhat in this matter, which I mean only to touch but not presently to answer. For this so great a demand needeth both great and grave advice. I read of a philosopher, whose deeds upon this occasion I remember better than his name, who always, when he was required to give answer in any hard question of school points, would rehearse over his alphabet before he would proceed to any further answer therein: not for that he could not presently have answered, but to have his wit the riper and better sharpened to answer the matter withal. If he, a common man, but in matters of school took such delay, the better to show his eloquent tale, great cause may justly move me in this so great a matter, touching the benefit of this realm and the safety of you all, to defer mine answer till some other time; wherein, I

---

[1] Northants Record Soc. MS. F. (M). P. 169 (Fitzwilliam of Milton Papers). Other copies in S.P. Dom. Eliz. 27/35, and elsewhere.
[2] *C.J.* i. 64; *Spanish Cal. Eliz.* i. 296.

assure you, the consideration of my own safety (although I thank you for the great care that you seem to have thereof) shall be little in comparison of that great regard that I mean to have of the safety and surety of you all.

'And though God of late seemed to touch me, rather like one that He chastised than one that He punished, and though death possessed almost every joint of me, so as I wished then that the feeble thread of life, which lasted (methought) all too long, might by Cloe's hand have quietly been cut off; yet desired I not then life (as I have some witnesses here) so much for mine own safety as for yours. For I knew that in exchanging of this reign I should have enjoyed a better reign, where residence is perpetual. There needs no boding of my bane.[1] I know now as well as I did before that I am mortal. I know also that I must seek to discharge myself of that great burthen that God hath laid upon me. For of them to whom much is committed much is required. Think not that I, that in other matters have had convenient care of you all, will in this matter, touching the safety of myself and you all, be careless. For I know that this matter toucheth me much nearer than it doth you all, who, if the worst happen, can lose but your bodies; but if I take not that convenient care that it behoveth me to have therein, I hazard to lose both body and soul.

'And though I am determined in this so great and weighty a matter to defer mine answer till some other time, because I will not in so deep a matter wade with so shallow a wit; yet have I thought good to use these few words, as well to show you that I am neither careless nor unmindful of your safety in this case — as I trust you likewise do not forget that by me you were delivered whilst you were hanging on the bough ready to fall into the mud, yea to be drowned in the dung, neither yet [do you forget] the promise which you have here made concerning your duties and due obedience, wherewith, I assure you, I mean to charge you — as further to let you understand that I neither mislike any of your requests herein, nor the great care that you seem to have of the surety and safety of yourselves in this matter. Lastly — because I will discharge some restless heads, in whose brains the needless hammers beat with vain judgment,

---

[1] i.e. 'There is no need to prate about my death': an allusion to many passages in the Commons' petition.

that I should mislike this their petition — I say that of the matter and sum thereof I like and allow very well. As to the circumstances, if any be, I mean upon further advice further to answer. And so I assure you all that, though after my death you may have many stepdames, yet shall you never have a more natural mother than I mean to be unto you all.'[1]

A typical Elizabethan composition, with its involved sentences, its vigour, its astuteness, its irony, its affection. 'The restless heads in whose brains the needless hammers beat with vain judgment' undoubtedly included many of our 'choir'. The speech is more than a hint that the debate in the Commons had run a little wild.

Meanwhile, in fulfilment of their promise to the Commons, the Lords had been drafting their own petition. It was read by the Lord Keeper, Sir Nicholas Bacon, at an audience, probably on February 1st.[2] Their suits, he said, tended 'to the preservation of these three things, your person, crown and realm, the dearest jewels that my Lords have on the earth'. They wanted her assent to two points. The first — and here, as became their staider assembly, they got the subject of marriage into more attractive and acceptable perspective than the Commons — is 'that it would please your Majesty to dispose yourself to marry, where it shall please you, to whom it shall please you, and as soon as it shall please you'. The second was the limitation of the succession. They asked for the Queen's licence and favour to discuss the subject in this Parliament.

'The former of these two, which is your marriage, they do in their hearts most earnestly wish and pray for, as a thing that must needs breed and bring great and singular comfort to yourself and unspeakable joy and gladness to all true English hearts. But the second carrieth with it such necessity that without it they cannot see how the safety of your royal person and the preservation of your imperial crown shall be or can be sufficiently or certainly provided for. Most gracious and sovereign Lady, the lamentable and pitiful state and condition wherein all your nobles and Commons late were, when it pleased God to lay his heavy hand upon you, and the amazed-

---

[1] S.P. Dom. Eliz. 27/36. Copy in Fitzwilliam Papers, F. (M). P. 170.
[2] *Spanish Cal. Eliz.* i. 296 proves that the audience took place before February 7th. *H.M.C. Pepys MSS.* p. 10, if it refers to this occasion, establishes the date as February 1st.

ness that most men of understanding were by the bruit that grew by that sickness brought unto, is one cause of this our petition. The second, the aptness and opportunity of this time, by reason of this Parliament.'

Not to limit the succession — he went on — would, in the event of the Queen's death without heirs of her body, result in 'factious, seditious, and intestine war' and the shedding of much innocent blood. Moreover, in such circumstances the realm would be left without governance, for 'upon the death of princes the law dieth', all offices of justice, etc., lose their force. 'Strength and will must rule', and it is to be feared that the realm may become a prey to strangers. If now 'no sufficient remedy should be by your Highness provided, it must needs be a dangerous burden before God to your Majesty, and you are to yield a straight accompt to God for the same'. Earnestly praying her to have consideration of their petition, 'in time most gracious sovereign — in time, in time', they asked for such a favourable and comfortable answer that 'good effect and conclusion may grow thereof before the end of the session of this Parliament, the uttermost day of their greatest hope'. 'God bless and save your Majesty', he ended.[1]

According to the Spanish ambassador, Elizabeth was extremely angry, and 'told them that the marks they saw on her face were not wrinkles but pits of smallpox, and that although she might be old, God could send her children as He did to Saint Elizabeth' — one of the historical allusions made in the Lords' petition. 'They had better consider well what they were asking.' 'If she declared a successor, it would cost much blood to England.'[2] Probably the ambassador got his story from the same malicious, ill-informed source as before, for on February 2nd the time-serving Lord Rich, exercising the privilege of a peer and writing to the Queen for audience in which to give his personal advice on the subject, was encouraged — so he wrote — by 'perceiving yesterday your most godly inclination, great care and study to leave your imperial crown, your realm, and your loving and faithful subjects . . . in unity, concord, and quietness if God should call your Highness from us without heirs of your most royal body'.[3] The reference was probably

---

[1] B.M. Additional MS. 32379, fols. 17-20. Many manuscript copies exist.
[2] *Spanish Cal. Eliz.* i. 296.     [3] *H.M.C. Pepys MSS.* p. 10

to the reception of the Lords' petition, when Lord Rich, it seems, was present; and it hardly accords with the ambassador's story. Such was the universal concern about the subject that he was not the only peer moved to exercise the privilege of his class. We possess a long, anonymous letter written by one who had been kept from Parliament by illness, proffering his advice to the Queen both on her marriage and the succession.[1]

As the days passed and the definitive reply that the Queen had promised did not come, the Commons grew restive. On February 12th they commissioned the Councillors in the House to remind her that they looked for her answer. Perhaps — if on this occasion we may accept a hint from the Spanish ambassador — their tactically-minded leaders had their eyes on the subsidy bill, which was reaching its final stages in their House, and were regretting that they had not adopted an earlier proposal to hold up supplies until the succession was settled. On February 16th Elizabeth sent a rejoinder to their reminder. 'Mr. Comptroller and Mr. Secretary declared from the Queen's Highness that she doubted not but the grave heads of this House did right well consider that she forgot not the suit of this House for the succession, the matter being so weighty; nor could forget it. But she willed the young heads to take example of the ancients.'[2]

Could Sovereign have been in a more harassing situation? virtually isolated and under remorseless, if loyal pressure. She was unable to remit the problem to her Council for unfettered advice. She dared not take the risk. Their counsel would almost certainly have conflicted with her judgment. It was in this mental torment that the device of marrying Dudley to Mary Queen of Scots was conceived. She seems also to have made a tentative move towards conceding legislative action, though not the sort that was demanded. Unfortunately, at this point our sources fail us and uncertainty enters the story. In a dispatch of March 28th the Spanish ambassador reported that a proposal had been made to the Lords on behalf of the Queen to regulate the succession by an act of Parliament which would limit the right to four families, leaving the Queen power to

---

[1] B.M. Cotton MS. Titus B. II, fol. 255. Printed in *Egerton Papers* (Camden Soc.), pp. 34 seqq. and STRYPE, *Annals*, II. ii. 652 seqq.
[2] *Spanish Cal. Eliz.* i. 294; *C.J.* i. 65.

nominate among these the person whom she considered nearest and fittest to succeed her. If the report is true, it was an astute move, which would force them to face the practical difficulties involved in any decisive action: an apple of discord tossed among the factions.[1]

Perhaps it is here that another document should be inserted: a speech by Sir Nicholas Bacon, for which — if it was delivered, as seems likely — no better place can be found. We must assume that, disappointed with the Queen's legislative proposal, the Lords sought a second audience, and renewed their suit through the Lord Keeper, this time, however, limiting their supplication to her marriage: the wind had been taken out of their sails over the succession.

The occasion of this suit, said Bacon, 'grew upon the reading of a bill exhibited on Wednesday last — perhaps March 24th — before my Lords, containing matter concerning the succession of the crown of this realm, upon the well weighing and considering whereof it evidently appeared unto them that, neither by that bill nor by any other act already made, any certain and open declaration or limitation is made to whom the crown should remain . . . ' Renewing the earnest plea to Elizabeth to marry — sometimes in words borrowed from the earlier petition — he tried to speak to the woman in her: 'If your Highness could conceive or imagine the comfort, surety, and delight that should happen to yourself by beholding an imp of your own that should in time to come by God's grace inherit and enjoy the imperial crown of this realm, to the great rejoicing of all your loving subjects, it would (I am assured) sufficiently satisfy to amove all manner of lets, impediments, and scruples.'[2]

If, indeed, there had been an official proposal, tampering with the succession problem without solving it, then clearly it was dead; and doubtless the Queen was not sorry. But there remained an incidental danger, mentioned in the Lords' earlier petition, which might possibly be tackled. It was the lapse of all legitimate authority on the death of the Sovereign, thus threatening to turn an interregnum into anarchy. The Spanish ambassador reported that the Lords agreed to pass an act devised to remedy this. That seems an exaggeration; but there exists a document, endorsed by Cecil, 'A clause to have been

[1] *Spanish Cal. Eliz.* i. 315.     [2] B.M. Harleian MS. 5176, fol. 93.

inserted in an act meant for the succession, but not passed,' and from this we may assume that the Lords had such a bill before them. It evidently provided that if the Queen died without issue or before Parliament had settled the succession by law, certain principal and ordinary officials — judicial and royal household officers, said the ambassador — should continue in office; a Privy Council, consisting of existing Councillors along with any others named in the Queen's will, should remain in being, ten constituting a quorum; and this régime should continue until Parliament — which, says the ambassador, was to be summoned as last constituted, within thirty days — had authorized a proclamation naming the new Sovereign.[1]

The *Lords Journal* remains silent on the matter: unfortunately a silence that implies nothing. Sensible as the proposal may seem to us, it was evidently not liked. Perhaps, indeed, it was this bill that the Lord Keeper rejected in that second audience with the Queen. Apart from the constitutional novelty, in the circumstances of the time it gave the illusion of security without the substance: a situation likely to be more dangerous than desperation itself.

And so the great theme of this Parliament remained in suspense, waiting through the remaining few days of the session for the Queen's final pronouncement at the closing ceremony. Before describing this, we must turn to other business.

---

[1] *Spanish Cal. Eliz.* i. 317; S.P. Dom. Eliz. 28/20.

## CHAPTER III

# OTHER BUSINESS

THE Parliament of 1563 is a notable assembly in our economic history. It passed the famous Act of Artificers and an Act for the Relief of the Poor. Neither appears to have caused any trouble in its passage. The *Journals* of both Houses record only the stages of their progress and hint at nothing else. We may leave them at that. But another measure — an act touching certain politic constitutions made for the maintenance of the navy — did cause trouble and provides a rather interesting glimpse into the minds of many Members.

The bill seems to have arisen from a motion by Mr. William Winter, the admiral who had played Elizabeth's game so blatantly and successfully in the Firth of Forth in support of the Scottish rebellion. On February 6th, he moved that 'this House would have regard by some bill to the navy', and was put in charge of a committee to consider the matter. The bill they framed aimed at increasing the number of ships and sailors as a reservoir for the navy, employing several devices, including an additional compulsory fish-day in the week — Wednesday. It must have run into heavy weather from the start. Cecil took it under his direction on committal, and it re-emerged as a new bill. Still the going was difficult. The second-reading debate was prolonged over two sittings, with a day intervening for Cecil to draft a proviso; and only after long arguments was it ingrossed. On the third reading it was taken clause by clause. Begun one morning, in the afternoon the debate concentrated on the provision to make Wednesday a fish-day; and there were again long arguments about this on the two succeeding days.[1]

It was probably for this third-reading debate that Cecil prepared a speech which we possess; a unique specimen of his parliamentary oratory.[2] It was factual and cogent, marshalling information about foreign trade, analysing possible remedies, exploring obstacles. 'The very ground that naturally serveth to breed mariners is the trade and conversation upon the sea,

[1] *C.J.* i. 65-9.     [2] S.P. Dom. Eliz. 27/71.

which is divided into two sorts: the one is to carry and recarry merchandise; the other is to take fish: for the third, which is exercise of piracy, is detestable and cannot last.' The first, he argued, was in as good case as it had been in any age and could not be augmented; whereas the trade of fishing was manifestly decayed. The causes of this decay were two: small eating of fish at home and no selling of it abroad. By an examination of the fishing trade in other countries, he showed that there could be no hope of increased foreign sales: 'no selling can be where no buying will be'. Consequently, more fish must be eaten at home. He reminded younger Members — including, one is inclined to suspect, members of our 'choir' who were probably proving most rebellious — that their fathers, 'within these twenty-seven years', lived when more fish was eaten than was now proposed. Indeed, he went rather too far in depreciating the effect of the bill, urging that it amounted to so little, that he might have invited the obvious retort — 'Then why cause all this stir?' As a matter of fact, when the act became due for renewal in the Parliament of 1585, its main innovation was killed stone dead by this very argument. The Clerk of the House of Commons was evidently fascinated by the debate, for he jotted down on a blank fly-leaf of his little *Journal* some of the statistics, taken maybe from Cecil's speech as he elaborated his figures in delivery.[1]

Controversy centred on making Wednesday a fish-day; and at last this was put to the question as an isolated issue in the prolonged third-reading debate. The House divided: 179 voted for the clause, 97 against. On such an occasion, when the government was placing its weight behind a measure, we should generally regard opposition sentiment as stronger than the figures indicate. Mixed up in this sentiment there was manifestly not only gastronomic objection — in the 1585 debate, for example, it was said that people just ignored the law: there was also religious prejudice against a Popish practice. The sponsors of the bill tried to appease the former by permitting one dish of flesh along with three of fish. They hoped to placate the latter by adding an explanatory clause repudiating any superstitious meaning and even making it a punishable offence to give a

[1] Northants Record Soc. MS. F. (M). P. 192; my article, 'The Commons Journals of the Tudor Period', *Trans. Royal Hist. Soc.* 4th ser. iii. 139 n.3.

religious significance to this political act. 'Cecil's Fast', the
Papists called it: Cecil's Fast it had to be. One is reminded of
the Black Rubric on kneeling at the Communion which the
radicals got inserted into the Prayer Book of 1552. And here
at any rate it is not fanciful to suppose that some of our 'choir'
of forty-three were vociferous in opposition and faithful in
voting. The third-reading debate spread over two more meetings — six in all, an extraordinary number — before the bill
finally passed; and then it was only after a division, 149 voting
for, and 77 against. A struggle worthy of a more critical issue:
though opposition to authority, whatever the occasion, was
part of the parliamentary apprenticeship to independence.
Pity that we are too early for the private diarist to detail the
story, or the Clerk to do more than make the briefest entries of
readings.[1]

'I am so fully occupied to expedite matters in this Parliament,' wrote Cecil to his friend, Sir Thomas Smith, in France,
'that I have no leisure almost to attend any other things.' This
was on February 27th, before the navy bill had imposed its full
burden, though the succession and other questions had been
frittering time away. 'Expedition'; 'short session': these were
Cecil's objectives. They were not his to command; and our
symbolic 'choir' of forty-three discovered several other openings
for singing their song.[2]

One came through a measure ultimately entitled 'An act for
the assurance of the Queen's Majesty's royal power over all
estates and subjects within her Highness's dominions'; which
the Clerk descriptively called 'The bill against those that extol
the power of the Bishop of Rome, and refuse the oath of
allegiance'. It marked a further stage in the Protestant revolution, a stiffening of the law against Catholics in response to
increasing tension at home and abroad: the religious conflict in
France, the Council of Trent, the fear aroused by the Queen's
recent illness. The penalties imposed by the Act of Supremacy
in 1559 against those who in specified ways maintained the
authority of the Pope were stepped up, and the obligation to
take the oath of supremacy was extended — also with an
increase of penalties — to include not only the ecclesiastical and

---

[1] *Statutes of Realm*, IV. i. 426-7; WRIGHT, *Q. Elizabeth & Her Times*, i. 126n.
[2] WRIGHT, op. cit. i. 126.

secular officers and others mentioned in the Act of Supremacy, but all in or taking Holy Orders, all university graduates, all schoolmasters, lawyers, and other socially influential persons. The bill incidentally imposed the oath on future Members of the House of Commons, thus excluding avowed Catholics from Parliament; though the Lords of the Upper House were exempt, since, as the text of the measure diplomatically asserted, 'the Queen's Majesty is otherwise sufficiently assured' of their faith and loyalty. Thus, Viscount Montague could remain in the House of Lords; but, after future elections, his opposite number in the House of Commons could no longer sit there.[1]

We may recall that in 1559 the Commons had objected to the mild penalties of the government's Supremacy bill and had tried to extend them to include the death penalty. They failed on that occasion. Radical opinion, however, remained unchanged. In his parliamentary sermon Dr. Nowell had given voice to it: 'maintainers of false religion ought to die by the sword'. And the Commons, in their petition on the succession, had spoken of devising 'the most penal, sharp, and terrible statutes' for the Queen's preservation.

This bill of 1563 was probably a government measure, as the brief official type of preamble suggests; and in its original form it may well have been relatively mild, stopping short of imposing the death penalty for refusal of the oath. On its second reading it was committed, with the passionate Sir Francis Knollys in charge of the committee. It emerged as a new bill. Its penalties were now those of praemunire (loss of lands and goods and imprisonment during pleasure) for the first offence, and treason for the second. Death for a second refusal of the oath: the Queen certainly did not want such severity, nor perhaps did her more responsible ministers. 'A law is passed for sharpening laws against Papists', wrote Cecil, 'wherein some difficulty hath been, because they be made very penal; but such be the humours of the Commons House, as they think nothing sharp enough against Papists.' If Cecil's letter can be taken to imply that the Commons had rewritten the original measure to make it 'most penal, sharp, and terrible', then our Protestant zealots were once more running away with things.[2]

---

[1] 5 Eliz. c. 1 (*Statutes of Realm*, IV. i. 402-5); *C.J.* i. 65.
[2] WRIGHT, op. cit. i. 126.

But there was opposition. Mr. Robert Atkinson, Member for Appleby, a lawyer of the Inner Temple who was expelled from that body for recusancy in 1570, was courageous enough to attack the bill. He was evidently a Catholic, but also a temporizer. Much of his speech was nearer in sentiment to his Queen than to the passionate majority who listened to him. The maintenance of foreign — that is, of Papal — jurisdiction, he argued, was never accounted treason. It should be regarded as an offence in religion, and against the Act of Supremacy. Turning first to what 'the express laws of God' had to say about the punishment for such an offence, he summoned the recent past to refute today. He had heard the present Protestant preachers then say that 'the greatest punishment that hath been taught by the Apostles in case of religion hath been by excommunication'. Religion, they had declared, 'must sink in by persuasion: it cannot be pressed in by violence'. They had disliked the dealings in Mary Tudor's reign, 'calling the bishops "bloodsuckers", and bade "Fie on these tormentors that delighted in nothing else but in the death of innocents; that threatened the whole realm with their fire and faggots; murderers; . . . worse than the traitors that put Christ to death". And that with such vehemency and stomach, as I assure you I marvel how it can possibly come to pass that they should now desire to establish that as a law which they thought then so far unlawful.'

In Christian realms, continued Atkinson, religious offenders had indeed been punished by death; but in this bill, though a man intended to live under a law and keep his conscience to himself, yet by the oath will we grope him and see what secretly lieth in his breast. The penalties of the Act of Supremacy were sufficient and had kept the peace. 'Let us follow the example of the Queen's Majesty, whose gracious Highness hath with such clemency ruled us, and so tempered her justice with mercy, as I ween never prince since the Conquest (I speak it without flattery) hath . . . reigned over us in a quieter peace, with more love and less exaction.'

But suppose the bill were passed, what good, he asked, would come of it? 'You will say, a sort of stubborn Papists should be rid out of the way, who, if they lived, would be causers of sedition . . . Surely, if the whole number that think against the oath in their conscience should refuse the oath and for the offence be executed, the realm could not choose but be much weakened.' Think you, however, 'that all that take it will upon the taking of it change their consciences? Nay, many a false shrew there is that will lay his hand to the book when his heart shall be far off . . . And if men were seditious before, now will they become ten times more seditious'.

'Let us, for the love of God, forget and forgive all griefs for the Commonwealth's sake, and let us love one another; for so shall no division work the desolation of our kingdom . . . We see in Germany, where after so long contention and so great destruction and waste of their country, at last they are come to this point, that the Papist and Protestant can now quietly talk together and never fall out about the matter . . . Since you have the sword in your hand to strike, be well ware whom you strike. For some shall you strike that are your near friends, some your kinsmen, but all your countrymen, and even Christian. And though you may like these doings, yet may it be that your heirs after you shall mislike them; and then farewell your name and worship.'[1]

An anonymous speech has survived which shows that, among the majority opposed to Atkinson, there were some who thought that, severe as the bill was, it did not go far enough. Concerning the section directed against those who extolled the Pope's authority, all, said this speaker, agree that the penalty is not unreasonable. Only the penalties against those refusing the oath arouse opposition; 'which, they say, toucheth the conscience, which should not be searched'. But it was a temporal, not a spiritual matter: a question of recognizing the prince's sovereignty, which is the duty of every subject, and to refuse which is treason. 'Shall a man have a conscience in cases of treason?' A first refusal of the oath was treason in Henry VIII's reign. To make the first offence merely praemunire, as they were now doing, was too mild. A 'bloodsucker' this speaker certainly was; and there were many like him.[2]

In a report of his, the Spanish ambassador would almost have us believe that Sir William Cecil sided with the extremists; but Cecil's own letter, from which we have quoted, implies that he favoured milder penalties. 'Vice-Chamberlain Knollys', the ambassador added, 'rose after Cecil and said this business must

[1] STRYPE, *Annals*, I. i. 446-55.  [2] Ibid. pp. 455-9.

be settled sword in hand and not by words, and that he would be foremost in the struggle.' That we can believe. Foremost he was. At its passing, the bill was taken to a division and was carried by 186 to 83. Though the opposition may have drawn encouragement from the more moderate intentions of the government, or, as Mr. Atkinson's speech might imply, from the Queen's known desire for clemency, they were a valiant minority in so passionate an assembly.[1]

In the Upper House, Lord Montague, the lone temporal peer who had consistently registered his dissent from the ecclesiastical bills of 1559, spoke against the measure. 'The prince or commonwealth that will make a new law, ought', he declared, 'to consider three things': that it be necessary, just and reasonable, and apt and fit to be put in execution. The law was unnecessary for 'the Catholics of this realm disturb not, nor hinder the public affairs of the realm, neither spiritual nor temporal'. It was neither just nor reasonable, for it was contrary and repugnant to all laws of man, natural and civil. No man ought to be constrained in a matter which he held to be doubtful. And here, though his intent was not to argue that Protestantism was false or schismatical, he made his belief quite clear. For his third point: 'What man', he asked, 'is there so without courage and stomach, or void of all honour, that can consent . . . to receive an opinion and new religion by force and compulsion? . . . And it is to be feared, rather than to die they will seek how to defend themselves.' He acknowledged that the greater part of the House, including the twenty-five bishops, were in favour of the bill. The bishops were partisans and could not be judges: moreover, they had no business with temporal penalties of confiscation, banishment, or death. As for the lay Lords, 'Let them . . . take good heed and not suffer themselves to be led by such men that are full of affection and passions and that look to wax mighty and of power by the confiscation, spoil, and ruin of the houses of noble and ancient men'.[2]

As Lord Montague anticipated, the Lords passed the bill. They added four provisions, which we may presume to be certain clauses softening its effects.[3]

---

[1] *Spanish Cal. Eliz.* i. 303; *C.J.* i. 65-6.  [2] STRYPE, *Annals*, I. i. 442-6.
[3] *L.J.* i. 593-604; *C.J.* i. 67-8.

The voice of moderation had been decisively beaten, and the government had no option but to accept the result. They were in serious need of the measure: of the extension of the oath, and, as they no doubt thought, of severer penalties against Catholic propagandists. The Queen could not employ the royal veto in such a situation. However, she had other ways of asserting her will. She could be rigorous or slack in the execution of the law. The death penalty for a second refusal of the oath was directed principally against the bishops and higher dignitaries of the Marian church: Bonner and his like, whom the zealots hated. 'There is no doubt some will die', wrote the Spanish ambassador on April 24th. But already, ten days before, Archbishop Parker, on the Queen's instructions, had ordered his bishops — who were charged by the act with administering the oath to ecclesiastics — not to tender it a second time and so put anyone in peril of death, without his written mandate. In other words, Elizabeth was refusing to execute a legal provision of which she disapproved. Parker, by no means an extremist, was sad. In order not to discourage 'honest Protestants', nor to rejoice the adversary — 'her adversaries, indeed', as he bitterly added — he issued the order in his own name, suppressing the Queen's. If Archbishop Parker felt like this, we can rest assured that Lord Montague was right in saying that all the bishops supported the bill.[1]

As the reign of Elizabeth progressed, the Queen kept an increasingly vigilant eye on any attempts by Parliament — which invariably began in the Lower House — to encroach by statutory enactment on the sphere of administration: to encroach, that is to say, on the prerogative. In this Parliament of 1563 there were two such occasions. One was a bill — from its title it seems innocuous to us — 'for allowance to sheriffs upon their accounts for Justices' diets'. It began in the Commons, was recast into a new bill on committal, passed, and had been twice read in the Upper House and was being 'called for to be read a third time', when the Lord Keeper intervened, declaring 'that the Queen's Majesty would take order therein herself; which her pleasure and determination she willed him to signify unto them, on her Majesty's behalf'. On the same day the Commons received a royal message to the same effect. The

[1] *Spanish Cal. Eliz.* i. 322; *Parker Correspondence* (Parker Soc.), pp. 173-5.

action was quite legitimate, and probably gave no more offence than did the exercise of the royal veto. But as an early occasion of the Queen's intervention in proceedings to defend the royal prerogative, it is worth noting.[1]

The second attempt was over a centuries-old grievance, purveyance: an ancient prerogative by which the Crown was entitled to preempt goods — principally food — for the maintenance of the royal household, buying them at customary prices, below the market rate. Purveyors were continually out in the shires commandeering supplies. At best it was an onerous, antiquated custom; often a cruel burden in the inflationary conditions of the Elizabethan period. But the corrupt and unreasonable practices of the purveyors, who descended like harpies on the countryside, made it a perennial source of complaint. Parliament had protested in the past, time and again, and parliamentary legislation had hedged the prerogative about with increasing restrictions. The last statute had been in Mary Tudor's reign. Any further legislation might have made the system unworkable. And indeed, short of a fundamental change, such as Cecil carried out in the latter part of the reign, substituting compounding by counties for the indiscriminate raids of the purveyors, what was needed was the observance of existing statutes. Elizabeth, with her acute sensitiveness about the royal prerogative, therefore resolutely defended purveyance from further statutory encroachment.[2]

In this Parliament of 1563 the Commons introduced two bills against the abuses of purveyors: independent moves, undoubtedly. The reign was young, the Queen was feeling her way, and perhaps, with the succession agitation on her, she was being cautious. In later Parliaments she intervened to stop such threats to the prerogative. But on this occasion she let the bills proceed. One of them passed the Commons and then the Lords. She vetoed it. But an accident took the sting out of her action. It was one of four bills which only reached their final stage an hour or so before she prorogued the Parliament. She vetoed the lot, presumably on the ground that there had not been time to scrutinize

[1] *C.J.* i. 63-9; *L.J.* i. 596-605.
[2] On this subject, see ALLEGRA WOODWORTH's *Purveyance for the Royal Household in the Reign of Elizabeth* (Philadelphia, 1945).

them. In all probability she would have vetoed the purveyors bill in any case.[1]

Peter Wentworth, a character whom we shall be meeting
later, was fond of quoting 'the spirit of God in Solomon': 'The
wounds of a lover are faithful; and the kisses of an enemy are
deceitful'. To which he added that he preferred 'to wound
her Majesty faithfully, thereby seeking her preservation'.
Wound her, our ardent Members in 1563 had not hesitated to
do. That they were lovers' wounds they made abundantly
clear: not least, in that seemingly strange place, the subsidy or
money bill.

Normally, it was a Privy Councillor who made the first proposal for a money grant: a form of procedure which has persisted to this day. In the course of Elizabeth's reign this became
so settled a habit that unofficial initiative was resented by the
House as an attempt to curry personal favour at Court. But in
1563 spontaneous loyalty, the loyalty perhaps of a Puritan
zealot, seems to have led to 'a motion made by a burgess for a
subsidy'. Our private Member was followed by the voice of
authority: 'an excellent declaration, made by Mr. Secretary
Cecil, of the great charges defrayed by the Queen's Majesty,
and of the causes of the wars in France, for not keeping the
edict there made by the Parliament; and also touching the
charges at Berwick, Newhaven [i.e. Havre], the provision of
armour and the navy, the cavillation of the French for Calais;
concluding to consider for the aid'. Alas! this 'excellent
declaration' — presumably a set oration of considerable length
and high quality — has perished in the ruins of time. Five days
elapsed before the House appointed its committee — all of
them knights of the shire, along with Councillor-Members — to
draft the bill. Perhaps the delay was due to Councillors being
busy with the petition on the succession; perhaps it was a
deliberate slowing down of supplies to give time for the succession agitation to achieve results. The latter seems more likely.[2]

The committee probably found the bill already drafted for
it on Cecil's instructions.[3] Whether the preamble was also in
draft we cannot even guess, but if it was, the committee almost

---

[1] *C.J.* i. 67-72; *L.J.* i. 618.                    [2] *C.J.* i. 63.

[3] Cf. S.P. Dom. Eliz. 40/68, 'A memorial of things fit to be considered of against
the Parliament'. '1. To have the book of subsidy put in a readiness': against
which is written, 'Mr. Attorney and Mr. Solicitor', who were to do the drafting.

certainly rewrote it, converting it into a song of loyalty, a paean of praise. 'Bliss was it in that dawn to be alive.'

'The certain knowledge and perfect sense that we your Majesty's most humble subjects have and feel of the great felicity which since your reign we . . . have enjoyed . . . far beyond all other nations, our neighbours . . . doth vehemently press and enforce us, first and principally, with all our hearts and souls, to acknowledge our most bounden duties to Almighty God, the King of Kings, for his exceeding, singular, and divine goodness showed to us his creatures in preserving for our safety, after so many storms, your royal princely person, our most gracious Queen.' Such were the opening words of the bill. For these their great benefits they offered themselves, 'most ready, with all obeisance and loyalty, to serve and most humbly to obey your Majesty, as God's immediate minister in earth and supreme governor over us, to the uttermost of our power and end of our lives'. Then followed a long, eulogistic recital of her princely and notable acts, beginning with the restoring of them 'to the favour, knowledge, and true service of Almighty God', and the delivery of them and their consciences 'from a foreign, unnatural tyranny and power, notwithstanding the many and great threatenings of worldly powers to the contrary'. The taxes they granted were their 'small gift', which 'may not be measured with your acts or with our own debts to your Majesty; but, of your accustomed clemency, accepted jointly with the treasure of our humble, infinite, and immeasurable thoughts and intentions of our hearts towards your Majesty'.[1]

It was a genuine outburst of feeling, a novelty in subsidy preambles; or rather, a revival and improvement upon the romantic note of Henry VIII's reign. Those of Mary Tudor's time had been matter of fact; under Edward VI, though touching on the theme of true religion, and of some warmth, they lacked the personal touch. Even the first Elizabethan preamble of 1559 was a different type: a brief expression of hope for the future, not a long savouring and glorification of the present. In the next session of this Parliament, we shall see that these men of 1563 were fully alive to the propaganda possibilities of a subsidy preamble, which was set up in print and sent into all the shires of the land. That being so, we may perhaps perceive

[1] *Statutes of Realm*, IV. i. 464-5.

a similar motive in the ardent stylists who poured out their emotion on this occasion.

Theoretically, the subsidy was a more liberal one than the last, since the tax on personalty now fell on subjects worth above £3 instead of £5. In its passing the Puritan conscience of the House proved troublesome. Not about the taxes: these they gladly gave. But this breed of men had tender scruples about oaths, especially if they were likely to lead to the heinous sin of perjury. They accordingly jibbed at the oath customarily and statutorily imposed on those charged with the assessments for the subsidy, which, indeed, must in general have been a mockery, for the assessments were a mockery. Presumably they were not much disturbed by the question whether the spiritual profit of lying without an oath would be offset by additional material loss to the Queen. At any rate, they debated the matter on the second reading of the bill, took out the oath, and by specific words forbade its imposition; and their successors, in the subsequent Parliaments of the reign, followed their godly example. Mr. Atkinson, in his speech on the bill against Catholics, had something to say about their behaviour, chiding them for objecting to the oath in the subsidy bill while at the same time approving of such severe penalties over the oath of supremacy that the same objectionable consequence was bound to follow.[1]

The parliamentary session ended on Saturday, April 10th, Easter eve. The Queen came by water from Whitehall to Westminster about 3 p.m. and after the Lords had donned their robes and she had taken her place in the Parliament Chamber, the Commons appeared at the bar, with their Speaker, Mr. Williams. His speech opened the proceedings. 'Thus it is, most excellent and virtuous princess, as nature giveth to every reasonable creature to speak, so is it a grace to be well learned. And I, representing the mouth of such a body as cannot speak for itself, and in the presence of your Majesty's person and nobles, must most humbly desire and crave of your Highness to bear with my imperfection.'

Describing Elizabeth as 'the fourth Queen, establisher of good laws', he made a sudden transition into a plea to her to marry. Then came a passage on the work of the Parliament,

[1] *C.J.* i. 65; STRYPE, *Annals*, I. i. 453; *Statutes of Realm*, IV. i. 469.

ornamented with a story about Alexander the Great and a tale from Xenophon about Cyrus and Croesus. Thanking the Queen for bearing with his unworthy service, and last of all with his 'unfitting words, uplandish and rude speech', he once more, and — if our report of the speech be a faithful reflection — as inconsequently introduced a plea that God would incline her heart to marriage and bless her with children, 'so that you and they may prosperously and as long time reign over us as ever did any kings or princes'.

The Queen then called the Lord Keeper to her, commanding him in her name to answer 'as she then declared unto him'. 'Her Majesty', he said, 'considereth how wisely you have done for the abolishing of the Romish power, the common enemy of this realm, remembering your care for the defence of the same realm, your respect for the maintenance of victual' — an allusion to a bill for the maintenance and increase of tillage — 'the banishment of vagabonds and relief of the poor, with other; and therefore alloweth your worthy proceedings herein.' He then thanked them at greater length for their grant of taxes, and went on to talk about the necessity of applying the laws, which 'without execution be as a torch unlighted or body without a soul'. In reply to the Speaker's petition to the Queen to accept in good part the travails and doings of the Nether House in this Parliament, 'she answereth how she doth not only accept them in good part, but also thanketh both you and them for the same'.

He then came to the petitions — as yet unanswered — made during the session for the Queen's marriage and succession. As the matter was of such importance, and he doubted his own exposition of it — a doubt one thoroughly appreciates — he had asked her Majesty 'that her meaning might be written, which she hath done and delivered to me to be read'.[1] It was from a manuscript in the Queen's own hand that he read this further specimen of Elizabethan prose:

'Since there can by no duer debt than Prince's word, to keep that unspotted for my part, as one that would be loth that the self thing which keepeth merchants' credit from craze should be the cause that Princes' speech should merit blame and so their honour quail, therefore I will an answer give. And this

[1] The proceedings and speeches to this point are from B.M. Cotton MS. Titus F. I, fols. 77 seqq.

it is. The two petitions that you presented me, expressed in many words, contained in sum these two things, as of your cares the greatest: my marriage, and my succession. Of which two I think best the last to be touched, and of the other a silent thought may serve. For I had thought it had been so desired as none other tree's blossom should have been minded or[1] ever hope of my fruit had been denied you. And yet, by the way, if any here doubt that I am as it were by vow or determination bent never to trade that kind of life, put out that heresy, for your belief is therein awry. For though I can think it best for a private woman, yet do I strive with myself to think it not meet for a Prince. And if I can bend my liking to your need, I will not resist such a mind.'

Turning to the subject of the succession, she continued: 'But to the last think not that you had needed this desire if I had seen a time so fit, and it so ripe to be denounced. The greatness of the cause, therefore, and need of your returns,[2] doth make me say that which I think the wise may easily guess: that as a short time for so long continuance ought not to pass by rote, as many tell their tales; even so, as cause by conference with the learned shall show me matter worthy utterance for your behoofs, so shall I more gladly pursue your good after my days, than with my prayers whilst I live be mean to linger my living thread. And thus much more than I had thought will I add for your comfort: I have good record in this place that other means than ye mentioned have been thought of, perchance for your good as much, and for my surety no less, which, if presently and conveniently could have been executed, it had not now been deferred or overslipped. But I hope I shall die in quiet with *nunc dimittis*, which cannot be without I see some glimpse of your following surety after my graved bones.'[3]

Among the Burghley papers in the British Museum there survives an early, perhaps the first, draft of the answer, written in the Queen's own hand with many deletions and insertions, showing with what labour and care, and — according to her canons — with what anxiety for stylistic niceties she arrived at her final text. She made at least three attempts to get the open-

---

[1] i.e. 'ere'.          [2] i.e. the need for Members to return to their homes.
[3] B.M. Harleian MS. 5176, fol. 97. There are several other manuscript copies of the speech.

ing phrase right. 'The two petitions that you presented', started off as 'The great', and then in a satirical mood, and perhaps in mounting annoyance as she recalled them, changed to 'The two huge scrolls'; whereupon discretion sobered it down. 'None other tree's blossom' started with an unpromising 'not', was instantly transformed into 'none other fruit', and as an after-thought blossomed. The three sentences beginning 'And yet, by the way, if any here doubt . . .' were a later addition, written in the margin. 'Other means than ye mentioned', which was surely a covert reference to her as-yet secret plan for marrying Dudley to Mary Stuart, began as 'other ways have been thought of'; while the words, 'in quiet', were inserted before 'with *nunc dimittis*' in order to make explicit a point only implied before.[1]

After the reading of Elizabeth's answer – if 'a silent thought' and baffling evasion can be called an answer – the royal assent was given to bills, two private bills being vetoed as well as the four concluded too late for scrutiny. The Lord Keeper then announced that the Queen had commanded him to prorogue the Parliament. The same House of Commons was to return for another session.

How grave a blunder Elizabeth made in retaining a body of men who had learnt to work together under radical leadership, who had proved so independent and insistent, and who had reason, not so much to trust a prince's word as to fear her prevarications: this the session of 1566 was to demonstrate. But in April 1563 she was probably hoping, before meeting them again, to have Dudley married to Mary and the succession ripe for settlement: perchance to be married herself or well on the way to it. It may be that some such thought caused her to prorogue rather than dissolve the Parliament. She was young – twenty-nine; and youth is optimistic.

[1] B.M. Lansdowne MS. 94, fol. 30.

# PART THREE

# THE PARLIAMENT OF 1566

## CHAPTER I

## THE SUCCESSION QUESTION RENEWED

THREE and a half years elapsed before the Parliament met for its second session, during which time it was kept in being by a series of prorogations. In the interval no solution had been reached either about the Queen's marriage or the succession. Wan were the hopes Elizabeth had cherished in 1563; and as time was the essence of the problem, it is hardly to be wondered at that her subjects felt desperate.

In 1563 the Queen had all but promised to marry. It was not bluff. Previous negotiations had sorted out the Archduke Charles of Austria as the most suitable candidate, and in the autumn of 1563 Cecil had been instructed to revive the suit. Far from being romance, this type of marriage was statecraft, subject to the cautions and interminable ways of diplomacy, be-devilled by factional intrigues at home, impeded by religion, and complicated always by the intimate feelings of a woman of personality. Negotiations dragged on and on. They were still doing so when Parliament met in 1566; and they were to continue for another year before the gathering difficulties — and not least the opposition of Protestant zealots, who had been the most clamorous for marriage in abstract — smothered them.[1] The irony in one of Elizabeth's speeches to this Parliament was not uncalled for.

As for the succession question, the passing years had not simplified it. On the contrary, it had been aggravated by the beginnings of a pamphlet literature. John Hales, Clerk of the Hanaper — an important Chancery office — had, as we have noticed, written a tract in favour of Lady Catherine Grey's

[1] Cf. my *Queen Elizabeth I*, chap. IX.

claim, during the Parliament of 1563. This came to light, along with certain dangerous intrigues over Lady Catherine's marriage, in the spring of 1564. Investigations implicated Sir Nicholas Bacon, Hales's official chief, and for a time Cecil was under suspicion. Bacon was excluded from Court and Council; Hales himself was indicted on a charge of sedition, and though the indictment may not have been prosecuted, he was imprisoned in the Tower for a time and was still under restraint as late as February 1568. The Queen feared a conspiracy to have Lady Catherine Grey's clandestine marriage declared legitimate and her claim to the succession recognized: the one claim to which she was certainly opposed, and of which a majority of the House of Commons — who, as the Spanish ambassador reported, were 'nearly all heretics and adherents of Catherine' — approved.[1]

The tract by Hales, of which manuscript copies had begun to circulate, was answered by Anthony Browne, a Catholic judge, who had been retained on the bench at Elizabeth's accession, though degraded from the office of Chief Justice. His tract advocated the claim of Mary Queen of Scots; and if the Queen knew of its existence, it is perhaps some comment on her views that she knighted its author in 1566.[2] Then in December 1565 the inevitable happened: that relatively new medium of propaganda, the printing press, whose startling potentialities had already been exploited by the religious controversialists of the age, was brought into play with a tract against Mary.[3] There was a manuscript reply from one of her supporters;[4] and about the same time two other pamphlets were written in her favour, one of which was published in March 1566.[5] To cap all, in June of that year, when Mary gave birth to her son James, Patrick Adamson, a Scottish minister in Paris, published a poem of thanksgiving in which he styled the infant, 'Prince

---

[1] WRIGHT, Q. Elizabeth & Her Times, i. 173-4, 179; HAYNES, Burghley Papers, pp. 411 seqq.; H.M.C. Hatfield MSS. i. 290; S.P. Dom. Eliz. 46/30; Spanish Cal. Eliz. i. 365, 602.
[2] Cf. D.N.B. sub Browne, Anthony. Copies of his tract are in B.M. Lansdowne MS. 254, fol. 185; Harleian MS. 555, fol. 11.
[3] B.M. ref. C.55. c.3. Manuscript copies, B.M. Cotton MS. Caligula B. IX, fol. 250; Harleian MSS. 4243, fol. 27; 4267, fol. 11. Cf. SCOTT, Bibliography of Works relating to Mary Q. of Scots.
[4] B.M. Harleian MS. 4243, fol. 32b.
[5] Ibid. 849, fol. 1; Cotton MS. Caligula B. IV, fol. 1. A copy of the other (printed) tract is in Cotton MS. Caligula B. IX, fol. 280.

of Scotland, England, France, and Ireland'.[1]    We shall hear
more of this poem.

Is it surprising that anxiety deepened among English Protestants? Moreover, like most people Elizabeth was occasionally
unwell, and the issues dependent on her life magnified the concern of those about her. In December 1564 she 'fell perilously
sick'. 'For the time she made us sore afraid', wrote Cecil to a
friend. It is as certain as historical speculation can be that had
Elizabeth died at or about this time there would have been
civil war. But that does not mean that the case for settling the
succession was either clear or sound. The conundrums of life
sometimes impose a gamble; and Elizabeth's gamble ultimately
succeeded.[2]

The hopes about Scotland which the Queen had entertained
when she prorogued the Parliament of 1563 had received a
severe setback. Although she had raised Lord Robert Dudley
to the peerage with the impressive title of Earl of Leicester in
order to make him more acceptable as Mary Stuart's husband,
the Queen of Scots had spurned the offer, taken control of her
own fortunes, and in July 1565 had married Lord Darnley, in
flat defiance of Elizabeth and England. She won a resounding
diplomatic victory, marred only, but fatally, by her utter mis-
judgment of Darnley's character. Tragedy was to be the terrible
price of that headstrong, foolish act; and in March 1566 the
first instalment had been exacted in the murder of David
Riccio. However, with her astonishing energy, courage, and
endurance Mary had recovered control of affairs, and in the
autumn of 1566, when the English Parliament met, was in a
stronger diplomatic position than ever. In the June she had
given birth to a prince — the future James I of England —
before whose baby eyes ranged a glittering prospect. Elizabeth
needed good relations with Scotland. That meant, as a minimum condition, no hostile declaration on the English succession;
and while Mary was prepared to acquiesce in this negative
policy, she demanded the right to send her representatives to
London if Parliament were to proceed with a settlement.[3]

To call Parliament at such a juncture was to invite trouble.

---

[1] Cf. *D.N.B.* sub Adamson, Patrick.

[2] WRIGHT, *Q. Elizabeth & Her Times*, i. 181.

[3] *Spanish Cal. Eliz.* i. 587, 590-1; CHÉRUEL, *Marie Stuart et Catherine de Médicis*,
p. 48.

On the one hand there was the Queen, who had recovered her poise and command, which in 1563 seem to have been undermined by her recent skirmish with death. She was her father's daughter. She knew what she wanted, or rather, what she did not want. If she favoured any claim, it was the Scottish. But she was resolutely set against the declaration of a successor; and her policy had the invaluable merit of avoiding a break with Scotland. On the other hand were the Commons, the overwhelming majority of whom were opposed to both trends of her policy. They were hostile to the Scottish claim; and they were determined to have the succession settled. The risk of a clash was not hidden from observers. The Spanish and French ambassadors both mentioned it in their dispatches before Parliament met.[1]

What is more, there was a public opinion behind Parliament — a significant feature — and perhaps a measure of organized agitation. Among the surviving papers of Thomas Sampson, the eminent Puritan divine and Marian exile, is an exceptionally long and wearisome tract, entitled, 'The common cry of Englishmen made to the most noble lady, Queen Elizabeth, and the High Court of Parliament . . .' Sampson may have been the author. He was a rigid, a temperamentally difficult man, who had refused a bishopric and recently been deprived of the deanery of Christ Church, Oxford, for his cast-iron nonconformity: a man whose dull, literary verbosity suggests authorship of the tract. 'And if the Queen . . . should seem not to be willing to hear and help, as we desire, presently', runs one passage, 'then turn we our cry to you our Lords and Commons . . . Though the delay made upon your last most godly request in this behalf [in 1563] did daunt and grieve the hearts of you and of thousands which loved you for your good attempt', yet try again. Was the Queen's answer on that occasion a promise? If so, then 'it is time to claim the performance . . . Was it a delay, peradventure but to try whether you did heartily affect the thing desired? Show forth again that affection which the cause requireth . . . If there should be such difficulty in the Queen that she would not of herself incline to help this misery, then is the wisdom and power of the Parliament to be showed

---

[1] *Spanish Cal. Eliz.* i. 571, 574, 577, 580, 581; P.R.O. Baschet Transcripts, Bdle. 26, La Forêt to Charles IX, September 22nd, 1566.

. . .' It looks as if Sampson also drafted a petition for the House of Commons to make to the Queen; thus demonstrating that instinct of the agitator to be ready with everything, which in due course we shall notice as a trait of another Puritan, Peter Wentworth. One sentence in the petition is instructive for its scepticism: 'We may despair of your marriage, we may despair of your issue.' These documents suggest that the clergy were using their zeal and their skill in propaganda to egg on Members of the House of Commons.[1]

In the city of London also there were outsiders ready to do their bit. Under October 6th, Cecil entered in his diary the note: 'Certain lewd bills thrown abroad against the Queen's Majesty for not assenting to have the matter of succession proceed in Parliament.' An ominous entry. This scattering of broadsheets — sometimes in the Queen's rooms at Court — was one way in which popular discontent had expressed itself in Mary Tudor's reign; and an insidious, unnerving sort of attack it was. Cecil went on: 'and bills also to charge Sir William Cecil, the Secretary, with the occasion thereof'. At much the same time the law students at Lincoln's Inn held a disputation on the succession — a sort of 'moot', for at least one senior was there — and 'found, by all the laws and customs of England that as a foreigner, born outside the realm, Mary Queen of Scots could not succeed to the crown, even if she were the nearest in birth and the ablest'. Mary was driven to lodge a formal complaint, and one, Thornton, a Reader at the Inn, was imprisoned for the offence.[2]

Why, in such an atmosphere, did the Queen summon Parliament? The answer is money. In spite of the subsidy of 1563 the royal finances had not recovered from the strain imposed by the war in France. But, however justified nationally and morally, Elizabeth was here on dangerous ground. She would be asking for taxes in time of peace: for extraordinary revenue in ordinary circumstances. Apart from the mood likely to be created in Parliament by the succession question, she could not count on that ready and unanimous response which had come on previous occasions. Altogether, it was a sorry outlook.

---

[1] B.M. Egerton MS. 2836, fols. 66-8, 72.
[2] MURDIN, *Burghley Papers*, p. 762; CHÉRUEL, op. cit. p. 48, quoting a dispatch from La Forêt, October 21st, 1566.

Since Parliament met on prorogation, there was no formal opening when both Houses assembled on September 30th, 1566. But the Commons found themselves in a peculiar position, for their Speaker, Thomas Williams, had died on July 1st, and procedure had to be devised to replace him. The Privy Council had evidently given thought to the problem, and it was the senior Councillor present who propounded the solution. This was to send a delegation to the Upper House, ask the Lords to notify the situation to the Queen, and so secure her licence to undertake a new election. The procedure was followed, letters patent issued, and the next day the Commons were summoned to the Upper House where the Lord Keeper charged them to set about the election.

The man selected by the government for nomination was Mr. Richard Onslow, a youngish person of thirty-eight; 'a furious heretic' as the Spanish ambassador wrote, but a royal official. Though a Member for the borough of Steyning, his recent appointment as Solicitor General had brought him a writ of assistance to attend in the Upper House. Consequently, the Comptroller, Sir Edward Rogers, had to preface his nomination by moving that the Commons should ask the Lords to restore this Member to them so that he might 'join in their election'. The farce was then gone through of bringing Onslow down from the Lords 'to show for himself' why he should not be in the Commons. His objections were overruled and the nomination proceeded, whereupon he made the customary disabling speech, arguing in addition that his oath to the Queen unfitted him for the office. As we know, this was a singularly independent, not to say rebellious, House of Commons, and Onslow had made much of his obligations to the Queen, which cannot have appealed to men set on coercing their Sovereign. Whatever the reason — a dispassionate appraisal of the speech, or, more likely, hostility to an official — the nomination was challenged, taken to a division, and carried by the narrow majority of 82 to 70. The Spanish ambassador reported that two rival nominations were made: a startling innovation, if true, but the Clerk records no such move, and it is best to be sceptical. In any case, what a start to the session! Our 'choir', we may be sure, aided that hostile vote.[1]

---

[1] *C.J.* i. 73; *L.J.* i. 627; *Spanish Cal. Eliz.* i. 583.

The Speaker-elect was presented to the Queen at a formal sitting of Parliament on October 2nd, and after a choice disabling speech, in which he once more stressed the objection of his legal office — perhaps what he said three times was true! — his excuse was denied on behalf of the Queen. 'An eloquent oration', noted the Clerk; and, indeed, as the unusual occasion robbed Mr. Onslow of the customary full-blown 'oration', he put his best literary endeavour into this first speech. His second was merely a brief, though well-phrased presentation of the Speaker's two personal petitions: for access to the Queen and for the right to correct any errors he might make in his reports. The privileges of the House survived, without repetition, from the previous session. After granting his requests, the Lord Keeper bade both Houses settle themselves 'wholly to weighty matters and those which be necessary, and to spare superfluous things and which needeth not'. He was probably girding at debates on marriage and the succession; but when told 'to prefer the most weighty matters first', the Commons knew none more weighty than these two. A short session to avoid great expense, was the Lord Keeper's injunction: short it would have been if the Commons had kept to the official agenda.[1]

Almost immediately there was a symbolical move from the zealots. 'This day Mr. Speaker took the oath', noted the Clerk on October 2nd. As an officer of a court he was compelled under the act of 1563 to take the oath of supremacy. The obligation also applied to anyone 'hereafter' elected to Parliament, and therefore to Members who had come in through by-elections since 1563. Next day business began with 'arguments touching the oath to the new burgesses'; and they were renewed a few days later. The zealots were trying to have the oath imposed on all Members, old and new, wanting to rid themselves of the very few Catholics elected in 1563, who in truth were an offence but certainly no danger to them. They failed: the law prevailed.[2]

Apart from this episode, the first fortnight passed in a strangely lax way, as though there was not enough business to fill in the time. The opposition seems to have been waiting its

---

[1] B.M. Cotton MS. Titus F. 1, fols. 100 seqq.
[2] *C.J.* i. 73-4; *Spanish Cal. Eliz.* i. 585-6.

cue, the government reluctant to give it. Conscious of the storm
that was gathering, the Council was apparently trying to soften
up the Queen's resistance. The French ambassador reported
that at a Council meeting on Saturday, October 12th, with the
Queen herself present, after Irish business had been discussed,
the Duke of Norfolk addressed Elizabeth on behalf of the whole
nobility. 'Madam,' he began, 'you know that I have taken an
oath to your Majesty as a Councillor, by which I am obliged
to have regard to your well-being and that of your subjects.
Pardon me, therefore, if I take the liberty of putting this matter
before you.' He then reminded her of the petitions presented
in the last Parliament, the answer to which she had postponed
until the present session. So far they had taken no action,
because they awaited her answer. They most humbly begged
her to let Parliament discuss both the succession and her
marriage.

The Queen, reported the ambassador, retorted in anger that
she had governed the country well hitherto, that if there had
been a little warfare which had caused her subjects to complain
of her, that was their responsibility, not hers. As for handling
the succession, not one of them should do it: she would reserve
that for herself. She had no desire to be buried alive, like her
sister. Well she knew how people at that time had flocked to
her at Hatfield: she wanted no such journeyings in her reign.
Nor had she the slightest wish for their counsel on this subject.
Her marriage: they knew quite well that it was not far off.
Parliament: she bade each of them do his duty. With that, she
took her leave and went out of the Chamber.[1]

If the French ambassador's news was authentic — and he
seems to have been well-informed — then it offers an explanation of that curious fortnight's quiet in the House of Commons.
The cue for which Members were waiting was the subsidy bill;
and by October 17th the government could no longer withhold
it. Mr. Comptroller moved for aid to be given the Queen and
was followed by Mr. Secretary Cecil, who 'made an excellent
declaration' — alas! another lost speech — concerning the
Queen's charges at Newhaven, on the navy, and on munitions

---

[1] [La Forêt] to Charles IX, October 21st, 1566 (MS. volume in the possession
of the publisher, John Murray, to whom I am indebted for permission to inspect
these MSS.)

against Shane O'Neil in Ireland. According to the French ambassador, a Member rose and declared that he saw neither the occasion nor the need for the Queen to demand money from her subjects. The war, which, it was said, had consumed her treasure, had been made on her whim, not in defence of the realm. Better scrutinize how the last subsidy had been spent and call to account those who had handled it. Hereupon, Edward Baeshe, surveyor of victuals for the navy, rose to defend the motion. The Queen, he said, had spent, and was daily spending, great sums not only to maintain a large number of ships but to build new ones. He urged them to grant the money willingly and freely. Another Member got up. Baeshe, he retorted, had reason to speak for the Queen, since the more money he handled, the more he profited. There were too many purveyors in this realm, he complained: they have so long a nose, it would stretch from London to the West Country. Their activities should be examined.[1]

Whether these things were really said, there is no means of checking; but that there was trouble we can believe. By now the morning was spent, and a committee of supply was appointed.

The next morning, Mr. Molyneux, a member of our 'choir' — 'Molyneux the mover', as the pasquil calls him — made the opening, the crucial, and surely the pre-arranged move in the succession campaign, linking it immediately with supply. The Clerk noted in his *Journal*: 'A motion, made by Mr. Molyneux, for the reviving of the suit for succession and to proceed with the subsidy, was very well allowed of the House.' A long debate followed. The French ambassador reported one Member as saying that when the Queen received the last subsidy, she had promised and pledged her word that she would not take a single penny more from them, and would even abolish the duty on wine. There was much greater need in this Parliament to speak of succession and marriage than of a subsidy. Some Members declared that the succession was the chief cause of their meeting and its settlement should be one of the reasons for granting supplies; others — and the official voice no doubt spoke here — that supplies should be voted first. The Clerk notes that Sir Ralph Sadler — who had recently been made a

[1] *C.J.* i. 74; [La Forêt] to Charles IX, October 27th, 1566 (Murray MSS.).

Privy Councillor — spoke, declaring that he had heard the Queen say she intended for the good of the realm to marry: conceivably he was referring to the Council meeting on October 12th.[1] We possess his own text of a speech, which was probably this one.

Dealing first with the subsidy, he protested that no man living would be more loth than he to speak in favour of anything that might seem burdensome to his country. 'If I speak for the Queen's Majesty, in so doing I speak not against the common weal of my country.' His argument was attuned to his hearers. 'We see that the whole world, our neighbours round about us, of long time have been, and yet be, in arms, in hostility, and in great garboil.' Religion is the cause. 'The malice of the enemies and adversaries of God's gospel doth increase and waxeth very hot. The late accidents in France, the great tyranny and horrible and cruel murders and slaughters which have been committed and executed there upon those of the religion, the like whereof hath never been heard nor read of, doth plainly show and declare the deadly hatred and malice of the Papists against the professors of God's gospel and true religion . . . What faith, what trust is to be given to their words and promises, all men may see. Indeed, they do but watch their time.' We need to beware of them. 'We have heard and we hear daily of secret conspiracies and great confederacies between the Pope, the French king, and other princes of the Popish confederacy, against all princes, Protestants and professors of the gospel, of the which the Queen's Majesty is the chief patroness and protectrix at this day. It is not unlikely, nay it is not to be doubted, but that those princes . . . as soon as they can settle and establish the Romish religion within their own territories and dominions, will forthwith convert and employ all their forces to restore the same also in England, where they may be sure to find a great aid of our own nation of our English Papists . . . England, the Queen's Majesty, is the only and greatest mark which the adversaries of God's gospel do shoot at.' Ireland, also, called for money; and Sadler proceeded to deal with that subject. Expounding the accepted theory of national finance, he declared the charge to be an extraordinary one: 'the prince's ordinary revenue will not

[1] *C.J.* i. 74; [La Forêt] to Charles IX, October 27th, 1566 (Murray MSS.).

suffice nor extend to maintain such extraordinary charges'. After flattering his hearers for their wisdom and judgment, he turned to the question of the succession.

'Surely,' he said, 'I cannot but much commend the zealous and good mind of him that hath brought it here in question. And for mine own part, I wish and desire from the bottom of my heart that some good success and effect might follow it. And yet I am not of opinion that it is fit for us to deal with it at this time, especially not to mix or mingle it with the matter of the subsidy, whereby we might seem as it were to condition and covenant with her Majesty.' 'It is a matter far out of our reach', he added; and chiefly concerns the Queen and her nobility, whom we must not think to be less mindful of it than we be. Perhaps there was some great cause, 'hidden and un-known to us', which stayed her Majesty at this time. Proceed with the subsidy; and as for the succession, 'let us pray to God in whose hands the hearts of princes are'. In our text of the speech there is no mention of the Queen's marriage. It may have been an unpremeditated, though officially inspired, addition.[1]

There can be little doubt that making supplies depend on redress of grievances was the deliberate and concerted policy of the group organizing this agitation: of our 'choir', shall we say? Indeed, it was the tactical lesson taught them by the frustration of 1563: there had been those who wanted to apply it then, and at the end of the session they might have said, 'I told you so'. The debate continued. Some Members, at the prompting either of their stomachs or of courtiers, or of both, attempted to leave, saying it was too late to deal with so impor-tant a matter. Others insisted on shutting the door of the Chamber and keeping them in. They came to blows, reported the Spanish ambassador: which may or may not be true. In the end, as the Clerk noted, 'their mind was to recontinue their suit, and to know her Highness's answer'. The agitators had triumphed. The Queen was annoyed; the Spanish ambassador reflected that 'these heretics neither fear God nor obey their betters'.[2]

The next day, Saturday, they were at it again. A move from

---

[1] B.M. Additional MS. 33591, fols. 8-11 (printed, *Sadler Papers*, ii. 548-52).
[2] *Spanish Cal. Eliz.* i. 589; *C.J.* i. 74.

the Court probably precipitated the debate. 'Mr. Secretary
and Mr. Vicechamberlain' — the Clerk notes — 'declared that
the Queen's Majesty is by God's special providence moved to
marriage, and that she mindeth, for the wealth of her Commons,
to prosecute the same.' The Chancellor of the Duchy and the
Comptroller spoke in confirmation, and urged the House 'to
see the sequel of that, before further suit touching the succession'. From the French ambassador's report it seems that they
were merely wasting their breath. Ordinary Members were
unanimous and insistent, warning the Councillors that responsibility rested on them more than on anyone else in the Kingdom,
and that if trouble befell the country through lack of action
their persons would answer for it. One Councillor advised a
little patience and meanwhile to content the Queen by proceeding with the subsidy. 'No! no!' replied the Commons, 'we
have express charge to grant nothing before the Queen gives a
firm answer to our demands. Go to the Queen, and let her
know our intention, which we have in command from all the
towns and people of this Kingdom, whose deputies we are.'

The debate continued till 1 p.m., interspersed with confused
cries and voices. The Clerk summed it up: 'After long arguments by divers lawyers to recontinue the suit to get the Queen's
answer, order was taken that the Privy Council with forty-four
of this House should meet tomorrow' — tomorrow being Sunday, a token of extraordinary haste — 'to consult in what
manner suit may be made to the Lords to join in this matter.'
On that committee, though seniority might have been expected,
were twenty-one of our 'choir'. The House was indeed out of
hand.[1]

According to the French ambassador, the Councillors delivered the message to the Queen. Angrier than ever, Elizabeth
exclaimed that even her Council was betraying her by joining
in this game. It was her will that must prevail: and she would
on no account be coerced into naming a successor. They
deluded themselves: they would never extract consent from
her.

Two or three days later, Elizabeth poured out her story to
the Spanish ambassador. He happened to be a Spaniard with
whom she got on well, and the Austrian marriage suit was a

---

[1] C.J. i. 75; [La Forêt] to Charles IX, October 21st, 1566 (Murray MSS.).

link between them. But what a position for the Queen of England, to find his almost the only sympathetic ear! The Commons, she told him, were offering her £250,000 for her consent to their demands. She would accept no conditions. The ambassador put in a word for the Archduke Charles. Within a week, said Elizabeth, she would send to the Emperor signifying her intention to accept the marriage. With misplaced confidence in that bulwark of monarchy, the nobility, she expressed her belief that they would not join with the Commons. As for the latter, 'she did not know what these devils wanted'. 'Liberty', promptly answered the ambassador; and it behoved kings to look out for themselves. With a sudden surge of feeling for her subjects, the Queen confessed that there was some show of reason in their wishes. Needless to add, the ambassador got in a dig at heretics.[1]

On Monday, October 21st, the Commons' committee duly delivered their request to the Lords to join in the suit to the Queen, and were told that they would receive an answer the next day. The Upper House at this time was without its chairman, the Lord Keeper, who had succumbed to gout; and his place had been taken by the senior peer in precedence, the doddering Lord Treasurer, the Marquis of Winchester, over eighty years old, whose 'decay of memory and hearing, griefs accompanying hoary hairs and old age' — and perhaps his incapacity to maintain discipline at this critical time — led the Queen to replace him by the Chief Justice. Not indeed that the Lords acted hastily. Instead of receiving the Commons' committee on October 22nd, as promised, they sent an impressive deputation to the Queen.[2]

They found her in the Privy Chamber, and after her courtiers had withdrawn, the Lord Treasurer explained their mission, telling of the approach that the Commons had made, and saying that necessity constrained them to press her to answer. It was the custom of kings, her predecessors, to provide in good time for the succession, and the Commons were unanimously resolved to deal with the subject before treating of a subsidy or any other business. Few measures, and those of little impor-

---

[1] [La Forêt] to Charles IX, October 21st, 1566 (Murray MSS.); *Spanish Cal. Eliz.* i. 589-90.
[2] *L.J.* i. passim.

tance, had as yet been passed in Parliament: a comment
which the *Journal* of the Commons shows to be true. They were
wasting time, continued the Lord Treasurer, and witnessing a
great assembly reduced to futility. They begged the Queen
either to declare her will on this matter or to put an end to
Parliament and let everyone go home. The Duke of Norfolk
then took up the argument, and after him each in turn and
rank, all to the same purpose.

The Queen's answer showed no change of mind. The Commons, she said, were very rebels, and would not have dared to
act thus in her father's lifetime. It was not for them to meddle
in her affairs, nor did it pertain to a subject to constrain his
Prince. They were demanding that she should dig her own
grave. 'My Lords', she went on, 'do whatever you wish. As for
me, I shall do no otherwise than pleases me. Your bills can
have no force without my assent and authority.' The matter,
she added, is too important to be dealt in by so light-witted a
body. She intended to choose half a dozen of the ablest lawyers
in her kingdom, and after hearing their advice would tell them
her decision. Very angry, she dismissed them.[1]

The drama became more tense. The next day, October 23rd,
the Lords received and listened to the Commons' committee,
whose case — revealing fact — was expounded, not by its senior
members but by three of our 'choir': Bell, Monson, and Kingsmill. The Upper House took two days for reflection and then
decided to join with the Lower House in its suit to the Queen.[2]
The only dissentient voice, says the Spanish ambassador, was
that of the Lord Treasurer — the ancient time-server, who once
described himself as sprung from the willow, not the oak. And
he was heard unwillingly. Thus the monarch was left in isolation, the greatest peril that could befall a prince: defied by her
Council, defied by her nobility, defied by the Commons. Elizabeth was right: they would not have dared treat her father so.
The regiment of a woman displayed its inherent weakness.[3]

In Elizabeth's opinion, the chief culprit among the Lords
was the Duke of Norfolk; and it is little wonder that in the
family life of the Court she vented her wrath on him. The

[1] [La Forêt] to Charles IX, October 27th, 1566 (Murray MSS.).
[2] *C.J.* i. 75 and *L.J.* i. 638 are in conflict, the former giving the item under
October 25th, the latter under 26th. I think the former more likely to be right.
[3] *Spanish Cal. Eliz.* i. 591.

Spanish ambassador says that she went almost as far as calling him a traitor and conspirator. When the Earls of Leicester and Pembroke, along with the Marquis of Northampton and Lord Chamberlain Howard, remonstrated, she turned on Pembroke, telling him that he talked like a swaggering soldier. Addressing Leicester, she said that she had thought if all the world abandoned her, he would not: to which he answered that he would die at her feet. That, she retorted, had nothing to do with the matter. The Marquis of Northampton, who had twice invoked Parliament over his unfortunate matrimonial affairs, received a home thrust. He had better, said Elizabeth, talk about the arguments that got him married again when he had a wife living, instead of mincing words with her. She banned them from her company. Under October 27th, Cecil noted in his diary that the Earls of Pembroke and Leicester 'were excluded the Presence Chamber' for furthering the succession question in Parliament without the Queen's allowance. Elizabeth poured out her trouble to the Spanish ambassador, stressing especially the ingratitude of Leicester. They are all against me, she complained, except the Lord Treasurer.[1]

The leading noblemen — not the bishops, whose outlook was similar to that of the Commons — were evidently worried by the situation. Perhaps they shrank from the consequences of their decision: the isolation of their Sovereign. They moved slowly: too slowly for the House of Commons, who pursued their purpose by what we today would term a 'go-slow' strike. On October 26th their only business was the first reading of two bills — an hour's work at most; at the next sitting the same, though one bill was the subsidy bill, which they were to leave at this stage for a month, dangling like a bait. On October 30th it was one bill only. They must have risen very early on these mornings, unless, indeed, they spent the time talking about the succession. Their tactics succeeded. On October 31st — it was a Thursday — the Lords fixed the following Saturday afternoon for conference between the committees of both Houses. The Commons promptly adjourned their House till the Monday: an astounding act of insubordination, which under other circumstances would have provoked disciplinary action by the

---

[1] [La Forêt] to Charles IX, October 27th (Murray MSS.); *Spanish Cal. Eliz.* i. 591-2; MURDIN, *Burghley Papers*, p. 762.

Crown. They ordered their committee, however, to meet on the Saturday morning to agree on reasons to be set before the Lords' committee in the afternoon.[1]

It looks as if the Privy Council, about this time, was trying to find a way out of the impasse. Cecil clarified his thoughts in a memorandum. 'To require both marriage and stablishing of succession is the uttermost that can be desired. To deny both is the uttermost that can be denied. To require marriage is most natural, most easy, most plausible to the Queen's Majesty. To require certainty of succession is most plausible to all the people' but 'is hardest to be obtained both for the difficulty to discuss the right and for the lothsomeness in the Queen's Majesty to consent thereto . . . Corollary: the mean betwixt these is to determine effectually to marry, and if it succeed not, then proceed to discussion of the right of the successor.'[2]

From this line of thought proceeded another memorandum of his, which we may assume to have been a Council paper. It advocated threefold action: proceed with marriage; declare the necessity to establish the succession; then prorogue Parliament for a short time, see how the marriage negotiations prosper, and when Parliament reassembles deal with the succession as circumstances require. We know that some such idea was in the air, for the Earl of Sussex — who though not a Councillor was an influential peer and friend of Cecil — saw the Spanish ambassador and begged him, as one in Elizabeth's good graces, to urge her to get on with the marriage, and, using that as an excuse, to prorogue Parliament for six months. Responsible circles had been brought to the sorry expedient of advocating an 'Addled Parliament'.[3]

Somewhere or other — and the best place seems to be here, though November 11-13th is not impossible — we have to fit in a speech made by Sir Ralph Sadler at a Council meeting, with the Queen present. Excusing himself as a newcomer to the Council, whose role it was to learn rather than speak, he asked the Queen's leave to state his thoughts without dissimulation. He urged her to establish the succession, 'the thing that all your people of all degrees have long expected and looked

---

[1] *C.J.* i. 75-6; *L.J.* i. 640.    [2] S.P. Dom. Eliz. 40/91.
[3] Ibid. 40/102; *Spanish Cal. Eliz.* i. 592.

for'. He could not see how it should be dangerous to her person: rather the contrary, for she would thus win the hearts of all her people. If she should now end her Parliament, and nobles and Commons go home and when asked by their countrymen (for, be sure, all men hearken to this matter) 'What is done?' some rashly answer, 'We have done nothing but give away your money; the Queen hath that she looked for, but hath no care of us': how your people's hearts will be wounded with this! He then went on with further arguments for his — and Parliament's — case.[1]

The climax to these strange proceedings was near. At their meeting on Saturday, November 2nd, the committees of both Houses did not get as far as a decision: they adjourned till the Monday, and on that day, by common consent, resolved to petition the Queen to deal with the succession. Cecil sent an optimistic message to the Spanish ambassador.

He misjudged his mistress. The following day — November 5th — the Lords were told to arrange for thirty of each House to be at the Palace, before the Queen, that afternoon. Elizabeth had decided to forestall their petition: to deliver her answer without permitting them to state their case. Ethics apart, the tactics were sound, for the weakness of Elizabeth's position lay in the plausibility of her opponents' arguments.

In the Commons, instead of leaving the House to choose the delegation, the Speaker was empowered to select thirty from the committee which had been conferring with the Lords: the committee on which were twenty-one of our 'choir'. On the delegation there were only four, and those, so far as we can tell, the least active. The principle of rank and respectability kept out the others: doubtless to the relief of the official mind. The Speaker himself was excluded, in all probability on the Queen's explicit instructions: as she told them, she alone was to be a speaker on this occasion.[2]

We possess an odd sheet of paper on which Elizabeth started out to draft her speech to this parliamentary delegation. She was not the first, certainly not the last, to find that sort of exercise a cathartic for the first fury of her thoughts. There are only the opening sentences, with her customary deletions and interlineations:

[1] *Sadler Papers*, ii. 553-5.    [2] *Spanish Cal. Eliz.* i. 593, 594; *L.J.* i. 641; *C.J.* i. 76.

'If the order of your cause had matched the weight of your matter, the one might well have craved reward and the other much the sooner satisfied. But when I call to mind how far from dutiful care — yea, rather, how nigh a traitorous trick — this tumbling cast did spring, I muse how men of wit can so hardly use that gift they hold. I marvel not much that bridleless colts do not know their rider's hand, whom bit of kingly rein did never snaffle yet. Whether it was fit that so great a cause as this should have had his beginning in such a public place as that, let it be well weighed. Must all evil bodings that might be recited, be found little enough to hap to my share? Was it well meant, think you, that those that knew not how fit this matter was to be granted by the Prince, would prejudicate their Prince in aggravating the matter, so [that] all their arguments tended to my careless care of this my dear realm?'[1]

Fortunately, we also have what appears to be a full and faithful report of this remarkable speech, written by one of those present. It may be a little lacking in the authentic vocabulary and flavour, but there is no mistaking the source.

'If that order had been observed in the beginning of the matter, and such consideration had in the prosecuting of the same, as the gravity of the cause had required, the success thereof might have been otherwise than now it is. But those unbridled persons whose mouth was never snaffled by the rider, did rashly ride into it in the Common House, a public place; where Mr. Bell with his complices alleged that they were natural Englishmen and were bound to their country, which they saw must needs perish and come to confusion unless some order were taken for limitation of the succession of the crown. And further to help the matter, must needs prefer their speeches to the Upper House, to have you, my Lords, consent with them; whereby you were seduced, and of simplicity did assent unto it, which you would not have done if you had foreseen before considerately the importance of the matter. So that there was no malice in you, and so I do ascribe it. For we think and know you have just cause to love us, considering our mercifulness showed to all our subjects since our reign. But there, two bishops, with their long orations, sought to persuade you also with solemn matters, as though you, my Lords, had not known

[1] S.P. Dom. Eliz. 41/5.

that when my breath did fail me I had been dead unto you, and that then, dying without issue, what a danger it were to the whole State: which you had not known, before they told it you!

'And so it was easily to be seen *quo oratio tendit*. For those that should be stops and stays of this great good, and [responsible for] avoiding of so many dangers and perils, how evil might they seem to be! And so to aggravate the cause against me! Was I not born in the realm? Were my parents born in any foreign country? Is there any cause I should alienate myself from being careful over this country? Is not my kingdom here? Whom have I oppressed? Whom have I enriched to other's harm? What turmoil have I made in this Commonwealth that I should be suspected to have no regard to the same? How have I governed since my reign? I will be tried by envy itself. I need not to use many words, for my deeds do try me.'

From this fiery prologue, in which she vented her anger on the Commons and bishops, but not on the lay peers, she turned to business. 'Well, the matter whereof they would have made their petition (as I am informed) consisteth in two points — in my marriage and in the limitation of the succession of the Crown, wherein my marriage was first placed, as for manner's sake. I did send them answer by my Council I would marry (although of mine own disposition I was not inclined therunto). But that was not accepted nor credited, although spoken by their Prince. And yet I used so many words that I could say no more: and were it not now I had spoken those words, I would never speak them again. I will never break the word of a prince, spoken in a public place, for my honour's sake. And therefore I say again, I will marry as soon as I can conveniently, if God take not him away with whom I mind to marry, or myself, or else some other great let happen. I can say no more, except the party were present. And I hope to have children, otherwise I would never marry.

'A strange order of petitioners, that will make a request and cannot be otherwise ascertained but by their Prince's word, and yet will not believe it when it is spoken! But they (I think) that moveth the same will be as ready to mislike him with whom I shall marry, as they are now to move it. And then it will appear they nothing meant it. I thought they would have been rather ready to have given me thanks than to have made any new request for the same. There hath been some that have ere this said unto me they never required more than that they might once hear me say I would marry. Well, there was never so great a treason but might be covered under as fair a pretence.'

Turning to the succession question, she revealed how decisive an influence on her policy was her own experience in Mary Tudor's reign, hinting at intrigues which remain as secret from the historian as she now kept them from her audience. 'The second point was the limitation of the succession of the crown: wherein was nothing said for my safety but only for themselves. A strange thing that the foot should direct the head in so weighty a cause; which cause hath been so diligently weighed by us, for that it toucheth us more than them. I am sure there was not one of them that ever was a second person, as I have been, and have tasted of the practices against my sister — who, I would to God were alive again. I had great occasions to hearken to their motions, of whom some of them are of the Common House. But when friends fall out, truth doth appear, according to the old proverb; and were it not for my honour, their knavery should be known. There were occasions in me at that time. I stood in danger of my life, my sister was so incensed against me: I did differ from her in religion, and I was sought for divers ways. And so shall never be my successor.

'I have conferred before this time with those that are well learned, and have asked their opinions touching the limitation of succession; who have been silent — not that by their silence, after lawlike manner, they have seemed to assent to it, but that indeed they could not tell what to say, considering the great peril to the realm, and most danger to myself. But now the matter must needs go trimly and pleasantly when the bowl runneth all on the one side. And, alas, not one amongst them all would answer for us, but all their speeches were for the surety of their country. They would have twelve or fourteen limited in succession, and the more the better. And those shall be of such uprightness and so divine as in them shall be divinity itself. Kings were wont to honour philosophers; but if I had such I would honour them as angels, that should have such piety in them that they would not seek where they are the second to be the first, and where the third to be the second, and so forth.

'It is said, I am no divine. Indeed, I studied nothing else but divinity till I came to the crown; and then I gave myself to the study of that which was meet for government, and am not ignorant of stories wherein appeareth what hath fallen out for ambition of kingdoms — as in Spain, Naples, Portugal, and at home; and what cocking hath been between the father and the son for the same. You would have a limitation of succession. Truly, if reason did not subdue will in me, I would cause you to deal in it, so pleasant a thing it should be unto me. But I stay it for your benefit. For if you should have liberty to treat of it, there be so many competitors — some kinfolks, some servants, and some tenants; some would speak for their master, and some for their mistress, and every man for his friend — that it would be an occasion of a greater charge than a subsidy. And if my will did not yield to reason, it should be that thing I would gladliest desire to see you deal in.'

And now, her bitterness against the bishops — *Domini Doctores* — who presumably had been the leading agitators in the House of Lords, again declared itself. 'Well, there hath been error: I say not errors, for there were too many in the proceeding in this matter. But we will not judge that these attempts were done of any hatred to our person, but even for lack of good foresight. I do not marvel, though *Domini Doctores* with you, my Lords, did so use themselves therein, since after my brother's death they openly preached and set forth that my sister and I were bastards. Well, I wish not the death of any man, but only this I desire: that they which have been the practisers herein may before their deaths repent the same, and show some open confession of their fault, whereby the scabbed sheep may be known from the whole.

'As for my own part, I care not for death; for all men are mortal. And though I be a woman, yet I have as good a courage, answerable to my place, as ever my father had. I am your anointed Queen. I will never be by violence constrained to do anything. I thank God I am endued with such qualities that if I were turned out of the realm in my petticoat, I were able to live in any place in Christendom.

'Your petition is to deal in the limitation of the succession.

At this present it is not convenient; nor never shall be without some peril unto you and certain danger unto me. But were it not for your peril, at this time I would give place, notwithstanding my danger. Your perils are sundry ways; for some may be touched, who resteth now in such terms with us as is not meet to be disclosed, either in the Common House or in the Upper House. But as soon as there may be a convenient time, and that it may be done with least peril unto you — although never without great danger unto me — I will deal therein for your safety, and offer it unto you as your Prince and head, without request; for it is monstrous that the feet should direct the head.

'And therefore this is my mind and answer, which I would have to be showed in the two Houses. And for the doing thereof, you, my Lord Chief Justice, are meetest to do it in the Upper House, and you, Cecil, in the Nether House. And therewith, speaking of the Speaker, that the Lower House would have had their Speaker there, wherein they did not consider that he was not there to speak: she said she was a speaker, indeed; and there ended.'[1]

---

[1] Cambridge Univ. Library MS. Gg. III. 34, fols. 208 seqq. There is another copy of this version in B.M. Stowe MS. 354, fols. 18-19 (printed by me in *Eng. Hist. Rev.* xxxvi. 514-17). I have used the former (and better) text, with an occasional reading from the latter.

## CHAPTER II

# THE SUCCESSION QUESTION
## (CONTINUED)

THE day after the audience, the Queen's speech was reported to the House of Commons. The Clerk surprisingly tells us that 'Mr. Comptroller and, after, Mr. Secretary read in writing notes of the Queen's Majesty's sayings'. We know nothing of Mr. Comptroller, but we do of Secretary Cecil, whom the Queen specifically charged with conveying her 'mind and answer' to the House. He made a few notes of the speech, and then wrote out a *précis* of it. What a transmogrification! The vigour, the passion, the gibes — all the virtue had gone out of it. Nevertheless, in his offenceless English he had retained some of the Queen's criticisms. On reflection he was evidently afraid of their effect upon the House. 'This was not reported', he wrote on the document. He then drew up another version. Elizabeth was now roaring 'as gently as any sucking dove; . . . as 'twere any nightingale'. One single touch of gentle reproof: for the rest, a spirit of reasonableness and accommodation, far, indeed, from the Queen's 'mind and answer'.[1]

Cecil wrote at the head of his manuscript that the report was made 'with the consent' of the rest of the delegates, both Lords and Commons. If this means that the 'vetting' was done in concert, how thankful officials must have been that the hotheads of our 'choir' had been discreetly kept off the delegation. In any case, there was reason to be thankful.

But the best-laid schemes go astray. Our Clerk ends his simple entry: 'Whereupon all the House was silent.' A pregnant sentence! They remained silent on the subject during another sitting. And then, on November 8th, as the Clerk states, 'Mr. Lambert began a learned oration for iteration of the suit to the Queen's Majesty for limitation of succession; and thereupon [it was] strongly reasoned, for both parts'. This Member was the gentle antiquary William Lambarde, Member for Aldborough, a lawyer, then in the prime of his thirtieth year and perhaps not

[1] *C.J.* i. 76; S.P. Dom. Eliz. 41/8, 7, 9.

so gentle when young. In a tract of his on parliamentary procedure, he tells us that he made this speech: the bare fact, no more. A first reading to two bills — about an hour's work — was all the business that the House did that morning. They must have spent the rest of the sitting on the debate.[1]

The next day, Saturday, November 9th, came the riposte from Court. 'Mr. Vicechamberlain declared the Queen's express commandment to this House, that they should no further proceed in their suit, but to satisfy themselves with her Highness's promise of marriage. Mr. Secretary and Mr. Comptroller severally rehearsed the like matter.' Once more the opposition paused to consider their tactics. On the Monday, again after the first reading of two bills, by which time the tardy were in their places, Paul Wentworth — 'Wentworth the wrangler', worthy forerunner of his redoubtable brother, Peter — 'moved whether the Queen's commandment was not against the liberties'. He put three questions to the House:

'Whether her Highness's commandment, forbidding the Lower House to speak or treat any more of the succession and of any their excuses in that behalf, be a breach of the liberty of the free speech of the House, or not?

'Whether Mr. Comptroller, the Vicechamberlain, and Mr. Secretary, pronouncing in the House the said commandment in her Highness's name, are of authority sufficient to bind the House to silence in that behalf, or to bind the House to acknowledge the same to be a direct and sufficient commandment, or not?

'If her Highness's said commandment be no breach of the liberty of the House, or if the commandment, pronounced as afore is said, be . . . sufficient . . . to bind the House to take knowledge thereof, then what offence is it for any of the House to err in declaring his opinion to be otherwise?'

Wentworth, it seems, was supported by the lawyer, James Dalton, another of our 'choir'; a youngish man, probably in his early thirties, as was Wentworth.[2]

Here was something fundamental: an innovation in parliamentary tactics; dawn of a new age; harbinger of Stuart conflicts. How rapidly we are moving away from the days of Sir

[1] *C.J.* i. 76; B.M. Additional MS. 5123, fols. 10b-11.
[2] *C.J.* i. 76; S.P. Dom. Eliz. 41/16; Additional MS. 5123, fols. 10b-11.

Thomas More! Alas! no account of the debate is known, but the Clerk's bald entry in his *Journal* stirs the imagination: 'Whereupon arose divers arguments, continuing from nine of the clock till two afternoon. And then, resolved to cease till on the morrow, the House did rise.' Those last two hours, on empty stomachs, are eloquent of the temper that morning. And the world without was following the struggle. The previous night, so the Spanish ambassador reported, a paper was thrown down in the Presence Chamber at Court, stating that Parliament had discussed the succession question because the country's good required it, and that if the Queen would not give way, she would witness disagreeable things.[1]

On the morrow, to which they had adjourned their debate, the House assembled to find no Speaker present. About 9 o'clock came a message from him saying that he had been summoned to attend upon her Majesty at Court, and begging them to have patience. It was after 10 a.m. when he arrived, bringing a special commandment from the Queen, in which she repeated her previous order that there should be no further talk of the succession. 'And if any person thought not himself satisfied, but had further reasons,' the message continued, 'let him come before the Privy Council, there to show them.'[2]

This was the high hand. Already, Elizabeth's speech to the parliamentary delegation had sufficed to bring the Lords to heel. Many of them, she told the Spanish ambassador, had asked pardon, protesting no intention of offending her: rather, as they explained, they had followed the lead of her Councillors, who had spoken first. It was a different matter with 'the Protestant gentlemen', as she sometimes called the Commons. The Council, so the ambassador was told, tried to persuade her to let them discuss the succession and other questions freely, since she could always veto their acts: a dangerous argument. She chose discipline instead.[3]

No business was done that morning, although one or two or even more hours remained for work after the Speaker's return from the Court. Members may have sat stunned and silent, and then adjourned. They may have recovered in time to think of their next move. The Clerk, for some reason, quite

<hr/>

[1] *C.J.* i. 76; *Spanish Cal. Eliz.* i. 596.    [2] *C.J.* i. 76-7.
[3] *Spanish Cal. Eliz.* i. 595, 597.

fails us at this point, but we know that within a day or two a committee of thirty was at work drafting a petition; and, judging from its language, one imagines that the hotheads had been kept off this body. It would not be surprising if, at such a moment of crisis, leadership in the House swung over to the moderates. Sir William Cecil acted as draftsman, and three versions of the petition exist, drawn up on successive days and embodying the amendments made in committee. Though many, these corrections are not of great importance, but in a text which may have owed its initial verbal qualities to Cecil, they do tend to modify the obsequiousness a little and add to the bite, without diminishing the adulation. In the end, it read as follows:[1]

'We your Majesty's most humble, faithful, and obedient subjects, being limited by Almighty God's order to resort to your Majesty only, for succour in all our common distresses, could find no quietness nor rest in our minds until we had obtained this access to your Majesty's presence; to whom we come in most lowly manner to declare our inward general sorrow, conceived of some doubt of your Majesty's favourable meaning towards us, upon certain conferences lately had in our Common House. And knowing by good experience the abundance, not only of your mercy but also of your dexterity and justice in giving gracious ear to all parties before you will make any determination, we do here in the presence of Almighty God (whose vicegerent we know you to be), on our knees, and with our hearts full of all humility, manifest and make assured to your Majesty that we . . . have no wise intended or prosecuted anything in our late conference but the renewing of a former suit made in the last session . . . ; which we are fully persuaded, being obtained, should tend to the glory of God, to your Majesty's honour and surety, and to the tranquility and perpetual quietness of all your realm. And though your Majesty might . . . for a time conceive . . . otherwise of our meaning, yet we, best knowing the very truth and certainty of our own hearts and intentions, do most humbly' require you 'to accept this our most faithful and true declaration of our whole intentions, . . . regarding rather our own testimonies in the simplicity of truth, than any other conjectures which in such cases, by

[1] S.P. Dom. Eliz. 41/20, 21, 22.

misreporting or mistaking of speeches, may . . . stir up and nourish doubtfulness of our meanings. . . .'

Then followed thanks for her promise to marry, 'in which we do behold, as in a glass, by God's grace the success of most certain comfort and surety to your Majesty's own royal person, and of felicity perpetual — by hope of God's blessing of your Majesty with children — to us your poor subjects now living and all our posterity after us'. They prayed for 'a speedy, honourable, good end' to this intention of hers.

Next they referred to her resolve to postpone any decision about the succession, stressing that it was no more than a postponement. 'We your Majesty's most humble subjects do receive this your Majesty's answer according as we are bound by our obedience, being most sorry that any manner of impediment hath appeared to your Majesty so great as to stay you from proceeding in the same.'

The next passage, with its far-reaching claim about freedom of speech — nearer to Pym and Eliot than Sir Thomas More — is of supreme importance; and the verbal corrections of successive drafts had here strengthened the text. 'We, your most loving subjects, have . . . received some messages and commandments, importing some doubts, not only that your Majesty might conceive of us some lack of duty in receiving . . . your answer, but also . . . that we deserved as it were to be deprived' of 'an ancient laudable custom, always from the beginning necessarily annexed to our assembly, and by your Majesty always confirmed: that is, a leeful sufferance and dutiful liberty to treat and devise of matters honourable for your Majesty and profitable for your realm.' They had been informed, they went on to say, 'that your Majesty meant not, by any your commandment, to diminish our accustomed lawful liberties'. They were 'persuaded that if your Majesty should find in us no lack of duty in receiving your answers obediently, you would withdraw from us all signification of misliking, and would rather augment, or at the least confirm, your grants, tending to our laudable liberties, than to diminish or abridge the same.

'And therefore, most gracious sovereign Lady, we are of necessity, as people stricken with a dutiful fear of your Majesty's displeasure, moved to make declaration . . . that before your message sent to us to stay further proceeding in our former suit,

we had made no determination to deal therein anywise to your
discontentation. And therefore we beseech your Majesty . . .
that we may continue on this course of our humble duty, as
your faithful, lowly subjects, honouring, serving, and obeying
you, like children, for duty, reverence, and love, without the
burden of any unnecessary, unaccustomed, or undeserved yoke
of commandment; that it may be hereby confirmed to the
world, to your immortal praise, how your Majesty doth excel all
your progenitors in quiet governing and ruling, and we also all
our forefathers, subjects of this realm, in universal, hearty, free,
and unconstrained obedience.'

Though what they, precociously and unhistorically, regarded
as a violation of their liberties, was the occasion of their
petition, they had, with remarkable nerve and adroitness,
come very near to including an 'iteration of their suit' for
the succession.

But the petition was not presented. There is some obscurity
about what really happened. The last draft was dated by
Cecil November 16th, a Saturday. Presumably, the committee reported this to the House early in the following week.
The House took action: that we know. According to Cecil,
they sent a request to the Queen for 'leave to confer upon the
liberties of the House'. Either this was a loose way of saying
that they asked for audience to present their petition; or it
implies some modification of tactics. Whatever the explanation, the Queen was now confronted with a situation in which
the issue had become sharply defined as that of liberty: whereof,
as Cecil and his fellow-Councillors justly noted, 'must needs
have ensued more inconvenience than were meet'. 'The
insolence of these heretics', the Spanish ambassador was told,
'and their hankering after liberty in everything, is greatly dis-
gusting the Queen.'[1]

Elizabeth had been driven into the last ditch. There were
two ways open to her: an 'Addled Parliament', as her Councillors had suggested earlier, though now it could only be an
act of desperation; either that, or surrender. She surrendered.
We possess three quite distinct texts of the document in which
she announced her change of policy, including one in Cecil's
hand, composed perhaps on the Queen's verbal instructions

[1] S.P. Dom. Eliz. 41/30; *Spanish Cal. Eliz.* i. 598.

and containing corrections in her own hand. It is rather chilly and grudging in tone, whereas the third, which corresponds more with the brief entry of it in the *Commons Journal*, sets out to woo her very disgruntled Commons. Perhaps a night's reflection brought her round to the view that if she had to surrender, it was wiser to do so with good grace. The first draft contains a note at the end: 'This manner of answer her Majesty hath thought best, without any further answer to the request that hath been made to have leave to confer upon the liberties of the House, forasmuch as thereof must needs have ensued more inconvenience than were meet.' The answer took the form of a royal message to be delivered by the Speaker. The most friendly version reads as follows:[1]

'The Queen's Majesty, being informed that, notwithstanding her late answer made to a chosen number of the Upper and Lower Houses in the matter of succession, the same nevertheless by some speeches in the Nether House seemed to be revived; and doubting lest it might further proceed than were convenient, her Majesty in that respect sent two commandments for silence therein, the one by certain of her Privy Council, the other by the Speaker. Nevertheless, her Majesty understandeth now, by good information, that albeit the speeches of some particular men seemed to incline to reiterate that suit, yet there followed no general consent nor resolution of the whole House, whereby she findeth that those commandments were not necessary ... And therefore, both for that cause, and for that no scruple or doubt should remain in the minds of her loving subjects, either of her Majesty's displeasure towards them, or of any other thing that might prejudice them, contrary to her good meaning, [she] is pleased to revoke and cancel those commandments as needless to be sent, assuring herself that all her good and loving subjects will stay themselves upon her said answer, without pressing her Majesty any further therein at this time.'

On Monday, November 25th, after three bills had been read, the Speaker received a summons from the Queen, and when he returned delivered this message of hers. The Clerk noted that

---

[1] S.P. Dom. Eliz. 41/30 (Cecil's draft, with Elizabeth's corrections, dated November 24th – Sunday); 41/31; 27/45 (misplaced under 1563). The order of the texts is conjectural, but the last is the one I quote.

it 'was taken of all the House most joyfully, with most hearty prayer and thanks for the same'.[1]

Meanwhile, fresh trouble was blowing up. On the previous Friday there had been a motion in the Commons 'against corrupt and wicked books that came from beyond the sea', whereupon James Dalton, the lawyer who had supported Paul Wentworth's questions on the liberty of the House, happening to see in a Member's hand a copy of Patrick Adamson's poem on the birth of Prince James of Scotland, and being, as he confessed, 'very much moved therewith', poured out his wrath. Robert Melville, the Queen of Scots' representative in London, lodged an official complaint, accusing him of using the following words: 'God forbid, and I never trust to see the day that ever any Scot or stranger shall have any interest in the Crown of this realm, for it is against the law that any person other than such as be born the Prince's subjects hold merit in this land.'[2] Dalton, for the information of the Council, wrote his own account of the speech. It was as follows:

'How say you to a libel lately set forth in print, calling the infant of Scotland, "Prince of Scotland, England, and Ireland"? "Prince of Scotland, England, and Ireland"? quoth I. What enemy to the peace and quietness of the realm of England, what traitor to the Crown of this realm hath devised, set forth, and published this dishonour against the Queen's most excellent Majesty and the Crown of England? "Prince of England"; and Queen Elizabeth as yet having no child? "Prince of England"; and the Scottish Queen's child? "Prince of Scotland and England"; and Scotland before England? Who ever heard or read that before this time? What true English heart may sustain to hear of this villainy and reproach against the Queen's Highness and this her realm? It is so that it hath pleased her Highness at this time in part to bar our speech, but if our mouths shall be stopped, and in the meantime such despite shall happen and pass without revenge, it will make the heart of a true Englishman break within his breast.

'With the indignity of this matter being as it were set afire', he added, 'I was carried with the flame thereof, well I know not whither, but I suspect something escaped me unawares that made some doubt that I would have entered into some title of

<hr />

[1] *C.J.* i. 78.    [2] S.P. Dom. Eliz. 41/28.

the Crown; insomuch that Mr. Speaker said to me, "It were not well you enter into any title." But what I said I do not remember, but sure I am that I did not speak these words: "That no person might inherit the Crown of this realm, except he were a subject of the realm of England." For I answered Mr. Speaker that I did not mind to deal with any title of the Crown. And thereupon making my conclusion, that it were good there were provision against such spreading of infamous libels, I did leave to speak any further.'[1]

'Dalton the denier': 'Not I, Lord'; says our pasquil. Little doubt he was set afire with the indignity of the matter; and, one suspects, carried with the flame thereof into an attack on the Scottish title. After all, had not Sir Ralph Sadler, now a Councillor, been as blunt in the previous session? and were not most Members of like opinion? But new factors had since appeared: the greater delicacy of the subject and the severer taboo on it; the stricter discipline of the Queen; the stronger diplomatic pressure from Scotland. Melville made his protest on Sunday, November 24th, and it presumably led Cecil to insert 'An Addition' into his first draft of the Queen's message lifting her veto, dated the same day: 'If any person after this message shall either presently or at any time . . . begin any speech tending directly or indirectly to make any declaration of any particular title to the succession . . . the Speaker shall forthwith, in her Majesty's name, command the party to cease . . . and shall declare to the whole House that so is her Majesty's express commandment.' The 'Addition' disappeared in the other, less chilly drafts of the message.

The Council proceeded to take action on Melville's formal complaint.[2] Dalton was called before some of that body, produced the report of his speech, and denied the crucial charge. Consequently, it was decided to demand from the House itself, in the name of the Queen, whether he had in fact made the statement of which Melville complained. Cecil drew up a message to this effect on November 26th. While denouncing Patrick Adamson's poem as 'infamous' and 'very derogatory to the crown and dignity royal of her Majesty', the draft message

---

[1] S.P. Dom. Eliz. 41/29.
[2] *Scottish Cal.* ii. 310 (cf. *Foreign Cal. 1566-8*, p. 164) shows that Mary demanded punishment of Dalton.

declared that it was 'far unmeet and dangerous for any person of his own head to set forth or abase any particular title of this crown, the consideration whereof belongeth properly to her Majesty and the three estates of the realm'. 'The case toucheth a prince [Mary] with whom her Majesty is in good amity.'[1]

In all likelihood the Council was acting on its own initiative. Perhaps Cecil expected to get Dalton's denial confirmed by the House, and thus furnish diplomatic, if not intellectual satisfaction to Scotland. If so, he was lacking in imagination, for such a *démarche* was calculated to jar the frayed nerves of the Commons and spoil the soothing effect of the Queen's message of surrender. His mistress, in contrast, saw the danger. On November 27th the Earl of Leicester wrote to Cecil: 'Mr. Secretary, Since your departure, the Queen's Majesty called me unto her and asked what Dalton had done and what order was taken by us. I declared to her Majesty all things as near as I could remember, as we proceeded with him. And having occasion to speak touching the bringing the matter in question in the House tomorrow for trial of his speech, I found her Highness well liking that it should stay, and not proceed further to any question or trial; and so commanded, and to signify unto you.' That, so far as we know, ended the Dalton affair. Appeasement was now Elizabeth's game; and there was to be no fumbling.[2]

The same day she made a further move to re-establish her hold over the House of Commons. Her message on November 25th, seductive as it had been, and received most joyfully, with most hearty prayers, had not revived the subsidy bill, which after its first reading on October 28th had lain uncalled-for, derelict. The charm had not been potent enough. Consequently, in the middle of the morning, on November 27th, Cecil rose to deliver a further royal message. The subsidy, as already rated, provided for payment in three instalments. The Queen, he announced, remitted the third payment. Her 'gracious and most princely' message, as described by the Commons in a draft preamble to their subsidy bill, was to this effect: 'That you [the Queen] made more estimation of our carefulness in the devising, and dutifulness in the free offering,

[1] HAYNES, *Burghley Papers*, p. 449; *H.M.C. Hatfield MSS.* i. 341.
[2] S.P. Dom. Eliz. Addenda, 13/39.

than of the substance and value thereof. And to make a plain demonstration of your Majesty's princely judgment to be such in very deed, you were graciously, beyond all examples within any memory, contented (notwithstanding your public affairs might require more) that we should at this time retain to ourselves some portion of that which we intended, esteeming us your storers or treasurers (as indeed we are most glad to be accounted) both of that and of all the rest that we have, to serve your Highness's person to the maintenance of your estate, crown, and dignity.'

The effect was electric. For 'her great clemency', wrote the Clerk in his *Journal*, 'most hearty thanks was given by the House. And immediately', as he noted, the subsidy bill was read.[1]

Elizabeth had stooped to conquer. She had withdrawn her veto on the succession debate: the result, as William Lambarde tells us, was that 'upon consultation amongst themselves' Members 'spared to proceed any further therein'. She had remitted a third of the subsidy, sacrificing money she desperately needed: immediately the derelict measure was re-floated. She had also stayed proceedings against Dalton for his rash speech. The magic worked. Elizabeth had got her way; and that without an 'Addled Parliament', which the less supple James I might have incurred, and her own Councillors, in their despondency, had suggested.[2]

But these men of 1563 and 1566 were pertinacious, and almost too fertile in ideas. Subsidy bills carried preambles, and, as we have noticed, they had made the preamble of 1563 a vehicle of propaganda. They now had the inspiration — no doubt 'upon consultation amongst themselves' — of incorporating in the preamble to the present bill the Queen's promises to marry and to determine the succession as soon as circumstances permitted. They would thus place on record the fugitive words of their beloved but wily mistress, compel her to confirm them by the solemn and public process of the royal assent in Parliament, disseminate them in print throughout the realm, and render to an anxious people an account of their stewardship.[3]

---

[1] Discarded preamble in House of Lords MSS.; *C.J.* i. 78.
[2] B.M. Additional MS. 5123, fols. 10b-11.
[3] In 1628 there was a proposal to make the Petition of Right a preamble to the subsidy bill, so that it would be published in the counties (cf. RELF, *The Petition of Right*, p. 55).

They seem to have evolved their ingenious and audacious plan during the day following the revival of the bill. 'Argument for a preamble to be had to the subsidy', noted the Clerk on November 29th; and two hours or more may have been spent overcoming the doubts of the timid.

Two lawyer-members of our 'choir', Robert Monson and Robert Bell — the two men, both of them Puritans, selected by Cecil for notice in his diary as causing trouble in Parliament about the succession — were leaders in this latest agitation. In the evening following the debate, Sir William Cordell, Master of the Rolls, wrote to Cecil to say that he had shown these two 'the notes conceived of the day's resolution in the Parliament House', and told them of Cecil's decision to have a draft ready by the morning. Monson, he stated, voiced misgiving on one point: 'that if it should be opened unto the world that the Commons granted more than her Majesty would receive, that then it should appear that we were more ready to grant than her Highness was to ask or than her necessity required, and that her Majesty thought the burden too great for her subjects to bear; which might argue in us, by such as shall be charged with the payment thereof, want of consideration'. It is an interesting sidelight on an Elizabethan M.P.'s sensitiveness to public opinion. Cordell quietened his scruple and told Cecil that the three of them would therefore wait upon him the next day.[1]

Much labour went into drawing up this preamble. There are three drafts of one model — Cordell's presumably — on which Cecil worked, amending the wording. And then in committee (as one must suppose) this model was discarded in favour of another, which in turn was subjected to amendments.[2] Ultimately, the independent rather than the official mind was mirrored in the text: though it must be added that Cordell and Cecil, in their drafts, wrote as Members of Parliament rather than ministers of the Crown. They were under instructions from the House. All versions, after some opening sentences, contained three sections: thanking the Queen for remitting part of the subsidy, for determining to marry, and for promising to

[1] C.J. i. 78; Hatfield MS. cxviii, fol. 122 (cf. Hatfield MSS. i. 341). I am indebted to Mr. J. Hurstfield for a transcript of this document.
[2] S.P. Dom. Eliz. 41/40, 41, 41a; House of Lords MSS.; B.M. Lansdowne MS. 1236, fol. 42. On these, cf. my article 'Parliament and the Succession Question . . .', Eng. Hist. Rev. xxxvi. 512 seqq. where the House of Lords MS. is printed.

THE SUBSIDY PREAMBLE 1566

With the Queen's comment at the foot

settle the succession. The crucial third section, in what was possibly the final text, was worded as follows:

'Thirdly, we cannot but also thankfully remember to your Majesty that it pleased the same to signify unto us that you did not mislike of us for our desire in this Parliament to have the succession of the crown declared, for that you rightly conceived the same our desire to proceed from us (as indeed it did) of mere duty and love towards your Highness, your realms and countries, and not of any other disposition or pretensed purpose. And signified further of your godly disposition and natural love towards us, to our great comfort, that rather than your realm should threat ruin for lack of declaration of succession — which you trusted Almighty God would show of your own body in due time after your marriage — you would by God's help, though it should appear some peril to yourself (which God defend), declare the succession in such convenient time as your Highness, with the advice of your Council and assent of your realm, should think most meet . . . to the joyful comfort of us all.'

Someone — Cecil, perhaps, who, whatever his private inclinations, would be compelled by his oath and duty as a Councillor — showed this text to the Queen, and at the foot of the last sheet, in what the endorsement of the manuscript not inappropriately calls 'Queen Elizabeth's running hand' — a very different script from her characteristic and legible Roman hand — she scribbled her flaming comment:

'Set these two conceivings into one meaning, and my counsel is all given. Let not other regard themselves so holy as I have no corner left for me. Let them know that I knew, though I followed not, that some of them would my pure conscience better served me than their lewd practices could avail with me. I know no reason why any my private answers to the realm should serve for prologue to a subsidies-book. Neither yet do I understand why such audacity should be used to make without my licence an act of my words. Are my words like lawyers' books, which nowadays go to the wire-drawers to make subtle doings more plain? Is there no hold of my speech without an act compel me to confirm? Shall my princely consent be turned to strengthen my words that be not of themselves substantives? I say no more at this time; but if these fellows were well answered, and paid with lawful coin, there would be fewer counterfeits among them.'[1]

Evidently, the Queen's views, if not her winged words, were told to the committee before it reported back to the House. The proposed preamble was scrapped and its place taken by uninspired, devitalized brevity. The threefold thanks were kept. The crucial section on the succession was whittled down to a promise, 'when time shall thereunto serve conveniently', 'to have due regard' to the problem. A miserable little mouse to come from such mountainous labour! The House clearly thought the same when the preamble came before it for a double reading on December 10th. The Clerk records 'long arguments'; and they probably spent all but about an hour of that sitting on the subject. The independents went down fighting.[2]

[1] B.M. Lansdowne MS. 1236, fol. 42.
[2] *Statutes of Realm*, IV. i. 505-6; *C.J.* i. 79.

## CHAPTER III

# RELIGION: END OF THE SESSION

THE Queen's troubles were not yet at an end. If the attention and efforts of left-wing Protestants, in and out of Parliament, had not been absorbed by the succession question — incomparably the most urgent national issue — the odds are that the campaign for a radical adjustment of the religious settlement of 1559, vainly attempted in the Lower House of Convocation in 1563, would have been renewed, this time through Parliament. Bishop Horne of Winchester, a Marian exile, wrote to the eminent Swiss Reformer, Rudolph Gualter, at Zurich on July 17th, 1565. After explaining that the ornaments clause of the Act of Uniformity imposed on them the dilemma of either complying with its injunction to wear the abhorrent caps and surplices or of giving way to others and seeing their enemies take their places, he went on to say: 'We certainly hope to repeal this clause of the act' in the next session of Parliament. And Theodore Beza at Geneva, prompted by the tales of a clerical emissary from England, wrote to Bullinger at Zurich on September 3rd, 1566, with a doleful account of the Papistical practices and shortcomings of the Anglican Church, urging him to send Gualter on a mission to England to convert the Queen and bishops to reform. 'The time', he remarked — and here his English informant must have been prompting him — is 'very favourable, as the Parliament in that country is about to assemble, when it is certain that all these things will be brought forward for consideration'.[1]

Can one doubt that the radical clergy, both high and low, had been preparing for action? But two such ticklish agitations as the succession and Church reform could not be conducted simultaneously; and by the time the succession manœuvres had been brought to a standstill, the session was near its end. In any case, the parliamentary atmosphere was too unpromising for anything like radical reform. Nevertheless, the will to do

---

[1] *Zurich Letters* (Parker Soc.), i. 143, ii. 132; cf. KNAPPEN, *Tudor Puritanism*, p. 206.

something was there. On December 5th, ten days after the Queen's surrender over parliamentary liberties, and eight after the revival of the subsidy bill — just about the time required for an organizing group to adjust itself to the new situation and prepare a programme to suit it — there was introduced and read a first time, at the end of the morning, 'The bill, with a little book printed 1562, for the sound Christian religion.' Bill A it was called, and the next day Bills B, C, D, E and F were given a first reading. A whole code, all unofficial bills! It would take a simpleton not to suspect a planned drive.[1]

Bill A gave statutory confirmation to the Articles of Religion agreed on in the Convocation of 1562-63, and its incidental purpose in imposing uniformity of doctrine was to purge the Church of any of the Marian clergy who would not conform. The other bills concerned the quality of ministers, non-residence, corrupt presentation to livings, simony, and pensions paid from benefices: the sort of evils referred to in Beza's letter to Bullinger. They were Puritan reforms in the sense that Puritans desired them; but they were that part of the Puritan programme which might appeal to any earnest Churchman, whatever his views on vestments, etc. The bills did not originate officially from Convocation, nor from the bishops: that we know. But the clergymen who had attempted to get a Puritan programme through Convocation in 1563 were in London again for the present Convocation; and it seems likely that some or all of them devised this moderate reforming code, wooing their lay friends and supporters in the House of Commons to sponsor it there.[2]

Those who introduced and supported the bills may or may not have anticipated trouble with the Queen. They may or may not have understood clearly the nature of the royal supremacy: the constitutional doctrine that ecclesiastical legislation rightly fell not within the parliamentary sphere but within that of Crown and Convocation. After all, the Settlement of 1559 had been effected in Parliament without recourse to Convocation; and the Statute Book, since the Reformation, bulged with ecclesiastical legislation. It was a little subtle to argue that these statutes and the procedure by which they were brought

[1] *C.J.* i. 79.
[2] *Spanish Cal. Eliz.* i. 603; *Parker Correspondence* (Parker Soc.), p. 291.

into being were determined by two considerations: the need for secular sanctions behind religious changes, and the occasional need for revolutionary methods. Until they clashed with Elizabeth, Members may easily have overlooked this abstruse, but none the less sound point in constitutional law. Perhaps Speaker or Councillors did issue a warning; or perhaps the House was simply being practical, calculating that they could not deal with all their letters of the alphabet in the time remaining to them: whatever the reason, they chose out Bill A, and left the rest to sleep until the next Parliament.

Bill A was read a second time on December 10th, ingrossed, read a third time and passed on December 13th, and sent to the Lords, with special commendation, the next day. The Lords got down to it at once, and with the bishops strongly in favour of the measure, gave it a first reading the day they received it. Then the Queen took action.

Elizabeth had sighed for someone to check the bill's progress, fearing that if it passed she would be unable to exercise her veto owing to the pressure that would be brought to bear upon her. But wishful thinking could get her nowhere, and she therefore now gave a 'special commandment' to the Lord Keeper that the bill was to proceed no further, thus exercising her constitutional right to stop any action involving the royal prerogative, taken without consulting her — *rege non consulto*. She probably hoped that the bill would just be allowed to sleep, with no questions asked and no fuss made. But the Commons had their eyes on its progress. They sent up a further recommendation to the Lords to proceed with it, and the bishops, too, pressed for a second reading. Consequently, the Lord Keeper had to reveal that the Queen had stopped it.[1]

Elizabeth struck again. Cecil was away from Court, unwell, and, as Archbishop Parker lamented, there was need of his moderating influence. Some mischief-maker had suggested — erroneously, as it turned out — that the bishops had been responsible for putting this bill into Parliament; and after the drubbing that Elizabeth had administered to them for their part in the succession agitation, she cannot have been feeling kindly disposed towards them. On December 20th she sent for

---

[1] *C.J.* i. 79; *L.J.* i. 658; *Parker Correspondence*, p. 293; *Spanish Cal. Eliz.* i. 604, 606.

Parker and some of his colleagues. She was careful to empha-
size that she had no dislike for the Articles of Religion, which in
fact expressed the faith that she openly professed, but she made
her views clear about introducing a bill of religion into Parliament without her knowledge and assent. When those present
denied any personal responsibility, she ordered an inquiry to
be made among the rest of the bishops. It says much for the
courage of these prelates that, in spite of the intimidating
audience, four days later the two archbishops and thirteen
bishops addressed to her a petition begging her to lift her veto,
let the bill proceed with all expedition, and then give the royal
assent to it.[1]

As for the Commons, they employed their own way of exercising pressure. It was essential to keep the Queen from ending
Parliament while efforts were being made to save Bill A. And
the end might come any day. On December 2nd the Spanish
ambassador was expecting it in a week's time; on the 15th
Elizabeth told him that she hoped for it before Christmas; and
on the 23rd he reported that Parliament was to end 'tomorrow'.
There was only one thing to do: hold up essential legislation.[2]

After the Queen's generous action in scaling down the subsidy, the Commons for very shame could not do much with the
money bill. However, after passing it on December 12th, they
delayed five days before sending it up to the Lords; and a
comparison of dates leaves little doubt that the delay was
deliberately intended to give the Lords time to pass the bill on
the Articles of Religion. The manœuvre failed. The subsidy
bill had been read and passed in the Upper House by the
afternoon of December 18th.[3]

There remained a trump card: a major government bill. It
was a bill for continuing divers statutes which were due to
expire either at the end of this session or this Parliament.
Probably eleven statutes were involved, including the important
laws for the relief of the poor and the increase of tillage enacted
in 1563.[4] The government had secured a first reading for the

---

[1] *Parker Correspondence*, pp. 291-4.    [2] *Spanish Cal. Eliz.* i. 599, 603, 606.
[3] *C.J.* i. 79-80 (though the subsidy bill was ready, the Commons did not send
it to the Lords on December 14th with other bills); *L.J.* i. 660.
[4] Cf. 13 Eliz. c. 25 (*Statutes of Realm*, IV. i. 560-1). This states that the act for the
relief of the poor expired at the end of the 1566 session; but the act itself (ibid. p.
414) gives its duration as 'to the end of the first session of the next Parliament'.
This surely would be 1571.

bill as early as October 10th, but at that stage the Commons
had left it in suspense. During the succession agitation they
had obviously used it, along with the crucial subsidy bill, as a
means of coercing the Queen. Now, with the subsidy bill
passed, it remained their only weapon. Writing on December
28th, the Spanish ambassador explained that the delay in
ending Parliament was due to this bill, which the Commons had
refused to pass owing to their anger at the stoppage of Bill A
in the Upper House.

Clearly, the House timed this new strike to allow their own
representations to the Lords, and the bishops' to the Queen,
the opportunity of succeeding. The bill was brought out for a
second reading on December 23rd — nearly eleven weeks after
the first. It was read a third time, passed, and immediately sent
to the Lords early on December 24th, but with 'provisions and
articles' attached, which the government, or at any rate the
Lords, would not agree to. The Upper House immediately
gave it three readings, and sent it back the same morning to
have all the provisions and articles removed: that is — if we
may indulge in a guess — to have the text restored as the
government had drafted it. With a last, and, one suspects,
quite irresponsible flash of their rebellious spirit, the Commons
rejected the Lords' amendments in a division where 97 voted
against the bill and 61 for. In consequence, all the eleven
statutes which the government wished to continue — and
wished so strongly that the Queen had been compelled to prolong this exasperating session — lapsed and could only be
revived when a similar act was passed in the next Parliament of
1571.[1]

The Commons achieved one of their objects. It was now too
late to close Parliament before Christmas. In their main purpose they failed. Elizabeth refused to surrender either to the
prayers of her bishops or the blackmail of her faithful and
loving Commons. No more business was transacted before
Parliament closed on January 2nd, though the Lower House
met twice after Christmas and the Higher once, possibly in the
hope of a last-minute repentance by their mistress.

It was probably about this time — between December 14th

---

[1] *C.J.* i. 74, 81; *L.J.* i. 664; *Spanish Cal. Eliz.* i. 606; *Statutes of Realm*, IV. i.
560-1.

and 21st,[1] possibly when he was away from Court — that Sir William Cecil (who was prone to wring his hands when his mistress was going her own, or someone else's way) drew up a catalogue of lamentations, which he endorsed, 'Memorial to the Queen at the end of the Parliament'. Whether Elizabeth ever saw it may be doubted; but that Cecil and other Councillors were so many Cassandras crying doom, we can readily understand.

'The succession not answered.
The marriage not followed.
A subsidy to be levied.
The oppression of the informers not amended.
The commission of inquisitors: to unmeet persons.
The bill of religion [Bill A] stayed, to the comfort of the adversaries.
The abridgement of such parcel of the [bill of General] Pardon, as, though it be no profit greatly to the Queen's Majesty, yet was it most plausible to the Commons.
Dangers ensuing:
General discontentations.
The slender execution of the subsidy.
Danger of sedition in summer by persons discontented.
. . . . . . . . . . . . . . . . . . . . . . . . . . . . . .,'

The 'commission of inquisitors' was an allusion to a commission for the execution of penal laws, which had been issued by the Queen on December 3rd and had caused an outburst of angry criticism in the House of Commons on December 21st, directed against three of the commissioners whose names were cited. It was probably a rather scandalous piece of jobbery by some courtier; and if, as one suspects, the culprit was the Earl of Leicester, Cecil's bitterness would be doubly explained. The House of Commons sent a committee up to the Lords to ask them to intervene for the revocation of all such commissions; which they agreed to do, agreeing also that the three commissioners concerned were 'not convenient persons'.[2] The Queen's

---

[1] S.P. Dom. Eliz. 41/36. The reference to Bill A fixes the earlier date. The insertion later of 'the commission of inquisition' proves that the memorandum was already written by December 21st. Cecil dated the document 'November': undoubtedly an error.

[2] *C.J.* i. 81. Cf. *H.M.C. Hatfield MSS.* i. 350 where the reference to 'Elliott and others' may be to this commission.

reaction to this impertinent meddling with her letters patent will be seen in the Lord Keeper's subsequent speech. Another of Cecil's items — the oppression of informers — may have been prompted by a bill which started with the Commons early in the session, was ultimately passed by that House, but being amended by the Lords was apparently no longer acceptable and was allowed to lapse. Perhaps here, also, there was a strong sense of grievance among Members.[1]

It had been an altogether unprofitable session. For much of the time the Commons had been deliberately obstructive over normal business. Consequently, more bills seem to have been started in the Lords: they were not too well received by the Commons. Thirty-six bills seem to have passed both Houses, and of these the Queen apparently vetoed two.[2] In quality, and even in number, the harvest was poor: certainly poor for twelve weeks' work.

'The world is full of offences and displeasure contained', wrote Archbishop Parker, after seeing the Queen.[3] In this gloomy atmosphere, with her Privy Councillors critical of her, and Lord Keeper Bacon in official displeasure over the succession, with Lords and Commons also critical, and Elizabeth herself critical of them all, Parliament assembled between 2 p.m. and 3 p.m. on January 2nd, 1567, for the closing ceremony.

The Speaker's oration opened the proceedings. When elected Mr. Onslow had been denied a full revelation of his talents, but on this occasion he let himself go. He spoke for two hours; and the Clerk, a worthy representative of that hardy generation, thought it 'an excellent oration'.[4] After belittling himself and reflecting wistfully on the proverb that there is no difference between a wise man and a fool if they keep silence, he declared himself the mouth of men to whom the people 'have committed the care and charge of themselves, wives, and children, lands and goods . . . to take order in and for all things necessary': a vague and ambitious claim, which might leave little room for the Sovereign. God, he said, hath blessed this our native

---

[1] *C.J.* i. 73-7, 79-80; *L.J.* i. 645-6, 654-5 (the entry of *expedit* in the margin is an error).

[2] (*a*) concerning the writ of *Latitat* (cf. *C.J.* i. 80; *L.J.* i. 661); (*b*) gaol-delivery in Wales (cf. *L.J.* i. 663).

[3] *Parker Correspondence*, p. 291.

[4] *C.J.* i. 81.

country with manifold and great benefits and much more fruit-fulness than any other. Aided by the much-worked simile of the human body, he discoursed on the subject of monarchy, hereditary or elective, perhaps prompted by a debate last September before the Queen and Court at Oxford, when, to the bewilderment of the courtiers, the verdict was in favour of an elected Sovereign: students — was the French ambassador's sage comment on that occasion — think nothing so fine as to say what they like. Monarchy, concluded Onslow, was the best form of government, and hereditary monarchy better than election: as witness 'the most holiest election', that of the Pope, 'called indeed holy and quiet, but utterly unholy and unquiet'.

In a passage on religion he revealed his Reformist political theory by enunciating the doctrine of passive obedience: obedience even to evil rulers, and therefore how much more to those that be good. This no doubt pleased Elizabeth, but she must have been uneasy when this 'furious heretic' went on to describe a king's special duty, as 'God's special creature', to be that of ensuring 'quietness among the ministers of the Church' and extinguishing and putting away 'all hurtful or unprofitable ceremonies in any wise contrary to God's word': a palpable reference to the Vestiarian Controversy, with Puritan sympathies hardly concealed by the praise in which they were set. Nor was he the complete courtier in his laudation of the English Common Law, 'grounded on God's laws and nature': 'Although thereby for the Prince is provided many princely prerogatives and royalties, yet is it not such as the Prince can take money or other things or do as he will at his own pleasure without order.'

The speech ended with mention of two occasions for thanks: the Queen's remittance of part of the subsidy, and her promise to marry. 'I must not omit to do that which never Speaker did before: namely, to desire your Majesty not to regard this simple offer of ours, but therein to accept our good wills. Wherein your Highness hath . . . required us to retain in our hands part of our gift; and so rather yourself and your revenues [suffer] than us, accounting it in our purses to be as in your own.' After thanking her for her inclination to marriage — 'which afore you were not given unto, which is done for our safeguard, that when God shall call you, you may leave of your own body to succeed you' — he went on: 'God grant, as your Majesty hath defended the faith of Abraham, you may have the like desire of issue with him, and for that purpose that you would most shortly embrace the holy state of matrimony.' Truly, this man spoke as the mouth of the House of Commons rather than the Queen's Solicitor General.

'After the Queen had called him and told him her mind', the Lord Keeper replied. Seizing on the word 'policy' used by the Speaker, he administered a rebuke to the Commons. 'Politic orders be rules of all good acts; and touching those that you have made to the overthrowing of good laws' — a reference to their high-handed treatment of many bills, and particularly to their quashing of the bill to continue the life of lapsing statutes — 'they deserve reproof, as well as the others deserve praise. In which like case you err in bringing her Majesty's prerogative in question' — here the offence was Bill A — 'and for that thing wherein she meant not to hurt any of your liberties; and again, the grant of her letters patent to be in question is not a little marvel . . . Howbeit, as her Majesty, according to her nature, is mild and full of clemency, so is she loth herein to be too austere. And therefore, although at this time she suffer you all to depart quietly into your countries . . . she hopeth that the offenders will hereafter use themselves well.'

The speech went on to stress the need for executing the laws that had been made and for gathering in the money granted; it echoed the Speaker's thanks for the hope of seeing the Queen married, and ended with a reminder of the benefits they enjoyed and the loyalty they owed.

Then, while the Queen stood, holding in her hand 'the brief' or list of the acts passed, the two Clerks intoned the antiphony of the royal assent.

Standing again, Elizabeth herself spoke. 'My Lords and others, the Commons of this assembly, although the Lord Keeper hath according to order very well answered in my name, yet as a periphrasis I have a few words further to speak unto you, which notwithstanding that I have not been used nor love to do it in such open assemblies, yet now, not to the end to amend his talk, but remembering that commonly Prince's own words be better printed in the hearer's memory than those spoken by her commandment, I mean to say thus much unto you.'[1]

After this prologue, she delivered a prepared speech. Perhaps she trusted her memory: we possess a report which is sufficiently different in text and clarity to suggest a free rendering of a conned oration. Possibly she read her manuscript. The draft of this survives, written in her 'running' hand, with her usual verbal amendments.[2] She had sent a copy to the Lord Keeper by his wife when Lady Bacon came to Court, carrying her husband's submission, he 'being in displeasure' about the succession.[3] Either it was to serve Bacon in preparing his own reply to the Speaker, or he was to take it to Parliament and hand it to Elizabeth at the proper moment. She evidently felt an author's pride in her composition, for another copy survives, written in the hand of the Lord High Admiral, Lord Clinton, and endorsed by him: 'This is the true copy of a bill delivered me by the Queen's Majesty's own hands; which for my better understanding' — he was aged 54 and she 33! — 'her pleasure was I should copy out. The bill delivered me was written all of her own hand.'[4] This is what Elizabeth wrote:

'I love so evil counterfeiting, and hate so much dissimulation, that I may not suffer you [to] depart without that my admonitions may show your harms and cause you shun unseen peril. Two visors have blinded the eyes of the lookers on in this present session, so far forth as under pretence of saving all, they have done none good. And these they be: succession and liberties.

'As to the first, the Prince's opinion and good will ought, in good order, have been felt in other sort than in so public a place [to] be uttered. It had been convenient that so weighty a cause had had his original from a zealous Prince's consideration, not from so lip-laboured orations out of such subjects'[5] mouths; which, what they be, time may teach you know, and their demerits will make them acknowledge how they have done their lewd endeavour to make all my realm suppose that their care was much, when mine was none at all.

---

[1] The foregoing proceedings and speeches are from B.M. Cotton MS. Titus F. I, fols. 117 seqq.

[2] B.M. Cotton Charter IV. 38 (2). Copies, with a few variant readings, in Harleian MSS. 1877, fol. 26; 5176, fol. 96b.

[3] B.M. Harleian MS. 1877, fol. 26. Cf. ibid. 5176, fol. 96b.

[4] H.M.C. Hatfield MSS. xiii. 215, wrongly dated.

[5] Elizabeth first wrote, more caustically, 'wrangling subjects'.

'Their handling of this doth well show (they being wholly ignorant) how fit my grant at this time should be to such a demand. In this one thing their imperfect dealings are to be excused, for I think this be the first time that so weighty a cause passed from so simple men's mouths, as began this cause.

'As to liberties, who is so simple that doubts whether a Prince that is head of all the body may not command the feet not to stray when they would slip? God forbid that your liberty should make my bondage, or that your lawful liberties should anyways have been infringed. No, no, my commandment tended no whit to that end: the lawfulness of which commandment, if I had not more pitied you than blamed you, might easily by good right be showed you, perchance to their shame that bred you that coloured doubt.

'You were sore seduced. You have met with a gentle Prince, else your needless scruple might perchance have bred your cause blame. And albeit the soothing[1] of such be reprovable in all, yet I would not you should think my simplicity such as I cannot make distinctions among you — as of some that broached the vessel not well fined, and began these attempts, not foreseeing well the end; others that respected the necessary facies[2] of the matters, and no whit understood circumstances expedient not to have been forgotten therein; others whose ears were deluded by pleasing persuasions of common good, when the very yielding to their own inventions might have bred all your woes; others whose capacities, I suppose, yielded their judgment to their friends' wit; some other that served an echo's place.

'Well, among all these sundry affects,[3] I assure you there be none (the beginners only except) whom I either condemn for evil-minded to me, or do suspect not to be my most loyal subjects. Therefore I conclude with this opinion, which I will you to think unfeignedly true: that as I have tried[4] that you may be deceived, so am I persuaded you will not beguile[5] the assured joy that ever I took to see my subjects' love to me more staunch than ever I felt the care in myself for myself to be great; which alone hath made my heavy burden light, and a kingdom's care but easy carriage for me.

---

[1] i.e. maintaining, putting forward.  [2] i.e. face, appearance.
[3] i.e. intentions, dispositions.  [4] i.e. demonstrated, proved.
[5] i.e. cheat or disappoint me of the assured joy.

'Let this my discipline stand you in stead of sorer strokes, never to tempt too far a Prince's patience;[1] and let my comfort pluck up your dismayed spirit, and cause you think that, in hope that your following behaviours shall make amends for past actions, you return with your Prince's grace; whose care for you, doubt you not to be such as she shall not need a remembrancer for your weal.'[2]

Her speech ended, the Queen said openly to the Lord Keeper, 'My Lord, you will do as I bade you'; whereupon he dissolved the Parliament. Many people had thought that it would merely be prorogued. That would have been gladly received as an earnest of Elizabeth's intention to fulfil in the near future her promises about marriage and the succession. Moreover, it would have had the solid practical advantage of preventing from lapse the majority of those eleven statutes which the government wished to continue; and one is indeed tempted to ask whether our ninety-seven obstreperous Members who quashed the government's bill, knowing this, had not deliberately indulged in a last and impudent act of coercion. In any case, Elizabeth was inflexible. She sacrificed her statutes to be rid of an intolerable House of Commons, sharing the Spanish ambassador's opinion that the depths had been plumbed and that no future general election could produce a worse body of men than these.[3]

And so our 'choir', and 'the rest that be at devotion' — those, to use Elizabeth's phrases, who 'yielded their judgment to their friends' wit', and those others 'that served an echo's place' — returned to their homes, having conceived and employed such arts of opposition and displayed so resolute a spirit that no House of Commons before their time could furnish the like. The men of 1566 deserve place pre-eminent in our country's parliamentary history.

---

[1] Elizabeth evidently first intended to write 'power' instead of 'patience'.
[2] The text is from the Cotton Charter.    [3] *Spanish Cal. Eliz.* i. 607, 602.

# PART FOUR

# THE PARLIAMENT OF 1571

---

## CHAPTER I

## INTRODUCTORY

EXPERIENCE had not taught Elizabeth to love Parliaments, and had she been able to carry on the government of the country without them she would probably have done so. On February 2nd, 1570, Cecil drew up 'A memorial' in which he inserted the item, 'To consider for summoning of a Parliament'.[1] There were most urgent financial and political reasons for the note, but a full year elapsed before the Queen would consent to face another ordeal, and the writs went out for a new Parliament.

Superficially there were grounds for expecting even heavier weather than on the last occasion. In 1566 Elizabeth had promised to marry, while her evasive words about settling the succession had been construed to imply action at no distant time. Neither promise had been fulfilled. The marriage negotiations with the Archduke Charles of Austria, which had then been regarded as offering a solution of both problems, had foundered in 1567; and though this was owing, in no small part, to the religious prejudice and agitation of those very people who had pressed her hardest in Parliament, there was little consolation in that.

As for naming an heir to the throne, the strident happenings in Scotland had silenced official thought on the subject. In February 1567 Darnley, the King, had been blown up — or strangled — at Kirk o'Field, and Mary Queen of Scots had begun those few months of reckless indiscretion with Bothwell before revolt ended her career as a Queen regnant and began her life of intrigue as a captive. Eleven months passed. After escape from Loch Leven, defeat, and panic flight across the Solway Firth, this fascinating, artful, and dangerous young

[1] S.P. Dom. Eliz. 66/42.

woman had transferred her captivity to England, where she remained a magnet for religious and political discontents and an insoluble problem for statecraft.

Mary's flight to England in May 1568 marked a turning point in Elizabeth's reign. The period of relative quiet was over. The central period of storm and stress — of 'cold war', as we might term it today — had begun. The fate of neighbouring countries cast its shadow over the land. In 1567 the second religious war had broken out in France, while in the same year the Revolt of the Netherlands had started, bringing upon friends of English Protestants and customers of English merchants the bloody rule of the Duke of Alva, and sending refugees flying to England, there to create among zealots the sense of impending conflict with the powers of Catholic darkness. The arrival of Mary Queen of Scots — 'the daughter of debate that eke discord doth sow' — brought the conflict nearer. Within eighteen months, the intrigues that grew around her and the apparent drift of England towards war with Spain — in the opinion of many, made all but certain by the seizure of money on the way to Alva — had provoked the strange conspiracy which culminated in the Northern Rebellion of November 1569; while the Northern Rebellion had drawn from the Pope a declaration of spiritual war and act of comfort for the Queen's enemies, the Bull of 1570, depriving Elizabeth of her throne and releasing her subjects from their allegiance.

These were the circumstances in which the Parliament of 1571 met. It had to be called, because, apart from the need for legislation to deal with the leaders of the Rebellion and to counter the Papal Bull, the cost of suppressing the revolt, which had been met temporarily by a forced loan, required the aid of a subsidy. If we can accept a hint from the Spanish ambassador, the delay in summoning it was caused by Elizabeth's fear that Members would insist on a settlement of the succession; and while her former preference for the Scottish claim had been stilled by the violent course of events, her opposition to any other claim remained as firm — and as prudent — as ever.[1]

She need not have worried. The question of the succession did indeed arise, but only in a negative, not a positive form. Her marriage was not even mentioned. The common peril in

[1] *Spanish Cal. Eliz.* ii. 237, 273.

which English Protestants and their Queen now stood drew them closer together and sobered the zealots into some degree of responsibility. The impulse to defy and coerce their Sovereign — perhaps a manifestation of parliamentary adolescence, certainly a consequence of the Queen's youth and sex — was not so general after 1566. Though the experience and maturity that had come to the House of Commons in past Parliaments were not lost; though a sufficient number of the men of 1566 reappeared to allow continuity of policy; and though, in all conscience, Members could be troublesome; the bond between them and their Sovereign was now too intimate and their respect for her too deep to permit such liberties as were taken in 1566.

But these men were like nature: they abhorred a vacuum. The critical character of the times might suggest discretion about marriage and the succession: it equally emphasized the urgency of the religious issue. As we have noticed, there is reason to think that if the succession agitation had not absorbed the energies of the Commons in 1566, there would have been a concerted move, in which many bishops would have joined with their radical clergy, to reform the Act of Uniformity, purge the Church of offensive rites and ceremonies, and achieve that kind of life and worship, akin to 'the best-reformed' churches on the continent, which they had tried to secure in the Parliament of 1559. 'The interimistical state of our Church', was how a Puritan thought of it in 1573; and there were many, both high and low, who had been inclined to view the Religious Settlement of 1559 as temporary.[1]

The bishops, who as late as 1565-66 were hoping for a further step in reform, expected to end the distressing Vestiarian Controversy in this way. In principle they did not differ from their nonconforming brethren over vestments, any more than they differed over doctrine. Moreover, all were agreed — at any rate at first, though, as tempers sharpened, the nonconformists qualified their view — that the quarrel was over 'matters indifferent'. Since we have the essentials of a true Church, why be so stiff-necked over inessentials? asked the bishops, who found themselves obliged to carry out the Queen's demand for uniformity. Since these things are 'indifferent', retorted their

[1] *A Parte of a Register* (1593), p. 376.

opponents, why force them upon us? It was a tragic dilemma for the bishops: some of the keenest Protestants, men who had shared exile with them in Mary Tudor's reign, were being put in jeopardy of their ministry and even deprived.

The demand for rigorous uniformity had arisen at the beginning of 1565 on the initiative of the Queen. It came to a head with the issue of the orders known as Parker's *Advertisements* in 1566. 'These precise folk', the Archbishop told Elizabeth, 'would offer their goods and bodies to prison rather than they should relent.' Then imprison them, answered the Queen.[1]

In the ensuing conflict the nonconformists were painfully inflexible and sometimes outrageous in their vituperation. From his safe refuge in the living at Ashby-de-la-Zouche, the Puritan Earl of Huntingdon's estate, Anthony Gilby, 'a fast and furious stickler against church discipline', commented as follows on vestments: 'That wolf Winchester [the late Stephen Gardiner] and his butcher Bonner fought once against us for the grounds of this gear; but lo! how the Lord, within two or three years, overthrew them all to give us courage to go forward. We are too slack and negligent. That monster [Bonner] remaineth, and is fed, as the Papists say, for their sakes . . . We do cry, "Kill this traitor, enemy to the Crown, to the realm, to God and man . . ." We are answered: "Nay, yourselves shall be compelled to turn your cloth, your coats and caps, and to get you into his livery. . . ." '[2]

In their anger, these Puritans turned against their persecutors, the bishops, and against their office. It meant the collapse of the common front displayed by the *émigrés* and their parliamentary supporters in 1559, and still recoverable as late as the Parliament of 1566. Had not the Puritan House of Commons in that Parliament passed a bill to give statutory confirmation to the whole of the Articles of Religion, and worked in intimate accord with the bishops? By 1571 such bishops as Horne and Jewel and Sandys, under the virulent attacks on them, were tending to the right: the radical clergy, and with them their parliamentary supporters, moved to the left. The House of Commons was no longer willing to confirm all the Articles. The change that was coming over the scene was of profound

---

[1] *Parker Correspondence*, p. 278. Cf. Dixon, *History of Church of England*, vi. 44 seqq.
[2] *A Parte of a Register*, pp. 14-15.

significance. In their attacks upon episcopacy the radicals were drawing towards Geneva and Presbyterianism; and it was in 1570 that the prophet of this new phase in the Puritan movement, a Cambridge professor of the post-exile generation, Thomas Cartwright, delivered his famous course of lectures on the Acts of the Apostles, in which he expounded the Calvinistic form of church organization. The Parliament of 1571 was the hinge between the past and the future. Presbyterianism had not yet developed its parliamentary propaganda; but lack of sympathy with the bishops was clear.

Of the 438 Members elected to the new Parliament, approximately 165 had had previous parliamentary experience, and of these, about 115 had sat in the sessions of 1563 and 1566 and so become skilled in the art of opposition. Of our 'choir' of 46, slightly less than half — 19 is the minimum, 22 the maximum estimate — reappeared. John Hales had had his fill of freelance politics; the two Kingsmill brothers, with their intimate Puritan connections, were absent; and the disputatious Paul Wentworth was taking a rest. But Bell, Dalton, Monson, and Norton were back; so were Fleetwood, Strickland — the hero of this new Parliament — the golden-tongued Yelverton, and others. No Parliament could be drab with these men about.

The newcomers more than made up for the absentees. Paul Wentworth's place was taken by his elder brother, Peter, of Lillingstone-Lovell — a village near the town of Buckingham, though at that time in a detached part of Oxfordshire. All his associations proclaimed his radical Protestant interests. His first wife was a cousin of Katherine Parr, his second a sister of the dour and puritanical Francis Walsingham, the Queen's Secretary. A married sister had been one of the Marian exiles, and a daughter of his was to marry the son of William Strickland, his Puritan fellow-Member in this Parliament.[1]

Born in 1524, like others of his class he had rounded off his education at the Inns of Court. Parliament had not attracted him until now, when he was forty-six or forty-seven years of age. It may have been the tales his brother Paul told him of the previous Parliament, or the solicitations of Puritan ministers and gentlemen, wanting to build up their party in Parliament,

---

[1] Cf. my two articles on 'Peter Wentworth', *Eng. Hist. Rev.* xxxix. 36, 175; GARRETT, *Marian Exiles*, p. 95.

which induced him —and possibly induced another zealous Puritan in his neighbourhood, Anthony Cope, Member for Banbury — to seek election. Writing of the succession question in 1593, he explained: 'I was first stirred up to deal in it thirty-one years past, by God's good motion, then by sundry grave and wise men unknown unto me, and also by lamentable messages sent unto me by men likewise unknown unto me.' The allusion was to the period of the 1563 Parliament. It adds to the traces, already noticed, of external activity behind the agitation of that and the following session, and makes one readier to believe that some at any rate of the Puritans in Parliament were there in response to a call of duty. Indeed, those radical clergymen who had lived a life of propaganda abroad in Mary's reign, who recently had sent an emissary to Switzerland to organize from that country pressure on their Queen and bishops, and had tried to secure, and this year were to succeed in securing, the intervention of the Count Palatine in their interests[1] — such men, whose organizing genius deserves the closest study, were not likely to overlook the obvious strategy of persuading their friends and patrons among the gentry to find seats in Parliament. In later days, when they had constructed their 'classical' or Presbyterian organization, there is evidence of election campaigning. May we not, as early as 1571, suspect the existence of more restricted, more nebulous, yet none the less purposeful endeavours to provide themselves with the agents for their parliamentary campaign?[2]

Wentworth was described by a contemporary as a man 'of a whet and vehement spirit'. As a parliamentarian he was to be in constant trouble with his Queen, and he ultimately died a prisoner in the Tower at the age of seventy-three, refusing liberty at the price of keeping silent over the succession question. Like others of his colleagues, he presents that paradox of the age: passionate conflict with his Sovereign coupled with a love and reverence this side of idolatry. In the 1580s, when he was on a commission to take evidence in a Chancery case, he re-

---

[1] *Zurich Letters*, ii. 339 seqq.; KNAPPEN, *Tudor Puritanism*, p. 232.
[2] We know that Wentworth, at any rate in later years, corresponded with Thomas Wilcox, one of the London organizers of the Puritan party and joint-author of *The Admonition to Parliament* (Roger Morrice MSS. Dr. Williams's Library, vol. II. Letters of Eminent Persons, II. 617 (2) – a reference I owe to the late Edna Bibby's papers).

buked his fellow-commissioner for wanting, in the interest of speed, to write a 'brief titling' before the depositions, omitting 'Our Sovereign Lady' before 'Queen Elizabeth'. 'What!' said he, 'shall we not acknowledge her to be our sovereign Lady? This is well indeed. I think some of us are weary of her. I am not weary of her for my part; and therefore I will have it set down "Our Sovereign Lady".' And when this commissioner administered the oath to a witness in the form, 'to say the truth and the whole truth, as God should help him and the holy contents of the book', the Puritan in Wentworth broke forth with the objection 'that there was no help but of God, and therefore he should not speak of the holy contents of the book'.[1]

Peter Wentworth was the most colourful and courageous of the Puritan group among our newcomers, but there were others who in this or subsequent Parliaments played an active part in the drama. There was Anthony Cope of Hanwell near Ban-bury, a neighbour (as country distances go) of Wentworth's, and a man who helped to make the Banbury district a strong-hold of Puritanism. There was also Tristram Pistor of Hamp-shire, Member for Stockbridge, a man 'with a grave and seemly countenance and a good natural eloquence', whose melodious language and fervid zeal we shall be able to judge for ourselves. The Puritan Earl of Huntingdon had two of his brothers, Sir Edward, and that notable parliamentarian Francis Hastings, sitting for the first time; and the Earl of Bedford placed at Poole a Northamptonshire gentleman, George Carleton, whose activity in the cause we shall often have occasion to note. Carleton was to choose his 'beloved in the Lord', Peter Went-worth, as one of the overseers of his will: a sign of the close affinity between these men. There were also Robert Bainbridge, Member for Derby, who was to get into trouble in a later Parlia-ment for his connection with the Wentworth and Cope group; Edward Lewkenor, another of that group and a Suffolk gentle-man; and Thomas Cromwell, a younger brother of Lord Crom-well and grandson of Henry VIII's famous minister — a man whose sympathies were Puritan, and who in his will desired no funeral pomp or sumptuousness, 'being not willing to have vanities continue for me after my death, whereto I have been too much subject in my lifetime'. Cromwell interests us because

[1] P.R.O. Star Chamber, Eliz. W.18/1.

we now know him as the most remarkable parliamentary
diarist of the age. He was a conspicuous House of Commons
man, whose deepening knowledge of procedure and sound judgment got him placed on innumerable committees and whose
religious zeal rarely or never exceeded discretion.

There were other notable newcomers. One of Gloriana's
prime favourites, Christopher Hatton, who according to legend
danced his way into the Queen's favour, began a distinguished
parliamentary service, which redounds to his credit; and three
of England's most famous seamen, Richard Grenville, John
Hawkins, and Sir Humphrey Gilbert — each of whom, oddly
enough, sat in two Parliaments — sampled Westminster for the
first time. Gilbert we shall see in a rather indecorous role,
hardly in keeping with the immortal story of his last hours on
the little ship *Squirrel*. Sir Thomas Lucy, of Shakespearian
myth, was a newcomer, and so was John Hooker of Exeter,
the admirable antiquary.

Hooker, who was one of the Members for Exeter, wrote a
diary of the Parliament's proceedings for his town authorities,[1]
in this imitating the burgesses for Colchester who did the same
as far back as 1485. Perhaps other borough Members in the
past had committed their reports to writing — we know that
some of them made verbal reports; but if so, none seems to have
survived. Valuable as Hooker's diary is, it is another, an
anonymous, Member of this Parliament — whose identity quite
eludes us — to whom the credit must go of being the true
pioneer of the private-Member's diary. He was a Puritan.
That we can see; and it is significant. Such men were not only
making the proceedings of the House of Commons worth recording: they were themselves becoming the recorders. Alas! our
first diary is incomplete in the copies we possess; but it is a
worthy fragment.

One recession from the House of Commons commands
notice. In February of this year, 1571, the Queen had raised
Cecil to the peerage as Lord Burghley. From the House of
Lords he continued to keep a vigilant eye on proceedings. It
was needed. The House of Commons in 1571 was a remarkable
body of Englishmen. In quality, character, and experience
they were a tribute to a great age and to the curious, illogical

[1] It is printed in *Trans. Devon. Assoc.* xi. 442 seqq.

electoral system that selected them. But an excess of talent can be the enemy of time and business: procedural refinements and rigidities have to be invented to counter the tendency. As yet, parliamentary procedure was extremely flexible, and these men almost talked themselves to a standstill in the early days of the session.

The Parliament opened on April 2nd, 1571. It was the first in which every Member had to take the oath of supremacy: the first English Parliament, therefore, in which not a single avowed Catholic sat. While the royal procession made its impressive, decorative way to Westminster Abbey and to the initial religious service, the Lord Steward and his deputies administered the oath to the elected representatives of shires and boroughs.

At the Abbey the sermon was preached by Edwin Sandys, one of the Marian exiles, who in the previous year had been translated to the see of London. It was a fine sermon, not unlike the opening parliamentary orations of Lord Keeper Bacon in structure, except that a theologian was speaking. Discoursing on the Church, perhaps with knowledge of the bills that were likely to be brought before Parliament, he declared that 'it must be purged from all false doctrine, from all idolatry and superstition'. 'The primitive Church, casting away Judaical and heathenish rites, was simple in her ceremonies. The Pope hath polluted and burthened the Church with both. We may have no other than such as are comely, and serve for the furtherance of true religion.' This surely was the Sandys of the Marian exile and of 1559 speaking: one who like Horne and Jewel would still have been glad to see the ornaments proviso of the Act of Uniformity rescinded. The Church, he added, needed to be purged of simony: advance-support, perhaps, for reviving one of the bills of religion of 1566. 'Such in authority as truly fear God will purge His Church from false doctrine, from idolatry, from superstition, and from simony.'

Toleration, an axiomatic conception in the modern liberal tradition, had no place in his philosophy: theology apart, it was a time of ideological warfare. 'This liberty, that men may openly profess diversity of religion, must needs be dangerous to the Commonwealth ... One God, one king, one faith, one profession, is fit for one Monarchy and Commonwealth. Division weakeneth: concord strengtheneth ... Let conformity and unity in religion be provided for; and it shall be as a wall of defence unto this realm.' What he meant by 'unity in religion', he made clearer later on: 'compelling all subjects to hear God's word and receive His sacraments'. There was a bill to this effect put into Parliament; and we shall note its fate.

The Northern Rebellion and the Papal Bull were in his mind as he touched the chords of patriotism: 'If we, linked together in the fear of God and in true concord and amity among ourselves, put to our helping hands, every one dutifully in his calling, to the supporting of this State and defending thereof, doubtless no enemy, no foreign power can hurt us, no bull of Basan shall prevail against us; but we and our Commonwealth, in despite of all both corporal and spiritual enemies, shall be strengthened and stablished for ever.'[1]

When the Lords and Commons were assembled in the Parliament Chamber, the Queen herself spoke a few introductory words, and then Sir Nicholas Bacon began his oration on the causes for assembling Parliament. It was in two sections, lawmaking and supply, with the former — divided under the headings of religious and temporal matters — but briefly developed and most of his exhortation reserved for taxation. 'You are to consider first', he declared, 'whether the ecclesiastical laws concerning the discipline of the Church be sufficient or no; and if any want shall be found, to supply the same.' What he had in mind, it is difficult to guess: not as much, we may be sure, as some of those without the bar read into his words. Both he and the Queen must have anticipated an unofficial move for reform of the Church; and the weightier command, made — who can doubt it? — on the express instructions of the Queen, came in the words that followed: 'Thereof the greatest care ought to depend of my Lords the bishops, to whom the execution thereof especially pertains, and to whom the imperfections of the same be best known.'

The appeal for money was expounded in a declaration of the great benefits that the country had received from the Queen's rule, and the necessity for financial aid. The restoring

---

[1] *Sermons of Edwin Sandys* (Parker Soc.), pp. 34 seqq. It is without date, but Hooker's reference to the text (*Trans. Devon. Assoc.* xi. 472), and the contents, leave no doubt of the occasion.

SIR CHRISTOPHER WRAY

Speaker in 1571

and setting at liberty of God's holy word; ten whole years and more of peace; the contrast to be seen between England and 'neighbours round about us'; clemency and mercy: these were the benefits. Had it not been for 'the raging Romanist rebels', peace and clemency might have continued twenty years longer. The necessity for aid lay in the charge of suppressing the Northern Rebellion; in action against the Scottish friends of the rebels; in the growing expense of Ireland; in other items, including the navy; and in the breach of trade with the Netherlands and with Spain, which had diminished receipts from the customs. An encomium followed on the Queen's financial prudence: on her eschewing of 'gorgeous, sumptuous, superfluous buildings', the pomps of expensive embassies, and such like. God had given them a phoenix, 'a blessed bird', *rara avis*.[1]

Back in their own House, the Commons set about the election of a Speaker.[2] On the nomination of Sir Francis Knollys, Treasurer of the Royal Household, they chose Christopher Wray, aged forty-seven, an experienced Parliament-man, but not, if we may judge from a few signs, a very astute chairman. He was a Queen's serjeant, who subsequently became a distinguished judge; a Yorkshireman by birth, who made his principal home in Lincolnshire, and was a generous patron of his old college at Cambridge.

His election was confirmed by the Queen in the afternoon of April 4th; and in his main oration on that occasion 'he desired', as our diarist put it, 'to say somewhat concerning the orderly government of a Commonwealth'. He divided his discourse under the headings of 'religion, authority, and laws', and under the first of these described the Queen's power in spiritual and ecclesiastical causes as 'absolute' — meaning by that, free from Papal supremacy. 'Leaving all proofs of divinity to the bishops and Fathers . . . he proved the same by the practice of princes within this realm', beginning with Lucius the (legendary) Christian king, thirteen hundred years past, and citing William the Conqueror, Henry III, and the law reports. It was as though he was set on expounding the preamble to Henry VIII's Act in Restraint of Appeals: 'Where by divers sundry old

---

[1] B.M. Cotton MS. Titus F. I, fols. 123-6.
[2] The following proceedings and speeches are from the Anonymous Diary, ibid. fols. 129 seqq.

authentic histories and chronicles it is manifestly declared and expressed that this realm of England is an empire.' His historical argument was part of the Queen's case for claiming that the royal supremacy was not bestowed by Parliament but was inherent in the prerogative.

Plato came into his discourse on laws, and he concluded this section with praise of the Queen for not interfering with the course of justice, as her progenitors had sometimes done, and for not pardoning offenders without first taking the advice of the judges who had tried them. At the end of the oration came the customary petition for privileges.

Hitherto the granting of this petition had caused little or no anxiety to the Queen. A caution about abusing freedom from arrest, a proviso that speech be reverent and dutiful: that seemed enough. And if the Commons had not laid claim to a broader privilege than Sir Thomas More described in 1523, it would have continued to be enough. But in the previous session they had not only strayed in their actions beyond their constitutional bounds: in Paul Wentworth's questions and in the unpresented petition about their liberties they had defined freedom of speech in a novel way, claiming rather vaguely, and, in the circumstances of the time, very dangerously, a liberty to 'treat and devise' of matters honourable to the Queen and profitable to the realm: a claim which threatened to make them the arbiters of state policy and to transform the character of Tudor monarchy. A more or less unrestricted right of initiation; a royal veto paralysed by the fear of seeming to withstand the nation's will (and on this latter point Queen Elizabeth was already a little sensitive): where could these lead, except to constitutional in place of personal monarchy?

In the interests of her prerogative the Queen could no longer be content with a vague reply to a vague petition. In the longer of two versions of the petition made by Serjeant Wray on this occasion, he asked 'that every man might have free speech, and without interruption or trouble to speak his mind freely'.[1] Into such language Members of the House of Commons could easily read a justification for almost any agitation or any bill that they cared to promote. For this reason the Crown came forward with the first of its definitions of freedom of speech.

[1] *Trans. Devon Assoc.* xi. 474.

In his reply to the Speaker, the Lord Keeper, as our anonymous diarist records the speech, dealt with freedom of speech as follows: 'The fourth [petition] was such, that her Majesty, having some experience of late of some disorder and certain offences — which, though they were not punished, yet were they offences still, and so must be accounted — therefore said, they should do well to meddle with no matters of state but such as should be proponed unto them, and to occupy themselves in other matters concerning the commonwealth.'

The distinction drawn was between matters of state — or, as we should say, the prerogative — and commonwealth matters. Matters of state included the Church, where by the constitutional theory of the Reformation the Queen's supremacy was part of the royal prerogative; they included questions of high policy, such as the succession; they included the royal administration — the Exchequer, purveyors, licences, monopolies, and such-like grants by royal letters patent, to mention some of the subjects on which the Commons were tempted to trespass. On such matters the Queen was denying to Parliament the right of initiation. Correctly denying; for (to take a parallel instance) in the law courts no case affecting the prerogative could proceed *rege non consulto* — without royal licence.

In the version of Bacon's speech given by John Hooker the point is put more crudely: 'Her Highness thinketh it not meet that any should have further liberty to speak or talk in that House of any matter other than that which is there to be proponed.' If we add that this applied only to 'matters of state', it expresses the Queen's point more clearly.[1]

There can be no doubt that Elizabeth was justified constitutionally and historically in her definition. The privilege for which More asked in 1523 claimed no right of initiative. He sought freedom of speech 'in every thing incident among' them: or as Sir Nicholas Bacon — in Hooker's version — now put it, in 'that which is there to be proponed'.

Of course, the operation of the prerogative might injure or distress the people; and Parliament was an organ for expressing grievances. In that case, the proper procedure was to petition the Sovereign for remedy, not frame bills to legislate on the subject. If legislation was deemed expedient, it was for the

---

[1] *Trans. Devon Assoc.* xi. 474.

government to initiate it. And even in petitioning there were limits. The point should not be passed, as had happened in 1566, where such action became coercion.

But constitutional niceties make little appeal in passionate, revolutionary times. Doctrinaire clergy and their doctrinaire friends in the House of Commons obeyed a higher loyalty, as the emotional speech of Tristram Pistor in this Parliament so clearly reveals. Queen Elizabeth was trying to contain a heady new wine in an old bottle.

In his version of the Lord Keeper's speech, Hooker reports some more admonitions: 'that they should leave to talk *rhetoricè* and speak *logicè*; to leave long tales, which is rather an ostentation of wit than to any effect, and to deal with those things as there were to be proponed; that, going effectually to the matter, they might dispatch that they were sent for, and that they might the sooner return home'.

'Speak *logicè* and not *rhetoricè*; leave long tales': we shall judge for ourselves how much heed was paid to these words. As the Queen rose to depart, she expressed a hope 'that they would be more quiet than they were at the last time'.[1]

---

[1] *Trans. Devon Assoc.* xi. 475.

## CHAPTER II

# RELIGION

INEVITABLY, the dominant topic of this Parliament was religion. The Papal Bull, coinciding in intention though not precisely in time with the Northern Rebellion, had not only heightened the conflict of creeds: theoretically it had converted every Catholic into a potential rebel and made his faith tantamount to treason. 'Let conformity and unity in religion be provided for': that had been the injunction of Bishop Sandys in his Westminster sermon, and as an anti-Catholic text it doubtless echoed the opinion of Privy Councillors. Ecclesiastical laws and Church discipline had been spoken of in the Lord Keeper's speech: he, too, was probably thinking of the Catholic menace, not of radical nonconformists who were more Protestant than their Protestant Queen. Indeed, these perfervid patriots had reason to think the omens propitious. Now was the acceptable hour to stop appeasement, suppress all compromise with the enemy, and stand in the strength of a purified church against 'the remnants of Antichrist'.

What of the Queen? In January 1570, between the Northern Rebellion and its aftermath, the Dacres revolt, she had had a 'Declaration of the Queen's proceedings since her reign' prepared for general dissemination, and had carefully corrected the text in her own hand, emphasizing its liberal doctrine by her amendments. 'In the word of a Prince and the presence of God', she had assured her subjects that so long as they showed themselves in their outward conversation quiet and conformable to the law by attendance at church, they should enjoy her accustomed favour, mildness, and grace, 'without any molestation . . . by way of . . . inquisition of their opinions for their consciences in matters of their faith, remitting that to the supreme and singular authority of Almighty God, who is the only searcher of hearts'. The outbreak of the Dacres revolt may have cancelled this particular piece of propaganda, but not her policy. In June, following the publication of the Papal Bull in England, she ordered the Lord Keeper to make a similar declaration publicly in the Star Chamber. 'Her Majesty would have all her loving subjects to understand that as long as they shall openly continue in the observation of her laws and shall not wilfully and manifestly break them by their open acts, her Majesty's meaning is not to have any of them molested by any inquisition or examination of their consciences in causes of religion . . ; being very loth to be provoked by the overmuch boldness and wilfulness of her subjects to alter her natural clemency into a princely severity.'[1]

With passions astir, a Puritan Parliament in session, and her advisers set on severity, would the Queen be able to maintain her broad and tolerant policy? Would she manage to retain indulgence for loyal conservatives and keep the rein of discipline on radicals? This session gave the answer.

When, after the admission of the Speaker, the Commons returned to their chamber, the customary formal reading of a bill was not, as usual, devoted to a measure of little consequence, but to one 'concerning coming to the church and receiving of the Communion'. Under the Act of Uniformity everyone was already liable to a fine of one shilling for absence from church; but, as a speaker complained, churchwardens, who for the most part were 'simple, mean men', were prone to neglect their duty and 'would rather commit perjury than give their neighbours cause for offence' by reporting them. The new bill was supplementary: apparently, its object was to enforce attendance at least once a quarter by a stiffer fine, levied in a surer way.[2] But its notable feature was the extension of compulsion to attendance at the Communion. Everyone was to receive this sacrament at least once a year under the stringent penalty of a fine of 100 marks (£66.13.4). Here, indeed, was a novelty. It threatened Catholics, if only indirectly, with that very inquisition in matters of conscience from which Elizabeth had promised 'in the word of a Prince and the presence of God' to protect them.

Who was responsible for the bill, we do not know. Bishop Sandys, in his sermon, had advocated it; Burghley, there is reason to think, favoured it. It won episcopal and official

---

[1] Q. Elizabeth's Defence of her Proceedings in Church & State, ed. W. E. Collins (Church Hist. Soc.); S.P. Dom. Eliz. 71/16.

[2] The Cotton copy of the Anonymous Diary, April 9th, gives the fine as xiid., a Bodleian copy as £12; Hooker, April 4th, gives it as 30s.

blessing. But it was not what we should call a 'bishops' bill': though that does not exclude the possibility that a bishop — say Sandys — was one of its sponsors. Nor, one imagines, was it a formal government measure, for the Queen cannot have been consulted about it: all the same, some of the Privy Councillors may have devised it. It was certainly not a specifically Puritan bill. Those free-lance nuisances had their own radical programme, to which we must now turn.[1]

The Puritan leaders must have been delighted when the Speaker chose this bill to inaugurate the session. It got the right spirit into the House at once; and before they rose that day the Commons arranged for the Litany to be said every morning, as had been done in previous Parliaments of the reign, and for the Speaker to compose an appropriate prayer. Five days later they took steps to intensify the devotional atmosphere by asking the congenially-minded Bishop of London to supply them with a preacher to read a three-quarters-of-an-hour lecture every morning at 7 o'clock.[2]

Then came the first full working day: April 5th. The whole morning was spent calling the House, since it seemed over-full, and in dealing with points that emerged therefrom, including the trespass into their company of two gentlemen from the Inner Temple.[3] This too was propitious for the Puritans, for it engendered the very opposite mood to that of crisp business-like efficiency which the Lord Keeper had tried to instil into Members. How the Queen must have fretted, if told of it! Worse followed. Next morning, instead of checking the incipient demoralization by instantly reading a bill, the Speaker allowed the sitting to begin with a number of motions. It was wretched leadership. Before he realized what was happening, William Strickland, Member for Scarborough, was on his feet. The Puritan campaign had begun.

'One Mr. Strickland' — wrote our anonymous diarist — 'a grave and ancient man of great zeal and perhaps (as he himself thought) not unlearned, first stood up.' 'In a long discourse', he recalled 'God's goodness in giving to us the light of His

---

[1] *C.J.* i. 82; Anon. Diary, April 5th, 6th, 9th; *Trans. Devon. Assoc.* xi. 475 (hereafter cited as Hooker); S.P. Dom. Eliz. 77/54.

[2] *C.J.* i. 82; Hooker, p. 476.

[3] *C.J.* i. 83; Hooker, p. 475. The Anonymous Diary, April 5th, erroneously gives a reading of the bill for coming to church.

word'; 'the gracious disposition of her Majesty, by whom, as by His instrument, God had wrought so great things; and our slackness and carelessness' in not seizing 'the time and blessing offered', nor protesting the truth openly. This was by way of preface to a motion that Thomas Norton, 'a man neither ill-disposed to religion nor a negligent keeper of such matters of charge', should be asked to produce before the House the Edwardian *Reformatio Legum*, that corpus of radical canons, which, as we have noticed, the reform party had tried to revive in the Parliament of 1559 and in the Convocation of 1563. It was hot from the press, having just been edited by the renowned martyrologist, John Foxe, especially for this Parliament.

'After so many years', Strickland continued, 'as now by God's providence we have been learning the purity of God's truth, we should not permit, for any cause of policy or other pretence, any errors in matters of doctrine to continue amongst us. And therefore, said he, although the Book of Common Prayer is (God be praised) drawn very near to the sincerity of the truth, yet there are some things inserted more superstitious or erroneous than in so high matters be tolerable.' Enumerating a few, he asked 'to have all things brought to the purity of the primitive church'. 'He spake at large of the abuses of the Church of England and of the churchmen', instancing known Papists in great livings, 'honest, godly and learned Protestants' with little or nothing, boys with dispensations to have spiritual promotions, and so on.

Though our report of the speech is neither as full nor as lucid as we might wish, the implications are clear. The Parliament of 1559 had fallen short of radical hopes in details of the Prayer Book; also in failing to enact a body of Reformist Canon Law. The Puritans were intent on remedying both short-comings. In other words, the Settlement of 1559 was now to be treated as an *interim* and be replaced by a final, Puritan Settlement: 1559 was to achieve fulfilment in 1571. Moreover, certain practical defects and abuses had become apparent in the Church. A party in the Lower House of Convocation had tried but failed to apply the remedies in 1563, and these had therefore been formulated in the code of alphabetical bills introduced into the House of Commons in 1566. They were now to be revived.

The policy was thorough-going: it was the complete Puritan programme in its pre-Presbyterian phase. To assume that it sprang from Strickland's mind alone would be childish. There must have been party organization behind him, and if only we could penetrate to that background we should probably find the leaders of the radical clergy in consultation with a group of Members of Parliament. When Parliament ended, Archbishop Parker summoned some of these ministers before the High Commission: to examine them, he told Burghley. They included men of the old guard, such as Dean Sampson and the equally renowned Thomas Lever, and one of the brilliant organizers of the future Presbyterian movement, John Field, a younger London clergyman who may one day appear in our histories as the Francis Place of the Elizabethan period. Can they have been among the agitators behind this Parliament? And was Parker's attack on them retaliation?[1]

Strickland ended his speech by moving for a committee to confer with the bishops about reform of the Church. It may seem an anticlimax. No doubt he and his friends had been influenced in their tactics by the injunction given in the Lord Keeper's speech; but also they do not appear as yet to have abandoned all hope in the bishops. Were not the circumstances of the time such as to wean the leaders of the Church from their conservatism? Certainly, the parliamentary sermon of Bishop Sandys seemed full of promise.

Strickland was followed by Thomas Norton — 'a man wise, bold, and eloquent', says our diarist — who, after explaining what the *Reformatio Legum* was, offered a copy to the House: surely prearranged action. A committee of about twenty was then appointed to take charge of the book and consult with the bishops. It contained a firm core of Puritans, including Bell, Monson, and Strickland, balanced, however, by five Privy Councillors and other staider heads.

The topic of religion practically monopolized that morning of April 6th, for the House read only two bills, and one of those was the bill for coming to church, now at its second reading. Sir Thomas Smith, Privy Councillor and distinguished scholar, gave it his support, but suggested consulting the bishops: an

[1] *Parker Correspondence*, pp. 381-2; KNAPPEN, *Tudor Puritanism*, p. 230 and references there.

indication that the bill came officially neither from the bishops nor the Council. This brought to his feet our loquacious and precedent-quoting lawyer, William Fleetwood. After opposing one of its details — enforcement by 'promoters', or, as we should say, 'informers', a device which he believed to be no older than the first year of Henry VIII's reign, and which he denounced as nothing more than the prospect of 'private gain to the worst of men' — he turned on Smith's suggestion about the bishops. The question of attendance at church and the service of God was, he affirmed, the direct concern of the House of Commons. 'We all have as well learned this lesson — that there is a God who is to be served — as have the bishops.' He thereupon undertook to prove 'by the old laws vouched from King Edgar' that Princes in their Parliaments have made ecclesiastical constitutions. He urged them to commit the bill to some of the House and to ignore the bishops, 'who perhaps would be slow'. So it was done; and in thus flouting the Lord Keeper's injunction Fleetwood proclaimed himself a rebel and probably got into bad odour with authority.

Next morning, April 7th, the radical leaders were at it again. The Speaker let them seize the initiative, and once more it was Strickland. Business seems to have begun with a motion of his that Mr. Norton should produce the alphabetical bills of 1566: bills A, B, C, D, E, and F. For the second time, Strickland and Norton! It is curious that the bills were in Norton's custody. Can this most prolific of unofficial parliamentary draftsmen have been the lawyer employed to draw them up in 1566, or was he no more than aide in the present campaign? Whichever it was, he now handed in the bills; and nothing would satisfy the House but to have them all read immediately. True, there was a royal ban on such action. How they got round it the Clerk records: 'this not to stand for any reading'. The naivety or effrontery of these men! What with this and other diversions, there was no formal reading to any bill that morning; and the House certainly deserved the royal reprimand which descended on it two sittings later for spending too much time in motions and long speeches.[1]

Interest now shifts to the Commons' committee appointed to consult with the bishops. The discussions did not go well.

[1] Anon. Diary, April 6th-7th; Hooker, pp. 475-6; *C.J.* i. 83.

First, the proposal to revive the *Reformatio Legum* must have been quashed. Doubtless it was clear to all except the fanatics that the Queen would on no account allow Parliament to meddle with the canons of the Church. As likely as not, the bishops softened the blow by promising to frame some new canons in the present Convocation: which in fact they did. Next, the Prayer Book: here also nothing came of the talks. On these two subjects there was probably no specific commission from the House, tying the hands of the committee. The real clash was over Bill A — the bill to confirm the Articles of Religion — on which there is reason to think that the House had expressed its views.

Here the bishops were standing where they stood in 1566. The Commons, however, were no longer prepared simply to confirm the Articles — 'the little book' of 1563. There were certain non-doctrinal Articles which had become offensive to Puritans since 1566; and they were determined not to give statutory sanction to them. Moreover, it seems likely that the Commons had taken over some of the proposals made by a group of radical clergy in the Convocation of 1563, who wanted to impose uniformity of doctrine on the laity in general and the test of subscription on all graduates of the universities as well as clergymen. The bishops may not have been averse to proposals of the latter kind: like the Commons they did not draw the Queen's liberal-minded distinction between outward conformity and inward freedom, and like them they were obsessed by the perils of the time. But attrition of their 'Thirty-nine Articles' was something to which they could not possibly agree.[1]

In order to strengthen their hand, the bishops suggested that the Commons should broaden the conference, making it one between committees of both Houses (in which, of course, they would be included). This was done, the Commons reinforcing their committee for the purpose, adding, among others, the redoubtable Peter Wentworth. They met on April 10th and evidently could still not agree. The Commons were given two alternatives, neither very hopeful: to continue the two-House conference, or to 'stand at the direction of the bishops'. Next

[1] Hooker, p. 476; *C.J.* i. 83; STRYPE, *Annals*, I. i. 508-12, and cf. pp. 474 seqq. On the proceedings about the Articles, cf. my article, 'Parliament and the Articles of Religion, 1571', *Eng. Hist. Rev.* lxvii. 510-21, and references there given.

day there was a debate about this in the Lower House and many spoke. Thomas Norton gave them their lead, revealing how little co-operation the Puritan leaders now expected from the bishops. Let them continue in conference with the Lords' committee, he urged, and not 'stand at the direction of the bishops further than their consciences should be satisfied'. To retain freedom of action, he wanted the procedure termed 'a suit', not a conference. Yelverton agreed: adding that they should keep authority over the proposals in their House.

Meanwhile, a start had been made — possibly with the good will of the bishops — in reading the other, less controversial alphabetical bills. But it was only too clear that things were going wrong with the main Puritan effort. Strickland himself had suggested approaching the bishops: the consequence had merely been to erect an impenetrable barrier. Even the common front of 1566 could not be resuscitated, much less that of 1559. Egged on — as we may guess — by their clerical friends without, the Puritan leaders now decided to ignore the Lord Keeper's injunction and proceed to action themselves.

On April 14th, the intrepid Strickland exhibited a bill for the reformation of the Book of Common Prayer: the main item in their programme, the summit of their aspirations. Our diarist describes its purpose: 'first, for taking away of copes, surplices, etc.: then, for [taking away] the needless confirmation of children, as he termed it; the childish asking of questions of the children at baptism; the ministration of the sacraments in private houses; the giving of a ring at marriage, etc.'. It abolished kneeling at Communion, private baptism, and obviously everything to which the Puritans had been objecting in their Vestiarian Conflict and to which the Queen, and Matthew Parker under royal compulsion, had been clinging tenaciously. The Prayer Book was to 'be established', 'without these matters'. The House gave the bill a first reading.

This was rank insubordination. In his heart Sir Francis Knollys must have sympathized with all Strickland's proposals, but the official prevailed over the Puritan in him. And no wonder. He knew only too well that the Queen would be scandalized; and probably he had already, as a member of the committee, lent a hand in restraining the hotheads. Now, as senior Privy Councillor, he rose in opposition. If the matters mentioned were heretical, he said, then verily they were presently to be condemned. If merely matters of ceremony, it behoved them to refer the same to the Queen who, as chief of the Church, had authority to deal therein. 'For us to meddle with matters of her prerogative, quoth he, it were not expedient.' With a touch of practical wisdom, he suggested that the Queen might have reason for her *via media*: she might be hoping 'in time and order' to carry all dissidents with her. What 'secret cause or scruple there may be in the hearts of princes, it is not for all people to know'.

The Comptroller of the Household, Sir James Croft, followed. He spoke to the same effect, but, as became his nature and outlook, less sympathetically, insinuating that their 'heady and hasty proceedings, contrary to and before the law, did rather hinder than help'.

Authority had frowned, but Strickland was not left deserted. 'Hereupon one Pistor . . . showed how conscience enforced him to speak, and rather to hazard his credit than to the offence of his conscience to be silent: albeit, he would willingly acknowledge that many hundred of that honourable and worshipful assembly were well able to teach him, and he indeed willing to learn of them all. The matter of his grief was that matters of most importance, standing us upon for our souls, stretching further and higher to every of us than the monarchy of the whole world, were either not treated of, or so slenderly, that now after more than ten days continual consultation nothing was thereon concluded. Those causes he showed to be God's. The rest are all but terrene; yea, trifles in comparison. Call ye them never so great, or pretend ye that they import never so much: subsidies, crowns, kingdoms, he knew not, he said, what they were in comparison of this. This, he said, he knew, whereof he most thanked God: *primum quaerite regnum dei et caetera omnia adjicientur vobis* [seek ye first the kingdom of God, and all things shall be added unto you]. This rule is the direction, and this desire shall bring us to the light whereupon we may stay and then proceed unto the rest, for in His word and by Him we learn . . . Our true home certainly is not here, for *non habemus hic permanentem civitatem* [we have not here an abiding city]. And the justice of God, he said, moved terror unto all: which he seemed to mean concerning the bill before mentioned

of Strickland's propositions. And so did he set it forth with
vehemency that there lacked no modesty, and with such
eloquence that it neither seemed studied, nor over-much
affected, but grave and learned throughout, and no whit too
long, but very good liking.'

'After him', continues our diarist, 'Mr. Robert Snagge spake;
and far after him indeed, either for order, proof or matter.'
Snagge was the less eminent of two lawyer brothers, M.P.s,
both 'earnest in religion'. Our diarist, clearly a connoisseur of
oratory, was not much impressed. Perhaps, *inter alia*, he objected to Snagge's facetiousness in repeating a favourite Puritan
quip: that if there must be a law about the posture at Communion, then instead of kneeling let it be 'to lie prostrate', thus
shunning 'the old superstition'. Snagge was entirely with
Strickland, and declared that there was 'nothing derogatory or
contrary to the prerogative' in his proposals.

The diary mentions no more speeches, though the debate
seems to have been a prolonged one. There were 'many arguments', the Clerk noted. We miss the name of Thomas Norton.
Perhaps he spoke; perhaps he kept silent. Most Members were
in favour of Strickland's bill, but the defiant mood of 1566 had
mellowed. They shrank from open conflict with their Queen —
their Deborah; and in the end, as the Clerk noted, the House
decided 'that petition be made . . . unto the Queen's Majesty
for her licence and privity to proceed in this bill, before it be
any further dealt in'.[1]

It was Saturday and Easter Eve, and the House adjourned
till the following Thursday. Our diarist — and doubtless many
other Members, for this was one of the season's attractions for
people fortunate enough to be in London — made the round of
sermons, preached by famous divines over the festive period.
He noted them in the part of the diary that is lost.

He also noted something else: the fate of Strickland. 'During
which time of Easter' — his entry runs — 'Mr. Strickland, so
often before mentioned, for the exhibiting of the bill for
reformation of ceremonies and his speech thereupon was called
before the lords of the Privy Council and required to attend
upon them and to make stay from coming to the House in the
mean season.' In thus sequestering Strickland, the Council

[1] Anon. Diary, April 14th; *C.J.* i. 84; Hooker, p. 478.

may have acted on its own authority, but more likely the Queen was behind the move. She knew that she could defend her position against doctrinaires only by constant vigilance and discipline. After her experience in 1566, however, she might have foreseen the result.

The Commons reassembled on April 19th. On the 20th, when the tardy had returned to duty and the House was at its fullest, Peter Wentworth, who, unlike Norton, Fleetwood, and others, was not a ready debater but rather a man of premeditated speeches, made a merciless attack on Sir Humphrey Gilbert: we shall notice this later on. He roused the House. The Speaker tried to calm them with assurance of the Queen's approval of their proceedings; but when he sat down, Wentworth's friend and fellow-Puritan, George Carleton, rose to challenge the action taken against Strickland.

'Mr. Carleton', says our diarist, 'with a very good zeal and orderly show of obedience', explained that 'a member of the House was detained from them: by whose commandment, or for what cause, he knew not. But forasmuch as he was not now a private man, but to supply the room, person, or place of a multitude, specially chosen . . . he thought that neither in regard of the country, which was not to be wronged, nor for the liberty of the House, which was not to be infringed, we should permit him to be detained.' Whatever his offence, 'he should be sent for to the bar of that House, there to be heard, and there to answer'.

Here, indeed, was novel doctrine: that the House possessed disciplinary jurisdiction over its members, to the exclusion of the Crown. Coupled with their new-fangled ideas on freedom of speech it threatened mortal danger to Tudor monarchy.

Sir Francis Knollys rose. He warned them to be wary in their proceedings, and neither to venture further than their assured warrant might stretch, nor to hazard their reputation with the Queen in any doubtful cause. He tried to stay alarm by the assurance that Strickland was not 'detained nor misused, but on considerations is required to expect the Queen's pleasure', and that 'so much favour was meant unto him as he reasonably could wish'. Drawing a significant distinction which it would be well for us to mark, he declared that he 'was in no sort stayed for any words or speech by him in that place

uttered, but for the exhibiting of a bill into the House against
the prerogative of the Queen, which was not to be tolerated'.
Nevertheless, added he, the Council were construing his action
rather as excess of zeal than intentional malice to the dignity
royal. He concluded by remarking that 'oft it hath been seen
that speeches have been examined and considered of'.

Perhaps his concluding remark destroyed the effect of the
studied moderation in the rest of the speech. At any rate, Sir
Nicholas Arnold, an elderly Gloucestershire gentleman and an
old parliamentarian of distinguished public service, 'with some
vehemency moved care to be had for the liberty of the House,
which he was enforced rather to utter and so to run into any
danger of offence of others, than to be offended with himself'.
A gentleman of Suffolk suggested defining the liberty of the
House.

Sir James Croft now intervened to echo Sir Francis Knollys —
maladroitly, one suspects. He was followed by one of the Duke
of Norfolk's followers, who 'told a long tale, how the prerogative
is not disputable', going on to prate about divinity being the
preserve of bishops — 'where', acidly comments our diarist, 'he
utterly forgot the place he spake in and the person who was
meant, for that place required and permitted free speech with
authority, and the person [i.e. Strickland] was not himself a
private man, but a public, by whom even the ordinary himself
[the bishop] was to be directed'.

This courtier-like speech brought the orator Yelverton into
the attack, who roundly asserted that Strickland was to be
sent for, arguing as follows. First, the precedent was perilous.
In this happy time of lenity, under so gracious a prince, extremity of injury was not to be feared. But times might alter,
and what they acquiesced in now might be construed against
them. 'All matter not treason, or too much to the derogation
of the imperial crown, was tolerable there, where all things
came to be considered of, and where there was such fullness of
power as even the right of the Crown was to be determined.'
'It was fit, princes to have their prerogatives; but yet the same
to be straitened within reasonable limits. The prince, he
showed, could not of herself make laws, neither might she by
like reason break laws.' He defended Strickland's speech and
his introduction of the bill. 'Among the Papists', he bitterly

added, 'it was bruited that, by the judgment of the Council, Strickland was taken for an heretic.' Let Members ruminate thereon.

Fleetwood then spoke, the antiquary in him getting the better of the radical: indeed, prosperity — and possibly advancing years — were in due course to cure him of radicalism. He cited precedents for the imprisonment of Parliament-men, and concluded that they had no remedy other than to be humble suitors to her Majesty. They should neither send for Strickland, nor demand him of right.

During this speech, Privy Councillors — staggered by the hornets' nest they had stirred up, and perhaps reflecting on the precedents of 1566 — 'whispered together, and thereupon the Speaker made this motion, that the House should stay of any further consultation hereupon'.

Next morning, as the House was appointing a committee on the bill for coming to church — appropriate moment! — Strickland walked into the chamber. 'Whereupon, many of the House, even upon first sight of him, in grateful sort cried out that he might be one of the committees in that bill.' And so he was. Thus ended another episode on liberty, with the Sovereign again making a tactful retreat; though not surrendering her principle, nor abandoning the Church to its critics.[1]

There was still work for Strickland and his friends to do. Among the alphabetical bills on religion, the two most important were Bill A and Bill B. We must look at these rather closely, in order to extract their strange story.[2] There is reason to think that in 1566 they had been quite distinct measures: Bill A confirming the Articles of Religion, with certain subordinate provisions; Bill B simply laying down age and other qualifications for the clergy. The Commons by 1571 were no longer satisfied with Bill A. As we have already noted, they wanted to limit the number of Articles it confirmed, and probably also to use it as some sort of religious test for people in general. In the end, they scrapped the old bill, along with its alphabetical title, replacing it by a new measure entitled, 'The bill for conservation of order and uniformity in the Church'.

[1] Also cf. *C.J.* i. 85; Hooker, p. 479.
[2] For a more detailed narrative and appropriate references, see my article, *Eng. Hist. Rev.* lxvii. 510 seqq.

Though we are ignorant of its contents, the odds are that it was the sort of measure that would not seem out of place in the modern totalitarian State.

But in the political circumstances of 1571 it was the ideological reliability of the clergy that was of paramount importance. A Protestant régime could not tolerate crypto-Catholics among them. Consequently, it was decided that the Henrician and Marian clergy must all be compelled to subscribe to the Articles by Christmas next, on pain of automatic deprivation. Also, in order to prevent lay patrons with Catholic sympathies from intruding doubtful candidates into the ministry, it was decided to impose subscription on all new ministers. There remained the Edwardian and Elizabethan clergy already instituted under Protestant ordinals. For these it was thought sufficient to provide for their deprivation if they maintained any doctrine directly contrary to the Articles. The question arose, which Bill — A or B — should be saddled with these provisions? As Bill B already imposed other qualifications on the clergy, it was decided to incorporate them in that one.

Consequently — and the unfolding of our story turns on the point — there were two bills dealing with the Articles of Religion in the Parliament of 1571. The first was the main bill: 'the bill for conservation of order and uniformity in the Church'. It gave statutory confirmation to most, but not all of the Articles, and probably imposed a religious test for laymen. On the first count it was obnoxious to the bishops, on both counts abhorrent to the Queen; and therefore doomed. The second bill was Bill B: ultimately to become a statute, as 'An act to reform certain disorders touching ministers of the Church'. It dealt with clerical subscription to the Articles. Being needed for national defence, it was, though unpalatable to the Queen, safe from the oblivion awaiting the main bill.

At this stage in its progress, Bill B was a dependent bill: it was worded in terms of the main bill. Having been drafted in consultation with the Lords' committee and the bishops, it was a compromise. It permitted the clergy to subscribe to *all* the Articles — either in their 1563 version or as they were being amended in the present Convocation of 1571. But the House of Commons had instructed their representatives not to 'stand at the direction of the bishops further than their consciences' permitted. They loyally and stoutly carried out the instruction by adding a further option which permitted the clergy to subscribe to 'so many of those said Articles' as were confirmed in the main bill. In other words, Puritan ministers, by choosing this option, could not be compelled by statute to subscribe to any Articles obnoxious to men of their views.

'So many of those said Articles' as were confirmed in the main bill: the main bill confirmed only the doctrinal Articles, over which there was no quarrel between Anglican and Puritan. Peter Wentworth throws a flood of light on the subject in a speech that he delivered in the Parliament of 1576. Apparently, after drafting their main bill the Commons submitted it to Archbishop Parker, and on April 25th Wentworth was one of six Members deputed to hear his comments. He tells us: 'I was amongst others, the last Parliament, sent unto the bishop of Canterbury for the Articles of Religion that then passed this House. He asked us why we did put out of the book the Articles for the Homilies, consecrating of bishops, and such like.

' "Surely, sir," said I, "because we were so occupied in other matters that we had no time to examine them, how they agreed with the word of God."

' "What!" said he, "surely you mistook the matter. You will refer yourselves wholly to us therein."

' "No, by the faith I bear to God!" said I: "we will pass nothing before we understand what it is, for that were but to make you Popes. Make you Popes who list," said I, "for we will make you none." '

When Wentworth and his colleagues reported back to the Commons, the House proved no less stout-hearted. They may have spent much of the morning in discussion, but they decided to go ahead. Next day they gave the bill two readings and ordered its ingrossment; the following day they passed it; and this despite their own order of April 9th that no bill should be read twice within three days.[1] Their precipitate procedure was, and was meant to be, an unmistakable sign of solidarity and determination.

The bill went to the Lords, and there on April 28th was given a first reading. It got no further: which is not surprising, for it was intolerable that the Commons should act as censors of

[1] Hooker, p. 476.

the articles of faith. On May 1st the Lords transmitted to the Commons a message to the effect 'that the Queen's Majesty, having been made privy to the said Articles, liketh very well of them, and mindeth to publish them and have them executed by the bishops, by direction of her Highness's regal authority of supremacy of the Church of England, and not to have the same dealt in by Parliament'. The voice was mild: tribute to the perilous times, the touchiness of the Commons over the Strickland affair, and perhaps to the fact that the subsidy bill was not yet through the Lower House. The voice was mild; but what anger must have been in the heart!

The loss of this main bill threatened to have a grievous effect on the dependent Bill B. It left the option for Puritan clergymen inoperative, and, unless the wording were changed, would subject them to subscription to the whole of the Articles. The bill, however, was still with the Commons. They had probably held up its progress with the deliberate purpose of watching the fate of their main bill. At the moment, Bill B stood at the ingrossing stage. It had been given an extra reading: perhaps a reflection of the criticism to which its compromise with the bishops had exposed it. It came before the House for a fourth and final reading on May 3rd, two days after the Queen's message. The Puritan leaders now had an angry, resolute House behind them. They proceeded to take their revenge by a major operation on the ingrossed text.

For more than three centuries the final wording of this famous act has puzzled people. Its meaning has been disputed; its historical background has been a mystery. And yet all the time the original parchment bill on which the Commons operated — now and for many years kept in the Victoria Tower at Westminster — has been at hand to yield up the secret. There we can see what they did. They struck out the three optional ways of subscribing to the Articles, renounced their former compromise with the bishops, and substituted the celebrated words of the statute, limiting subscription 'to all the Articles of Religion which only concern the confession of the true Christian faith and the doctrine of the sacraments' — that is, limiting all clerical subscription to the doctrinal Articles. On that roll of parchment we can see the triumph of Peter Wentworth and his colleagues: their determination to safeguard Puritan ministers, and their revolt against the bishops. Alas for them! They might be able to restrain the action of the State but not of the Church; and ecclesiastical discipline soon came to ignore the implication of their statute.

That fourth reading of the bill on May 3rd must have been a tempestuous occasion. Hooker tells us that 'there was much ado' concerning the words 'minister' and 'priest'. Our parchment tells the rest. Nothing would satisfy these men but for the Clerk, then and there during the debate, to take a knife and erase the word 'priest'. For the main amendment they probably had to send a committee into the Lobby or the Upper Chamber, and while at their task they eliminated the word 'minister' where they could. When their Clerk came to give the bill a normal title, consistently, deliberately, he called it 'A bill for *pastors* . . .': in the Lords, the higher Clerk changed the word to '*ministers*'. What Puritan-minded folk these Commons were!

A final point. Elizabeth could have outmanœuvred and outwitted the Lower House by arranging for the main bill to pass in the Lords, when Bill B would presumably have been left unchanged. She could then have vetoed the main bill at the end of the session, thus effectively nullifying the limiting provision for Puritan consciences in Bill B. She was surely astute enough to see this possibility, but did not dare to employ it. The moral is worthy of reflection.

## CHAPTER III

# RELIGION
## (CONTINUED)

WITH its lack of a sense of time and its failure to get on with essential business, this Parliament seems to have driven the Queen and Burghley almost to despair. The Queen tried to jolt them into action by a message on April 10th, which the Speaker did his poor best to implement by moving 'that from henceforth men making motions should bring them in writing'. Judging from our diary, neither had much effect. True, that morning the House set to and read twelve bills, as well as dealing with other business. On Good Friday — the 13th — they sat till 10 o'clock, got through six more bills, but then trooped off to hear the sermon at Court. They had done little before Easter, and made a wretched start again on April 19th, after Easter. On the 21st Burghley tried to ginger things up by asking the Speaker for a list of the bills in his House, showing the stage each had reached: to which list the unhappy man added a postscript — 'Note, we have sitten but eleven days'. The same day — on the Queen's instructions, says Hooker — the Lords asked for a conference and told Members that 'as the season of the year waxed very hot and dangerous for sickness, so they desired that this House would spend the time in proceeding with necessary bills for the Commonwealth, and lay aside all private bills in the meantime'. On April 26th they followed this up by demanding bills 'with speed': so far, however, only one had been passed! A shrewd parliamentary manager, Burghley may have expected something of the sort, for one notices that, from the first day of the session, presumably to escape hopeless delay, bills were being started in the Lords which normally would have been introduced through the Lower House. For example, the bill for continuation of statutes — whose dismal and embarrassing fate in 1566 may be remembered — was the first measure read in that House.[1]

One of the principal reasons why the Commons failed to

---

[1] *C.J.* i. 83-6; S.P. Dom. Eliz. 77/54; Hooker, pp. 479-80.

move quickly was the campaign for reforming the Church.
There were all those alphabetical bills from the last parliament.
By Easter a start had been made with Bills B, D, and E. Having
apparently incorporated the gist of Bill F in Bill E, F fell out of
the alphabet. But on May 10th they restored the score by pro-
ducing a Bill G, the purpose of which was to restrain the
'ordinary' — the bishop or his deputy — from commuting
penance without the advice of two J.P.s: surely a remarkable
example of lay effrontery.[1] They managed to get Bill C started
on May 12th.

Their reforming zeal, however, was not limited to these bills,
nor to the bill for coming to Church, and Strickland's bill on
the Prayer Book. At the end of the morning on April 14th,
before rising for the few days' recess over Easter — psychologically a favourable moment for another sally — George
Carleton, our active Puritan, exhibited a bill against licences,
dispensations, faculties, and rescripts granted by the Archbishop of Canterbury: that prerogative right of sanctioning
breaches of the Canon Law which had belonged to the Papacy
and had been transferred to the Archbishop by Henry VIII's
Dispensations Act in 1534. Carleton's bill reversed this act:
'by which statute' 'procured by the bishop of that time', 'the
Bishop of Canterbury', he declared, 'is made as it were a Pope':
surely a curious slight upon the memory of Cranmer to come
from a Protestant. The bill, by a typical Puritan limitation
that was much stricter than the corresponding limitation in
Henry VIII's statute, forbade any such grant 'contrary to the
word of God'.

The Speaker seems to have done his best to counter Carleton's action, putting a question to the House whether the bill
should be read. But bishop-baiting was evidently much to their
liking. They agreed to a formal reading. In the long run the
bill was passed (though in a form redrafted by a committee)
and got as far as a second reading in the Upper House. The
Lords had plenty of time to pass it, if they had so wished.
Clearly, a second reading was as far as they were willing to go
to humour the Lower House.

[1] *C.J.* i. 88; Hooker, p. 485. The entry under May 15th in *C.J.* i. 89 for the
second reading of Bill C is a misprint for Bill G. The second reading of Bill C was
on the previous day.

The debate provoked by this bill is not without interest. At its first reading, after Carleton's speech, it was immediately criticized by a civil lawyer, Francis Alford, a man with experience in ecclesiastical courts and an inveterate conservative. He thought the measure impracticable. Dispensations for marriage and for clerical non-residence, he argued, had to depend on somebody's discretion. They could not be precisely limited as in the bill.

This brought Yelverton — a common lawyer — to his feet. No Christian, he declared, would reason contrary to a bill which provided only that licences should not be granted against the word of God. As for discretion, he knew not what it meant; but Alford's speech was not an example of it. He thought the bill did not get to the root of the evil. It might, indeed, be a delicate matter to probe, but no Christian bishop had need of a liberty contrary to the express word of God.

Others spoke. Dalton, in cynical mood, was inclined to think that the bill accomplished nothing; another Member valued it for its penalties; Serjeant Manwood, an outstanding lawyer, was for first elucidating their griefs and the abuses of the system and then devising remedies.

Fleetwood intervened, 'learnedly and withal pleasantly', entertaining the House with a display of his knowledge, wit, and irrelevance. He discussed the word 'discretion', saying he had read it often. 'The Queen is sworne to minister justice with mercy and discretion. What mercy is, he said he knew; but what discretion was he would gladly learn.' It came 'out of the word *discerno*, to see; but that is uncertain'. 'A good *quorum* of England — a bench of J.P.s — was governed by wisdom and discretion . . . The law is, it should be so.' But 'if a poor man have law on his side, then they say their discretions will not serve them; and when conscience doth give it him, then they say the law is against them'. This pleasantry led him to have a dig at some nameless person — 'whom he meant, many did guess', says our diarist — who had said publicly to him: 'You are a lawyer, but I am a judge.' 'This man', added Fleetwood, 'might have wit, but he neither had law, wisdom, nor discretion, other than in his own judgment.' And so he meandered on, to finish by supporting Serjeant Manwood's suggestion.

Another serjeant-at-law, William Lovelace, joined in. He

obviously sympathized with the grievance but thought the remedy useless, pointing out that a temporal judge, given trial of licences that were contrary to the word of God, would nevertheless, 'by the ancient laws of the realm and by order', need a certificate from the bishop, and no bishop would testify against himself. How far all the criticisms were met in the subsequent re-drafting of the bill, we have no means of knowing.[1]

Much time must have been spent on this debate, and the hour was probably late, but the House, like an inebriate, succumbed to further indulgence. Thomas Norton asked that 'by warrant of this Court', and 'by the wisdom and godly care' which was to be used in matters of weight, order should be taken against benefit of clergy: that ancient privilege of the clergy, which in effect allowed 'clerks' (in a very broad construction of the word) to escape punishment for many crimes, including murder and most felonies.

He described it as 'the shameful and most hateful usage among the ecclesiastical judges for delivering of clerks convict upon their oaths': 'manifest perjury by their law against all law'. As a common lawyer and a Puritan, the whole business seemed to him outrageous. It could not be said to be a liberty of the Church, 'except they will claim a liberty to sin: wherein, indeed, their principal liberty hath stood, for the which they have not spared to hazard, nay to give, both their bodies and souls to become traitors to God and man'. He instanced Thomas Becket in Henry II's reign: 'Thus did that rebel, Bishop Becket, whose principal quarrel and chief cause of all his stir was that the King would have punished one of his mark, a priest, for an abominable incest . . .: which trifling fault, forsooth, this holy Saint could not brook to be rebuked by a temporal judge.' The final passage of the speech, exposing the procedure by which convicted clerks were 'purged', and 'declaring, of truth' — as our diarist remarks — 'so disordered and hateful doings', stirred the House into a resolve to redress the abuse. They authorized Norton to make inquiries and 'deal therein accordingly': that is, to draft a bill.

With so much business to get through, it is not surprising that Norton's bill — 'against perjury in clerks convict' — did not emerge until May 11th. But the House then made up for lost

[1] C.J. i. 84, 87, 88; L.J. i. 684, 685, 698; Anon. Diary, April 14th.

time. They immediately read it twice and ordered its ingrossment, and passed it on May 14th. In the Lords it got as far as
a second reading and a committee. That — understandably —
was the end of it. And the moral? How readily this House of
Commons responded when one of their radical leaders gave
the cry, 'The hunt is up!'[1]

After Easter, once they had got William Strickland safely
back into their company, they behaved more responsibly and
thought rather more about getting through with their business.
They agreed to start work at 7 a.m., and from May 11th added
afternoon sessions to their labours. On April 21st came the
Lords' injunction to make haste, and a list of ten bills which
their lordships hoped would be given priority. The only
religious bill included was the one for coming to church. On
the 24th the Commons themselves ordered a list of the bills
offered into their House to be prepared against the morrow;
but as the morrow proved to be the day when Archbishop
Parker's angry comments were made on their main Articles
bill, it was not until the 26th that the list was read. A committee
was then appointed to place the bills in order of priority, not
rejecting any. Perhaps the committee was too heavily weighted
with staider Members to suit either the radicals or the majority
of the House. At any rate, two days later, by which time this
committee must have made its choice — perhaps a disappointing one — the House set up another committee, consisting of
only four Members, all Puritans and including Strickland and
Yelverton, to sort the bills for religion into what they thought
the best order of precedence. There was not a single Privy
Councillor to act as a brake on the zealots.[2]

Of all the religious bills, the one for coming to church and
receiving the Communion occupied most time in passing. This
bill, after its second reading on April 6th, had been committed
to a small, responsible committee, containing no hotheads.
They recast it, and it was given a first reading as a new bill on
April 9th.

There followed 'sundry motions and many long arguments'.
Mr. Aglionby, Member for Warwick, made a notable speech.
He began on a theme congenial to most, criticizing a proviso

[1] Anon. Diary, April 14th; *C.J.* i. 84, 89; *L.J.* i. 688, 691, 692.
[2] *C.J.* i. 85-6.

which exempted gentlemen possessing private chapels. Plato, Cicero, and Lactantius Firmianus were cited in favour of his argument for equality between prince and poor man: 'all men do know and acknowledge that there is a God, and in this respect there should be no difference between man and man'. He approved of compulsory attendance at church. 'But for the other matter, concerning the receiving of the sacrament, he argued that it was not convenient to enforce consciences; and to that purpose he showed the authority of Doctors, which he vouched without quoting the place or sentence.' No law, he asserted, could make a man fit to receive the great mystery of God above. 'This whole speech', adds our diarist, 'he tempered with such discretion as in such a case was seemly, and whatsoever he spake, he spake the same under correction.'

Aglionby's discordant note aroused Strickland: 'to speak on a sudden and unprovided', he said. With the egalitarian proposal he of course agreed, but against the citation of Doctors on the issue of conscience 'he vouched out of Esdras that the . . . consciences of men were by the Prophet restrained'. 'Conscience may be free', he added, 'but not to disturb the common quiet. He showed the practice and doings of the Pope: the banishment of the Arians, etc. That the sword of the Prince, for lack of law, must not be tied. The Israelites', he said, 'were constrained to eat the Passover.' And finally, with a switch of argument, 'he concluded that it was no straitening of their consciences but a charge or loss of their goods, if they would not vouchsafe to be, as they should be, good men and true Christians'. How apt was our diarist's description of Strickland: 'a grave and ancient man of great zeal, and perhaps (as he himself thought) not unlearned'.

Dalton also answered Aglionby, in a less biblical manner. His argument seems to have been that as law-makers they should not worry about other people's consciences or the oddities and obstinacy of evil, ignorant, or froward persons, but should 'proceed orderly to the discharge of their own consciences in making the law' and 'let them care for the rest whom it behoveth'. In short: a fig for conscience!

An earlier speaker had been afraid — unnecessarily some thought — of the dilemma that would be created should any minister, as frequently happened, depart from the prescribed order of the Prayer Book, thus making his parishioners liable to a fine under this bill if they stayed away, or a heavy penalty under the Act of Uniformity if they attended and so 'maintained' the minister in his breach of the law.

Fleetwood also spoke, seizing the opportunity to attack the ornaments rubric in the Book of Common Prayer, which had caused the deprivation of some of his clerical friends. 'Great consideration', he argued, 'was to be had of the old Book of Common Prayer, wherein some hidden things were carried as matters of no account, and yet are indeed laws. For, said he, coming to the Bishop of London, and desirous to learn the warrant' for 'deprivation of such as refused to fulfil some of the prescribed orders, I was willed to look on the Book of Common Prayer. Of all things under Heaven, I never looked (quoth he) for a law in the rubrics of a Matins book. But since it is so, let it be better looked to.' With words singularly appropriate to our present society, he urged 'that no authority should be given to others in hidden sort to ordain anything having the force of a law'.

The next day, as an appendix to this debate, a bill was read, which ultimately was to be attached to the main bill, permitting people in danger of arrest for debt — a situation in which so many Elizabethans found themselves — to go to and from church in safety.[1]

On April 20th, the main bill, in its new form, was read a second time, along with a proviso; and the debate stretched over into the next day when a new proviso and an addition were also read. All were committed, and it is significant that on this occasion the Puritan leaders got some of their own number on to the committee.

The second-reading debate had brought another excellent speech from Mr. Aglionby, deploring the assault upon conscience. Attendance at church he described as tolerable and convenient: it but proves a man a Christian and distinguishes him from the brute beasts. 'But the conscience of man is internal, invisible, and not in the power of the greatest monarch in the world; in no limits to be straitened, in no bonds to be contained.' Neither Jew nor Turk requires more than sub-

[1] *C.J.* i. 83-4; Anon. Diary, April 9th-10th.

mission to outward observance, and a convenient silence. 'To
enforce any to do the act which may tend to the discovery of
his conscience, it is never found.' Moreover, 'to be fit for so
great a mystery [as the Communion], God above of his free
gift may make a man. To come unworthily, the penalty is
appointed: St. Paul hath pronounced it to be death and damna-
tion, as guilty of the blood and death of Christ'.

Thomas Norton spoke. He conceded that 'where many men
be, there must be many minds': surely an impressive tribute to
Aglionby's manner and discretion, for Norton was rarely
tolerant. On the point at issue, he contended that 'not only the
external and outward show is to be sought, but the very secrets
of the heart in God's cause . . . must come to a reckoning, and
the good seed so sifted from the cockle that the one may be
known from the other'. Straying from the point, he moved that
all suspected of Papistry should be subject to an oath, acknowledging the Queen to be Queen for anything the Pope in any
respect might do. Receiving the Communion must be the very
touchstone of trial as to 'who be those rebellious calves whom the
[Papal] Bull hath begotten'.

To meet the dilemma, mentioned earlier, about attendance
at irregularly conducted services, Norton suggested a proviso
that 'mistaking of chapters, misreading, etc., should be reckoned
for no offence, so that there be no Mass sung or Popish service
used in Latin, etc.' He seems to have devised a proviso along
these lines, which was added to the bill; and one suspects that
he may have drafted it in such a way as to excuse or countenance
some of the irregularities of Puritan ministers, for a Privy Councillor, Sir Thomas Smith, objected to it next day.[1]

Alas! the incomplete state of our diary prevents us from
following the debates any further. The bill was read a third
time on April 30th and ingrossed. It was read again and passed
on May 4th, and the following day was sent to the Lords with
an impressive escort of twenty-nine Members to signify the
importance attached to it.[2]

The Lords put it through the normal routine of three readings
and a committal before passing it with amendments and
against the formal dissent of four lay peers. The French am-

---

[1] *C.J.* i. 85; Anon. Diary, April 20th-21st.
[2] *C.J.* i. 86-8; Hooker, p. 481.

bassador — a disappointing guide for this Parliament — reports some of the peers as saying that it was intolerable that bishops and ministers, who at the beginning of the reign pretended nought save to preach the word of God in fear and humility, should have now become so arrogant that they are not content with lording it over the people, but also wish to subject the nobility to their authority.[1]

The ambassador's report may perhaps indicate that the Commons had deleted the proviso exempting gentlemen with private chapels, to which Aglionby and others had objected, and had made the bill apply to all subjects, noble and simple: in which case, the odds are that the Upper House reinserted the proviso. At any rate, they had clearly made alterations to which the Commons objected, for on the return of the bill to them they immediately sought a conference with the Lords. Two days later, after much discussion, they remained discontented; and on one particular point — this one of exemption, it would seem — they actually carried a resolution, deciding that the Bill was 'to be general as to the body thereof'. Another conference with the Lords seems to have led to some sort of compromise; and, after passing to and fro between the two Houses, agreed amendments were made, and on May 25th the bill was formally 'concluded'. It now awaited the royal answer at the end of the session.[2]

Elizabeth vetoed it. The trouble taken by the Lords to ensure that the bill should not be lost through any vital disagreement between the two Houses is certain proof that a substantial majority in their House ardently desired the law. There is reason to think that Lord Burghley and the Privy Council were in favour of it. Most, perhaps all, of the bishops were; and we know only too well that the Commons were. The veto was therefore imposed by the Queen in defiance of her advisers: a striking illustration of personal monarchy. Tolerance was undoubtedly her motive. She refused to go back on her liberal declarations of 1570; she would open no window into men's souls.

The fortunes of the alphabetical bills on religion can be quickly told. Bill C — 'against pluralities of benefices, non-

[1] L.J. i. 681-8; La Mothe Fénélon, Correspondance Diplomatique, iv. 106.
[2] C.J. i. 91-2; L.J. i. 695-7; Hooker, pp. 486-7.

residence, and . . . [for] sermons to be had in every parish'[1] —
got no further than a first reading in the Lords. It cannot have
been attractive either to the bishops or the more orthodox
peers. It was probably impracticable and obnoxious: its pedigree
was proclaimed by the tell-tale word 'pastors' in its title. Bill D
— 'against corrupt presentations' — got through the Lords with
amendments on a majority vote, but as the Commons, after a
conference of both Houses, would not agree to the changes, the
Lords received it back and rejected it.[2]  Bill E, known during
its passage as a bill against simony, ultimately became a statute
with the longer title of 'An Act touching leases of benefices and
other ecclesiastical livings with cure'. Apart from Bill B, it was
the only one of the series to succeed. Bill G did not emerge
from the committee to which the Lords sent it.[3]

A poor harvest after so much labour; yet profoundly significant. Viewed as a whole, the programme of reform this
session had envisaged the sort of Church for which the Marian
exiles and the House of Commons had toiled in the first Parliament of the reign, and, under a less resolute or more radically-
minded Sovereign, might have achieved. Hitherto, the Elizabethan Religious Settlement had seemed to depend, and depend
almost solely, on the determination of the Queen. The significance of 1571 is that though the Queen herself was directly
responsible for the failure of the campaign, the bishops also
emerged as its critics and opponents. The common front of
1559 was dissolved. Conditions were ripe for nonconformity to
move on to Presbyterianism; for radicals to become revolutionaries.

---

[1] This is the descriptive title in a list of bills prepared for Burghley (S.P. Dom.
Eliz. 78/11). Its proper title was 'For the residence of pastors upon their benefices'
(cf. *L.J.* i. 688).
[2] *L.J.* i. 689, 699 (the marginal entry of 'conclusa' proves, on examination of the
MS. Journal, to be an error, and really belongs to the previous bill); *C.J.* i. 91, 92.
[3] *L.J.* i. 692.

## CHAPTER IV

# THE TREASONS BILL AND OTHER TOPICS

THE Government had its legislative programme. It wanted money. It also wanted certain measures made necessary by the recent national crisis. Proceedings did not go according to plan: and one reason was the tactless enthusiasm, or obsequiousness, of a gentleman, Mr. Robert Newdigate, Member for Buckingham.

On April 7th, after Strickland had got the House started with the alphabetical bills on religion — and perhaps while Members were still intent on pursuing that absorbing topic — Mr. Newdigate, instead of awaiting the customary official motion for supply, 'moved that where one of the causes for the calling of the Parliament (and perhaps the chiefest) was for a subsidy, he thought it not amiss to make offer' of the grant 'before it should be required'. Both our anonymous diarist and Hooker note that the motion 'was much misliked'. It may well be that some Members were ready in any case to couple supply with grievances, but irritation at what was regarded as an attempt to curry favour at Court must have soured the humour of the assembly.

Sir Francis Knollys, surprised into doing his duty as senior Privy Councillor, rose after Newdigate. A wordy man at the best of times, his effect on the House was laconically reported by our diarist: 'a long needless discourse concerning the subsidy'. He was followed by the radical lawyer, Robert Bell, whose prominent part in the succession agitation of 1566 had provoked a scathing comment by the Queen. 'A subsidy', said he, 'was by every good subject to be yielded unto'; but it would be difficult to levy, because the people were robbed by two means. One was licences: royal letters patent granting privileges to individuals contrary to some law — a practice sound enough within reason. The other was the abuse of promoters or informers. 'By licences', he declared, 'a few only were enriched and the multitude impoverished'; adding, 'that if a burthen should be laid on the backs of the commons, and no

redress of the common evils, then there might haply ensue that
they would lay down the burthen in the midst of the way and
turn to the contrary of their duty.' Not a diplomatic speech;
and his attack on licences struck at courtiers' perquisites as well
as the Queen's prerogative.

Bell's courageous lead was infectious. Another lawyer, Mr.
Popham — and if John, not brother Edward, then a future
Speaker like Bell — confirmed what had been said, and added
another abuse. This was the practice of 'treasurers of the
Crown, who have in their hands great masses of money, with
the which either they themselves or some friends of theirs do
purchase lands to their own use, and after become bankrupt',
causing their debt to be enstalled. He instanced a recent case of
a debt of £30,000, which, he said, had occasioned the present
lack of money in the Exchequer. In fact, he was denouncing a
chronic evil of the times, one that resisted all attempts at
eradication. Holders of Crown moneys seem to have postponed accounting as long as possible, meanwhile employing the
cash in their private transactions. Periodically there was a
gross scandal, like the one mentioned by Popham: minor cases
must have been many. The Crown might be said to have been
acting, willy-nilly, as a benevolent, non-interest-charging, all-
risks-bearing bank to supply its officials and others with
capital. Some — perhaps most — of those cases of public servants dying heavily in debt to the Queen, which have drawn
from posterity many tears and barbed criticism of royal
ingratitude, derive from this type of fraud. Each age and each
society has its stubborn ills: this was one from which the
immature Elizabethan state machinery could not free itself.

After Popham, Serjeant Lovelace: 'Every loyal subject ought
to yield to the relief of the Prince, and that without any condition or limitation.' Having uttered this fine sentiment, he
added to the tale 'three abuses more'. They all touched the
prerogative. The old yet ever new grief of purveyance was the
first. And here he was far-sighted enough to suggest the solution which ultimately became Burghley's policy: replace the
whole system by county compositions. His other two abuses
were in the royal Exchequer: the fleecing of tenants-in-chief of
the Crown by the charges for respite of homage and the
expenses involved by the writ *quo titulo ingressus est*.

The Comptroller of the Royal Household, the official responsible for purveyance, now intervened to promise his best endeavours over that grievance. But when he sat down, another gentleman got up to voice another complaint, or rather, an extension of Popham's. He added collectors of subsidies to Crown treasurers. They retained the money a year or more in their hands, often converted it to their own use, and, being mean men, defaulted. People were therefore unwilling to pay. Better quality collectors and prompt payment were his remedy.

There were probably other speeches and other grievances, but the debate ended as it began, Newdigate's role being played by Henry Goodere, a gentleman who had fallen under the spell of Mary Queen of Scots since we last met him as 'Goodere the glorious', a member of our 1566 'choir'. He wanted immediate action on the subsidy and on that alone, 'without the hearing of any more complaints . . . They might be infinite; and already more were remembered than in one Parliament could be reformed'. 'Wherein, surely', adds our diarist, 'he showed a great desire to win favour.'

About the sentiment of the House there was no doubt. They appointed a committee 'for motions of griefs and petitions' to draft the necessary bills, and authorized those who had made the motions to collect notes and hand them to the committee. Here was the first committee for grievances: a procedure which was to develop in later Elizabethan and early Stuart Parliaments, and, as one of the Commons' standing committees, was to be a prime factor in winning the initiative in public, as distinct from private, legislation. Of course, Parliament had always been an organ for the expression of grievances, and in medieval times the initiative in petitioning, on which statutory action was based, had belonged to the Commons. We must therefore beware of implying too much novelty in Elizabethan days. But under the newer conditions of the modern State, it was the Crown which so far had been accustomed to give the necessary thought to first-line legislation at each Parliament. The new device of a committee for grievances was calculated to appropriate a share in that role for the House of Commons: to provide the House, as it were, with a Privy Council of its own.[1]

Before we follow the activities of our committee, we must hear

[1] Anon. Diary, April 7th; Hooker, p. 476; *C.J.* i. 83.

about the repercussions of the debate itself. Bell had been the most conspicuous of the speakers. He began it all. In attacking licences he probed the prerogative to the quick. Peter Wentworth is our sole authority for what followed. He told the story to a committee of the House when he himself was in trouble for an indiscreet speech in 1576.

'The last Parliament, he that is now Speaker — Bell — uttered a very good speech for the calling in of certain licences granted to four courtiers, to the utter undoing of six or eight thousand of the Queen's Majesty's subjects. This speech was so disliked of some of the Council that he was sent for and so hardly dealt with that he came into the House with such an amazed countenance that it daunted all . . . For ten, twelve, or sixteen days there was not one of the House that durst deal in any matter of importance, and in those simple matters that they dealt in, they spent more words and time in their preamble, requiring that they might not be mistaken, than they did in the matter they spake unto . . . This rumour grew in the House: "Sirs, you may not speak against licences: the Queen's Majesty will be angry; the Council will be too, too angry".' The Committee examining Wentworth acknowledged that they had heard the rumour; and doubtless the chastening of Mr. Bell did lead to apologetic preambles and a certain restraint in speech. But the men of 1571, as our narrative has surely shown, were far from supine. Fanatics like Wentworth and Pistor were not good judges of the subtle difference between the atmosphere of 1566 (which would have pleased them better) and that of 1571.[1]

Our diarist tells us that the Queen's message of April 10th, enjoining Members 'to speak of matters already proponed only, and not to make new motions, every man at his own pleasure' — in other words, freedom of speech but not of initiative — grew out of Bell's speech. While admitting that Bell 'seemed to speak against her prerogative', the diarist added: 'but surely, so orderly did he utter what he spake, as those who were touched might be angry, but justly to blame him might not be'.[2]

If we can believe the diarist, on April 14th, as the final item before rising for Easter, Sir Humphrey Gilbert put up some

---

[1] Inner Temple Petyt MS. 538/17, fol. 252b.
[2] Anon. Diary, April 10th.

unknown and obviously dim lackey to remind the House of the grievances mentioned in the debate of April 7th, in order that he, Sir Humphrey, might deliver himself, 'in fine speech', of a prepared — and much detested — lecture on the prerogative.

Alluding back to Bell's motion, Gilbert endeavoured to prove it a vain device and perilous, 'since it tended to be derogatory of the prerogative imperial, which whoso should attempt, in his fancy could not otherwise be accounted than for an open enemy'. To say the Queen is not to use the privilege of the Crown, is to say she is not Queen. 'If we should in any sort meddle with these matters, her Majesty might look to her own power . . . and do as did Lewis of France, who (as he termed it) delivered the Crown there out of wardship.' Other kings had absolute power, for example, in Denmark and Portugal, where, as the Crown became more free, so all subjects were thereby rather made slaves.[1]

The late hour allowed of no adequate reply, but during the Easter break Peter Wentworth addressed himself to the task. On April 20th he interrupted the reading of bills to speak 'touching the liberties and privileges of the House'. He was concerned at the false information given to the Queen about Bell's speech and at the disclosure of 'the secrets of the House': a theme which implied another novel claim, namely, that their proceedings, or at any rate their speeches, should not be reported to the Crown. So far as we know, it was Wentworth's maiden speech. As became his nature it was forthright. Says Hooker, he called Gilbert 'a flatterer, a liar, and a naughty man'.

'Mr. Wentworth', reports our diarist, 'very orderly, in many words, remembered the speech of Sir Humphrey Gilbert, delivered some days before. He proved his speech (without naming him) to be an injury to the House. He noted his disposition to flatter or fawn on the Prince, comparing him to the chameleon, which can change himself into all colours saving white: even so, said he, this reporter can change himself to all fashions but honesty. He showed further the great wrong done to one of the House by a misreport made to the Queen (meaning Mr. Bell). He showed his [Gilbert's] speech to tend to no other end than to inculcate fear into those which should be

[1] Anon. Diary, April 14th.

free. He requested care for the credit of the House and for the maintenance of free speech (the only means of orderly proceedings), and to preserve the liberty of the House to reprove liars, inveighing greatly out of the Scriptures and otherwise . . .: as thus of David — "Thou, O Lord, shalt destroy liars!" '

Sir Humphrey Gilbert may have played the sycophant, but he was no coward. He attempted to reply, but, as Hooker tells us, 'he had the denial three times by the House': which we may interpret as a very noisy barracking. The Speaker tried to restore agreement and unity, 'making signification that the Queen's Majesty had in plain words declared to him that she had good intelligence of the orderly proceedings amongst us, whereof she had as good liking as ever she had of any Parliament since she came unto the crown'. It was not saying much, seeing how difficult all her three previous Parliaments had been: however, a little diplomatic prevarication rarely comes amiss. The Speaker added a wish that they would not give the Queen cause to change her opinion. And then he told them that she had promised to take order about licences, 'wherein she had been careful, and more careful would be': a placatory gesture, as well as an intimation that grievances arising from the operation of the prerogative must be remedied by royal and not legislative action.[1]

Normally, such an assurance of royal favour would have delighted and appeased the House; but the restraint of Strickland was an impediment to rapture, and the Speaker's seductive words merely evoked Carleton's motion on that subject. It looks very much as if Wentworth, Carleton, and others had spent the Easter recess preparing a concerted defence of parliamentary liberties.

But we must return to the committee on grievances. Two of the subjects referred to it had been removed by alternative action, or promise of action: licences, by the Queen's promise, and purveyance by the Comptroller's. A third had been anticipated in the House of Lords; for already when the Commons' debate took place, the Upper House had given a second reading to a government bill which ultimately became law as 'An act to make the lands, tenements, goods, and chattels of tellers, receivers, etc. liable to the payment of their debts'.

[1] Hooker, p. 479; Anon. Diary, April 20th; *C.J.* i. 85.

Burghley, one suspects, was its parent; and it is significant that he started it in the Lords, not the Commons. Though both Houses wanted the bill, it proved difficult to frame satisfactorily. The Lords discarded a first version and proceeded with a new bill. In the Commons there were 'many long arguments', and again a new bill was devised. Be it added that the abuse persisted, major scandals recurred, and despite this law the Crown failed to recoup itself.[1]

Concerning other grievances, the committee did draft bills. The first was a bill 'for reformation of promoters', which was ready in draft, though not read, on April 21st, and was included in the list of bills which the Lords that day asked the Commons to expedite. Again, though both Houses felt the grievance, devising a satisfactory remedy proved difficult: in this instance, too difficult. The Commons rejected the first bill 'after many long arguments', and appointed a committee to draft a new one. This was amended in the Lords, amended again in the Commons, and then lapsed, either because time was too pressing, or, more likely, because the Commons' amendments were not acceptable.[2]

The second bill dealt with the two Exchequer abuses — respite of homage, and the writ *quo titulo*. Here Parliament was on delicate ground, for throughout her reign Elizabeth regarded Exchequer affairs as an intimate part of the prerogative. Curiously enough, this bill was another of those which the Lords asked the Commons to hasten. The peers were the victims of such abuses quite as much as the country gentlemen, and they were clearly allowing their feelings as individuals to overcome constitutional niceties. Once more the bill presented difficulties. A new one had to be substituted. When it got to the Lords, they did not like it and, after conference with the Commons, drafted a third bill. Perhaps time was its enemy; perhaps — and this seems more likely — Burghley received a hint from the Queen. At any rate, it was allowed to sleep out the remaining few days of the session after being committed on its first reading. Certainly the Queen was told of the bill; and at the end of the session, during a curious personal intervention

---

[1] *L.J.* i. 669 seqq.; *C.J.* i. 84 seqq.; *Statutes of Realm*, IV. i. 535-7.
[2] *C.J.* i. 85 seqq.; *L.J.* i. 685 seqq. The former is defective in its entries for this bill. Hooker, p. 483, supplies one omission.

while the ceremony of the royal assent was in progress, she seems to have referred to the grievance and promised 'in time' to take order herself for its remedy. She made the same promise about a bill for limiting lawyers' fees, which, right at the end of the session, was rushed through the Upper House in two days, passed the Commons almost as quickly, and was sent back on the closing afternoon, perhaps with some alterations that the Lords had not time to confirm: an odd episode.[1]

The Commons had another pet grievance which they vainly tried to be rid of. This was the clause in Burghley's navy act of 1563, which made Wednesday an additional fish day: 'Cecil's Fast'. It will be remembered that they had disliked this provision on both gastronomic and religious grounds. Their gastronomic objections presumably remained as firm; their detestation of Popish practices was fiercer than ever; and Burghley was no longer among them to counter passion with statistics, though they might have reflected that he was in 'another place'. In three days, with the greatest of ease, they passed a bill which the Clerk delightfully and expressively entitled, 'against Wednesdays'. The Lords read it once: then oblivion. Burghley was in that House.[2]

But it is time that we turned to the main government bills of the session. One of them furnishes a dramatic story. The government's legislative answer to the Northern Rebellion and the Papal Bull was contained in several measures: a new treasons act; an act against the bringing in and execution of Papal Bulls and other instruments; an act against fugitives over the sea, depriving them of their goods and their revenues from lands — the type of bill which the House of Commons rejected in Mary's reign, when Protestants were to be the victims; and an act to confirm the attainders of the northern rebels. It is the first of these — the treasons act — which provides our story.

This bill, we know, was drafted by the Queen's learned counsel. At the close of the session Elizabeth herself had something to say about its origin: 'In this Parliament it was showed us of a bill devised of for our safety against treasons, whereof, when we had the sight, it liked us not. Nevertheless, being persuaded by our Council of the necessity thereof, and that it

---

[1] Anon. Diary, April 12th; *C.J.* i. 84 seqq.; *L.J.* i. 681 seqq.; Hooker, p. 490.
[2] *C.J.* i. 89-90; *L.J.* i. 688, 690.

was for our safety, we were contented the same should proceed.'[1]
As presented to the Commons, it contained in substance only
the first clause of the final statute, making it high treason to
imagine or practise the death or bodily harm of the Queen, to
practise against the Crown or to write or signify that Elizabeth
was not lawful Queen, or to publish, speak, write, etc., that she
was an heretic, schismatic, tyrant, infidel, or usurper. The bill
was devised to meet the dangers revealed by the recent national
crisis, and its provisions were based principally on Henry
VIII's treasons act of 1534.[2]

After its first reading on April 9th, Thomas Norton immediately rose, and in 'a long discourse' declared 'that her Majesty
was and is the only pillar and stay of all our safety, as well for our
public good as for the state of religion; and for religion the very
basis and pillar throughout Christendom'. 'Our care, prayer,
and chief endeavour' must be for the preservation of her estate.
He liked the bill, but it did not go far enough, and he therefore
produced another bill, devised by himself, which he asked the
House to tack on to it.

Norton's 'addition' was about the succession to the throne.
It took away all right or title from anyone — and from the
children of such a person — who 'hath [made] or hereafter
shall make claim to the crown of England during her Majesty's
life, or shall say she hath not lawful right, or shall refuse to
acknowledge her to be undoubted Queen'. It was to be treason
to aid and maintain any such person, or 'to say or hold opinion
that the Queen's Majesty, with the Court of Parliament, hath
no authority' to determine the succession.

Since Mary Queen of Scots could be said to have laid claim
to Elizabeth's throne in 1558-59 — quite apart from her purpose in the intrigues accompanying the Northern Rebellion —
the retrospective character of these provisions was fatal to her
claim to the succession and to that of her son, James. Norton
intended it so: that we can be sure. And if he and the House
could have known that, while their discussions were proceeding
in these weeks, Burghley was actually on the track of the Ridolfi
conspiracy, already holding clues that led to Mary and a plot,
then indeed their vehemence would have passed all bounds.

Elizabeth herself must of course have shared Burghley's knowledge; and the magnanimity and statesmanship that she displayed during this Parliament will be seen dimly unless this is remembered.

Norton needed no stimulus — not even the Northern Rebellion, which had drawn two tracts from his pen — to direct his mind against Mary. Ten years before, he had collaborated with Thomas Sackville in writing the famous play *Gorboduc* — 'the first English tragedy' — the fifth act of which was nothing less than a tract on the succession, urging immediate parliamentary settlement of the question and the exclusion of Mary Queen of Scots.

> In which your parliament . . .
> Prefer the right, my lords . . .
> Right mean I his or hers, upon whose name
> The people rest by mean of native line,
> Or by the virtue of some former law,
> Already made their title to advance.
>
> Such one so born within your native land;
> Such one prefer, and in no wise admit
> The heavy yoke of foreign governance:
> Let foreign titles yield to public wealth.

The play was produced before Elizabeth in January 1561. If she listened to Act V in the later, printed version, one wonders what her reaction was: her reaction, for example, to the lines,

> These be the fruits your civil wars will bring.
> Hereto it comes when kings will not consent
> To grave advice, but follow wilful will.

Our diarist tells us that after Norton had spoken about his bill, 'Mr. Clere of Norfolk made hereupon a staggering speech: his conclusion I did not conceive.' Nor, of course, can we; but we can guess. Mr. Clere was a follower of the Duke of Norfolk;[1] and the last thing his group desired was any impediment to Mary Queen of Scots' prospects, with which were linked the Duke's and their own.

[1] Cf. my *Elizabethan House of Commons*, p. 195n.

Sir Francis Knollys spoke next, as a Privy Councillor who, though liking Norton's bill, felt constrained to urge that the two be kept separate. 'This', remarked our diarist, 'he uttered with many words.' Sir Nicholas Arnold then spoke, liking both bills, but shocked at the thought of revealing to posterity that Parliament believed there might be so wicked a man who would call so good a princess by so vile and hateful terms. Could not the government's bill achieve its purpose in general words? Sir Henry Norris, 'in a short, mild, and plain speech', expressed approval of the main bill and, from his recent experience as ambassador in France, suggested that it should be made treason to give aid to religious exiles. Fostered by help from England, these men were wholly bent on conspiring against the Queen and the State.

The two great debaters, Yelverton and Fleetwood, followed. Part of the government's bill, Yelverton thought, was already covered by Edward III's great Statute of Treasons; but he was in favour of both bills and of joining them as Norton proposed; and he commended the provision for excluding the heir — in effect, James of Scotland — from the succession. Fleetwood was all for caution; and he perhaps revealed the reason — in this lending some colour to Peter Wentworth's later complaint — by confessing that he himself 'for hasty speech' had recently sustained reproach. Alford, running true to form, echoed caution. The House concluded the debate by assigning a day for the second reading of the government's bill, leaving Norton's 'addition' as yet unread and unattached.[1]

On April 12th both bills were read, the one being given its second reading, the other its first. The opening speaker in the debate that followed was 'Goodere the glorious'. In September of this year he was to be imprisoned in the Tower for acting as intermediary between Mary and the Duke of Norfolk; and, appropriately enough, an apologetic poem which he wrote on his imprisonment was to be answered in a bitter parody by Thomas Norton.[2]

Both the sentiment and diction of Goodere's speech were evidently repulsive to our diarist, who reported that in 'a long speech' and 'with wrested eloquence', first protesting his loyalty

[1] Anon. Diary, April 9th, 12th; C.J. i. 83.
[2] B. H. NEWDIGATE, Michael Drayton & His Circle, pp. 27-9.

to the Queen, the State, and the House of Commons, he proceeded to criticize some of his fellow-Members, doubting their sincerity to the Crown and accusing them of being 'doubly disposed and with a favourable affection bent for some special body'. He entirely approved of the government bill: if, indeed, the existing law did not render it superfluous. He would even add a new treason: namely, to say 'that the Papists do not err in . . . speaking so slanderously of her Majesty'. But — as became his new loyalty — he denounced the retrospective character of Norton's addition. It was 'a precedent most perilous'. 'Of present time man's wisdom might judge, of future time man's policy may reach to, but to call again the times past . . . man may not.' He had read thousands of laws, 'yet did he never find such a precedent'. He pointed out that they had not been told the Queen's views. 'Withal, it may haply occasion dislike between her Majesty and the House, which were odious and hateful.' Certainly it would create great peril. He advised, and vehemently urged, them to stay, insinuating that Norton had a secret purpose — to deal with the title to the succession: a comment with which we must surely agree.

Goodere's partisan speech gave Sir Thomas Smith the opportunity of suggesting that the two bills should be kept apart, lest one hinder the other. But Norton then rose, and 'with his accustomed manner of natural eloquence' — to which our diarist likewise paid tribute by the length of his report — trounced Goodere. Free speech should be also free of unjust slanders. His sole purpose in his bill was, he asserted, the preservation of her Majesty, 'she being of this Realm not only, in respect of our goods and lives, the singular stay, but for truth and religion, yea of all Christendom, not *magna*, but in this world *spes sola*'. He defended the retrospective character of his bill with the reflection that 'where ambition hath once entered, such is the nature of the same that it never will be satisfied, and the thirst for a kingdom is unquenchable'. The overthrow of a Crown is not compassed in a day, 'and therefore what hereafter is thought or meant to be executed is already begun, compassed, and devised'. Little did he know how apt, how fearfully apt, these last words were. He quoted precedents from Mary Tudor's reign — one of which he got a little wrong — to show that retrospective legislation was not the innovation

Goodere claimed it to be. As for the charge of partiality against himself, he retorted with *tu quoque*: 'it might seem by the gentleman's earnestness who spake, that someone his friend, whom he was bent to serve, should be touched'.

Again the official voice intervened: this time the Comptroller of the Royal Household. 'After some declaration of grief, perceiving the matter grew to heat (as verily' — says our diarist — 'the greatest number of the House were more than moved with the vehemency of Mr. Goodere's speech)' he urged the separation of the two bills.

Mr. Snagge — probably the abler of the two brothers — then spoke, expressing his dislike both of retrospective legislation and Marian precedents. He thought Edward III's Statute of Treasons sufficient to meet Norton's fears. Sir Francis Knollys followed, and for once our diarist — a friend of Norton's — made no caustic comment on his verbosity. Knollys, in fact, was now his true self, allowing his conscience and not his office to speak. He revealed that the Queen had been told about the proposals before the House, and that the Council had conferred about them. There can be little doubt that both were opposed to tacking Norton's bill to the government's; but Knollys confessed that for his part 'he could not utterly dislike' it. He defended Norton's retrospective provision and denounced Goodere's vehemency. The Queen was mild. Her clemency should be tempered with authority. Together, they 'could never grow to cruelty'. With a hint that his real views were even more downright, he ended.

An anonymous speaker then made a long speech emphatically supporting the joining of the two bills. He had some detailed proposals to make for strengthening the law. He wanted to add 'Papist' to the treasonable words of slander, explaining that some 'do not spare to say her Majesty is of another religion than is published' and that her Councillors, not she, are solely responsible for the doctrine of the Church: an interesting comment in view of the occasional tendency in our day to revive this myth. Monson, the eminent leader of 1566, spoke to the same general effect.

Thomas Heneage now stood up, and as a rising favourite at Court advised the House either to keep the bills separate (which of course would have brought Norton's bill to a peaceful end in the House of Lords), or to refer both to the Queen's learned counsel (another, perhaps less peaceful, road to death). He found a supporter in William Fleetwood, who, in his new role of caution, piled up precedents for the argument. But such timidity was adequately countered — if that was needed — by a weighty speech from Serjeant Manwood. There were other speakers, says our diarist, citing the names of Alford and Dalton who must have cancelled each other out. They added nothing to the argument.[1]

In the end, the House was for Norton. They decided to join the two bills, and committed them to a large committee, which included all Privy Councillors and many of the debaters, even the egregious Goodere. At this point we lose the help of our diary, and the story becomes difficult to reconstruct. But on April 14th the House authorized the legal members of the committee to confer with the Queen's learned counsel. It was an ominous sign. The Norton party was probably in a minority on the committee, and it looks as if the voice of authority was prevailing there.

Sure enough, when the committee reported back to the House on April 26th, there were still two bills, not one. They had ignored their instructions. Now, however, there was the general body of Members to be faced. The fight was renewed. The first and fundamental issue was this one of joining the bills, and Hooker tells us that there 'was much ado' before it was carried to a division, and by a majority of 36 — Hooker gives the figures as 170 to 138, a majority of 32 — the House reaffirmed its former decision. There followed 'many long arguments'. Opponents probably wanted some crucial amendments in Norton's bill, and perhaps a majority of the committee had drafted them. But from subsequent events it would seem that the radicals triumphed again. The House decided to have the composite bill ingrossed, and the next day gave it a third reading and passed it.[2]

What could the Lords do? They dared not separate the bills: that would have brought the marginal voters over to Norton, thus jeopardizing the government bill; and Burghley knew that the Queen would shed no tears in consequence. Provided they did not go too far, they could weaken Norton's sting by amend-

---

[1] Anon. Diary, April 12th.     [2] *C.J.* i. 84, 86; Hooker, p. 480.

ments; and in fact, after committing the bill, they passed it, with a new proviso and certain amendments. The proviso may have been one which has come down to us. If so, it authorized Elizabeth, at any time during her life, to reinstate the heir of anyone disabled by the operation of the act: in effect, to reinstate James of Scotland in his claims to the succession. This was to be done by proclamation.[1]

And now the obscurity deepens. The Commons received the bill back from the Lords on May 9th, but instead of reading the amendments, two days later they appointed a committee to confer first among themselves and afterwards with the Lords. For several days a joint-committee of both Houses seems to have been active devising new amendments. What had happened?

In all probability Burghley had shown the Queen a copy of the bill as it passed the Lords, and she had refused to approve of it. This is not wholly guesswork, for at the end of the session, before the royal assent was given to the bill, Elizabeth made a personal explanation to the assembled Lords and Commons. 'This bill', she said, 'being brought into the Lower House, some one learned man [Norton] did put to the same one other bill additional, which stretched so far that others [i.e. James] might unawares be entrapped, full much against our good will and pleasure. And this being brought unto us, we misliked it very much; being not of the mind to offer extremity or injury to any person. For as we mind no harm to others, so we hope none will mind [it] unto us. And therefore, reserving to every his right, we thought it not good to deal so hardly with anybody as by that bill was meant.'[2]

In face of the Queen's disapproval, with its implied threat of the veto, Lords and Commons were compelled to get together and try to amend it in a way acceptable to all three parties. Hence the activity of that joint-committee. The episode is an instructive sign of the flexibility and informality that could still be imposed on parliamentary procedure when everyone wished it.

Among the State Papers is a document, with an amendment by Burghley, which probably belongs to these final consulta-

[1] *L.J.* i. 677-83; S.P. Dom. Eliz. 88/37.
[2] *C.J.* i. 88-90; *L.J.* i. 686; Hooker, p. 490.

tions. It contains draft proposals for a new version of the
Norton clauses. The principal provision took away all claim to
the succession from anyone to whom a present right to the
throne had been or should be attributed, if that person did not,
on request from Elizabeth, acknowledge such right to be false
and recognize the undoubted title of Elizabeth herself. The
Queen's views were met by excluding the heir from any
penalty. True, the wording was still retrospective, and would
have made Mary Queen of Scots liable at once to a formal
demand for recognition of Elizabeth's title. But what hardship
was there in that? Indeed, it is amazing that Burghley, engaged
as he then was in unravelling a plot against the throne, should
have associated himself with such a proposal. To allow a
conspirator to retain her claim to the succession merely by
recognizing Elizabeth as Queen was a naivety that surely did
not spring from his mind. Perhaps Elizabeth herself was
responsible. Not that she was naive: the proposal effectively
drew the sting from a bill that she disliked.[1]

Rather than agree to such futility, the joint-committee
evidently preferred to work on the original Norton text. Concerned now with avoiding the royal veto, they took out the
retrospective element of the bill and its penalty for the heir: the
sins of the parent were not to be visited on the child. As finally
approved, the measure disabled from inheriting the crown anyone who, after thirty days from the close of this Parliament and
during Elizabeth's life, claimed for themselves or any other a
right to the throne, usurped the royal title, or refused, on
demand by Elizabeth, to acknowledge her as lawful Queen.
Anyone maintaining the right of such a person to the succession
— provided Elizabeth denounced the person by proclamation
— was to be guilty of treason. Norton's provision about the
right of Parliament to settle the succession was, with a significant
amendment, retained: and a clause imposed heavy penalties on
writing tracts about the succession.[2]

Thus amended the Commons passed the bill. The ingrossed
parchment was by now in such a mess with amendments that
they asked the Lords to write it out anew; and after doing this
and scrutinizing the new text, they sent it back to the Commons

[1] S.P. Dom. Eliz. 229/89, wrongly dated.
[2] 13 Eliz. c. 1 (*Statutes of Realm*, IV. i. 526-8).

to be scrutinized and passed by them in turn. Alas! in being so tidy, what a wonderful historical document they denied to posterity. The bill at Westminster today is that clean copy. It tells no tale.[1]

In ruminating on this extraordinary story and on Elizabeth's personal part in it, let us never forget that the threads of the Ridolfi Plot were at that time in the Queen's hand, that they already led to Mary and were the more disturbing because their full ramifications were not yet known. If it be a mark of statesmanship to remain calm, tolerant, and high-principled while awaiting an explosion and when all around emotions ran high, here surely was an example.

[1] *C.J.* i. 90-1; *L.J.* i. 688, 694; Hooker, p. 486.

## CHAPTER V

# END OF THE SESSION

In spite of the dismal pace of the Commons during the early weeks of the session, the two Houses managed by the end of May to pass forty-six bills, two-thirds of which were public bills and a fair number highly important or controversial. Undoubtedly, this amount of work would not have been accomplished unless the House of Lords had taken a larger share than usual in initiating the main bills; but the surprising fact is that the Commons, with their galaxy of talent, their critical approach to everything, their love of long debates (or inability to save themselves from them), and their obstinacy, did not thwart the commendable endeavours of the Higher House. Certainly, when our anonymous diary abruptly ends on April 21st, Members were still talking hard on slight provocation, and thereafter, in the *Journal* and Hooker, there are sufficient allusions to 'long arguments' or 'much ado' to indicate that fatigue had not smitten the orators.

In later Elizabethan parliaments this sort of quandary drove the House to develop its committee system in order to transfer much of the debate from the Chamber. In 1571 they avoided paralysis by exploiting the device of conference between committees of both Houses. In this way, differences between Lords and Commons over details of their bills, which might have led to much debate about amendments and to the loss of a number of measures, were readily settled, if agreement was at all possible. The idea of turning this occasional procedure into a normal habit seems to have come to the Commons as a sudden inspiration on May 2nd. On that morning, a committee of theirs returned from such a conference and reported a suggestion made to them for 'the enlargement and better explanation' of parts of their bill: 'whereupon', notes the Clerk, 'the House, liking well of that course of proceeding', agreed that the committees for two specific bills and for 'such-like bills as hereafter shall come from their Lordships', needing consideration, addition, or alteration, should seek conference with the Lords as they in this instance had sought it with them.

Thereafter, many entries of conferences appear in the *Commons Journal*, sometimes sought by the one House, sometimes by the other. The Lords requested a conference about one of their bills while it was still at the second-reading stage in the Lower House. On another occasion they actually sent down to ask the Commons if they would agree in advance to a particular amendment to one of their bills, supposing the Lords made it. Here, indeed, was flexible procedure. It saved time: it saved bills.[1]

The session ended in the afternoon of Tuesday, May 29th. Though neither House finished reading all its bills until that afternoon, in the morning the Commons found themselves with a little time on their hands, and their hearts full of sentiment, like schoolboys at the end of term. Hooker describes the scene.

Sir Walter Mildmay — Chancellor of the Exchequer, and, as such, a junior Privy Councillor, perhaps left in charge by his seniors and betters at this unimportant sitting — 'made motion that as all they were met together in peace and love, [he] did wish they should so depart; and that no advantage should be taken of any words there passed, but all to the best. After him, Grimston' — the Bastille hero, and Nestor of Parliament in 1593 — 'did the like, making motion also that a collection should be made for the relief of the French church: which was done and amounted to about £30'. He also suggested that 'the Queen might be moved' — possibly in the Speaker's speech — 'for the recovery of Ireland into good order, whereby a gain would grow to her and an ease to all her subjects; towards which her subjects gladly would contribute of their goods another subsidy'. Thomas Norton, Sir Humphrey Gilbert, and the Lord Deputy, Sir Henry Sidney, supported him.

'At length the Speaker stood up, and he made the like requests of love and amity, as also craved the good will of every person there; and that if he had slipped in anything they should impute it to his ignorance and not to any wilfulness; and that he was and would be prest [i.e. ready] not only to do his best for that House, but also for every one of them to his uttermost, if he might stand them in stead.'[2]

Elizabeth came to end the session between 4 and 5 o'clock. In his oration, the Speaker, having commented on the work of the Commons and asked the Queen for her assent to bills, went

[1] *C.J.* i. 87, 92, 93.      [2] Hooker, pp. 488-9.

on to declare 'the good will and hearty love the Lower House bare unto her, and how that freely, without the denying of any one person, or of any demand or motion made, they have given her a subsidy and two tenths and fifteenths'. Though this was no more than her deserts, yet, seeing their good intentions, he hoped that her Highness would forgive those who by their rashness (which he knew proceeded rather of ignorance) had incurred her dislike.[1]

We possess the full text of Sir Nicholas Bacon's reply, which he had written out beforehand. According to this, he went directly to the subject of the Commons' behaviour in this Parliament.

'Her Majesty hath commanded me to say unto you that, like as the great number of them of the Lower House have in the proceedings in this session showed themselves modest, discreet, and dutiful, as becomes good and dutiful subjects, and meet for the places they be called unto, so there be certain of them, although not many in number, which . . . have showed themselves audacious, arrogant, and presumptuous, calling her Majesty's grants, and prerogatives also, into question, contrary to their duty . . . and contrary to the express admonition given in her Majesty's name in the beginning of this Parliament: which it might very well have become them to have had more regard unto. But Her Majesty saith, seeing they will thus wilfully forget themselves, they are otherwise to be remembered. And, like as her Majesty allows and much commends the former sort for the respects aforesaid, so doth her Highness utterly disallow and condemn the second sort for their audacious, arrogant, and presumptuous folly, thus by frivolous and superfluous speech spending the time and meddling with matters neither pertaining unto them nor within the capacity of their understanding.'

This is what Bacon evidently intended to say; but Hooker gives a summary of the speech which suggests that he must have departed a little from his prepared text, doubtless on the Queen's instructions: not to mollify its phrases — they retain their acerbity even in the partly obliterated words of the diary; but to be more specific about the offence. He criticized the Commons for their bills on religion: and one imagines that here

[1] Hooker, p. 489.

he voiced the Queen's annoyance with the Articles Bill (Bill B), to which she was having to consent, though its Puritan provision must have been gall and wormwood to her. These bills, he declared, 'should first have been debated in the Convocation and by the bishops, and not by them. Likewise,' he added, 'the prerogative toucheth her Majesty and her authority, which, without her favour, ought not to be had in question. These, therefore, that so audaciously and arrogantly have dealt in such matters may not look to receive further favour than by the statutes of this realm is ordained.'

If the modern reader, stranger to the curious Elizabethan idiom and even to stern ideas of parental discipline, is repelled by the language, let him reflect that in due course the Queen was to select, first as Speaker, and then judge, both Robert Bell, offender-in-chief, and Christopher Yelverton, in the front rank of the audacious. As Sir John Harington later wrote of his royal godmother: 'Anon came a storm from a sudden gathering of clouds, and the thunder fell in wondrous manner on all alike.' Soon again it was 'pure sunshine'.

'And thus much concerning Parliament-men of the Nether House', wrote Bacon at the end of his first paragraph. He turned, like a practitioner in chiaroscuro, to the Lords. 'As to my Lords here of the Upper House, her Majesty hath commanded me to let them know that her Highness taketh their diligence, discretion, and orderly proceedings to be such as redoundeth much to their honour and commendation, and much to her comfort and consolation.'

Bacon then expressed the Queen's thanks for the subsidy, saying, as he had been commanded, 'that she maketh a greater account of the good wills and benevolent minds of her good and loving subjects than she doth of ten subsidies'. She appreciated the readiness with which the money had been granted. 'If the service of the realm and your sureties would so permit . . . her Majesty would as gladly, as readily, and as frankly remit this grant as you have freely and liberally granted it.' These sentiments he expressed at some length, and proceeded to admonish his audience, also at some length, on the collection of the money.

The rest of the speech — quite half of it — was devoted to the ill execution of the laws, on which subject he spent his oratorical skill. The Queen, he said, does her part. She gives her royal assent to the laws; she proclaims and publishes the most material of them; she grants her Commission of the Peace in every shire to men who are or should be of the greatest consideration — men sworn to their execution: by her command, at least once a year, a number of these Justices are called into the Star Chamber and there exhorted, admonished, and commanded to see to the execution of their charge. The negligence was theirs. 'Is it not, trow you, a monstrous disguising to have . . . him that should by his oath and duty set forth justice and right, against his oath offer injury and wrong; to have him that is specially chosen . . . to appease all brabbling and controversies, to be a sower and maintainer of strife and sedition . . .; leading and swaying of juries according to his will, acquitting some for gain, indicting others for malice, bearing with him as his servant or friend, overthrowing the other as his enemy, procuring all questmongers to be of his livery' so that 'his winks, frownings, and countenances may direct all inquests?'

It is not a pleasant picture that Bacon drew, and his vehemence makes one wonder how extensive was the rot. For a tirade of the same kind a Member of the House of Commons got into hot water with his colleagues in the last Parliament of the reign. Bacon on this occasion was careful to add that 'like as this is not said to those that be good, so is this and much more to be said and done against those that be ill'.

For remedy he suggested greater care in the choice of J.P.s, sharp correction of offenders, and the device which he had advocated before — biennial or triennial visitations by special commissioners. In slack counties, negligent Justices should be removed from all governance; and in order to distinguish between 'the slothful, drowsy drones' and 'the diligent and careful bees', he suggested that a roll should be kept, recording the offences that each Justice prosecuted — 'how oft and how many' — to be shown at the visitation.

Perhaps, after all, Bacon's long jeremiad had no special significance. He had to write an oration, and he had to have a theme; and he happened to be in good form on this occasion. There is not even a hint of it all in Hooker's brief report.

During the ceremony of giving the royal assent, the Queen

herself intervened, as we have already noticed. It was another of those signs that 'Protocol' was still far from being King in Parliament: though, in any case, Elizabeth's instinct for the unconventional was that of a supreme leader, overflowing with personality. She broke into the antiphony of the Clerk of the Crown and the Clerk of Parliaments, after the title of the bill of treasons had been read: probably the first on the list. 'Then', wrote Hooker, 'the Queen stood up and spake herself as followeth.' His account of her words has already been quoted. 'And so, when she had said her mind, the bill (which indeed was amended before) was allowed.'[1]

The royal assent was given to forty-one bills. Five were vetoed. They included the bill for coming to church, and a bill to discharge sheriffs from the cost of diets for Justices of Assize.[2] This latter measure had been before the Parliament of 1563, but had been stopped in the House of Lords at the Queen's command. She had then promised to 'take order therein herself'. Evidently the promise had not been fulfilled, but her objection to parliamentary action remained.

The Parliament was then dissolved. In 1566 Elizabeth had preferred to let a number of her laws lapse rather than prorogue Parliament and face that obstreperous body of Commons again, thinking that a fresh dip into the lucky-bag of a parliamentary election would be sure to bring better fortune. It had not; and she was inclined to try again. When in the next Parliament she found a House more to her liking, she clung to it for eleven years: indeed, until the implacable erosion of death forced her hand. She was clearly not averse to proroguing Parliaments; but in her long reign she had little luck with her faithful (and troublesome) Commons.

---

[1] Corpus Christi Coll. Camb. MS. 543, fols. 21 seqq.; Hooker, p. 490.
[2] Also: for the town of Shrewsbury; for appointing two sheriffs for Hunts. and Cambs.; for the severance of sheriffs in Beds. and Bucks. (cf. *L.J.* i. 682, 691, 695, 698).

# PART FIVE

# THE PARLIAMENT OF 1572

## CHAPTER I

## INTRODUCTORY

LITTLE did Elizabeth imagine how soon she would be facing another Parliament. In the autumn of 1571 chance gave the government a clue to that mysterious conspiracy which it had been trying to fathom during the sitting of the 1571 Parliament. The nature and details of the Ridolfi Plot were discovered, involving insurrection, military aid from the Duke of Alva, the freeing of Mary Queen of Scots and her marriage to the Duke of Norfolk, the restoration of Catholicism in England, and doubtless, as a result, the deposition or death of Elizabeth. In January 1572 Norfolk was brought to trial for his part in it and was found guilty of high treason.

The following months were a period of intolerable suspense. Time and again, to the despair of her advisers, the Queen wavered over the Duke's execution, even rescinding a warrant that she had already signed. She shrank from the irrevocable stroke of death. Greater pressure was required than the Privy Council could exert; and Parliament alone was capable of that. There was also the problem of Mary Queen of Scots. 'If ye strike not at the root', John Knox had prophetically written, 'the branches that appear to be broken will bud again.'[1] Here was a second perplexity requiring Parliament. It was a moot point whether the laws of England — whether even a special Act of Parliament — could deal with the Sovereign of another country, though she had renounced her throne, was resident in England, and had committed what in another would undoubtedly have been treason.

How much pressure was needed to extract Elizabeth's consent to summon a Parliament, we can only surmise. Probably a great deal: she knew what to fear, and her Council what to

[1] *Scottish Cal.* iii. 40.

hope for. 'God preserve her Majesty long to reign over us by some unlooked-for miracle', wrote Sir Thomas Smith from France on March 22nd; 'for I cannot see by natural reason that her Highness goeth about to provide for it.' As though the strain on English statesmen was not already enough, just about the time that Smith was writing, Elizabeth fell seriously ill, possibly from food-poisoning. For five days, she told the French ambassador, she was in great pain, and she thought that she might die. Leicester and Burghley watched by her bed for three nights. It is clear that they were greatly alarmed, and that 'the uncertainty, the disorder, the peril and danger which had been like to follow' her death, haunted her statesmen's minds. Indeed, had the illness turned out to be fatal, the odds are that the cause of Mary Queen of Scots would have triumphed: her complicity in the Ridolfi Plot, along with her manifold offences, would have proved little hindrance to the throne.[1]

Hitherto Elizabeth may have been reluctant to summon Parliament while negotiations were proceeding in France for the Treaty of Blois. The clamour of an outraged House of Commons for Mary's death would not have constituted a harmonious background to that business. But the Queen's illness, stern reminder of the awful gamble with England's future, must have swept away any resistance to her Council on that score. It was already late in the season to start thinking of a Parliament, since summer sessions in plague-ridden London, abnormally congested on such occasions, were regarded as highly dangerous to everyone concerned and to the country at large. Nevertheless, the writs went out on March 28th, summoning a meeting for May 8th — more than a month later than any 'Spring' session of the reign. As it happened, because of some suspicion of plague the Court during this Parliament was established at St. James's, instead of Whitehall.[2] To Elizabeth, who by temperament had a strong aversion to decisive action so long as doubts obscured her mind and instinct, the sense of haste which this imposed upon proceedings was probably not unwelcome. It furnished an excuse for further delay.

---

[1] DIGGES, *Compleat Ambassador* (1655), pp. 198, 199; Fénélon, *Corres. Diplomatique*, iv. 411, 412.
[2] Fénélon, op. cit. iv. 459.

In the elections, nearly half of those chosen were new-comers to Parliament. They naturally included men of position and substance, but none who became great 'Parliament-men'. In this the new Parliament was a striking contrast to the last; and we may well suspect that here was a partial explanation of the Queen's desire to keep this particular House of Commons in being as long as possible. Not that she had at last got an amenable assembly, for just on two hundred of the 1571 Members were re-elected, including most of the radical leaders and great debaters, who returned with even more experience and mastery of the parliamentary art. Bell, Dalton, Fleetwood, Monson, Norton, Yelverton — the old incomparables — were back. From the remarkable group which first entered Parliament in 1571, there were Bainbridge, Carleton, Cope, Tristram Pistor, and Peter Wentworth, among many other staunch Puritans. William Strickland was taking a rest: a long rest the many prorogations made it. But there was compensation in the reappearance of Peter Wentworth's brother, Paul.

Thomas Cromwell, the Elizabethan parliamentary diarist *par excellence*, was again returned, and for this Parliament we have the first of four private journals that he kept.[1] As yet, parliamentary committees were not rendering him too busy, or familiarity with debate too *blasé*, to be interested in what Members said. The consequence is a diary which rivals the long-known and remarkable diary of the 1601 Parliament kept by Heywood Townshend. Another, an anonymous Member, also kept a private journal, superior in literary quality to Cromwell's, its match sometimes in the length of the report, though its inferior in thoroughness.[2] Since we also have a fragment of the private notes kept by Fulk Onslow, the Clerk of the House, this session vies with that of 1601 as the best-reported Parliament of the reign.[3] Happy the narrator when fullness of knowledge coincides with stirring drama.

In his opening speech on Thursday, May 8th, the Lord Keeper, Sir Nicholas Bacon, referred first to the Queen's concern at having a concourse of her people out of all quarters of her realm at so unseasonable a time of the year. 'The cause

[1] Trinity Coll. Dublin MS. N.2/12.
[2] Bodley, Tanner MS. 393, fols. 45 seqq. (hereafter cited as Anonymous Diary).
[3] Formerly among the MSS. of Lord Braye at Stanford Hall, but recently acquired for the House of Lords MSS.

was so necessary and so weighty as it could not otherwise be.' The chief reason for summoning Parliament was to devise laws for the safety of the Queen's Majesty, both the Privy Council and the wisest persons of the realm having agreed that the existing laws were inadequate to deal with the great treasons and notable conspiracies recently revealed through the providence of God. ¹A subordinate reason was normal legislation; but he warned them that once they had begun to deal with the main subject, they should meddle with other matters as little as possible. It was 'towards the heat of the year', and it rested with themselves to minimize the danger and secure as speedy a release as possible.

When they returned to their Chamber, the Commons set about electing a Speaker, and, on the recommendation of the senior Privy Councillor, Sir Francis Knollys, Robert Bell was chosen. That Burghley and other leading statesmen, with whom the nomination effectively lay, selected one of the most conspicuous radical leaders of the last Parliament is significant. They could rely in this crisis on the lead they wanted.

Bell was presented to the Queen on Saturday, May 10th, and after his disabling speech and the confirmation of his election, he began his oration with a historical review of legislative activity in England, reminding his hearers that there had been annual Parliaments in Edward III's reign, and Parliaments summoned for relatively unimportant causes. There was no occasion, therefore, to marvel at this one, meeting so soon after the last, and called for the preservation of the Queen's most royal person, 'assaulted with so many traitorous conspiracies and seditious practices', for remedy whereof her loving subjects 'do long more than the chased deer desireth the soil for his refreshing'. 'This error', he declared, 'was crept into the heads of a number: that there was a person in this land [Mary Queen of Scots] whom no law could touch.' If true, it was a perilous matter to our State. 'It hath been said of old that the Common Law should be common reason; but this I dare safely avow, that if any person, of what state, condition, or nation whatsoever, shall commit any felony within this realm, they shall die for the same. What reason, then, can allow that, seeking the destruction of your Majesty, whom the Almighty God long preserve, such offender should be without law? Sure it were much like as one should maintain that a killer of a phip [a sparrow] should be punished, and the murderer should go scot-free.'

Though, as he asserted, the law was able to deal with the matter, yet Parliament, he thought, was best: first, to rectify the common error and so stay the machinations of evil people; and secondly, because in such an assembly the whole circumstances of a cause could be considered and further remedy provided. He recalled the benefits they had received from the Queen's rule: in what state they were when the merciful providence of God first delivered the sceptre to her. 'You found us in war with foreign nations, subject to ignorant hypocrisy and un-sound doctrine, the best sort under great persecution, some imprisoned, some driven to exile for their conscience, the treasure . . . corrupt.' A miraculous change — and the more miraculous to be so easily achieved — had taken place. 'One benefit more I will recite: in my opinion not much inferior to some of the rest. God hath inclined your heart to be a defence to His afflicted Church throughout all Europe.' It is for love that your subjects obey you.

In asking for the accustomed privileges of Parliament, he placed freedom of speech first: and, indeed, quite forgot free-dom from arrest! The way he phrased his first petition is interesting: 'for liberty of speech to be freely had (due reverence always used to your Majesty), without which it is impossible any great matter be achieved in any conference; for except the objections on every part be heard, answered, and confuted, the counsel cannot be perfected. Some speech, perhaps singly and nakedly reported, hath [seemed] and may seem odious, which, the circumstances considered and well digested, carrieth no cause of offence.' His personal experience in the Parliament of 1571 was evidently still rankling in his mind.

In his reply, Sir Nicholas Bacon took the speech section by section. The first led him to repeat the warning that the time of year made a short session essential. And he was now — prob-ably on orders from the Queen — quite explicit about the busi-ness they were to undertake: 'no private bills to be received'. It was asking the impossible of an Elizabethan House of Com-mons. How could Members betray friends, clients, and con-stituencies by refusing to sponsor their bills?

Turning to the Speaker's eloquent recital of 'benefits', Bacon conveyed the Queen's response. 'She delighteth not' in such praise. The benefits were the work of God, and thanks were due to Him. But she wished that they were 'doubled, trebled, yea, quadrupled'; and as she had not hitherto pretermitted her care nor her ability, so in the future she heartily prayed that her power and will might advance the weal-public of her realm.

The Speaker's expository petition for freedom of speech brought a considered reply. 'Her Majesty hath willed me to declare that it hath been often moved, and men often warned, and yet not so great regard had as was convenient. She knoweth that speech fit for the state, well placed and used in matters convenient, is very necessary: which she granteth unto you. But there is a difference between staring and stark blind. Trifling digressions from matters proponed' — our witty William Fleetwood, now Recorder of London, was a prime sinner in this — 'idle and long discourses, her Majesty misliketh and condemneth, wherein she adviseth them to be more wary than they have been heretofore.'

'This oration ended', — Cromwell tells us in his diary — 'the Speaker was called for to the Queen's Majesty, and kneeling, her Majesty had a quarter of an hour's conference with him under the cloth of state.' Whether it was simply an informal, gracious gesture or whether she imparted instructions for this extraordinary session, we do not know. Cromwell also tells us that though Bell had already taken the oath as a burgess, he was sworn anew when he returned to the Chamber as Speaker. The customary bill was then read to give him seisin of his place, and so the Commons adjourned till Monday.[1]

---

[1] The foregoing speeches are generally epitomized from the lengthy reports in Cromwell's Diary, but I have incorporated occasional quotations from the Anonymous Diary. Also cf. *C.J.* i. 94.

## CHAPTER II

# MARY QUEEN OF SCOTS—I

'THE great cause', 'the great matter': that is how the two Houses referred to the business of Mary Queen of Scots, which absorbed this session. Proceedings began when towards the end of Monday morning, May 12th, the Lords sent to ask all the Commons with their Speaker to come up to their House. Here they were told that the Queen wished a committee from both Houses to meet her learned counsel the next morning at 8 o'clock in the Star Chamber; that the Lords proposed to send seven prelates, seven earls, and seven barons, and wished the Lower House to send forty. In specifying the size of the Commons' committee their Lordships ventured too far. 'Not thinking good to be directed in their number', reports Cromwell, the House chose forty-four. They were sensitive about punctilio. The Lords seem to have retorted by increasing their total to twenty-two, thus maintaining the traditional proportion of one peer to two commoners for such occasions. No prolonged ill will resulted from this petty clash over dignity, as was to happen later in the reign. Among the Members selected for the committee were Peter Wentworth and others whom we know, such as Dalton, Fleetwood, Monson, Norton and Yelverton.[1]

Before they rose for the day, Robert Snagge — 'Robin', as our anonymous diarist calls him — moved the appointment of certain Members for humble suit to the Queen that 'as she had already by ordinary course of law proceeded to judgment against certain malefactors, so likewise she would proceed further to the execution'. Otherwise, for fear of revenge men would be afraid to speak. It is notable as the first of the insistent calls for the execution of the Duke of Norfolk.[2]

'Upon this', says our diarist, 'Arthur Hall, as [if] he were moved, spake that the Queen, of herself being inclined to mercy,

---

[1] *L.J.* i. 706; *C.J.* i. 94-5.
[2] Except where indicated, my narrative of this Parliament is based on Cromwell's Diary and the Anonymous Diary. My version of speeches is often a conflation of both reports.

should not be stirred up to use the rigour of her laws towards any.' About this particular Member and his troubles we shall hear a good deal. A minor figure in English letters, as the first translator of Homer (from the French), he was a Lincolnshire gentleman, now aged thirty-two or three and representing Grantham. He had been a ward of William Cecil's, was brought up in that decorous household, married, and toured Europe as far as Constantinople. But there seems to have been a strain of insanity in his family, and he turned out to be a turbulent, unbalanced person, who could manage neither his fortune nor his temper.[1]

Hall's emotional outburst was like a spark to tinder. A Member was instantly on his feet to answer him. But Speaker Bell was an abler chairman than his predecessor. He stayed further proceedings with the remark that there would be a fitter occasion for Snagge's motion later on. For the moment Hall was saved; but, as we shall see, he could never learn discretion.

The next day, our anonymous diarist notes, 'little was done, for most part of the time was spent in calling the House; and beside, the whole forenoon and afternoon was employed to the conference had by the committees with the Lords and the Queen's learned counsel'. As a matter of fact, the Clerk's *Journal* shows that the House read six bills. They were already ignoring the Queen's explicit instructions and were using every opportunity to get a few private bills read. The diarist was probably away on the grand committee.

The following morning, May 14th, at the customary time for important business — namely, after reading a bill while the House filled — Sir Francis Knollys, the senior member of the committee, announced that its report would be made by Thomas Wilbraham, Attorney of the Court of Wards. Protesting that he was 'very suddenly taken', had kept no notes in writing and must trust to his memory, Wilbraham then began a very long speech — each of our main diarists required about 2500 words to epitomize it — recounting how the Queen's Attorney General and Solicitor had 'opened unto them by plain and great proofs the undue dealings of the Scottish Queen towards the Queen's Majesty'.

[1] Cf. H. G. WRIGHT, *Life of Arthur Hall of Grantham.*

The case against Mary was divided into five sections, the first of which dealt with her challenge to the crown of England, made in France at the beginning of Elizabeth's reign. It told in detail of the initial French claim that Mary was rightful heir to Mary Tudor, of the quartering of the arms of England and flaunting of them before great assemblies and the ambassadors of Christendom, and of her use of the title 'Queen of Scotland, of England and Ireland'. It told also of her many refusals to ratify the Treaty of Edinburgh, which contained a renunciation of this claim; and finished by recalling Patrick Adamson's description of Mary's newborn babe as son of the Queen of Scotland, England and Ireland. 'The proofs of these things rested chiefly in letters to and fro', which had been shown to the committee.

In itself this section of the case was not necessarily damning. It might have signified little more than diplomatic manœuvre. But set in the story of her subsequent intrigues and plots — as Protestant contemporaries were only too conscious, and as the subsequent sections in the case were calculated to demonstrate — there was a dormant threat in this old claim that could not be ignored.

The second section dealt with the plot to marry Mary to the Duke of Norfolk. Since this had been 'proved to the full' in the Duke's indictment, of which Wilbraham thought none of the House ignorant, he could be brief; but he took care to refer to a letter from Mary to her ambassador, the Bishop of Ross — confessed to by the latter — 'to bring the marriage about, either by fair means or else by force'.

The third and fourth sections covered her connections with the Northern Rebellion and her subsequent relations with, and sustenance of, the defeated rebels. The fifth was the longest of them all. It dealt with the Ridolfi Plot: citing confessions of the Bishop of Ross and the Duke of Norfolk; quoting a damaging letter from the Pope to Mary; telling of a ciphered letter from her to Norfolk, found under a mat in the Duke's house, which contained 'great discourses in matters of State (more than woman's wit doth commonly reach unto)' and affirmed 'that all the confidence she had in England was reposed in the Catholics'. The particulars of Ridolfi's activities and of those caught up in them were related in detail. It was told that 'six thousand

Spaniards were in readiness to have come under the commandment of the Duke of Medina', their ostensible purpose to go to the Netherlands, their real intent 'to invade this realm': the arrest of the Duke of Norfolk had stayed them. It was also said that the Bishop of Ross had planned for the Duke of Norfolk to cause a stir or tumult during the last Parliament, and to apprehend the Queen's Majesty.

After Wilbraham had ended his tale, Dalton and others added a few details that he had omitted; but, as 'the time was far spent', on the initiative of the Speaker and Sir Francis Knollys the House decided to postpone discussion until the next day. They read two bills, and then rose.

Next morning, the great debate was started at once, being opened by Richard Gallys, gentleman, aged sixty-six, Member for New Windsor, thrice mayor of that town and benefactor of its poor: he had appeared in our 'choir' of 1563-66 as 'Gallys the doctor'. 'In great congregations and assemblies', he said, 'the custom hath always been that the *puisne* doth begin to speak. I, though in age superior, yet in wisdom and understanding am of this society the most *puisne* and inferior.' He could not hold his peace. Yesterday, when he heard how the Scottish Queen had sought to dispossess the Queen's Majesty of her crown, he thought it not good that they should sleep before taking action. Quoting Theophrastus on the need for punishment in society, he asserted that the Scots were by right subject to the crown of England. He compared Mary to Clytemnestra, 'a killer of her husband and an adulteress'; denounced her as 'a common disturber of the peace of this realm'; and concluded with his advice, 'to cut off her head and make no more ado about her'.

Sir Thomas Scott of Scot's Hall, Kent, Member for that county, followed. He had been on the committee, but thought it needless to repeat the story of the Scottish Queen, 'through whom this whole realm is like to be brought into great thraldom'. Rather, as a good physician before prescribing medicine, he would seek out the causes. Papistry was the principal. He saw Papists placed in authority in all places: in Commissions of the Peace, in the seat of judgment, in noblemen's houses, in the Court, yea, about the Queen's person. This encouraged the Queen of Scots, the Pope, the rebels, the King of Spain and the

Duke of Alva. The second cause was the uncertainty of our state — the uncertainty, that is, of the succession after Elizabeth — which led noblemen and gentlemen to join with the Queen of Scots, seeing her pretend title to the crown and her likelihood to prevail. The ways for remedy were three: 'by cutting off the heads of the Scottish Queen and the Duke'; by taking away Mary's title to the succession; by the establishment of a certain successor. To adopt the second alone would do no good. Referring to the Greek who induced the Trojans to bring the wooden horse into Troy, he expressed his fear that 'some Sinon lay hid in the Court, who did secretly seek the undoing of his country'.

Robin Snagge — 'Snagge the indefatigable', we might be tempted to call him — eagerly re-entered the chorus. 'Warning hath already been given her by statute, and no good followed of it; and therefore the axe must give the next warning.' Cut off her faction, and let her title alone, for when she comes to claim it she will seek it, not by law but by conquest; 'and then will be pleading at the bar with a buckler'. 'She hath already been considered by twenty-one noblemen and forty-four of the best of our House: himself [Snagge] should have but twelve godfathers' — an ordinary jury of twelve — 'if he had made like offence.' 'She hath been put down in Scotland, and shall we sit her up?' 'She hath not spared her nobility, neither her bed nor board. A sower of sedition in France, hither she came, not as an enemy but worse — as a dissembling friend, and under friendship hath sought the destruction of the Queen's Majesty.' He could not see but that nature and reason permit her to be punished if she do amiss. 'What have we to do with *ius gentium*, having law of our own? Shall we say our law is not able to provide for this mischief? We might then say it hath defect in the highest degree.'

Sir Francis Knollys now intervened to express his approval of their zeal and policy, but to warn them off the subject of establishing the succession. He himself was in favour of it, but as former Parliaments had sufficiently shown, all was vain without the Queen's consent. They could only pray to God, who ruleth the hearts of princes.

The debate was here interrupted by a summons to their committee to go up to the Lords' Council Chamber, where a further meeting of the joint committee was arranged for that afternoon.[1] While their committee members were away, the House read a bill, resuming the debate when they returned.

Thomas Norton now entered on a great speech; and there could not be better testimony to the esteem in which this influential speaker was held than the space accorded it in both our diaries. Cromwell's epitome runs to 1600 words or more. Our anonymous diarist, after his long report, adds: 'wherein I omitted very much'. After applying Mr. Gallys's modest prologue to himself, Norton referred to the succession question, here answering Sir Francis Knollys. It had merely been moved, not urged. Leave it at that, and await the Queen's pleasure, 'who he doubteth not in good time will provide for the same'. In the mean season, strike down the bushes which lie in the way. It was the business of the House to provide for the Queen's safety. 'If she fall, he wisheth any heads off rather than hers; yea, though his own, and yet a great many others rather than his own.'

This brought him to the Duke of Norfolk. He was sorry to speak particularly, and he was sorry for the nobleman's fall; but he rejoiced that all the Duke's kinsfolk were found trusty to the Queen. There was no way left but his execution. 'Mercy hath been showed him and no good followed; submissions have not served; subscriptions have not served; oaths have not served; protestations and detestations have not served; and receiving of communions since his attainder hath been without repentance.' 'The example is ill, for men will be afraid to disclose treasons when traitors are not punished, but are suffered to live' and take revenge on 'those true subjects who have betrayed their traitorous attempts. Impunity is a great encouragement to the evil, not to give over but to proceed in their ill doings.' Moreover, it will be hard to remove the Scot without the Duke's execution. 'They are knit together so as while the one liveth the faction is strong. Take the one away, and weaken the other by all his friends.' 'Our Queen aboundeth in mercy'; but to increase this humour in her would be to cause that which is a virtue to abound too much.

Turning to the Queen of Scots, he pronounced her execution to be 'of necessity: it lawfully may be done . . . A general

[1] *C.J.* i. 95.

impunity to commit treason was never permitted to any'. If she die not, the Queen is endangered and the succession can never be established with safety: for if an heir apparent is named and kept weak in the interests of Elizabeth's safety, he will never be able to prevail against the Scottish faction; whereas, if he be made too strong for the Scot, he will be dangerous to the Queen. In this reflection, how wise Norton was! 'You will say', he continued, 'she is a Queen's daughter, and therefore to be spared: nay, then, spare the Queen's Majesty that is a King's daughter and our Queen.' As he reached his final proposal, he paused, and 'a great number' exclaimed 'Yea! Yea!' in approbation.

Then discord. As our anonymous diarist records it, the egregious Arthur Hall 'fell into the speech for which he was after called to answer. The House misliked so much of his talk that with shuffling of feet and hawking they had well nigh barred him to be heard'.

Seizing on Norton's phrase about 'two bushes', Hall said that two princes were meant. It was not convenient for them to direct her Majesty, or petition for the execution of him [the Duke] 'whose practices peradventure should not be prejudicial to the State . . . The cause touched the Queen only', not them. 'If both the bushes were removed, where is our assurance?' — or, as another version has it, 'where is ever a bush to hide us then?' 'You will hasten the execution of such whose feet hereafter you would be glad to have again to kiss.'[1] 'If others had been met with the same rod of justice' — an allusion to the Queen herself, in Mary Tudor's reign? — 'divers had not been, which now be. The nature of the lion [is] not to devour the prostrate.'

Francis Alford, a Member whose conservative leanings we have already observed, and whose wife, though not he, was a Catholic, rose to criticize Norton on procedural grounds and to crave, on Hall's behalf, 'freedom of speech without murmurings or other kind of interruption', and that 'every man may speak his conscience'. He was opposed to separate action by the Commons, and had this to say about putting Mary to death: 'he never read precedent of such dealing with kings, although he could allow it if there were no other remedy for

[1] S.P. Dom. Eliz. 147/52, wrongly dated. Printed in WRIGHT's *Arthur Hall*, p. 49.

the prince's preservation'. His closing words give the impression that he too was being barracked by the House.

Briefly but vigorously Dalton answered Alford. 'It did him good to hear the good liking' of Norton's motion.

The House then rose. The forty-four committee-men must have been left with little time for their dinner before meeting the Lords' committee at two o'clock.

The following morning, May 16th, business started with an echo from the previous day. Nicholas St. Leger — 'Sellenger' as the diarists spell it — Member for Maidstone and scion of a famous family, announced that he had a question to move. It was whether Arthur Hall was fit to be a Member of the House. For his own part he thought Hall's malady so great and his leprosy so perilous as to be incurable: for to doubt whether the Duke of Norfolk's practice was hurtful, after the proofs of treasons and conspiracies they had heard, was a manifest declaration that he belonged to that faction. 'Speech ought to be contained in bounds, canker not to be suffered.'

In this speech, St. Leger exposed a common failing and raised a nice issue. Were these men, who claimed indulgence from the Sovereign over freedom of speech, to display a like indulgence when the affront was to themselves? 'Hereupon', reports our anonymous diarist, 'divers men spake diversely, some for the liberty of the House in free speech, some that the liberty must be used in reverent and seemly sort; and so precedents were showed one way and [the] other.'

Cromwell gives a lengthy report of a speech by Edward Fenner, Esquire, Member for New Shoreham. While liking St. Leger's zeal, he nevertheless wished 'liberty of speech without restraint'. But that briefly said, he employed the tactics of Norton and seized the opportunity for a long argument and a motion for petitioning the Queen to execute the Duke of Norfolk, telling a story about Socrates and citing from history examples in which, though there was occasion for mercy, justice was executed.

The debate was interrupted at this point by a question of privilege; but it was then resumed, becoming, thanks to Fenner's tactics, rather muddled in its purpose, though tending to focus on his motion for petitioning the Queen. A newcomer, Mr. French, representing Old Sarum, brought in a biblical story. He was followed by Peter Wentworth, who demanded the execution of the Duke of Norfolk as a preliminary to dealing with Mary Queen of Scots, adding another biblical story with an appropriate moral.

Sir Francis Knollys then spoke. His main object was to divert them from petitioning the Queen and persuade them to let their desire come to her 'by way of opinion, not request. As it is spoken, it cannot', he assured them, 'be hid from her'. 'Urged or pressed it cannot be.' But he prefaced this advice with a personal defence against criticism which he took to have been directed against himself. 'It may be guessed that I arrogate authority to myself by reason of my often speeches . . . It was said, preeminence ought not to prevail in this place, and that there was equality amongst us; which I do confess . . . If I rubbed any man on the gall, let him heal the sore: the rubbing will not hurt him. I will not deny but both of us may lie, and both may play the knave.'

Evidently, Alford had been the critic, for he rose to explain his speech in Hall's defence and the remarks which Knollys had resented. He ended by expressing his opinion that those who wished to speak for the Queen of Scots should be heard in full, so that it might be said, for the honour of England, 'that as much hath been said for her as she could have said for herself'.

The Speaker now wisely broke in. Ignoring the matter of Hall's speech, he put a question to the House whether they wished their views about the Duke to come to the Queen's attention 'by opinion, or by request'. They decided for the former. Thereupon he gave this *caveat*, 'that though it had been alleged by some that the Queen of Scots was a subject or feodary, the same is not to be taken as allowed, for the law was not so'.

Here the matter ought to have rested, since it was clearly intended that the Queen should hear informally what the Commons had thought and said. But to Thomas Norton, with memories of past Parliaments, it seemed a feeble expedient. He tried bluff. With seeming innocence, he declared that they had still to decide how this 'opinion' was to come to the Queen: whether by the mouth of the Speaker, or through the Lords, or, as he preferred, by the Privy Council. Quite properly,

Knollys retorted that this was to propose a 'message', which was contrary to their resolution. With that the debate ended: at any rate, for the time being.

The next day, May 17th, they were at it again. Thomas Honywood, Member for Hythe, managed to sandwich into the reading of bills a renewal of the motion about Arthur Hall's speech, forgotten in the muddle of the previous day's debate. He quoted the qualifications laid down for Members in the election writs, pronounced Hall 'not fit for the House', and desired that he be called to answer for his speech. Sir Francis Knollys, playing the unrecognized role of leader of the House as senior Privy Councillor, tried to smother the motion. Wisely and temperately he declared that he wanted speech in the House to be free, and would rather know men by their speech than not know them by their silence. Let the perverse speak their fill. The House would neither be won from its course, nor abused by their sayings; and such people would then be unable to claim that they could, but durst not, answer their opponents.

He pleaded in vain. There were many eager to talk on the subject; and reason could not prevail against passion. A Shropshire gentleman spoke. He trusted that the House would not permit a man to speak treason. He was followed by a Member from Lincolnshire, who was of much the same opinion. 'He never knew in any Parliament liberty of speech so freely granted that a man might say what he listed.' After citing two precedents, he added the information — which, knowing a good deal about Hall's ways, we can readily believe to have had some substance — that outside the House Hall had given forth 'speech and slander of the nobility and of the whole State', and that he seemed 'at the least to be an abettor of a traitor'. George Grenville senior, from the West Country, Member for Launceston and a relative of the immortal hero of the *Revenge*, was as forthright. He had been a member of the grand committee that had heard all the evidence against Mary; and, following the tactics, which with a Norton were calculated and shrewd but with others may have been no more than unquenchable wrath, he seized the chance of straying from the debate. 'Temeris', he said, 'apprehending his son and another woman in adultery, cut off both their heads and then caused a coin to be made of two heads issuing out of one, for a perpetual monument of their adultery. He would have the like to be done with the Queen of Scots and the Duke, and some perpetual memory made for remembrance of the villainies of their acts.' We labour in vain without this be executed. 'If a man would bid us be merry this week for the next week we should die, I think we should hardly be merry.'

The two princes of debate followed, Norton to say briefly that Hall should be called to answer, and Recorder Fleetwood — who could never be brief — to cull more precedents from his inexhaustible memory. As regards speech inside the House, seeing that they had the arraignment of a Queen in hand, Fleetwood would have had it more liberally suffered. But speech outside was different. 'Words tolerable in this House are not sufferable at Blunt's table' — a tavern, presumably. Alford said much the same. But there was a return to the authentic radical note with Robin Snagge. 'If this be suffered, let sedition be sown': a sentiment shared by John Marsh, London mercer and Member for the City. The next speaker was perhaps wiser than he knew. He was for maintaining the liberty of the House by regarding Hall 'as a mad man'. He was answered by Sir Nicholas Arnold.

At this point the Speaker interposed, reciting the several motions and framing them into questions; whereupon it was resolved, as the *Journal* entry states, 'that Arthur Hall Esquire, for sundry lewd speeches, used as well in this House as also abroad elsewhere, shall have warning by the Serjeant to be here upon Monday next, and at the bar to answer to such things as he shall then and there be charged with'. Members who had noted his words were to assemble at once in the chamber above, put them in writing, and deliver them to the Speaker.[1]

That should have ended the business; but Robert Newdigate, Member for Berwick, rose to secure from the House a 'full resolution' of its opinion concerning the execution of the Duke. The question was put and 'passed without any negative voice'.

On the Monday, May 19th, another stage was reached in the great cause when Mr. Wilbraham reported on the further proceedings of the joint committee. At their last meeting, said he,

[1] *C.J.* i. 95.

they had consulted the judges, who agreed that the facts against
Mary Queen of Scots were 'treason in the highest degree in
any person, stranger or other'; and treason in her. 'Her estate
considered', they thought Parliament the fit medium for her
trial. Accordingly they had drawn up two bills, the one varying
from the other only in the variety of punishment. The first
attainted her of high treason and subjected her to its penalties.
It also disabled her from any claim to the crown, making it
treason to allow her title. The second pronounced her incapable
of succeeding to the throne.

Told of these alternatives, Wilbraham continued, the Queen
had preferred the second, not rejecting the first but postponing
it. She could not with honour attaint Mary without calling her
to answer; and to send a number from each House to examine
her would ask no small time. It would be perilous to keep
Parliament in session at this period of the year; the cost would
be great; and, besides, she wanted Parliament ended before the
special embassy arrived, which was coming from France to
conclude the Treaty of Blois. The committee, Wilbraham
added, thought it not good to hazard the Queen so long. They
were evidently under the impression that it was merely a question of postponing the death sentence, say until the autumn.

Norton at once spoke. No peril, he asserted, could be considered against the Queen's safety. And then, at his old tactics
again, he proposed that they should move the Queen to execute
the Duke of Norfolk 'in the mean season', and thus be rid of
one peril. Snagge, too, was adamant. He thought the greater
punishment — attainder — 'little enough'. As for the danger of
sickness by keeping Parliament in being, 'refer it to God'. The
trilogy was completed by Dalton. They should by no means
agree to the second alternative. It would do hurt rather than
good. It would not avert the peril; it might seem to affirm a
title in Mary; and in effect it would establish a succession,
which, he added, was 'never to be granted unto'. Presumably
he thought that by implicitly recognizing the validity of Mary's
claim, it would in effect nominate her son, James. What, asked
he, will Mary not attempt while her trial is pending? No sickness, no expense to themselves could countervail the danger.
'Surely, for his part he would follow the Queen upon his knees
to any place rather than leave the thing undone.'

DR. THOMAS WILSON

Master of Requests 1560-77

Secretary 1577-81

A sole discordant voice was raised. Francis Alford, again appearing as odd-man-out, after desiring 'favourable construction' of what he was to say, urged them to follow the Queen's advice. 'The Queen's Majesty is wise, she knoweth and considereth more than every one of us doth know or can conceive . . . To condemn a king is a matter of great weight. To condemn the Scottish Queen to die for faults, before she knew they were faults and that she offended by doing them, is a matter worthy of consideration . . . He thinketh her a king, though she be deposed and have resigned; for it were perilous for princes' that deposition by their subjects 'should make them no princes'. While he acknowledged that she had done 'lewdly and wickedly', and was sorry she wanted grace, he nevertheless described her offences as rather those of an enemy than a subject. 'Let her forfeit her estate, not her life.'

It was a speech which was long remembered, and made him — though closely connected with Burghley, and a friend of Christopher Hatton and other influential people — suspect in official circles six years later and even as late as 1590.[1]

He was answered by one of his own kind, the eminent civil lawyer, Dr. Thomas Wilson, a Master of Requests. He wished that Alford had been a member of the committee in this cause, for then he would have been better content with the first bill. The Queen, Wilson pointed out — perhaps truthfully, but surely not confidently — had made no decision, but merely shown her inclination to mercy. 'No man condemneth the Queen's opinion, nor thinketh her otherwise than wise; yet he doubteth whether she so fully seeth her own peril.' 'We ought importunately to cry for justice, justice.' 'The case of a king indeed is great, but if they do ill and be wicked, they must be dealt withal. The Scottish Queen shall be heard, and any man beside that will offer to speak for her. It is marvelled at by foreign princes that, her offences being so great and horrible, the Queen's Majesty suffereth her to live. A king, coming hither into England, is no king here.' The judges' opinion is 'that Mary Stuart, called Queen of Scots, is a traitor'. 'The law sayeth that dignity defends not him which liveth unhonestly.'

The debate continued. Monson spoke, and the subject of

[1] Cf. Alford's letter-book in Inner Temple Petyt MS. 538/10, fols. 13-14, 64, and passim.

the Duke was again raised. 'The Scottish Queen', it was argued, 'was much stronger within this realm by the Duke than the Duke by her.' Execute him, and 'though you cut not off her weasand, wherewith she breatheth, yet her sinews be cut off, whereby she moveth'.

Finally, 'by the whole voice of the House', it was resolved, 'for the better safety and preservation of the Queen's Majesty's person and the present state, to make choice of proceeding against the Scottish Queen in the highest degree of treason, and therein to touch her as well in life as in title and dignity, and that of necessity, with all possible speed'.[1]

'Act, insist, speak, in season and out': so the writer of our 'lewd pasquil' had diagnosed Norton's character in 1566. He now followed up this resolution of the House with the proposal 'that present motion may be made for execution in the mean season of the Duke, which he knoweth the Lords like well of', citing as a persuasive precedent the act for the attainder of Katherine Howard in 1542,[2] which provided for execution to be done while Parliament was still sitting. He did not get his way: perhaps the Speaker, or Knollys, prevented his motion being put to the House. But his remorseless pounding upon the one theme was astute policy.

The House now turned to deal with Arthur Hall, who was brought to the bar and charged with seven 'articles', excerpted from his speech or speeches. He confessed great folly in his utterance, and asked the House to believe that he was 'amazed' to be brought to answer in such an assembly. He thought he had enemies there, but was comforted that he had many indifferent hearers. Requiring them, for his credit's sake, to accept his submission, without particular answer to the questions, he explained that he had been so moved to anger by interruptions when speaking, he did not know what he had said. If his submission was not accepted, he wanted the House to be divided. The Speaker then asked him if he submitted himself generally to the House, to which he answered 'Yea': whereupon he was withdrawn.

His method of answer, with its undertone of surly defiance, was not liked. Sir Francis Knollys, however, counselled leniency, saying that he feared Hall 'had the disease of his

---

[1] *C.J.* i. 96.    [2] 33 Hen. VIII. c. 21 (*Statutes of Realm*, iii. 858).

father', who was 'somewhat inclined to madness'. 'He would have him condemned for a rash head and a fool.' After further suggestions, Hall was brought back, made to answer each 'article' in turn, and express contrition 'as well touching the said articles as also his other fond and unadvised speech at the bar'. He was then dismissed with 'a good exhortation given him by Mr. Speaker at large'.[1]

'The greatest reasons of this favourable dealing with Hall', says our anonymous diarist, 'were these: *i.* for freedom of the House in speech, lest otherwise it should seem to have been impugned; *ii.* for the honour of the cause wherein the speech was used, that it may not hereafter be said how men were barred of speech in the treating of the cause. For it may now justly be said that such favour was showed to one speaking in that cause as should have been permitted to none in any cause beside.'

[1] *C.J.* i. 96.

## CHAPTER III

# MARY QUEEN OF SCOTS: II

PARLIAMENT had been in session less than a fortnight. The joint-committee of both Houses had listened to the case against Mary, had devised two bills, one involving her execution as a traitor, the other exclusion from the succession, and had been told that Elizabeth preferred to proceed with the second, postponing the first. Like the Commons, the House of Lords had presumably received and discussed reports from their committee: with fewer words, we may suppose, and perhaps with less passion. Alas! their extraordinarily uninformative *Journal* contains not a hint of all this, nor does it seem that we can ever hope to know what happened in the Upper House. As we have seen, the Commons had decided to ignore their Sovereign's preference and to press for the first bill. It remained for them to ring up the curtain for the second act of the drama.

After waiting a day, probably in expectation of a move from the Lords, on May 21st, when sending Treasurer Knollys and others with bills to the Upper House, they instructed them to make their decision known, ask their Lordships' liking of it, and seek advice for further proceeding. Knollys and his colleagues returned with the information that the Lords had come to much the same decision and desired an immediate meeting of the joint-committee.

Thomas Norton promptly saw and seized a fresh opportunity for his relentless campaign against the Duke of Norfolk. He rose to move a motion. 'Sithence time is to be used in trial of the Queen of Scots, and that it is determined she shall come to her trial, it will occasion her to attempt what she may, for desperate necessity dareth the uttermost mischief that can be devised.' It is therefore necessary to execute the Duke in the mean season, 'which will be half an execution of the Queen of Scots', and, moreover, will give us some hope that the bill of attainder against her will succeed. He wanted the Lords informed of their opinion, and their co-operation sought.

This time he got his way, and the Commons' committee was

instructed accordingly. They did not carry out their charge. The unfolding drama stayed them.

As their first step the joint-committee evidently informed Elizabeth of the opinion of her Lords and Commons; and on May 23rd her reply was conveyed to each House through members of the Privy Council. In the Commons the Comptroller (Sir James Croft) delivered it. 'The Queen's Majesty', he reported, 'hath showed that she thought that never prince was more bound to subjects than herself.' She thankfully accepted their great care for her safety, but would not agree to the bill of attainder, 'partly for honour, partly for conscience, for causes to herself known; wishing therefore for the present to deal with' the second bill; 'not meaning to reject the first, but in time convenient to deal also therewith'.[1]

We today, knowing the end of the story, may easily fail to appreciate the emotional shock of this decision. It had been made known to the committee the day before, and a Member graphically described its effect. He wished 'that her Majesty, with her motherly pity, had beheld the fatherly eyes which he yesterday saw shed salt tears for her Majesty upon report of this message'. It was not any neurotic fear but ordinary prudence that told them of mortal peril: of the dire threat to their religion, of ruin and perhaps death for themselves. The hazards were grave. Let us, from the safe distance of the centuries — though not from an age immune from similar fears — concede that they were perhaps inclined to exaggerate the risks from plot and invasion. Still, their sole stay was the life of the Queen. The danger from a chance assassin was unpredictable. The danger from epidemic and other sickness threatened even the healthiest and best protected. 'In the midst of life we are in death': this was a passage that no Elizabethan could read with indifference. A month or two before Parliament met, the Queen had been seriously ill, and many could remember how near she seemed to death before the Parliament of 1563. These sombre thoughts formed the background to the impressive debate that followed.

George Ireland, a newcomer to this Parliament and a Shropshire gentleman representing a Wiltshire borough, seems to have spoken first. 'As we all are most bounden to her Majesty

---

[1] In addition to Cromwell's Diary, cf. *C.J.* i. 96-7.

to think so well of us', said he, 'so can we not but justly lament she hath so small regard unto herself.' He told a story of Philip of Macedon and the prophecy of Demosthenes that a barbarous nation would subdue the Commonwealth. The like he looked for in England. 'We shall become subjects to a treacherous generation'; and there is no Alexander to avenge us. He did not mean to provide for himself in Mary Stuart's court; and 'for his part had as lief be hanged in resisting the Queen of Scots as hunt after'. He adjured the Privy Councillors to do the duty of good subjects in stirring the Queen to action.

The occasion demanded the intervention and leadership of Norton. With his recollection of Elizabeth's obstinacy over the succession in 1566 and over religious reform in 1571, he was afraid of nothing effective being done, and therefore decided to concentrate his attack where it had best hope of success: on the execution of the Duke of Norfolk. Prefacing his speech with the remark that he too expected to be a victim should Mary attain the throne — a reflection which made him 'bold to show his opinion' — he went on to say that he was now persuaded that the first alternative (attainder) was the worst: not because it was so in its nature, but because he saw no likelihood of its execution. Indeed, both ways were now dangerous. The only remedy he saw was to make humble suit for the execution of the Duke. Though the will of the Queen of Scots be very great, we shall thus abate her power. 'Those that labour to save the Duke do it surely with intent to be themselves saved by the Duke, in whom they have expectation.' There was now no reason for the House to regard itself as bound to its former resolution merely to let their opinion reach the Queen informally. 'Execution of necessity is to be required during the session.' We must 'urge this importunately, either jointly with the Lords, or by our Speaker without them'. Otherwise, 'the Parliament may seem to be called to the end we should reveal ourselves' — make their views known to the Marian party, who were their enemies — 'to be hanged hereafter'.

Thomas Hussey, Member for Weymouth and Melcombe Regis, spoke next. They were concerned, he said, with two Queens, 'the one our sovereign Lady Elizabeth, the other a Scot, an enemy to England, an adulterous woman, a homicide, a traitor to the Queen, a subverter of the State, an underminer of titles'. The suddenness of its calling, the time of the year, the Queen's intimation through the mouth of the Lord Keeper, all proclaimed this to be a very necessary Parliament: he trusted that it was not intended to do nothing. He had hitherto forborne to speak, expecting a bill to be before them, but he was now urged to speak and to agree with Norton: 'No good can follow.' He wished the Queen to take example by the contention between York and Lancaster: between two kings, as this is between two queens. York was established heir apparent, but would not tarry for the crown. Such will be the sequel of the Queen of Scots. 'This disabling shall be an enabling; and that will she put in practice ere it be long. Great have been the victories which the Queen's Majesty hath had in spite of the Pope. He would have her as well to use victory as to get victory . . . Let the Queen, therefore, while she hath such an enemy in hand, execute her, lest hereafter herself come to be executed by her.'

Robin Snagge joined in with a long and characteristic contribution. No man was more sorry than he. He trusted that in duty of his zeal to the Queen's Majesty he might, without arrogancy, compare with any man. 'If her Majesty should command him to do anything which may tend to her safety, he would do it with adventure of his life. If her Majesty's pleasure were to command to do nothing, he would lay his hands under her feet. But to deal with this second bill were not to do nothing, but to do stark nought.' He had heard the wisest in this land confer with great diligence about Mary's title, and find nothing in it.

He noted in the message delivered to them that it was her Majesty's 'disposition', not her 'determination'. He therefore saw no reason why they should not proceed with the first bill. He then drew on historical examples to prove the wisdom of putting Mary to death. 'No determination of Parliament can restrain the ambitious mind.' To do as the Queen wished was to encourage traitors, for if they failed in their attempts they knew she was a merciful queen and would not execute them: 'a most dangerous state, when traitors live more surely than true men'. Let us 'proceed to incite her Majesty', in the hope she may change her opinion: St. Augustine changed his. 'This sore hath two heads, the one in the arm-hole, the other at the heart: . . . the one in the north [Mary], the other in London [the Duke]. The sores either to be cut out or the whole body to be lost.' Henceforward their case would not be that of persons suffering from agues — 'to have a good and a bad day' — but 'every day to expect our final destruction'. If all they were going to do was to pronounce that there was no title in Mary's claim before she got the crown, 'surely he will not resist her, but he will put his head between the Queen's Majesty's neck and the hatchet, for that will be the end of us both'.

'It is come to a common voice', he warned the House, that the Duke is ' "a true man, a great friend to the common weal, sought to be destroyed by some of the nobility who have unjustly condemned him: her Majesty will not, for half her revenue, execute him". He prayeth to God there be not those in London, which, if they durst, would pluck him out of the Tower; and the like in the north which would set her at liberty. He can say no more: but he looketh shortly for it, if better remedy be not provided.'

The next speaker, Robert Newdigate, bluntly declared that the report had appalled him, and he now looked for no good. He sorrowed to see so small care of herself in the Queen's Majesty. He feared she depended too much upon God's providence, 'refusing the means now miraculously by God offered unto her'. Mary Stuart was by nature a Scot, and Scots by nature enemies to England. Though for the present she pretend a title to the throne, if she should prevail she will claim it by conquest, as more gainful to her and fittest for her honour. And then all our lands will be lost, all our goods forfeit. Consequently, she must now not only be deposed, but 'her head cut off whilst she is in our hands'. 'Since the Queen, in respect of her own safety, is not to be induced hereunto, let us make petition she will do it in respect of our safety. I have heard she delighteth to be called our mother. Let us desire her to be pitiful over us her children, who have not deserved death.'

Paul Wentworth now spoke — let us hope, with the brevity of our diarist's report. He wished it to be put to the question, 'whether we should call for an axe or an act'.

If Wentworth was brief, the next speaker was not. He was Thomas Atkins, Town Clerk and Member for Gloucester, round whose representation of that city a story of faction can be told. Both our diarists give a lengthy report of his speech: indeed, it is the only one from this important debate recounted in the Anonymous Diary. It looks as if Paul Wentworth's pithy presentation of the case had imposed silence on the House: as if Members expected to go to a vote at once on his deadly motion. If so, the speech by Atkins, whatever its merits, was an impertinence: which is in keeping with what we know of him.

He began with the remark that the great silence now in the House gave him courage to speak, though haply it were more safe to be silent. He saw no reason why they should not stand upon their first resolution. They desired nothing but what was lawful and just. 'It may truly be said that this Scottish woman is the burden of the earth.' She was 'the whole hope of that called Holy, but indeed unholy League of Trent. Her head being cut off, their hope frustrate'. He concluded by bidding the House proceed without despair, stayed by no prohibition, incessantly crying out. God is oft inactive, but at length is stirred and listens. You that be Councillors, show yourselves true Councillors.

If God was not stirred, the Councillors were. Sir James Croft rose to bemoan his lot that he was the bearer of so uncomfortable a message. He suggested that they should marshal in written form the reasons for their refusal to agree with the Queen, and he hoped these would move her Majesty.

Sir Francis Knollys wound up the debate. He thought further speech needless. It only remained to settle how to proceed: whether to petition the Queen through their Speaker, or — which he preferred — 'to move the Lords to join with us in our motions, as well touching the Queen of Scots as the Duke'. As regards the Duke — and how secure Norton's triumph seemed now! — he declared that 'he would wish him dead though he were his brother'. He was allied to him, and near of kin to his children. He revealed that long ago he had told Norfolk that if he attempted this marriage, 'the realm must either destroy him or he destroy us'.

The Speaker now addressed the House. 'You have heard the effect of the Queen's message. You have heard divers very learnedly show cause why her disposition in the same is misliked. I have heard none show any liking thereof, so as by silence they have all confirmed that which hath been said by others.' 'You know it must finally proceed from the Prince.'

On the Speaker's motion the House agreed to send the members of their committee to the House of Lords to report that 'with one whole voice and consent' the Commons still relied on the first bill against Mary, 'as most necessary, without any liking or allowance of the second'. They were to ask whether the Lords held the same view; and, if so, to consult on further joint proceeding. They were also to signify 'that the whole opinion of this House is that her Majesty's safety cannot stand without the execution of the Duke this present session; and that it might please their Lordships in petition thereof unto her Highness, to join with this House'.[1]

The Lords gave their reply on the following day, Saturday, May 24th. They agreed to join with the Commons in a petition to the Queen about Mary, and appointed that afternoon for the joint-committee to meet, asking that the Commons authorize their members to select some of their number to join in presenting the petition. As regards the Duke of Norfolk, since many of the Lords had taken part in his trial, it was not appropriate for them to join in that petition; and besides, their verdict was sufficient declaration of their opinion. The Commons should proceed by themselves; and of this their Lordships had no misliking.[2]

It was Whitsuntide, and the House was to adjourn until the following Wednesday; but before they did so, Mr. Wentworth — whether Peter or Paul, we are not told — reminded them that they had still to take action about the execution of the Duke. It was decided that the petition should be made by Mr. Speaker. He was charged to think of the matter between then and Wednesday, and in the mean season every Member who wished was to deliver to him in writing any arguments they thought should be employed.[3]

Our anonymous diarist, who though not chosen for the smaller delegation sent to the Queen, seems to have been present at the meetings of the joint-committee, tells us about its procedure. It was agreed that every man should set down in writing such arguments as he thought most likely to influence the Queen. The bishops were to concern themselves with reasons of conscience, the laity with reasons of policy; and they

---

[1] *C.J.* i. 97.        [2] Ibid. p. 98.        [3] Also cf. ibid.

were tacitly to answer any objection which the Queen might be able to raise. The civil lawyers were to deal with the legal arguments, *pro et contra*. From all this material the principal arguments were to be selected. It was thought better to deliver these in writing rather than read them to the Queen. Speech might momentarily have more effect, but it was straightway gone and the reasons soon forgotten; whereas a written petition would be read with pauses, its arguments be reflected upon and thus better imprinted on the mind, and its ultimate effect be greater.

We possess the formidable dossier with which these optimists thought they could convince a singularly wilful woman, their Queen, in whom, though intelligence and education were of a very high order, intuition could operate as powerfully as reason.[1]

The bishops, as instructed and as became their office, addressed themselves to Elizabeth's conscience. Inevitably in that dogmatic rather than historically-minded age — was not the whole Bible the Word of God? — they drew on that fecund source of bloody precedents, the Old Testament, using as auxiliary aids classical writers and ancient history. According to the convention of theological controversy, they cited their references in the margin.

'The word of God', they began, 'which is the only director of consciences and a certain rule for all estates and offices, doth often and most earnestly teach that godly princes or magistrates not only in conscience safely may, but also in duty towards God ought, severely and uprightly to administer justice . . . The magistrate (as St. Paul saith) is the minister of God and the revenger of wrath towards him that hath done evil.' St. Peter was cited in confirmation of St. Paul, and from the Book of Wisdom came the warning that 'if the magistrate do not this, God threateneth heavy punishment'. The conclusion followed: 'Her Majesty must needs offend in conscience before God if she do not punish' the Scottish Queen 'according to the measure of her offence in the highest degree'. And for further reinforcement the Books of Leviticus, Proverbs, and Ecclesiastes were drawn upon.

---

[1] I take my version from B.M. Cotton MS. Titus F. I, fols. 172-86. There is a draft of the bishops' reasons in S.P. Scotland (Mary Q. of Scots), 8/47, endorsed by Burghley. I am inclined to think it represents an earlier stage in composition.

What they called 'the second reason' dealt with the wrath of God against Saul for sparing Agag and against Ahab for sparing Benhadad, King of Syria. 'In these examples', commented the bishops, 'great pretence might be made for mercy . . . and great reproach of bloodiness and cruelty . . ; but we see how God judged.' Mary Queen of Scots, a grievous offender, both before and after she came to England, 'hath been by God's especial and marvellous providence put into the Queen's Majesty's hands to be punished'. They feared that the fate of Ahab and Israel might fall upon Elizabeth and England if Mary escaped, as did Benhadad, under pretence of mercy and honourable dealing. And they ended their woeful prognostication with the report that the Prophet's words to Ahab had been spoken to James Stuart, Earl of Murray, late Regent of Scotland, who, ignoring them and sparing Mary, had himself been assassinated.

The theme was pursued in 'the third reason'. Quoting from the Book of the Covenant in Deuteronomy, they explained: 'Here you may perceive that God willeth his magistrates not to spare either brother or sister or son or daughter or wife or friend . . . if he seek to seduce the people of God from His true worship.' And Mary Stuart 'is the only hope of all the adversaries of God throughout all Europe, and the instrument whereby they trust to overthrow the gospel of Christ in all countries'. All histories, they added, highly commended Constantine the Great for putting to death his fellow-emperor Licinius.

'The fourth reason' dwelt on the danger of increasing like wickedness through hope of impunity; and here the story of David supplied the illustrations. 'The late Scottish Queen hath heaped up together all the sins of the licentious sons of David: adultery, murder, conspiracy, treasons, and blasphemies against God also.' If she escape with slight or no punishment, the Queen and her subjects ought to fear that God will reserve her as an instrument to put the Queen from her royal seat of this Kingdom and to plague the people.

Fifthly came an awful warning from the prophets Ezekiel and Jeremiah that 'if His people perish either in soul or body by slackness in administering justice or by any other misgovernment, God will require their blood at the Prince's hand'. For a 'sixth reason' they expounded the argument that it was dangerous for any Christian prince, and contrary to God's word, with colour of mercy and pity to do that which 'shall discourage and kill the hearts, not only of his own good subjects and faithful Councillors, but also of all other nations faithfully professing God's religion and His true worship'. King David was their illustration. By executing Mary, the Queen would 'abash and damp the minds of all the enemies of God and friends of Antichrist'.

Next, the bishops took a series of objections which they conceived might be influencing the Queen's mind, and with a similar wealth of biblical and other allusions answered them, one by one. With one 'objection' we might find ourselves in cordial agreement: 'it may appear very unseemly and worthy sharp reproof in a bishop to excite a prince to cruelty and blood, contrary to her merciful inclinations'. But, scanning the Old Testament, they found themselves in such a goodly company of prophets that the word of God refuted the argument. 'The prince in government must be like unto God himself, who is not only amiable by mercy, but terrible also by justice.'

From the argument of the bishops, with its repellent idiom of the ideologue and flavour of the Holy War — which it behoves us to understand and appreciate — one turns with relief to the layman's presentation of the case, beginning in language unmystical: 'We your Majesty's most humble and faithful subjects, assembled in Parliament for preservation of your royal person and estate. . . .'

In a long and sonorous preamble, they recited 'the great goodness of God that hath chosen and appointed such a Sovereign to reign over us as never subjects, by any record, ever had a better'; prayed that God would grant her the 'most perfect felicity that ever creature had or might have upon earth'; and reviewed the misdeeds of 'a very unnatural sister, Lady Mary Stuart, late Queen of Scots', a Lady 'born out of kind, as it should seem'. They rehearsed the provisions that it was proposed to embody in the second and milder bill against Mary. They appreciated that Elizabeth thought herself bound in honour not to proceed further against her, since she was her 'sister', and 'a Queen born', and had fallen into her hands from the violence of others, having 'as a bird followed by a hawk' sought succour at her Majesty's feet.

272 THE PARLIAMENT OF 1572

They described all this as 'rather a declaration of that most mild and gracious nature of yours than any assurance of your person or estate at all'; and they proceeded to a long series of 'reasons answering the former arguments', appended to which were reasons to prove that it stood not only with justice but with the Queen's Majesty's honour and safety to proceed criminally against Mary.

To disable her by name from any claim or title to the crown would in effect amount to confirmation of a right. 'We do take it for a known truth that both by the laws and statutes in this land now in force she is already disabled': a statement which — to illustrate the mutations of time and relativity of truth, and perhaps even the deeper wisdom of Elizabeth's instinct — might not inaptly be placed in juxtaposition with the Succession Act of 1604, where James I, whose hereditary claim came through his mother, was acknowledged 'as being lineally, justly, and lawfully next and sole heir of the blood royal of this realm'.

It would not do any good, our petitioners continued, to lay grievous pains on those espousing Mary's cause: 'desperation feareth no laws', and the only remedy is to remove the cause of all mischief. To threaten Mary with death if hereafter she attempt any evil or try to escape, was, by experience of her former life, useless: witness her escape from Loch Leven in spite of such a threat. Menacing and threatening words of law 'shall not keep her back from her malicious intent to subvert your Majesty and to give a push for the crown, come of her what will'. 'There will want no traitors to be always ready to bring this her device about and to do what they can for her liberty; and such as will not deal in mean matters will adventure deep for a kingdom, because the reward is great when the service is done.'

They dealt with the Queen's concern for her honour, re-butting the argument that all princes would speak well of her for dealing leniently with Mary. And against her desire to hazard her own self rather than deal with Mary according to her deserts, they declared: 'It behoveth all your good subjects, most gracious Sovereign, to call and cry to God for His heavenly assistance, that His power may be given unto you . . . to seek assuredly your own safety.' There followed twenty-four propositions from the Civil Law, succeeded by elaborations of some of them, with relevant quotations.

This laborious document may have been presented to Elizabeth on Whit Monday, May 26th, during the brief recess.[1] If so, she had time to study it before she gave her answer on the Wednesday. That morning — May 28th — when parliament reassembled, the Speaker, on arrival at the House, was told of the Queen's pleasure that the deputation, selected from their grand committee, should attend the Court at St. James's at 8 a.m.[2]

Elizabeth may have spoken extempore, not troubling to put her answer in writing, since the occasion, though important enough, was not formal: she was speaking to a delegation from a committee. At any rate, no trace of a written answer exists. All we possess are accounts of a report made to the House of Commons by Sir Francis Knollys, and a hint from Peter Wentworth that either in the report made by Knollys, or more likely in the original speech, there was such studied artistry, flattery, and affection, that, though they were plunged into despair, two Members at least were bewitched.

It was later that morning that Knollys announced the deputation's return from the Queen's presence, and made his report. The Queen's Majesty, he said, doth very thankfully accept the good will and zeal of this House in their carefulness for her safety and preservation. She wished them to think that in her opinion their device was the safest way; yet, weighing her estate in other respects, the time present, and other circumstances, she is resolved to defer, but not reject, the first way of proceeding, and in the mean time, with all convenient speed, to go forward with the second bill. She wanted this to be drawn by her learned counsel and to be so penned as not to give colour of title, one way or the other, either in Mary or any other person; and in the same bill, also, provision to be made for the safety of such as have spoken so earnestly against Mary's title. Though for the present they had not obtained as much as they desired, she bade them like wise men be content with what they could get. Pending the bringing in of this bill, they were not to

---

[1] Burghley's endorsement on S.P. Scotland (Mary Q. of Scots), 8/47 suggests this date.

[2] *C.J.* i. 98.

enter into any speeches or arguments on the matter. Knollys added that she had also signified this her pleasure to the Lords of the Higher House.[1]

Doubtless there were some few about Elizabeth at Court, in addition to the French ambassador, who were whispering rival advice to her. They cannot have been many or influential, nor can such intrigue detract from the sole credit or discredit for the decision. The formidable dossier presented to her voiced the collective Protestant wisdom of the nation. It was passionately supported by the overwhelming will of Council, Lords, and Commons. We are left with the reflection: what manner of person was this — nay more, what quality of woman in so masculine a society — that dared stand in the isolation of her own instinct and authority against her whole world?

---

[1] This is a composite account, from the two diaries and *C.J.* i. 98.

## CHAPTER IV

# MARY QUEEN OF SCOTS: III

THE Queen's message barred further talk about Mary Queen of Scots before the new bill appeared. It did not mention the Duke of Norfolk. Apparently it was Robin Snagge who perceived the opening this offered.

After Sir Francis Knollys had sat down, Snagge rose, and first saying that he submitted himself to her Majesty's pleasure and was glad that if time had allowed she would have been content to proceed against Mary — an optimistic or politic construction to put on the Queen's action — he went on to declare that it nevertheless remained to provide something for her safety. This was 'to cut off the heads of other her enemies, which are already condemned by law and for whom no such excuse can be made'. Experience, he said, showed that desperate men have killed themselves. Much rather would they adventure to kill the Queen. 'Dags [i.e. pistols] have already been taken in the Court; and that which hath been, may be. The Duke therefore to be executed in time, lest in time the Queen and we ourselves be destroyed.' They must petition for this; and he trusted the Queen would not be offended by their importunity, 'although for maidenly modesty she draw back'. He then hinted at the few discordant voices which were doubtless to be found at the Court, playing on Elizabeth's merciful instincts. 'Those that have persuaded with the Queen to stay the former proceedings' are 'never to be liked of: to do one thing here openly and persuade another secretly.'

Apparently there were more speeches than our diaries record. Our informant is none other than Peter Wentworth. In 1881 a manuscript was in existence containing three of his speeches, preceded by the Queen's message. Alas! since then, it seems to have disappeared, though let us hope that some day it will reappear and a precious episode in our parliamentary history be made known. Meanwhile, all we can do is to quote Wentworth's own heading to the document and sigh over our loss. 'Speech uttered by me the Wednesday, Thursday and Saturday in the Whitsun week [May 28th, 29th, 31st] ... upon a message sent by her Majesty in the Parliament House, whereupon two of the House made a motion that the Speaker and certain of the House should go to her Majesty and give her thanks in the behalf of the whole House for the good opinions conceived of us: the which for my part I did not think her Majesty had deserved, so that my speech was to stay thanks, and to other ends.'[1]

Our diarist, Thomas Cromwell, gives a short report of Wentworth's first speech. It follows Snagge's. Said Wentworth, he 'would have us hunger as we ought after righteousness'. He must needs be plain. This message was very sorrowful unto him. He was 'not satisfied to see the Queen forsake the better (which she seeth) and follow the worse', to the danger of her person, the subversion of religion, and the destruction of the realm and all her good subjects. 'For this he can give no thanks.' He thought that those persons were to be liked who would be plain with her Majesty to her preservation, and not such as dissemble with her to her destruction. Since she will not provide full remedy, it remained to do it at least in part by executing the Duke and so cutting off half Mary's head. He wanted the House to forbear dealing in any other matter until this was done: in other words, to employ the strike tactics of 1566. Otherwise, words of comfort to them were in vain. It was like saying, 'Eat, drink and be merry!': to which will be justly added, 'O fool! this night shall thy life be taken from thee'. He wanted the Speaker to petition, accompanied by the whole House.

Sir Francis Knollys now interposed, to save time, perhaps also to calm the House. It was already agreed, he said, that there should be a petition and that the Speaker should make it. All they had to decide was whether the whole House should accompany him to the Queen, or part. He preferred part, because it was difficult to accommodate all.

Our anonymous diarist tells us that the Speaker had no liking for the role allotted to him; and this seems true, for he now spoke, trying to divert the House back to its old decision against a petition. Fleetwood followed. After the courtier-like reflec-

---

[1] *H.M.C. Report viii.* p. 212. I owe warm thanks to Mr. Ralph Bankes for allowing me to look for this document at Kingston Lacy. I could not find it. If it survives anywhere, I should be grateful for the information.

tion that 'we ought to deal modestly when we deal with them that carry the sword', he transported Members far away from the passionate mood of Wentworth by inflicting on them a long historical disquisition on petitioning the Sovereign in Parliament, his precedents extending from Edward III's reign to Henry VIII's. He disliked the Speaker's suggestion about letting their 'opinion' be known. The gravity of the House called for 'conclusions', not 'opinions'.

In the end it was resolved, with only one negative voice, to petition 'for the present execution of the Duke', the petition to be digested and put in writing 'against tomorrow morning', when it was to be delivered to Mr. Speaker and arrangements made for its presentation.

That same morning the Lords had asked for a convenient number of those who had been to the Queen, along with others, to meet six of themselves in the afternoon, when the judges would be in attendance. They were evidently to confer over the drafting of the more moderate bill against Mary.[1]

On the Thursday, May 29th, the petition about the Duke ought to have been ready, but as the Commons seem to have omitted saddling anybody with the task, little wonder it did not appear. None of our sources gives any indication that the business was discussed, but one of Peter Wentworth's lost speeches belongs to this day and doubtless he saw that it was not forgotten.

Another isolated speech, maintaining the constant pressure, seems to have been made at the beginning of the next morning's sitting, when St. Leger addressed the House. We owe our epitome of it to the Clerk, Fulk Onslow's personal diary, which at this point becomes a valuable supplement to our information.[2] 'Since' — began St. Leger — 'the Queen's Majesty's will and pleasure is that we should not proceed nor deal with the first bill against the monstrous and huge dragon and mass of the earth, the Queen of Scots, yet my conscience urgeth and pricketh me to speak and move this House to be in hand with her Majesty with the execution of the roaring lion: I mean the Duke of Norfolk. And although her Majesty be lulled asleep and wrapped in the mantle of her own peril, yet for my part I

---

[1] Cf. *C.J.* i. 99.
[2] My narrative now becomes a fusion of all three diaries.

cannot be silent in uttering of my conscience.' He 'alleged the text of wicked Haman' which 'he applied to the Duke, and of the godly Queen Hester' which he applied to the Queen's Majesty.

Perhaps a remark by our anonymous diarist — who was now telescoping his report — belongs to this day. He says that 'the Speaker willed the House to put him in writing what they would have him utter, for more than they put him in writing he would not speak'. Speaker Bell was a Norfolk gentleman, Recorder of King's Lynn and Member for that borough; and this presumably explains his reluctance to figure as leader of the deadly agitation against that county's great magnate. His obstruction was holding up the House.

On the following day, Saturday, May 31st, Peter Wentworth was at it again, clamouring for execution of the Duke. And this time, as our anonymous diarist reports, the 'matter grew so far, as the House, without further delay, began wholly to incline to have committees appointed, which should consult upon and draw out the fittest reasons to be uttered by the Speaker'. Snagge spoke after Wentworth, 'to the same effect'. Norton followed. 'He brought forth a paper in writing, wherein he had written certain reasons which should be delivered to the Speaker to be considered of.' George Ireland, who had spoken so feelingly on May 23rd, joined in the chorus; and another newcomer to this Parliament, Thomas Digges, whose mathematical writings have secured him a place in *The Dictionary of National Biography* — a man ready with his pen — proposed the appointment of a committee to scrutinize any written arguments that Members had prepared. Robin Snagge intervened again, to urge that the whole House should go to the Queen; while John Marsh, the London mercer, spoke in support of Digges's motion.

Now it so happens that a copy of 'the paper in writing' which Norton delivered to the Speaker has been preserved among manuscripts once belonging to Christopher Yelverton; and along with it are papers prepared for the occasion by Digges and by the Member for Maidstone, Thomas Dannet, a cousin of Cecil, a former Marian exile, and — if, as seems likely, he be the father, not the son — a man who had been employed on missions abroad. These latter papers propound reasons for the execution, while Norton's — as was appropriate from the prime organizer of the agitation and an expert parliamentary draftsman — is 'a form or plat for the ground and order' of the petition: what, if it had been a bill, might have been termed 'articles'.

Digges was much concerned about the psychological effects of not executing the Duke. 'Reports vulgarly spread that his peers have wrongfully ... condemned him, and that the Queen, knowing it, is moved in conscience to keep him alive. The nature of the multitude being prone to credit rumours and favour such as are in misery, it cannot be but [that] this preserving of him augmenteth his well-willers and increaseth his faction ... It is an opinion, in many established, that God will not suffer the Prince to touch him.' The preachers are discredited and God's adversaries triumph when her Majesty will not give ear to the vehement exhortations of true prophets and the lamentable cry of her whole realm, craving 'to be delivered from the mouth of the dragon that, nuzzled in blood, expecteth but his time to satiate with the blood of her true subjects — God's people — his unsatiable, revengeful appetite'.

Dannet's paper was longer, more concrete, and abounded with classical illustrations of his arguments. He pointed out that 'her Majesty layeth a necessity upon her enemies to murder her own royal person', since they had only two ways of avoiding the danger of death and recovering liberty. These were rebellion and assassination, the former of which was ruled out because it would endanger Mary. He dealt in cogent and realistic manner — reminiscent at times of the penetrating but cold reason of a Francis Bacon — with two optimistic arguments: that Elizabeth's enemies would attempt nothing against her and that they could do her no harm. 'There are but two ways', he wrote, 'for a prince to deliver herself of enemies: mercy and justice.' Mercy is to be used as Vespasian and Octavian used it: that is, without open examination to forgive and forget the offence. But her Majesty, having taken a contrary course and, by the Duke's trial, touched the offender both in honour, blood, and lands, must now of force proceed to justice. 'The middle way ... cannot be but dangerous to her. ... Mercy, coming after honour stained, irritateth rather than appeaseth.' In answering the second of the optimists' arguments, he commented on the folly of building the Queen's preservation on this feeble pillar — 'that neither England, Spain, Italy, no, nor Rome (which both forgeth and dispenseth with all kind of treasons) are able to furnish one desperate person that dare either by sword or by poison attempt her Majesty's destruction'. His concluding paragraph rivals the frankness of Peter Wentworth: 'Last of all, it may please her Majesty to incline her gracious ears to the humble petition of her faithful subjects, lest her Majesty be recorded for the only prince of this land with whom the subjects thereof could never prevail in any one suit.'[1]

After Snagge and Marsh had spoken in the debate, Sir Francis Knollys rose, 'belike', as our anonymous diarist wrote, 'having some inkling that the execution of the Duke was toward'. 'I perceive', he said, that the motion 'proceedeth of very love and care you have to the Queen's person, which is the mark whereat all good subjects shoot. And although I do know nothing more convenient and needful than execution, and that with speed, yet I know the disposition of princes is rather of themselves to do such things than by way of pressing and urging. It may be, and it is like enough, her Majesty is of herself already disposed sooner to do it than you do perhaps think or believe . . . I know already her mind partly therein. The execution will be more honourable to her Majesty if the doing thereof come of her free mind without our motion.' He therefore urged them to stay. 'I trust we shall not repent it. If you go on . . . you may perhaps delay the thing you seek to further.'

Despite this authoritative hint, George Ireland was for instant action, believing that they would thus force rather than hinder a decision: if, he added, the Queen be bent that way, 'as I do greatly doubt'. Fleetwood — by now the model of caution — was opposed to action. Our diarist, Thomas Cromwell, resisted any delay at all. So did Robin Snagge and Paul Wentworth. Sir James Croft spoke in support of his fellow-Councillor, and the variable Newdigate backed him. There was 'much debating', and a call for a division, which itself provoked debate. At last, 'to ease the House of this trouble, a new question was made: . . . whether they were content to stay

---

[1] Yelverton MS. xxvi, fols. 159 seqq. at Elvetham Hall. There is an inferior copy in vol. xxxi of this valuable collection of manuscripts.

their proceeding for that day'. Out of credit for Knollys 'all, almost, consented'. The Wentworths and their friends were surely included in that word 'almost'.[1]

Pressure on Elizabeth had become irresistible. A price had to be paid for her lenity to Mary Stuart. On the Monday morning (June 2nd) 'straight after 7 o'clock', and before the House reassembled, England's sole Duke was led out to execution. Our anonymous diarist was present and reports 'somewhat of that which I heard him speak'. A sense of sorrow and tragedy possessed the Queen; and so far from leading to Mary's execution, as the over-rational orators of the House of Commons had anticipated, her revulsion probably made her more determined than ever to follow her instinct.

A momentary quiet now fell on proceedings while the Commons awaited the bill against Mary Queen of Scots. The bill was introduced in the House of Lords on Saturday, May 31st. Goodness knows what a fearsome gauntlet it would have had to run had it come first to the Commons: what a barrage of speeches, a plethora of amendments. The government was bent on speed. It was read a second time on June 2nd and perhaps committed then. On the 4th it was sent for ingrossing, and on the 5th was read a third time and passed, and sent to the Commons with 'recommendation' from their lordships, request also being made for a present reading thereof that day. The Lords further signified that 'the time of the year considered, the Queen's Majesty's pleasure is that this House [the Commons] do proceed in that and other weighty causes, laying aside all private matters'.[2]

The bill was entitled, an act 'concerning Mary, daughter of James the Fifth, late King of Scotland, called the Queen of Scots'. Its preamble, which ran to the extraordinary length of between 2000 and 2500 words, was a narrative epitome of the case against Mary presented to the joint committee of both Houses at the beginning of the session: a well-written, effective statement for the prosecution. A petition followed, praying the Queen 'not to bear in vain the sword of justice' but 'to punish and correct (which your Majesty justly and lawfully may do) all the treasons and wicked attempts of the said Mary condignly . . . as speedily and in such manner and form as may

[1] Also cf. *C.J.* i. 99.        [2] *L.J.* i. 715, 717; *C.J.* i. 100.

stand with your Majesty's good will and pleasure'. In the meantime, in order to remove the causes of high treasons and dangerous practices arising from the doubtful and uncertain hope of Mary and her adherents to possess or succeed to the crown, and as some part of the punishment of her offences, the following clauses were to be enacted.

These pronounced Mary unworthy and incapable of any title and interest in the crown of England. They provided that if hereafter, during Elizabeth's life, she pretend any interest or title in the crown, or procure or consent to the invasion of any foreign force, or stir any rebellion within England, or if any war, rebellion, or invasion be made for any causes concerning her, or if she do, or consent to the doing, of anything which would be deemed treason in any subject: that then Mary shall be deemed a traitor, and after indictment and conviction, suffer the pains of high treason. She was to be tried as the wife of a peer is tried. It was further provided that if at any time after Elizabeth's death she make claim to the crown, or any war or warlike forces be raised in England to advance her claim, then she and all her fautors to be deemed enemies of the realm and be utterly out of the protection of the law. The following clause was directed against her adherents, making it treason to support her title by speech or writing; or, during Elizabeth's lifetime, to conspire or assent to taking Mary away without licence; or to give Mary aid, comfort, or support by express words, writing, or deed in order to procure her deliverance; or to practice for her marriage without the Queen's consent. Then came a clause guaranteeing perpetual impunity at law for all persons maintaining and defending the provisions of this act to the uttermost of their power.

The next section expressed in the terms of that age the pervading sense of fundamental ideological conflict. Its preamble deserves to be quoted in full: 'And forasmuch as all the horrible treasons and conspiracies before in this act mentioned have grown by the said Mary and other her adherents, chiefly for this cause and purpose: to bring again into this realm the detestable and usurped authority of the see of Rome, and thereby to subject the imperial crown of this realm and the faithful and loving subjects of the same to the bondage, tyranny, and thraldom of the said see; and so to change and alter the true and

R. Dunkarton sculp.

SIR CHRISTOPHER YELVERTON KNIGHT

*of Gray's Inn.*

Justice of the King's Bench.

Anno Dom. 1602. Æt. 66.

*From an Original Painting by*

*JANSSEN, in the possession of the PUBLISHER*

London *Published by* S.Woodburn, 1811

sincere religion of God now established within this realm . . .'
The clause proceeded to make it high treason for anyone hereafter 'willingly, advisedly, and directly' to do, procure, or
assent to anything with the intent of re-establishing the authority of the see of Rome in England.

The final clause aimed at removing the fear, expressed in the
House of Commons, that those who had spoken and acted
against Mary might one day be called to account. All such
speeches and actions were to be deemed 'good and lawful
doings of honest, zealous, and true subjects'; and future behaviour in conformity with this act was likewise declared lawful. Little good this was likely to do if the occasion for fear —
the accession of Mary — came to pass.[1]

In asking the Commons to give an immediate reading to the
bill, the Lords, consciously or unconsciously, were furthering
the government's policy of little talk, few amendments, and
much speed. It was late in the morning. Ten bills had already
been read, and Members' stomachs must have been registering
the time for dinner. Later in the reign official tacticians tried to
plan the reading of controversial measures for that hour, when
drought was apt to stay the springs of eloquence. Success was
not always achieved; but on this occasion the bill was so in-
ordinately long that even the stalwarts can have been left with
no hope of a first-reading debate.

The next morning these forcing tactics were renewed. Our
anonymous diarist comments: 'About the middle part of the
sitting of the House, [Christopher] Hatton cometh in and
whispereth with the Speaker. By the sequel it was guessed he
brought a message from the Queen for the reading again of the
Scottish Queen's bill, for, presently after, the Speaker moved to
have the bill read; whereat there was much sticking, for it was
thought more haste than good speed that the matter, being of
so great weight and having received a reading but the day before, it should now proceed to the second reading. Yet at length
it was read, through the means of the Speaker especially.'

In the subsequent debate, Christopher Yelverton, the orator-
lawyer, seems to have been the first to speak. England, he said,

---

[1] My text is taken from Cotton MS. Caligula B VIII, fols. 240-6, which appears
to contain the later amendments by the Commons, but not the proviso which they
added. There is another, inferior copy in Cotton MS. Titus F. I.

was 'the spectacle of religion through all Christendom', though its glory was somewhat dimmed by the danger of alteration. He did not like the hasty procedure. The bill touched the Queen's Majesty, the whole State, and every man in particular, and was more fit for the beginning of a Parliament than to be speedily passed at the end. Judging by the one reading he had heard, it was very injurious at many points. 'The Queen of Scots', he declared, 'hath no title, neither in possession or reversion to the crown. If any man think otherwise, let him prove her title: he shall be answered.' And yet he found the contrary was covertly carried in the bill. He proceeded to detailed criticism. Consider well: either we shall seem, as the opinion of the whole Parliament, to allow that she hath title to the crown, which we now take away as punishment; or else we take away nothing, and then it is no punishment. He disliked the implication that at present there was uncertainty about their ability to try Mary. 'He hath been always, and is, of opinion she is a traitor; and then it were very impertinent to say she cannot be tried . . . She is to be tried as a subject of another nation. She is here no Queen.' And so he went on from item to item, exposing the dilemma in which the draftsmen of the bill had inevitably found themselves. He objected, for example, to the last clause, granting immunity to those who had spoken or written against Mary. 'It may carry a doubtfulness that before it was not lawful.' He himself would never claim benefit of this immunity. 'It is already lawful and hath always been; yea, even when she was in her best state.'

Snagge, the indefatigable, spoke again. He, too, we need hardly add, was critical. 'The words of the bill make her title stronger than before. The recital of the facts, treasons, and devilish practices will not touch her if she hap the crown. The facts [would then be] purged by dignity. The body politic confounds the property of a natural body.' The trial provided in the bill 'giveth a more honourable trial than is due to her before: a presumption we mean to honour and not punish her'. He wanted an oath included, to be taken of everyone, so that all outside Parliament should also declare their consent.

By now it was probably growing late, for Thomas Norton began a speech with the assurance that he would not be long. This Parliament, he said, was called for matters of great necessity, and therefore it was not good to do nothing; 'much worse to do stark nought'. He was thoroughly sceptical of the Queen taking drastic action against Mary. Their bill purported to be an interim measure: he feared that the 'meantime' in its wording 'will be too long a time'. He wanted all words of implication struck out. He also wanted a proviso to declare that the meaning of Parliament was 'not to affirm any title in her'. Referring back bitterly to the Treasons Act of the previous Parliament, he said it achieved nothing. Additions were then offered — his own bill, which the Commons tacked on to the government's. But the Queen was misinformed, being told that these additions aimed at establishing the succession, to her peril. He knew not what relics remained of the faction that then influenced her. 'He would, therefore, every man to make protestation [that] he meaneth not to advance any title; and yet to speak freely of the bill.'

There was evidently no more time for speeches that morning, but they had to decide how they were to deal with so long, so controversial, and so important a bill. Our anonymous diarist notes: it was moved 'that the bill might be drawn into articles, because it was so long, and that every man might speak to every article, and that by a man's speech to one article he might not be barred to speak to another. For otherwise, the length of the bill was such, and the occasions of speech therein so many, as two or three men speaking might spend a whole forenoon. It seemed hereupon good that certain of the ripest wits within the House' — the *Commons Journal* gives their names: Sadler, Mildmay, Bromley, among officials; Manwood, Popham, Monson, Yelverton and Norton from the rest — 'should be appointed to have conference upon every point in the bill; and after, upon the reading of it by articles, they should utter their opinions . . . and so to leave it to the House to judge upon. This resolution eased the House of much labour, and saved the expense of much time.' The *Commons Journal* notes another departure in procedure: 'all arguments [were] to be received as upon the second reading of the bill' — that is, the debate was not to be regarded as closed — 'until it shall be read the third time'. And Mildmay soon imposed a very heavy — and presumably unrewarded — burden on the Clerk by proposing that every member of the committee and every lawyer should have a copy of the bill and study it. Its words should 'be tried like drachms of gold'.[1]

The next day, Saturday, June 7th, after reading eight bills — mostly private bills, which in spite of the Queen's orders they were evidently determined to handle — they resumed their great debate, in accordance with the previous day's decision. Cromwell, the diarist, reports thirteen Members as speaking, including Norton, Alford, Wilbraham, Sir Thomas Scott, Dannet and Sir Walter Mildmay. Criticism tended to concentrate on several phrases. The anonymous diarist sums up fairly well in reporting that 'the occasion of speech against the bill grew most upon words which implied a title in the Scottish Queen, for the full remedy whereof no way could be devised; yet the best way was thought to have a proviso added to the end of the bill, whereby it should be enacted that no part of the bill should be construed by implication. And so it was agreed.'

Alford began his speech, which characteristically was opposed to any alteration, by remarking that he was 'grown in double suspicion in the House: as well in religion as for fancy and affection'. It is a reasonable assumption that, when he sat down, he had not dissipated the suspicion. Sir Thomas Scott talked about the crisis rather than the bill. He was afraid of delay; of Mary's strength in support from the Papists of England and Scotland, the Pope, the King of Spain, the Duke of Alva, the Guise party in France; he disliked her imprisonment in the north and begged Elizabeth's Councillors to incite her Majesty against this. A Member from the north supported him, saying that in his country it was a great deal more dangerous to be a Protestant than a Papist.

On the Monday, June 9th, the suggested proviso, stipulating that nothing in the bill should be expounded to affirm any title in the succession to any person, was offered to the House, certain articles of the bill itself were read, and a debate took place. Early among the speakers was Snagge, vigorous as ever. Since they could not obtain the best provision for the greatest sore, he would 'be content with any salve, but not with any medicine which carrieth poison'. Among other matters, he objected to the phrase, 'as though she were naturally dead', following the declaration of Mary's inability to claim the crown.

[1] Cf. *C.J.* i. 101.

'It may seem to help her son to the succession', he declared:
which tells us — if, indeed, we had doubted — what Snagge's
views were on that subject. Judging from the text of the bill
we possess, the Commons met this objection with an amendment: as they met most of the objections made in these debates.
Dalton spoke: briefly, it would seem. Fleetwood made a
typical speech, though not so egregious as on other occasions.
He declared himself 'amazed with a sentence of Tully. If
breach of laws a man should undertake, then break them boldly
for a kingdom's sake. Causes of kingdoms cannot be pleaded by
way of estoppel', he added; and he clearly, and rightly, thought
that facts could prove more powerful than their bill. Monson
spoke. The radical lawyer, Thomas Colby, urged 'that every
man may speak his fill. Corn, the more it is ground, the meal
will be the finer'. To which Norton retorted, 'Corn too long
ground makes burnt meal.' Peter Wentworth added his
contribution: 'he had rather commit some folly in speech than
do injury by silence'.

So the debate went on. Cromwell reports three more speeches
that morning. They decided to seek a conference with the
Lords over their proviso; and then in the afternoon — for, two
days before, they had begun afternoon sessions, from 3 p.m. till
6 p.m. to speed private bills, and those only[1] — they sand-
wiched in some more speeches on 'the great bill', including one
by Sir Thomas Scott and another by Dalton.

That apparently finished the second-reading debate, and
further work on the many criticisms and suggested amendments seems to have been undertaken by their committee,
which went into consultation with a committee of the Upper
House. On Wednesday, June 11th, another unusual feature
was added to this extraordinary session when the Queen
instructed both Houses to adjourn for thirteen days, owing to
the absorption of the Court in receiving the Duke of Mont-
morency, arrived on a special mission to ratify the Treaty of
Blois, offer the Duke of Alençon in marriage to the Queen, and
incidentally do what he could to protect Mary Queen of Scots.
His coming was no good omen for the cause that the Commons
had at heart.[2]

Parliament reassembled on Tuesday, June 24th — in full

[1] Cf. *C.J.* i. 101.    [2] Cf. ibid. pp. 101-2.

summer — and that morning the bill against Mary was sent up to the Lords 'to see and consider': again an extraordinary course of procedure, but calculated to save time and ease its passage.[1] It was back in the Commons the next morning, when it was given its third reading. Says our anonymous diarist, 'the bill had been so fully argued unto before, as it was thought there would have been no speech used against it; yet Alford, minding, as it seemed, the overthrow of the bill (for so, indeed, it fell out afterward) spake against two principal points of it'.

Alford began by desiring all men to mark his words, and that if any part of his speech were misliked, he might be charged while it was in remembrance. His first objection was to the provision that if any war be levied for Mary, whether with her consent or no, she shall be deemed a traitor. 'It might very well fall out', he said, 'that rebellion might be raised within this realm, the Scottish Queen not privy thereto, nothing at all knowing thereof, and so not to be blamed therefor.' 'If twenty lewd men should proclaim her Queen, she shall be condemned.' It would be accounted 'the greatest injustice in the world', would be 'against the honour of England', and be 'talked of in all Christendom'. His second objection was to the provision that 'if God should take away the Queen's Majesty, and the Scottish Queen should make any claim to the crown, or should make any trouble within this realm . . . she should be out of the protection of the law. Free liberty, without any peril of law, is given to every person for the killing of such'. It would 'be lawful for any man, were he never so mean a subject, to lay hand on her'.

'Hereupon he took occasion to tell how princes ought to be dealt withal, how men ought not to lay hands upon the anointed of the Lord.' 'First, we must consider what she [Mary] is, and what we be that thus deal against her. Her I take to be a Queen still *in esse*, although she be deposed by her subjects: a Queen, I mean, in England, not of England, a Scottish Queen, prisoner, that came hither for succour. We that deal against her are the Queen's Majesty (whom God long preserve) and the whole body of the realm, assembled in the High Court of Parliament, being the most noble and honourable court that we have in this land. And for my part, I think that to be safe

done for the realm that may be honourably done . . . Yea, and
it is seen that princes do as much esteem their honours as they
do their lives. I think her to be as vile and as naughty a creature
as ever the earth bare, and am as thoroughly persuaded of her
lewd demeanours as any man in this company; yet can I not
see how it can stand with the honour of England, for the avoiding of foreign slander, either to condemn her unheard, or to
touch her in life for that she never knew of.' He went on to
declare that he 'would not wish any man to inure a subject's
hands with prince's blood'; and this led him to recall David's
attitude to Saul and to tell the story of a Sovereign who,
immediately after executing a prisoner-King for treason, had
the hangman himself put to death, 'to this intent: that he should
not vaunt himself to have been the spiller of so noble blood'.

It was a significant, a disconcerting speech. All three of our
diarists pay it the compliment of a lengthy report. In exposing
the seeming injustice of the bill and its strain of lynch-law,
Alford, deliberately or fortuitously, was echoing the profound
repugnance which must already have been in Elizabeth's own
mind.

The speech shocked Members; the more so because Alford
had reserved these criticisms for the third reading. They
seemed the tactics of a wrecker. It brought Norton to his feet.
'Those which mean well, need not greatly to fear the mistaking
of their speech . . . No man's speech hath been oftener mistaken
than mine. Yet this advantage I have of some men . . . that my
speech tendeth not always to the overthrow of good matters, as
some other men's do.' With this thrust at Alford, he turned to
refute his arguments. Mary would be out of protection on the
Queen's death because there would be then no remedy by law,
and she was therefore to be deemed as an enemy. 'It hath been
said, we should do injustice if we should adjudge the punishment of treason to the Scottish Queen for every rebellion hereafter raised within this realm. For so perhaps we might punish
her for the offence of another. The matter is greatly mistaken
by the gentleman that thus spake. For if any tumult or rebellion hereafter grow, the pains of treason are laid upon her, not
for that rebellion but for those treasons which she hath hitherto
committed, for which, if the Queen's Majesty's lenity were not
the greater, she might now justly receive punishment. So that

the injustice which is done unto her is this: that she hath not presently the punishment which yet, perhaps, hereafter may fall upon her.' Moreover, 'at this present there is no likelihood of any rebellious attempt to be made but in respect of her, through the procurement either of herself or of her favourers'. 'Shall we ... provide no remedy until a new mischief or treason be wrought, and then provide remedy when it is too late; she living to the danger of our Queen daily?' 'The matter hath been considered by the bishops according to the word of God, by the civilians, and by the judges of the Common Law, and all have agreed that it is just and lawful. God forbid we should prefer the vain name of honour before the safety of the Queen's Majesty.' 'It may be doubted whether she [Mary] be a Queen at all ..., but sure I am she is no Queen of ours, she is none of our anointed. The examples of the Old Testament be not few for the putting of wicked kings to death.' He wanted the Speaker in his closing oration to declare to the Queen that this bill is no perfect safety for her; that it will be necessary for her to proceed further to execution, or otherwise she and we will continue in peril.

Another Member spoke, echoing Norton. Perhaps others did, though our diaries do not say so. On some occasion during this session Peter Wentworth bluntly denounced Mary as 'the most notorious whore in all the world'.[1]

The bill passed 'without any "No"', and the proviso was also passed. The consultations that had been going on between committees of both Houses secured that there would be no difficulties in the House of Lords either over the proviso or the amendments; and there, on the following day, June 26th, the bill was finally agreed to. It awaited its fate at the Queen's hands.[2]

---

[1] Inner Temple Petyt MS. 538/17, fol. 254.    [2] *C.J.* i. 102; *L.J.* i. 723.

## CHAPTER V

# RELIGION

No parliamentary time-table — not even that of 1566 — could have seemed less favourable to the Puritans in their desire to reform the Church. But the years were passing, and by the mere efflux of time the compromise of 1559 was shedding its interim character. It is little wonder that extremists, especially among the younger generation, were becoming impatient. To temporize over so vital an issue was not in their nature. They made this Parliament of 1572 the occasion for launching a full Presbyterian programme; and though in the end nothing was accomplished, the repercussions of the new policy were of profound importance.

Thomas Cartwright's lectures on the Acts of the Apostles, delivered at Cambridge in 1570, gave the first great stimulus, since the days of the Marian exile, to the conversion of left-wing clergymen. Vestments, rites, ceremonies — the objects of controversy hitherto — now appeared as incidentals. These lectures concentrated attention on a more fundamental matter: the structure and polity of the Church. They portrayed the apostolic and true Church as Calvinistic. To a generation that believed in the Bible as the word of God, the argument had a cogency quite alien to our mode of thought. Moreover, the times were revolutionary: minds were obsessed with the rival creeds of Protestantism and Catholicism, moderation and compromise out of season, and the keenest Protestants prone to be doctrinaire. Cartwright's lectures had such an immense effect at Cambridge that the authorities stepped in, silenced him, and deprived him of his professorship. He was driven abroad and was lecturing at Geneva in 1571.[1]

The new movement ought to have been dealt with firmly by episcopal discipline. It was not. The bishops were in a position which we today can appreciate: that of orthodox radical leaders trying to cope with an extremist left wing. An influential group of them had been exiles in Mary's reign; and though their

[1] Cf. A. F. Scott Pearson's *Thomas Cartwright*.

official duty compelled them to act otherwise, in their hearts they sympathized with many of the aspirations of their troublesome brethren. As late as August 1571 Bishop Horne was writing to Bullinger: 'Our church has not yet got free from those vestiarian rocks of offence on which she at first struck. Our excellent Queen, as you know, holds the helm and directs it hitherto according to her pleasure. But we are awaiting the guidance of the divine Spirit, which is all we can do; and we all daily implore Him with earnestness and importunity to turn at length our sails to another quarter.' Even Matthew Parker, writing to Burghley as late as 1575, revealed the radical within: 'Does your Lordship think that I care either for cap, tippet, surplice, or wafer-bread, or any such?' Such men could hardly be effective disciplinarians; and they tended to be long-lived, thus maintaining their indulgent control for a perilously long time.[1]

Moreover, the Privy Council that Elizabeth had constructed for her militant Protestant State contained sympathizers. The Earl of Bedford, Sir Francis Knollys, Sir Walter Mildmay, the Earl of Warwick, Francis Walsingham when he joined the Council, would all perhaps have welcomed some form of Presbyterian experiment. The Earl of Leicester was suspect: certainly, 'the chick that sitteth next the hen' was patron and protector of left-wing Puritans. Outside the Council, among the nobility, there was the powerful Earl of Huntingdon, and among ladies of great influence, the Duchess of Suffolk and Sir Anthony Cooke's two learned and indomitable daughters, Lady Ann Bacon, wife of the Lord Keeper, and Lady Elizabeth Hoby. These and others were all zealous radicals in religion. The bishops found them, individually or in collaboration, an obstacle to their disciplinary measures.

The radical cause was helped immeasurably by the intensified Catholic threat to Protestant England in the years 1569 to 1572. It caused some of the bishops, in their anxiety to improve the ability and influence of the clergy as the bulwark of their faith, to sanction a novel experiment known as Prophesyings or Exercises. These were periodic meetings of the ministers of an area for the purpose of biblical exposition, held under a moderator or chairman and controlled by regulations, both approved

---

[1] *Zurich Letters*, i. 248; *Parker Correspondence*, p. 478.

by the bishop. The laity, who had a lust for sermons that might astonish our busier and differently-minded age, were present. Afterwards, among themselves, the ministers criticized each other's expository efforts, thus helping to establish and preserve a common standard of belief; and they might even indulge in what the Calvinists called 'censures' — mutual criticisms of one another's mode of life, aimed at preserving a high level of conduct.[1] Now such meetings were a central feature of Calvinistic discipline: incidentally, they were not unlike the disciplinary devices of ideological movements in our own time. They were formidable in their potentialities, creating what might amount to revolutionary party-cells, or at the least giving to areas in which they were practised a taste — to keen Protestants a very attractive taste — of what might be accomplished under a Calvinistic church polity. If so many of the bishops had not experienced a rather similar type of life abroad in Mary Tudor's reign, and if they had not been confused by the need to combat Catholicism, they might have been more alive to the dangers than the advantages of Prophesyings. As it was, they unwittingly played the role of 'fellow-travellers' in a revolutionary movement.

These Prophesyings had probably been practised from early in the reign in various places where there were ministers of a Genevan cast of mind. The year 1571, with its sense of imminent national peril, seems to mark the time when the bishops were inveigled into lending them their patronage and authority. The initiative came from radical members of the lower clergy; and in some individual churches it seems clear that an even closer approximation to the Genevan pattern had been introduced by the incumbent. Indeed, in spite of episcopal authority and of the heavy penalties threatened by the Act of Uniformity, many ministers — as was blatantly confessed in the preamble of a bill framed by the Puritans in this Parliament — had ignored the Anglican Prayer Book, and 'conformed themselves more nearly to the imitation of the ancient apostolical Church and the best reformed Churches in Europe, as well in the form of common prayer, ministration of the sacraments', and so on. It was a case of

[1] Cf. the order for Northampton, 1571, in STRYPE, *Annals*, II. i. 133 seqq.; my *Age of Catherine de Medici*, pp. 19-20.

Wood, Williams, Whittingham and Sutton
Valued the Prayer Book not a button,
The Litany they grudg'd to say
And threw the surplice quite away,
Alter'd confession, chang'd the hymns
For old Jack Hopkins' pithy rhymes.

'Vouchsafe . . . to look upon these shires of Northampton and Rutland . . . and aid me with your counsel', wrote the Bishop of Peterborough to Burghley in April 1573, describing the troubles arising from 'those whom men do call Puritans and their fautors'. 'In the town of Overton, where Mr. Carleton dwelleth there is no divine service upon most Sundays and holidays according to the Book of Common Prayer, but instead thereof two sermons . . . When they are determined to receive the Communion, they repair to Whiston, where it is their joy to have many out of divers parishes, principally out of Northampton town and Overton . . . with other towns thereabout, there to receive the sacraments with preachers and ministers to their own liking and contrary to form prescribed . . . To their purposes they have drawn divers young ministers, to whom it is plausible to have absolute authority in their parishes. In their ways they be very bold and stout, like men that seem not to be without great friends.'[1]

The Mr. Carleton of Overton, mentioned in this letter, was none other than George Carleton, our active Puritan M.P. who owed his election at Poole in 1571 and at Dorchester in 1572 to the Puritan Earl of Bedford.

Though there was an element of spontaneity in all this, there was also collusion. Radical ministers knew one another, wrote to one another, visited one another. 'There is of late', wrote Bishop Aylmer in September 1576 — and one suspects that the picture was not fundamentally different four or five years earlier — 'a rank of rangers and posting apostles that go from shire to shire, from Exercise to Exercise, namely Patchet, Standon, etc., accompanied, countenanced, and backed with Sir R. Knightley, Mr. Carell [possibly our George Carleton] and others out of Warwickshire, Northamptonshire, and other

---

[1] FRERE & DOUGLAS, *Puritan Manifestoes*, pp. 150, xvii-xviii; *Camden Miscellany*, vi (Life of Whittington, p. 22, n. 3).

shires, to Ashby where Gilby'—the Earl of Huntingdon's notorious Puritan minister—'is bishop, to Leicestershire, where Johnson is superintendent, to another place where the monk Anderson reigneth, to Coventry, etc.'[1]

At the centre, in London, was John Field, the young Puritan minister whom we have already met as possibly connected with the Parliamentary agitation of 1571. About this time he seems to have been acting a part that might be described as organizing secretary to the movement. At any rate, in August 1572 we find him writing to Anthony Gilby of Ashby-de-la-Zouche, as he had written to others, mentioning a recent 'conference' and suggesting another, though he himself was at that time in prison. And in prison he was visited by a succession of Puritan divines. In August 1573 the Bishop of London reported to Burghley and Leicester: 'There is a conventicle or rather conspiracy breeding in London . . . The city will never be quiet until these authors of sedition, who are now esteemed as gods — as Field, Wilcox, Cartwright, and others — be far removed . . . The people resort unto them as in Popery they were wont to run on pilgrimage.' In the nature of things, the surviving evidence about this clandestine movement is fitful, but there can be little or no doubt that there was some form of organization and that the congenially-minded gentry in the House of Commons (and outside the House) were closely connected with its clerical members.[2]

When, in the latter part of the reign, Archbishop Whitgift's master-detective, the future Archbishop Bancroft, exposed the Presbyterian conspiracy and wrote its history from evidence and documents he possessed, he told how, before the Parliament of 1572, 'certain persons assembled themselves privately together in London (as I have been informed), namely, Gilby, Sampson, Lever, Field, Wilcox, and I wot not who besides': it was perhaps the conference to which Field was alluding in August. They decided, says Bancroft, to write and put out the famous *Admonition to Parliament*. 'Against which time it was also provided that Beza [Calvin's successor at Geneva] should write

---

[1] B.M. Additional MS. 29546, fols. 56-7. The MS. is a copy: hence my conjecture that 'Carlell' may be a slip for 'Carleton'. I owe this reference to Edna Bibby's papers.

[2] Scott Pearson, *Cartwright*, p. 61; Strype, *Parker*, ii. 240; *Puritan Manifestoes* p. xix.

his letter to a great man in this land.' The letter was probably
one we possess, to Burghley. It was mistimed, for it was dated
after the end of the Parliament; but it referred to news of a
Parliament being called in England, in which a consultation
was to be had concerning establishing religion: an indication
of Puritan hopes and intentions. These planners were also
calling on their master-theologian, Thomas Cartwright, to
return to England from Geneva; and he did return, probably
just in time for the Parliament.[1]

The *Admonition to Parliament*, referred to by Bancroft, is one
of the most important tracts — perhaps, indeed, the most
important — in the history of Elizabethan Puritanism.[2] It
marked the definite adoption by the party, or at least by its
clerical leaders, of a Presbyterian platform and therefore of a
revolutionary policy. Written in excellent prose, clear, succinct, vigorous, without the rollicking, vulgar, and embittered
wit of other Puritan pamphlets, it was the work of John Field
and another, even younger London minister, Thomas Wilcox.
It was constructed upon the declaration that 'the outward
marks whereby a true Christian Church is known are preaching
of the word purely, ministering of the sacraments sincerely, and
ecclesiastical discipline'. The first of these three points involved
certain Calvinistic, or, as they termed them, apostolic features
of the clergy: election by common consent of the Church and
'call' by the congregation; also equality of ministers and aboli-
tion of those 'titles, livings, and offices, by Antichrist devised',
such as archbishop, bishop, dean, archdeacon, etc., 'plainly in
God's word forbidden'. The third point involved the simple
triple ministry of ministers, elders, and deacons, to whom 'the
whole regiment of the Church is to be committed'.

The *Admonition* was accompanied by a second tract, entitled
'A view of Popish abuses yet remaining in the English church,
for the which godly ministers have refused to subscribe.' This
was an appeal to Parliament against the three articles which the
ecclesiastical authorities had been administering to suspect
clergymen, as a test of orthodoxy, since the Parliament of 1571.
Here indeed was bitterness and pungent language — Field's,

---

[1] BANCROFT, *Survey of the Pretended Holy Discipline* (1663 edn.), p. 42; STRYPE,
*Parker*, ii. 102; SCOTT PEARSON, *Cartwright*, pp. 50 seqq.
[2] Reprinted in FRERE & DOUGLAS, *Puritan Manifestoes* (1907).

one gathers. The Prayer Book was described as 'an unperfect book, culled and picked out of that Popish dunghill, the Mass book, full of abominations'. 'Drunken they are, and show their own shame, that strive so eagerly to defend' such things. Attacking the ecclesiastical courts, the tract describes the Commissary's Court as 'but a petty little stinking ditch that floweth out of that former great puddle', the filthy Archbishop's Court. 'Copes, caps, surplices, tippets, and such like baggage ... are as the garments of the idol, to which we would say, "Avaunt and get thee hence".'[1]

Written 'in the Parliament-time, which' — Field ingenuously claimed, when he and his fellow author were arrested — 'should be a free time of speaking or writing',[2] the secret press may have had difficulty with the printing, for the tract was published towards the end rather than the beginning of the session. Needless to say, it was not presented to Parliament, but it was certainly intended to influence opinion in the House of Commons. Moreover, Parliament-time was the supreme opportunity for securing the dissemination of propaganda. The *Admonition* proved a best-seller. Appearing in June, it was in a third edition by August; and the authorities could neither suppress it nor induce owners of copies to surrender them.

Field and his group almost certainly discussed what action could be taken in Parliament, and the odds are that they talked this over with their friends in the House of Commons. Whether their plans had to be modified because it was out of the question to make church reform a principal part of this Parliament's endeavours, we do not know. Their attack, however, was astute, and was not delayed.

On Saturday, May 17th, the Commons gave a first reading to a bill concerning rites and ceremonies. Its timing as the initial item in the morning's business was probably carefully chosen: before the more authoritative members of the House had arrived, and when, if the Speaker did not prove obstinate — and Speaker Bell leaned to the left in religion — a controversial measure might be launched successfully.[3]

---

[1] *Seconde Parte of a Register*, ed. A. Peel, i. 89; *Puritan Manifestoes*, pp. 20 seqq.
[2] PEEL, op. cit. i. 88.
[3] *C.J.* i. 95. Cromwell notes the reading in his diary.

The bill was an astounding piece of effrontery: no part more so than the preamble. The Book of Common Prayer, it asserted, though sound enough in substantial points of doctrine, contained 'divers orders of rites, ceremonies, and observations' which in 1559 had been 'permitted in respect of the great weakness of the people, then blinded with superstition'. But since that time the Gospel had progressed and there was now 'a great number of learned pastors and zealous ministers' who, in all humility and quietness and with the favourable permission of some godly bishops, had introduced 'godly exercises for the better instruction and edifying of their congregations', and had therefore 'omitted the precise rule and strait observation of the form and order prescribed in that book'. 'Malicious adversaries of the truth' had taken advantage of even slight departures from the Prayer Book service to prosecute them under the Act of Uniformity, thus greatly hindering the course of the Gospel and restraining 'divers godly-minded prelates' who otherwise 'would be right willing to favour and maintain the use of the same godly exercises'. For remedy of this situation the bill enacted that the Act of Uniformity should remain in force only against those using any manner of Papistical service, rites, or ceremonies, while permitting others, being preachers and having the charge of a congregation, with the consent of the bishop of the diocese, to omit parts of the established service or to use the form of service employed in French and Dutch congregations in England, which was Calvinistic.[1]

The place of this outrageous bill in the general pattern of the Puritan revolutionary conspiracy is clear. If it had been passed — an impossible 'if', for even supposing that the bishops could have been duped and the House of Lords with them, there was still the Queen, and it was anathema to her: if it had been passed, the law would have protected Puritan ministers and their lay patrons while they remorselessly destroyed the Anglican Church from within. Of course, they would have needed the consent of the bishop of the diocese; but a number were already countenancing Prophesyings.

Speed was the wish of its sponsors, and the House was disposed to back them. The bill was given its second reading at the next sitting, May 19th. Immediately it was attacked by

---

[1] *Puritan Manifestoes*, pp. 149-51.

Francis Alford. As an extreme conservative and a civil lawyer, he was doubly disposed against Puritans. Zeal and science, he began, were good when they met together; but the preferrers of this bill had the former without the latter. The matter belonged to divines, and Convocation was the place for it. He was aware that there had been great strife in the Church over trifles, but conformity was essential. They could not leave these matters to the choice of every curate or bishop; nor should they follow the example of other realms, since there were more learned men in England than in any other country he had visited.[1]

Robert Snagge replied. 'No honest man would disable those he knoweth not', he retorted. As for the contention that they had no authority to deal in matters of divinity, the bill affirmed the substance of the Prayer Book, and dealt only with the lamentable divisions about small matters. It was malice that made many trouble honest preachers about such trifles. He thought every church in England in danger by the Act of Uniformity. The bill required nothing unreasonable, nothing but what the bishop would allow.

Pistor then spoke. It grieved him to hear any mislike so good a bill. Alford was no 'sheep of the good shepherd'; but he trusted that the speech of one could not withdraw the House. With a confidence that was probably genuine, though staggering in its naivety, he expressed 'no doubt of the Queen's Majesty's or the bishops' good inclination to the furtherance of this bill'. The House seemed only too ready to share his credulity, for they ordered the bill to be ingrossed without troubling to commit it. In all probability the reading had taken place while the most weighty Members, who would have perceived the flaws, were elsewhere discussing the great matter of Mary Queen of Scots; and perhaps this was not accidental. Certainly, unless our diarist is misleading in reducing the debate to three speakers, there was something odd about the occasion. But, whatever may have happened, one thing stands out as remarkable: the alacrity with which so large a body of men followed the lead of those ardent irresponsibles, Robin Snagge and Tristram Pistor.

[1] The speeches on this bill are all from Cromwell's diary. Cf. also the entries under appropriate dates in *C.J.*

They were indeed moving too fast. The next day, 'being earnestly called upon' — as the Speaker reported — the bill went to its third reading. But the more distinguished and cautious members of the House — 'the higher sort', as our anonymous diarist calls them — were now present, and it was 'long debated'. Sir Francis Knollys spoke. Divers mischiefs grew by the Act of Uniformity, he said, and this bill offered remedy. Here spoke the Puritan; but as a courtier he realized that the preamble was a millstone about the bill and he wanted it reformed. Digges, the mathematician, with his matter of fact mind, declared that its obvious purpose was to help those ministers who refused to wear the appointed apparel. He wanted this plainly and not covertly done. He was opposed to the anarchy of letting every minister use what service he listed. Dalton, as an Englishman, disliked the reference to the Dutch and French churches. He was averse also to dissonancy. Let the imperfections of the Prayer Book be reformed. 'The best universal he liketh, but no best particular.'

A newcomer to this Parliament, John Audley, nephew of a former Lord Chancellor and a Member for a Cornish borough — a gentleman from Essex, where the Puritan movement was strong, and perhaps, as his speech might suggest, connected with the devisers of the bill — rose in defence. In his opinion, neither the preamble nor the body of the bill called for reform. There was nothing but the truth in the preamble. Then, to argue that reference to the service of the Dutch church involved slander to the learned men of this realm was 'the greatest derogation to the death of Christ which might be'. 'Although not directly from the bishops' — was he disingenuous or artless? — the bill had 'been considered by very grave learned men'. He disagreed with Dalton about the need for conformity. Answering Digges, he declared that the chief purpose of the bill was not for apparel but for a mischief: namely, measuring by one rod the obstinate despiser of the whole church service, and the minister who, while observing the whole in substance, varied a little in the accidents. Some think the bill 'will breed factions: we hope, being referred to the bishops, they will suffer none such to grow'.

Geoffrey Gate, another Cornish carpet-bagger, also a newcomer, and a nephew of Francis Walsingham, echoed Audley.

Uniformity, he said, could never be looked for in the Church.
It discouraged men from the study of divinity, for fear that they
might endanger themselves if they enter the ministry. To add
or take away one word of the service came within the compass of
the law. Another Member spoke, condemning the Act of
Uniformity for inflicting the same penalty on Papists and on
offenders in small matters. But he was no Puritan. He thought
rites and ceremonies trifles, and those who strove about them
nearer Judaism than those who yielded to them. Ceremonies
befitted monarchies. There should be one uniform order
throughout the realm.

Tristram Pistor again rose in defence of the bill, pouring out
his griefs in a speech reminiscent of his melodious oration in
1571, though our diarist's style empties the music from his
prose. 'He is sorry to see how, as well the last Parliament as
this, we are slow to further religion. He ascribeth it to the sins
of the time and punishment for our iniquity. The fear of the
Lord [is] the beginning of wisdom.' They were not seeking first
the kingdom of God. 'He feareth [that] the rod, which hath
yet but shaken us, will shortly destroy us for our iniquity . . .
The bill prayeth only that preachers, by the consent of the
ordinary [the bishop], may alter that which the word of God
hath directly warranted.' He still had no doubt of co-operation
from the bishops.

Marred as it was by the indiscretions of youth and enthusiasm, the bill was evidently now in peril; but, like Knollys, the
Speaker wanted to save it for the good that was in it. He
addressed the House, declaring that he was loth it should come
to the question as it was. He approved its principle, saying that
ministers were now troubled by every lewd man. But he wished
to have the bill amended, to secure 'the freer passage'. The
House accordingly committed it. Pistor and Audley were
members of the committee, and perhaps we should conclude
from this and from their speeches that one or both of them had
been responsible for its introduction.

This last-minute committal was rather a sign of discretion
than of revulsion in feeling. The House still wanted the bill:
wanted it with expedition, for they ordered the committee to
meet that same afternoon. While their delegates met, the first
sign was given of its ultimate fate. The Speaker received a letter

from Lord Burghley demanding particulars of the bill and the name of the Member who had introduced it into the House. Bell replied, summarizing its contents and reporting that in the long third-reading debate 'the greatest grief that was most generally allowed of was . . . that many preachers, for reading of a chapter at any time not permitted for that time by the Book [of Common Prayer] and for divers such like things, were indicted and grievously vexed before the justices of the assize by such as sought that advantage for malice in religion'. He added that as Mr. Treasurer Knollys was one of the committee he did not expect the bill to take any effect. As for the name of the Member who introduced it, he would wait upon Burghley 'and show you as much as shall become me'.[1]

Possibly, Bell imagined that the Queen had already issued some express command: at any rate, he was wrong in anticipating that Mr. Treasurer would stifle the bill. The committee, in fact, did more or less what Knollys had suggested in his speech. They purged the preamble so that it became inoffensive. In the body of the bill they substituted consent by a majority of the bishops of the realm for that of the bishop of the diocese, thus effectively removing its conspiratorial dangers; they entirely deleted permission to use any other prayer book, and made further omissions.[2]

It was now a moderate bill, dealing with a specific grievance under adequate safeguards; and as such, was given a first reading on the next day, May 21st. Then the Queen took action. The following morning the Speaker reported a message from her that henceforth no bills concerning religion were to be preferred or received in the House unless they had first been considered and liked by the bishops; and further that the two versions of this bill of theirs should be shown to her. The House thereupon ordered that the bills should be delivered to the Queen by certain of its members. Our anonymous diarist, who has a note on the episode, comments: 'The message that forbade the bringing of bills of religion into the House seemed much to impugn the liberty of the House, but nothing was said unto it.' He was of course quite wrong in his interpretation of the liberty of the House. That makes his comment the more

---

[1] *C.J.* i. 96; *Puritan Manifestoes*, p. 152.
[2] *Puritan Manifestoes*, pp. 149-51.

notable. Members were encroaching upon the royal prerogative in their theories as well as their actions.[1]

On the following day, May 23rd, Sir Francis Knollys reported
that the two bills had been delivered to the Queen. 'Her
Majesty', he said, 'did very much mislike' — 'utterly mislike',
says the *Journal* entry — 'the first, and the bringer in thereof.'
He told the House that he had delivered their message: namely,
that if there were anything in the original bill to be misliked,
'not to attribute the same to the House, who had made reformation thereof. If anything were in the other, to think it to be of
zeal to reform the mischiefs and inconveniences grown to her
good subjects for divers small causes, and not of malice. I
showed', he added, 'the order [of the Prayer Book] daily
broken as well in her own chapel as in her closet. Her Majesty
hereupon gave very good words of the good opinion she had of
the House and will take the good Protestants to her protection,
and is desirous to know if it be true that such indictments have
been preferred against any — yea or no — as is declared in the
preamble of the bill.'

Dr. Wilson, Master of Requests, who had been one of the
delegation from the House, then added that he was commanded
to inquire the truth of this charge, to bring to the Queen the
names of those indicted, of those who had preferred the indictments, and of those judges who had received them. This done,
'it shall be known to the world that as she is termed the defender
of the faith, so she will be found the protector of true Protestants'.

Elizabeth, it seems, had then switched her remarks to the
subject of the Duke of Norfolk and Mary Queen of Scots.
Wilson told the Commons that he was doubtful about reporting
this part of the interview. Nevertheless he continued: 'She said
further, she heard it had been given abroad that she could or
would do nothing; but it should appear ere long that she both
is able and will punish offenders according to our desires. It
pleased her to demand of me what matters were now in the
House. I desired pardon, for that the same were matters of
secrecy' (an interesting remark, for secrecy from the Sovereign
might flatter the Commons, but it was hardly sound constitutional doctrine). 'She was importunate', continued Wilson. 'I

[1] *C.J.* i. 96-7; Cromwell's Diary; Anonymous Diary.

declared how upon declaration of her message yesterday' — the message rejecting the bill of attainder against Mary — 'I saw great mourning and lamenting, yea to the shedding of tears, that her Majesty would leave so notorious treasons and conspiracies unpunished. She confessed the offence was heinous: so, she thought, the disablement [of Mary's title] would be a great punishment to her. I replied: "If further proceedings were not, no safety could follow, the Protestant in great danger." Finally, she concluded she had but advised, not debarred us to use any other way. And for the Protestants, they should find that, as she hath found them true, so will she be their defence.'[1]

After so indulgent a message, no wonder 'nothing was said' by Members about the liberty of the House: no wonder some of them were bewitched, and wanted to send the Queen their thanks.

That was the end of religious matters for the Commons this Parliament. But they were not the only interested parties. The same fear for their faith which had already led some of the bishops to countenance Prophesyings, was now exercising their whole bench and the lay peers, also, in the Upper House, and their minds cast back to that bill for coming to church and receiving the Communion which the Queen had vetoed in the last Parliament. Unfortunately, the wretched *Lords Journal* tells us nothing, but a letter from the Archbishop of York to Burghley on June 2nd is explicit. 'I and some other bishops', he wrote, 'according to the order taken by the Higher House, were yesternight with the Queen's Majesty, to move her Highness that the bill for coming to divine service might by her assent be propounded. We had the articles of the bill there ready to have read to her Majesty, but for want of time her commandments were that the bill should be delivered to your Lordship, and that at your hands we should know further of her pleasure.' The Archbishop went on to ask Burghley's support.[2]

Nothing came of the move. Elizabeth evidently refused to let the bill go forward, still holding firm to her policy of freedom of conscience, though the argument for coercion was even stronger than in 1571, and fear nearer panic.

---

[1] Cromwell's Diary; *C.J.* i. 97.          [2] S.P. Dom. Eliz. 88/5.

## CHAPTER VI

# END OF THE SESSION

How sensitive and loquacious Members could be about questions of privilege or liberty was shown by an episode centring on Robin Snagge. He had suggested in one of his speeches that everyone throughout the realm should give individual assent to the act concerning Mary Queen of Scots, by way of a general oath. In Parliament, he had remarked, Queen and Lords spoke for themselves only, whereas the knights and burgesses represented the commonalty of the realm; and though the people were bound by the assent of their representatives, nevertheless on this special occasion he thought that they should reinforce that assent by their own voices. Mischief-makers, carrying tales to the nobility, had twisted his words into a declaration that the Lords 'had not to do with the commonwealth, but that we in the Common House had only the care thereof', the Lords being but 'shadows'. Snagge asked for a deputation to be sent to the Upper House to purge him of these sinister reports.

It was the sort of grievance to touch off that stout champion of liberty, Peter Wentworth. The freedom of the House, he declared, was taken away by tale-tellers. It was very necessary to search them out. Send to the Lords, he urged, to know whence they received this information.

Speaker Bell, who had been a victim of similar treatment in the last Parliament and was still sore about it, broke in. He also took the matter seriously, declaring that it impeached the credit of the House to suppose that such statements as Snagge was accused of could pass unreproved by them. If no one else had objected, it would have been his duty, as Speaker, to do so. But he remembered the speech very well, and it was as Snagge claimed.

After this lead from their commander, the big guns of the House thundered. Considering the first institution of Parliaments, and what was happening nowadays, Christopher Yelverton was led to think that great injury had been offered in recent

Parliaments. Fortified by this curious illusion, which placed historical fiction at the service of liberty, he went on to support the idea of petitioning the Lords for the name of the tale-carrier. In his opinion it was not lawful for a Member to utter out of the House any speech that might tend to the reproach of another Member. 'Zeal may carry a man sometime in speech in weighty causes beyond discretion; yet were it not honest the words should be reported, believed, or revenged. It may breed disgrace to the whole Parliament. What can be a more detestable act than to set dissension and debate or to procure displeasure between the Queen, the nobility, and us which represent the commonalty? This kind of offence hath been too common a burden; but no amendment groweth because none hath been punished for the same.' On the subject of intemperate speech, he declared that 'for his part he thinketh it more convenient to bear with offence than to breed dumb silence; and then bad laws are to be looked for'. It was the same line of argument employed by Sir Thomas More half a century before. Apparently, too, there had been talk of bribery in the House: a charge made previously, in 1571. Yelverton suggested that they should also inquire into the origin of this.

Digges, succinct as usual, now spoke. He agreed with Yelverton over Snagge. As for the charge of bribery, he himself 'was the first utterer thereof in the House'. He was not its deviser, though he was 'warranted to say more than he did'. Fain would we know that 'more'; but it seems that the House let the matter drop in its eager pursuit of the main object.

Clearly, here was an occasion for Recorder Fleetwood to perambulate among his precedents. And he did. He threw in a parenthesis on summoning noblemen to the bar of the House as witnesses, as they had just done with the Earl of Bedford: quite out of order, was his view. Then he turned to the subject under discussion. 'These tale-tellers [had been] very rife in Queen Mary's time. It was the practice of the Papists, and they were traitors. Some of them be dead since, and some of them walk now in Westminster Hall. Messages were sent to the House, great trouble grew; some men troubled by speaking, some men by silence, and generally every man offended': a picture, be it added, which we have no means of testing. 'He is assured, whensoever the tale-teller is found, it shall appear he is an errant Papist that seeks to set dissension. Himself hath been in like sort used: God forgive him!' Then came a couple of precedents, one involving a fifteenth-century Speaker. 'Some such punishments in these days would make better Parliaments.'

Monson added his opinion that this was a matter of great moment, concerning every member of the House; and he, too, blamed it all on the Papists. 'Misreports have been made of divers. He [Monson] hath tasted thereof, and is fully resolved they be Papists.' Thomas Honywood, Member for Hythe, rose to prove their grievance sound. He had supped the previous night at my Lord Wentworth's and his Lordship had there mentioned Snagge's speech. Another Member, also at the supper, confirmed this, and then Sir Ralph Sadler added his authoritative endorsement.

At length, the House decided to send Sir Francis Knollys up to the House of Lords. On his return he reported that he had delivered their message. The Lord Keeper had answered that he himself had heard nothing about Snagge's speech, but two or three Lords confessed that they had, though they would not name their informers. Very sensibly Sir Nicholas Bacon suggested that if Snagge had not said anything offensive, the matter should be dropped.

Silent the Commons would not be. 'After further motions made', they agreed to inform the Lords that 'the House could not be so satisfied'. Either they must know the name of the informer, or they would take action 'to try out the truth'. However, when their representatives arrived at the Upper House with this message they found 'the Lords were up', having adjourned for the short recess in honour of the French ambassador's visit. The thirteen-days' interval before the Houses reassembled restored a sense of proportion and the matter was allowed to sleep: an end to the story which must appeal to the human frailty in most of us, though it rankled in the mind of Peter Wentworth and he ruminated on it for four years.[1]

When Parliament returned on June 24th, this extraordinary session was near its end. The Queen came to close it in the afternoon of June 30th.[2]

---

[1] Cromwell's Diary, June 11th; *C.J.* i. 102.
[2] Speeches and proceedings from Cromwell's Diary.

'It hath pleased your excellent Majesty', began Speaker Bell in his final oration, 'to call this Parliament especially and principally for one only cause, and the same the weightiest that I have known any Parliament called [for] in my time.' He referred to the bill which they had passed against Mary Stuart, with its long recital of horrible practices and treasons and its makeshift remedies. 'Although your Majesty hath thought good at this present to stay us from farther proceeding in the cause, yet we all have received hope that lack of time only hath stayed your Majesty, for such further correction [i.e. a bill of attainder] were more correspondent to the qualities of the crimes. We therefore most humbly beseech your Highness . . . speedily to proceed to the execution thereof accordingly, sith long tract of time may not only renew the former hazard but increase courage and boldness to new attempts, more perilous than the former.' He then went on to subject the Queen to yet another dose of historical parallels, plus a fable from Æsop, adding that 'to avoid tediousness' he would forbear the application of these histories. 'Seeing the imminent danger to your person and therein the utter ruin and subversion of the State and the present peril and destruction of your people, who love you as dutifully as this your known enemy doth horribly hate you', they were fearful. They appealed to her, 'with motherly pity to behold your afflicted children' and so 'leave a perpetual monument . . . of your providence, love, and zeal borne to your people, which, except the joys of Heaven, is the greatest glory which can be to any prince.' Why 'should not your Majesty execute that by judgment which both the laws of God and of your realm do permit and suffer? Your Majesty beareth the name of pity, and not unworthily. Our whole prayer is [that] it be not extended to your destruction . . . Blame us not, most mighty sovereign Lady, although we use importunity in a matter of great importance'.

From this discourse on the 'great bill', which, even in our diarist's report, was of considerable length and great insistence, Bell turned to ask for the royal assent to other bills, concluding 'with one petition more'. 'It may please your Highness to conceive that we all, subjects of the Lower House, most lovingly and entirely, with all humility, honour and tender your Highness's preservation, without any will to offend in any small cause, whatsoever hath been or shall be reported to the contrary.' He evidently had in mind the offence given by their bill on rites and ceremonies.

'Mr. Speaker', said Sir Nicholas Bacon in his reply, 'the Queen's Majesty doth well understand your petition . . . But afore I enter thereunto, her Majesty hath thought good, and commanded me to let you well understand, first the Lords and then you her good subjects of the Lower House, that your labour and travail . . . is most acceptable to her Highness; which she cannot but take in thankful part, as things proceeding of so tender zeal as are in no wise to be forgotten or passed in oblivion. And therefore commanded me from her own mouth to give unto you as hearty thanks as I could devise, adding further that neither I nor any other can by speech utter how thankfully she accepteth the same, with promise of recompense to her power; and showeth that her love towards you is as tender as yours towards her.'

Turning to the Speaker's concluding petition, he said that it seemed very strange to the Queen, implying that she had been told tales to their detriment. This was not true, and if she knew who had spread such reports she would take order for their punishment according to their demerits. After an exhortation to those of his audience who were Justices, he announced that the Queen's pleasure about their bills would be signified as the Clerk read them.

The titles of the bills were then read and the royal answers given. The bill against Mary Queen of Scots was reserved till the last, and before the answer was given the Queen called the Lord Keeper to her. Bacon then addressed the company:

'The Queen's Highness's pleasure is, I wish you not to be moved though upon a strange occasion a strange answer have been made.' 'Here', notes our diarist, 'the Queen interrupted him and told him that no answer at all was made as yet.'

Bacon had another try. 'Turning his speech to the answer which should be made, which was *La roigne se avisera*', he wished them 'not to take the same in such sense as it hath heretofore been commonly understood, applied, and taken.' The formula was to be construed literally, as a mere suspension of judgment. Used hitherto for rejecting a bill, she now meant not to reject or refuse, 'she liketh so well of the substance thereof'. There were some points in the bill on which she was not fully resolved, 'some things so excluded, some so concluded, as hath not as yet her whole and perfect liking'. In short, she perceived flaws in the bill. 'The greatest part thereof', continued Bacon, 'is to her contentation.' However, 'the time of year considered, she is compelled to prolong the performance thereof to a further deliberation. And for that purpose, her pleasure is [that] the Parliament be prorogued until the Feast of All Saints next ensuing [November 1st], when her pleasure is, you repair hither again for the further accomplishment of her pleasure'.

It had proved an unproductive session. Concentration on 'the great cause' was mainly responsible, though the Commons had done their utmost to get a fair proportion of private bills through, turning a deaf ear to repeated orders against this from the Queen, and extending their sittings into the afternoon. Only seventeen bills received the royal assent, two of which — one for the punishment of those rebelliously taking or conspiring to take any of the Queen's castles, and another against conspiring to enlarge a prisoner committed for high treason — were subordinate pieces to the main concern of the session. Three only were private acts. The Queen vetoed seven bills[1] — a very high proportion; and four or five of these were private measures, compared with the mere three to which she gave her consent. Was this excessive use of the veto her retort to the flagrant defiance of her orders? The endearments showered on the Commons in the Lord Keeper's speech might suggest not; but the figures are impressive.

The outstanding, the shattering fact was her response to the bill against Mary. In 1586 she was to speak of an 'answer-answerless': here was a 'veto-vetoless'. 'For our Parliament' — wrote Burghley when the session was over, unburdening his grief to Walsingham, then in France — 'I cannot write patiently. All that we have laboured for and had with full consent brought to fashion — I mean a law to make the Scottish Queen unable and unworthy of succession of the crown — was by her Majesty

---

[1] For inserting name and manor of Havering at Bowre (cf. *L.J.* i. 714); touching presentation to benefices by lapse (ibid. p. 720); for severance of sheriffs of Cambs. and Hunts. (ibid. p. 720); lands of Lord Latimer and Sir R. Wingfield (ibid. p. 722); for Plumstead Marsh (ibid. p. 723); assizes at Stafford (ibid. p. 723); a sermon at St. Paul's (ibid. p. 726).

neither assented to nor rejected, but deferred until the Feast of All Saints; but what all other wise and good men may think thereof, you may guess. Some here have, as it seemeth, abused their favour about her Majesty to make herself her worst enemy. God amend them. I will not write to you who are suspected. I am sorry for them, and so would you also [be], if you thought the suspicion to be true.'

Burghley had kept up what, for those days when reticence was a wise habit — *littera scripta manet* — might almost be called a running commentary on the Parliament. On May 21st: 'there can be found no more soundness than in the Common House, and no lack appearing in the Higher House; but in the highest person such slowness in the offers of surety and such stay in resolution as it seemeth God is not pleased that the surety shall succeed. To lament that secretly I cannot forbear, and thereby with it, and such like, I am [so] overthrown in heart as I have no spark almost of good spirits left in me to nourish health in my body . . . Now I am forced to be carried into the Parliament House and to her Majesty's presence' — he was only 51 years of age. The fault, he added, was not in 'us that are accounted inward counsellors'; and yet, to save 'the honour of the highest', we must take the blame. The same day Leicester wrote to Walsingham that he saw 'no likelihood' of the Queen acquiescing in the Commons' demand for Norfolk's head. Four days after the Duke's execution, Burghley reported Elizabeth as still 'sad' about it. At this moment he seemed to harbour no doubt that the second bill against Mary would become law, but he was utterly sceptical of its value: 'it will not draw her to any more fear to offend than words will do'.[1]

The attitude of Burghley and the other 'inward counsellors', indeed of the Privy Council as a whole, to 'the great matter' of this session allows of no doubt. Nor does that of the House of Lords; nor — how needless to say it! — that of the House of Commons. Parliament had demanded Mary's head: they had been as importunate as subjects dared to be. With stubborn reluctance — a reluctance pervading the Speaker's closing speech — they had consented to the milder treatment of the second bill. And in the end Elizabeth could not bring herself even to that degree of severity. Few of the 'old Parliament-men'

---

[1] DIGGES, *Compleat Ambassador*, pp. 219, 203, 213 (*recte* 212).

can have believed in her veto-vetoless; and in fact, the Feast of All Saints came and went and almost four years elapsed before this Parliament, ostensibly prorogued for the summer months, met again. The 'monstrous and huge dragon' was to be left untouched. The Commons had got neither an axe nor an act.

# PART SIX
# THE PARLIAMENT OF 1576

---

## CHAPTER I
## INTRODUCTORY

'THE Queen of Scotland still remains among us', wrote Bishop Parkhurst to the eminent Swiss reformer, Bullinger, in January 1573. 'She was in great alarm for herself last Parliament, and not without reason; for had not the extreme clemency of our Queen prevented it, it would have been all over with her. What will be done respecting her in the next Parliament, I cannot tell. She has certainly very few friends in this country. And what wonder, when she has been hankering after this kingdom, and is defiled and almost overwhelmed with so many and great crimes.'[1]

It was fortunate for Mary that the Parliament of 1572 had met when it did rather than a few months later, for on August 24th in that year there took place in France the infamous Massacre of St. Bartholomew: an event which was to retain something of its initial poignancy and horror throughout the centuries, until the greater crimes of our own time dulled man's sensitiveness. To Elizabethan Protestants it was a nightmare of terror, presage of a dark future. Little imagination is needed to conceive the cyclonic effect it would have had on the debates of 1572. Though Parliament was no longer in session, 'all men', Burghley told Mary's custodian, 'now cry out of your prisoner': that 'dangerous traitress and pestilence of Christendom'.[2] Under the panic fear of the occasion and the pressure of those about her — whose advice had for background the preamble of the suspended bill against Mary and the battery of parliamentary argument, now endowed with something of the quality of prophecy — Elizabeth momentarily surrendered. She agreed to a secret plan to hand Mary back to the Protestant

---

[1] *Zurich Letters*, i. 278.
[2] LODGE, *Illustrations of British History* (1791 edn.), ii. 75; *Scottish Cal.* iv. 389.

government of Scotland, provided that government consented to put her to death immediately, without the ignominy of the act falling on Elizabeth. This dubious manœuvre — not so repellent in its day as it appears in the retrospect of the centuries — failed. Two months passed without the Heavens falling; and Elizabeth, whose policy was essentially a gamble on her own life and on the expectation that events would not turn out so calamitous as fear, or even reason, anticipated, resumed her poise and personal mastery of the situation.

The Feast of All Saints, to which Parliament and the bill against Mary stood prorogued, passed: with another prorogation instead of another session. Who can doubt that if its Members had reassembled on November 1st, 1572, it would indeed have been all over with the Queen of Scotland? The prorogation was perhaps excusable in the circumstances because the negotiations for Mary's return to Scotland were not then finally known to be hopeless. On November 8th, when this became clear, Burghley opened his heart to Leicester: 'If her Majesty will continue her delays for providing for her own surety by just means given to her by God, she and we all shall vainly call upon God when the calamity shall fall upon us . . . God be merciful to us.'[1] But instead of providing for her own surety, Elizabeth continued proroguing Parliament. The months, the years passed by. Her gambler's luck held. The bill against Mary expired from mere inanition; and eventually the main purpose for resummoning Parliament resolved itself into the undramatic need for money. In February 1576, when they met again, all was so quiet on the Marian front that even the men of 1572 could find no pretext for reopening their campaign.

Though in a very different way, a comparable quiet descended on the second campaign of 1572: for reform of the Church. For a year or so the young revolutionaries of the Presbyterian movement sat their saddles in confidence: as well they might, in the post-Bartholomew atmosphere. There was a *Second Admonition to Parliament* published, and when John Whitgift, Master of Trinity College, Cambridge, Cartwright's principal opponent and the future Archbishop of Canterbury, took on himself to answer the first *Admonition*, Cartwright replied, and a resounding literary battle was joined.

[1] *Scottish Cal.* iv. 431-2.

The less responsible Puritan tracts were outrageous in the way they addressed the bishops: 'Look throughout all the Evangelists', declared *An Exhortation to the Byshops to deale brotherly with theyr Brethren*, 'and you shall see how vehemently Christ Jesus, and His, deal with the Pharisees, your great grandsires and famous forefathers, whose children ye are without doubt, and as like them as if you were spewed out of their mouths.' Then followed line upon line of biblical vituperation against the Pharisees, ending with the reflection that the Puritans, in their sharp speech against bishops, but followed 'the examples of the Apostles and Prophets, and Christ himself'.[1]

In *A friendly caveat to Bishop Sands*, evidently written and printed in the summer of 1573, the 'godly, learned, and zealous gentleman', its anonymous author, drained the sink of his wit in trouncing the radically-minded Bishop of London, whose period of exile and whose sympathies with the simpler ways of Swiss protestantism might have pleaded against abuse from such quarters: though, indeed, extremists are never so venomous as when attacking quondam friends. 'We hoped alway better and better from Parliament to Parliament of you', he wrote. 'But now, forasmuch as like blind Bayard ye hop — the longer the worse — I am right glad that divers good and godly men set to their hand to make an end of the rod, which I hope, afore it be long, will make your proud buttocks to smart. And this insure yourself of me, that if at the next Parliament you behave not yourself the better, I will deliver the Queen's Grace a little treatise as concerning your usurped titles and other abuses, to the end that . . . she may pay you according to your deserts: that is, put down and out of office all the men-pleasing mongrels and own-belly-filling but small-flock-feeding divines.'

'Therefore now, my Lords', ran another passage, addressed to the bishops at large, 'purchase what you can: enrich your legitimates and kinsfolks, and provide for afterclaps. For if in King Henry's days idle, loiterous and hypocritical friars and monks (for all their great authority and undeserved estimation they were in) were in despite of the Pope put down, why should you think it an impossible matter in Queen Elizabeth's days to make a search amongst those that are their successors and to saw off some of your branches that make you all to be as evil,

[1] *Puritan Manifestoes*, pp. 59-60.

if not worse than a great sort of your predecessors were: that is, idle overseers, slow-preaching pastors, vainglorious prelates, refusers of reformation, and maliciously and wilfully blind bishops. I am somewhat plain with you, my Lords, and therefore I pray you bear with me if you list, for I cannot bear no longer with you.'[1]

Fanatical movements are prone to develop a hysterical fringe: it was so in 1591, it was so on this occasion, it is so today. The frail mind topples under the impact of Revelation. In October 1573, a godly, lunatic lawyer, straight from a Puritan lecture and fired by the example of Old Testament heroes, stabbed the famous seaman John Hawkins — a grievous, not fatal wound — mistaking him for Christopher Hatton, who was reputed a Papist and hinderer of God's glory. The event stirred and enraged the Queen. It discredited the Puritans; and the authorities, who had been handicapped in dealing with the Presbyterian conspiracy while Bartholomew fears monopolized so many minds, saw their opportunity and struck. The bishops were ordered to enforce discipline, and a warrant was issued for the arrest of the acknowledged leader of the Presbyterian movement, Thomas Cartwright. He fled abroad. The next year, a couple of precious rascals, one a 'lewd scrivener', invented a Puritan plot against eminent opponents in Church and State, forged letters to make it seem specious, and momentarily succeeded in fooling the authorities. The fraud was soon exposed, and something of a *détente* followed. But in this atmosphere of alarm, Field and his company of organizing brethren were unable to proceed with open daring.[2]

The Prophesyings went on, the insidious undermining of the Anglican Church continued, until the Queen herself took drastic action: not, however, until after the 1576 Parliament, which in itself is perhaps significant. For these reasons — and for another, which we shall have occasion to note — agitation about the Church, though not absent from the new parliamentary session, was more circumspect in its scope, and, so far as we can tell, more considerate in its presentation.

So far as we can tell: though our invaluable new informant,

---

[1] *Parte of a Register* (1593), pp. 375, 377. For date of tract, cf. KNAPPEN, *Tudor Puritanism*, p. 241, n. 78.

[2] STRYPE, *Parker*, ii. 327-8, 368-72; PEARSON, *Cartwright*, pp. 125-9; KNAPPEN, op. cit. p. 245.

Thomas Cromwell, kept a diary of this Parliament and of subsequent ones in which he sat, and though he noted an occasional speech, he never again reported debates as he had done in 1572. The land seems arid after the oasis in which we have recently lingered. Apart from a few outstanding incidents, about which there is special evidence, we cannot be sure of the everyday life of this Parliament. But, after an initial dramatic outburst, it was evidently a relatively quiet session; and the Queen was pleased to go on proroguing it.

## CHAPTER II

# PETER WENTWORTH

BEING held on prorogation, there was no formal opening to the session. On the first day, February 8th, 1576, the Commons immediately got down to business. Speaker Bell — perhaps on instruction from Privy Councillors, perhaps in the light of experience — first proposed, for expedition's sake, that whenever a motion was made and before further argument, a committee should be appointed to consider whether the matter moved was fit to be embodied in a bill.[1] After this decorous start they proceeded to read their first bill. Then trouble started. Peter Wentworth rose to make a motion about liberty of speech.

His speech, he tells us, had been in writing two or three years: evidently since it became apparent that Elizabeth did not intend to proceed against Mary Queen of Scots, and since her repression of the Puritans. He had been ruminating on his experience in the last two Parliaments, inspired by the wrath of Elihu in the Book of Job: 'Behold, I am as the new wine which hath no vent and bursteth the new vessels in sunder. Therefore I will speak, that I may have a vent. I will open my lips and make answer. I will regard no manner of person, no man will I spare; for if I should go about to please men, I know not how soon my maker will take me away.' Twenty times and more, when he walked in his grounds revolving the speech in his mind against this day, his own fearful conceit, as he confessed, foretold the consequence of his action. 'Then I weighed whether in conscience and the duty of a faithful subject, I might keep myself out of prison and not warn my Prince from walking in a dangerous course', but 'I was made bold and went forward'.[2] As we shall see, he was not permitted to go as far forward as he intended; but the speech he wrote — which has deservedly found a place among our great parliamentary orations — was as follows:

'Mr. Speaker, I find written in a little volume these words

[1] Cromwell's Diary.
[2] Inner Temple Petyt MS. 538/17, fols. 1b, 255.

in effect: "Sweet indeed is the name of liberty and the thing itself a value beyond all inestimable treasure." So much the more it behoveth us to take heed lest we, contenting ourselves with the sweetness of the name only, do not lose and forgo the value of the thing. And the greatest value that can come unto this noble realm . . . is the use of it in this House. . . .

'I was never of Parliament but the last and the last session [i.e. 1571 and 1572], at both which times I saw the liberty of free speech, the which is the only salve to heal all the sores of this Commonwealth, so much and so many ways infringed, and so many abuses offered to this honourable Council . . . that my mind . . . hath not been a little aggrieved . . . Wherefore, to avoid the like, I do think it expedient to open the commodities that grow to the Prince and whole State by free speech used in this place. . . .

'First, all matters that concern God's honour through free speech shall be propagated here and set forward, and all things that do hinder it removed, repulsed, and taken away.

'Next, there is nothing commodious, profitable, or any way beneficial for the Prince or State but faithful and loving subjects will offer it in this place.

'Thirdly, all things discommodious, perilous, or hurtful . . . shall be prevented. . . .

'Fourthly, if the envious do offer anything hurtful . . . what incommodity doth grow thereby? Verily, I think none . . . for by the darkness of the night the brightness of the sun sheweth more excellent and clear; and how can the truth appear and conquer until falsehood and all subtleties that should shadow and darken it be found out? . . .

'I conclude that in this House, which is termed a place of free speech, there is nothing so necessary for the preservation of the Prince and State as free speech, and without it it is a scorn and mockery to call it a Parliament House, for in truth it is none, but a very school of flattery and dissimulation, and so a fit place to serve the Devil and his angels in and not to glorify God and benefit the Commonwealth. . . .

'Amongst other, Mr. Speaker, two things do very great hurt in this place, of the which I do mean to speak. The one is a rumour that runneth about the House, and this it is: "Take heed what you do. The Queen's Majesty liketh not of such a

matter: whosoever preferreth it, she will be much offended
with him." Or the contrary: "Her Majesty liketh of such a
matter: whosoever speaketh against it, she will be much
offended with him." The other is: sometimes a message is
brought into the House, either of commanding or inhibiting,
very injurious unto the freedom of speech and consultation. I
would to God, Mr. Speaker, that these two were buried in Hell:
I mean rumours and messages. For wicked undoubtedly they
are: the reason is, the Devil was the first author of them, from
whom proceedeth nothing but wickedness.

'Now I will set down reasons to prove them wicked. First,
if we be in hand with anything for the advancement of God's
glory, were it not wicked to say the Queen's Majesty liketh not
of it, or commandeth that we shall not deal in it? Greatly were
these speeches to her Majesty's dishonour; and an hard opinion
were it, Mr. Speaker, thus to conceive of the Queen's Majesty.
And hardest of all were it, Mr. Speaker, that these things should
enter into her Majesty's thought . . . Solomon saith, the King's
displeasure is a messenger of death. This is a terrible thing to
the weak nature of frail flesh. Why so? for who is able to abide
the fierce countenance of his Prince? . . . He that dissembleth
to her Majesty's peril is to be counted as an hateful enemy, for
that he giveth unto her Majesty a detestable Judas his kiss.
And he that contrarieth her mind, to her preservation — yea,
though her Majesty would be much offended with him — is to
be adjudged an approved lover. For faithful are the wounds
of a lover, saith Solomon, but the kisses of an enemy are deceitful. And it is better, saith Antisthenes, to fall amongst ravens
than amongst flatterers; for ravens do devour but the dead
corpse, but flatterers do devour the living. And it is both
traitorous and hellish through flattery to seek to devour our
natural Prince. . . .

'Now I will show you a precedent of the last Parliament, to
prove it a perilous rumour and much more perilous to give
place unto it. It was foreseen by divers of this House that if the
supposed title of the Scottish King or Queen to the Crown of
England were not by act of Parliament overthrown and mani-
fested to the whole Realm, that it had possessed such number
of traitorous hearts that it would one day break out to the
danger of the Prince and State. For of the wicked Isaiah saith,

"they weave the spider's web and breed cockatrice's eggs". And what falleth out of it? Truly, they long to see their good brood hatched. Even so, this wicked brood of Scottish hearts in English bodies, a detestable and unnatural thing, Mr. Speaker: what web did they weave and what brood did they breed? . . . Even abominable treason: namely, the life of our noble Prince (whom God long preserve) was, and, I do fear, is yet sought for, and the subversion of the whole State.'

He that utters rumour, Wentworth continued, should be regarded as a liar, 'what credit soever he be of', 'for the Queen's Majesty is the head of the law and must of necessity maintain the law'. He went on to quote the great medieval legist, Bracton: 'The King ought not to be under man but under God and under the law because the law maketh him a king.' 'He is God's vicegerent here upon earth . . . to execute and do His will, the which is law or justice; and thereunto was her Majesty sworn at her coronation, as I have heard learned men in this place sundry times affirm.' This led Wentworth to claim for freedom of speech a fundamental, entrenched place in the constitution, entirely removed from its historical status as a privilege resting on the grant of the monarch and subject to definition by him. 'Free speech and conscience in this place are granted by a special law, as that without the which the Prince and State cannot be preserved or maintained.' In other words, it was immune from legitimate interference by the Crown: a doctrine whose far-reaching effects Wentworth himself can scarcely have foreseen, though they are clear enough to us.

He continued: another inconvenience arising from wicked rumour was that it put into their heads the idea that the Queen had conceived an evil opinion or mistrust of them, for otherwise her Majesty would wish all things dangerous to herself to be laid open before them, 'assuring herself that so loving subjects as we are would, without schooling and direction, with careful minds to our powers, prevent and withstand all perils that might happen unto her Majesty. And this opinion I doubt not but her Majesty hath conceived of us, for undoubtedly there was never Prince that had faithfuller hearts than her Majesty hath here; and surely there were never subjects had more cause heartily to love their Prince for her quiet government.'

Returning to his precedents: 'There was a message, Mr. Speaker, brought the last session into the House, that we should not deal in any matter of religion, but first to receive it from the bishops. Surely, this was a doleful message, for it was as much to say as, "Sirs, ye shall not deal in God's causes: no, ye shall in no wise seek to advance His glory" . . . There were divers of this House that said with grievous hearts, immediately upon the message, that God of His justice could not prosper the session . . . God was the last session shut out of the doors. But what fell out of it? Forsooth, His great indignation was therefore poured upon this House, for He did put into the Queen's Majesty's heart to refuse good and wholesome laws for her own preservation, the which caused many faithful hearts for grief to burst out with sorrowful tears, and moved all Papists, traitors to God and her Majesty and every good Christian government, in their sleeves to laugh all the whole Parliament House to scorn. And shall I pass over this weighty matter so lightly? . . . May I discharge my conscience and duty to God, my Prince and country so?

'Certain it is, Mr. Speaker, that none is without fault: no, not our noble Queen. Since, then, her Majesty hath committed great faults — yea, dangerous faults to herself and the State — love, even perfect love, void of dissimulation, will not suffer me to hide them to her Majesty's peril, but to utter them to her Majesty's safety. And these they are. It is a dangerous thing in a Prince unkindly to intreat and abuse his or her nobility and people, as her Majesty did the last Parliament. And it is a dangerous thing in a Prince to oppose or bend herself against her nobility and people, yea against most loving and faithful nobility and people. And how could any Prince more unkindly intreat, abuse, and oppose herself against her nobility and people than her Majesty did the last Parliament?

'Did she not call it of purpose to prevent traitorous perils to her person, and for no other cause? Did not her Majesty send unto us two bills, willing us to make a choice of that we liked best for her safety, and thereof to make a law, promising her Majesty's royal consent thereto? And did we not first choose the one and her Majesty refuse it, yielding no reason: nay, yielding great reasons why she ought to have yielded to it? Yet did not we nevertheless receive the other, and agreeing to make a law thereof, did not her Majesty in the end refuse all our travails? And did not we, her Majesty's faithful nobility and subjects, plainly and openly decipher ourselves unto her Majesty and our hateful enemy? And hath not her Majesty left us all to her open revenge? . . . Will not this her Majesty's handling, think you Mr. Speaker, make cold dealing in many of her Majesty's subjects toward her again? I fear it will. And hath it not caused many already, think you Mr. Speaker, to seek a salve for the head that they have broken? I fear it hath . . . And hath it not marvellously rejoiced and encouraged the hollow hearts of her Majesty's hateful enemies and traitorous subjects? No doubt but it hath . . . I doubt not but that some of her Majesty's Council have dealt plainly and faithfully with her Majesty herein. If any have, let it be a sure token to her Majesty to know them for approved lovers. And whatsoever they be that did . . . commend her Majesty for so doing, let it be a sure token to her Majesty to know them for sure traitors and underminers of her Majesty's life and safety. God remove them. . . .

'But was this all? No: for God would not vouchsafe that His holy spirit should all that session descend upon our bishops, so that the session nothing was done to the advancement of His glory. I have heard of old Parliament men that the banishment of the Pope and Popery and the restoring of true religion had their beginning from this House, and not from the bishops; and I have heard that few laws for religion had their foundation from them. And I do surely think — before God I speak it — that the bishops were the cause of that doleful message.' Wentworth was evidently alluding to the ban on bills of religion. In support of his surmise, he went on to tell the story of the interview with Archbishop Parker about the Articles of Religion in 1571. 'And sure, Mr. Speaker', the Archbishop's speech 'seemed to me to be a very Popelike speech, and I fear lest our bishops do attribute this of the Pope's canons unto themselves, *Papa non potest errare* [The Pope cannot err] . . . But I can tell them news. They do but kick against the prick, for undoubtedly they both have [erred] and do err; and God reveals his truth maugre the hearts of them and all his enemies, for great is the truth and it will prevail. . . .

'It is a great and special part of our duty and office, Mr. Speaker, to maintain freedom of consultation and speech . . . I desire you from the bottom of your hearts to hate all messengers, tale-carriers, or any other thing, whatsoever it be, that any manner of way infringe the liberties of this honourable Council. Yea, hate it or them, I say, as venomous and poison unto our Commonwealth, for they are venomous beasts that do use it. Therefore I say, again and again, hate that that is evil and cleave to that that is good . . . We are incorporated into this place to serve God and all England, and not to be time-servers and humour-feeders . . . Let us show ourselves to be a people endued with faith: I mean, with a lively faith that bringeth forth good works . . . Therefore I would have none spared or forborne that shall from henceforth offend herein, of what calling soever he be, for the higher place he hath, the more harm he may do: therefore, if he will not eschew offences, the higher I wish him hanged. I speak this in charity, Mr. Speaker, for it is better that one should be hanged than that this noble State should be subverted . . . God, for his great mercy sake, grant that we may from henceforth show ourselves neither bastards nor dastards.'

He turned finally to another great fault that he had noticed in the last Parliament, connected with divisions, in which the House voted by one side going out of the Chamber, while their opponents stayed in their seats. 'I have seen right good men . . . sit in an evil matter, against which they had most earnestly spoken. I mused at it and asked what it meant, for I do think it a shameful thing to serve God, their Prince, or country with the tongue only and not with the heart and body. I was answered that it was a common policy in this House to mark the best sort of the same and either to sit or arise with them. That same common policy I would gladly have banished this House . . . My humble and hearty suit unto you all', he ended, 'is to accept my good will and that this that I have here spoken, of conscience and great zeal unto my Prince and State, may not be buried in the pit of oblivion and so no good come thereof.'[1]

It was surely the most remarkable speech hitherto conceived

---

[1] Petyt MS. 538/17, fols. 1-6 with an occasional superior reading from copies in B.M. Stowe MS. 302 and S.P. Dom. Eliz. 107/30.

in the Parliament of England: a measure of the mental progress made by more ardent members in seventeen years of revolutionary endeavour and excitement, under a Sovereign at once obstructive, indulgent, and passionately loved: a distillation in startling and prophetic terms of all the radical utterances and yearnings that we have followed in the debates. Wentworth's brother, Paul, in the questions he put to the House in 1566, had sought to lead Members in the same direction; Yelverton and others had defined freedom of speech in novel ways; and in their agitation over the succession and over Mary Queen of Scots many had tried to make their will prevail over that of their Sovereign. But no one — at least, we know of no one — had previously thought these questions fearlessly through to the simplicity and clarity of Peter Wentworth's conclusions. He was wrong, utterly wrong in his own generation; but the future hallowed his doctrine. He, indeed, as much as any of his colleagues, shaped that future.

His speech evidently made a deep impression. It was reported in diplomatic dispatches sent abroad: by the Spanish agent at considerable length. And in one of these reports we are told that there had been others of the company ready to support him, and one, a great favourite of Burghley's, cast for the role of seconder: which, if true, might suggest that on this, as on later occasions in the reign, Wentworth was trying to stage an organized campaign. He was not beyond writing his seconder's speech, as well as his own! The Queen once made the caustic remark, 'Mr. Wentworth has a good opinion of his own wit.'[1]

Speaker, Privy Councillors, and others listened to the speech with growing uneasiness, mounting to consternation as it moved into direct attack on the Queen. Wentworth was well launched on this personal criticism and was beginning to censure Elizabeth's treatment of the bills against Mary Queen of Scots in the last session, when he was stopped and secluded from the Chamber while the House considered what they should do. They decided to commit him to the Serjeant's ward, and appointed a weighty committee, including all Privy-Councillor

---

[1] KERVYNE DE LETTENHOVE, *Relations Politiques des Pays-Bas et de l'Angleterre*, viii. 164; *Spanish Cal. Eliz.* ii. 524; *Roman Cal. Eliz.* ii. 258. The French ambassador's dispatch does not survive. Cf. my articles on Peter Wentworth, *Eng. Hist. Rev.* xxxix. 36, 175.

Members and other officials, to examine him that afternoon.[1]

Like many of the Puritan clergy, after their examinations before Ecclesiastical Commissioners, Wentworth wrote an account of his ordeal in dialogue form. It was part of the propaganda technique of the Puritan party that made them so dangerous in their own day, and provides so fascinating a study in the comparable conditions of our own times.

'*Committee.* Where is your tale you promised to deliver in writing?

'*Wentworth.* Here it is, and I deliver it upon two conditions. The first is that you shall peruse it all, and if you find any want of good will to my Prince or State in any part thereof, let me answer all . . . as if I had uttered all. The second is that you shall deliver it unto the Queen's Majesty. . . .

'*Committee.* We will deal with no more than you uttered in the House.

'*Wentworth.* Your Honours cannot refuse to deliver it to her Majesty, for I do send it to her Majesty as my heart and mind, knowing that it will do her Majesty good. It will hurt no man but myself. . . .

'*Committee.* Then, the speech being read, one said, "Here you have uttered certain rumours of the Queen's Majesty. Where, or of whom, heard you them?"

'*Wentworth.* If your Honours ask me as Councillors to her Majesty, you shall pardon me: I will make you no answer. I will do no such injury to the place from whence I came. For I am no private person: I am a public, and a counsellor to the whole State, in that place where it is lawful for me to speak my mind freely and not for you, as Councillors, to call me to account . . . But if you ask me as committees from the House, I will then willingly make you the best answer I can.

'*Committee.* We ask you as committees from the House.'

The committee pressed him to reveal the source of the rumours. One of their questions is not without interest for its suggestion of collusion between Puritans in and out of Parliament: 'Belike you have heard some speeches in the town of her Majesty's misliking of religion and succession, and you are loth to utter of whom.' To this Wentworth replied that his speech

---

[1] Cromwell, who gives a report of the speech in his diary, indicates the point at which he was stopped; *C.J.* i. 104.

had been in writing two or three years, and owed nothing to what he had heard since coming to town. In fact, he had picked up the rumours in the Parliament House, from one or two hundred members. The questioner — doubtless a Privy Councillor — evidently suspected that they were dealing with the opening move of an organized campaign.

'*Committee*. Then of so many, you can name some.

'*Wentworth*. No, surely. Because it was so general a speech I marked none ... And I assure you, if I could tell, I would not, for I will never utter anything told me, to the hurt of any man.'

Still protesting ignorance, and ready to take an oath on the point — provided it was voluntary and not imposed by authority, for that would be an infringement of the liberties of the House — he offered to cite one instance of such rumours; and with this the committee promised to be satisfied. He instanced the occasion of Bell's speech in 1571: and the committee acknowledged he was right. They then turned to his 'hard interpretation' of the Queen's message about matters of religion in 1572.

'*Wentworth*. "So hard a message could not have too hard an interpretation ... for can there by any possible means be sent a harder message to a Council, gathered together to serve God, than to say, you shall not seek to advance the glory of God? I am of this opinion, that there cannot be a more wicked message than it was.

'*Committee*. You may not speak against messages, for none sendeth them but the Queen's Majesty.

'*Wentworth*. If the message be against the glory of God, against the Prince's safety, or against the liberty of the Parliament House, whereby the State is maintained, I neither may nor will hold my peace ... And I say that I heartily repent me for that I have hitherto held my peace in these causes, and that I do promise you all (if God forsake me not) that I will never during life hold my peace if any [such] message be sent ... Everyone of you here present ought to repent you of these faults and to amend them.

'*Committee*. It is no new precedent to have the Prince to send messages. There were two or three messages recited sent by two or three Princes.

'*Wentworth*. Said I: You do very evil to allege your precedents in this order. You ought to allege good precedents, to comfort and embolden men in good doing, and not evil precedents to discourage and terrify men. . . .'

The committee turned to a remark of his, not in our texts of the speech.

'*Committee.* You called the Scottish Queen Jezebel. What meant you by that?

'*Wentworth.* Did I not publish her openly in the last Parliament to be the most notorious whore in all the world; and wherefore should I then be afraid to call her so now again?

'*Committee.* She is a Queen. You ought to speak reverently of her.

'*Wentworth.* Let him take her part that list. I will speak the truth boldly.'

The committee next tackled him about his criticism of the Queen for rejecting the two bills against Mary. He did not give way an inch, but put a series of questions to them with which they were forced to agree. He told of his victory over his own fears when composing the speech, and then of its delivery.

'*Wentworth.* When I uttered these words in the House — "that there was none without fault; no, not our noble Queen" — I paused, and beheld all your countenances, and saw plainly that those words did amaze you all. Then I was afraid with you for company, and fear bade me put out those words that followed; for your countenances did assure me that not one of you would stay me of my journey. Yet the consideration of a good conscience and of a faithful subject did make me bold to utter that, in such sort as your Honours heard. With this heart and mind I spake it, and I praise God for it; and if it were to do again, I would with the same mind speak it again.

'*Committee.* Yea: but you might have uttered it in better terms. Why did you not so?

'*Wentworth.* Would you have me to have done as you of her Majesty's Privy Council do? to utter a weighty matter in such terms as she should not have understood to have made a fault? Then it would have done her Majesty no good, and my intent was to do her good.

'*Committee.* You have answered us: we are satisfied.

'*Wentworth.* Then I praise God for it.     — And as I made a curtsy, another spake these words:

'*Seckford* [Master of Requests]. Mr. Wentworth will never acknowledge himself to make a fault, nor say that he is sorry for anything that he doth speak. You shall hear none of these things come out of his mouth.

'*Wentworth.* Mr. Seckford, I will never confess it to be a fault to love the Queen's Majesty, while I live; neither will I be sorry for giving her Majesty warning to avoid her danger, while the breath is in my belly. If you do think it a fault . . . say so, for I cannot. Speak for yourself, Mr. Seckford.'[1]

The next day Sir Francis Knollys reported back to the House on behalf of the committee. They had made a collection of 'the violent and wicked words' used about the Queen, which Wentworth had acknowledged, taking all the burden on himself: he had been able to say nothing at all in extenuation. They were read to the House, and Knollys moved that he be imprisoned in the Tower. 'Sundry disputations and speeches' followed. Our diarist, Cromwell, tells us that one member was for bringing the offence within the statute of Philip and Mary for raising seditious rumours, or alternatively, passing a special act, there and then. Possibly this one proposal was noticed because of its singularity and extravagance. It is hard to believe that, however much the majority deplored the diction of the speech, they did not feel a sneaking regard for its sentiments. In the end they followed their official lead. Wentworth was brought to the bar by the Serjeant and there submitted himself to the censure of the House, 'acknowledging that he could not as much as think evil of the same', but desiring 'that his rash speech might not be a cause of prejudice' to liberty of speech in others. He protested 'that whatsoever he had said, his fault did grow in abundance of zeal and love and good will to the Queen's Majesty, and that whensoever any service of hers were required, he would adventure himself with the foremost'. He desired the whole House to be suitors to the Queen for him. And so he was handed over to Mr. Lieutenant of the Tower to be kept close prisoner.[2]

If there had indeed been a pre-arranged plan among Puritan extremists and their friends out of doors, directed either towards

---

[1] Petyt MS. 538/17, fols. 251-6. This MS. gives the name as Sackville instead of Seckford, as in Harleian MS. 1877. The latter is right.

[2] Cromwell's Diary; *C.J.* i. 104.

the Church, or the succession, or both, then its opening move had been a sad failure.[1] In any case, Wentworth's fate was calculated to damp down other hot-gospellers; and the evident decorum of the session presumably owed something to this initial cautionary tale. Intemperate advocates hamper many good causes.

The Spanish agent, after his report of the episode and the scandal it had caused, added that it had 'given rise to an order that no bill shall be submitted unless it is signed by two commissioners appointed for the purpose, in order that nothing shall be discussed in the House except by the Queen's will'. Fiddlesticks! might be the normal response to such a story from such a source: and, indeed, it is possibly a distorted version of the motion with which the Speaker opened the session. But it so happens that among the State Papers there is a curious petition to the House of Lords from the sponsors of a private bill, explaining that, though the 'abridgement' or breviate had been read in the Commons, the Speaker would not allow the body of the bill to be read, 'alleging that he may not read the same without order from her Majesty or from your Honours'. Whatever its significance — probably very little, being concerned merely with a private bill — it certainly seems to suggest that Speaker Bell was disposed to be ultra-cautious this session.[2]

Wentworth remained in the Tower for just over a month: his first of several sojourns there. On March 12th — two days before the end of the session — Christopher Hatton, after telling the House of the Queen's 'great good acceptation' of their 'temperate usage', announced that she had sent Mr. Wentworth back to them. 'She was absolutely persuaded that his speech proceeded of abundance of zeal towards her', and she had 'not only forgiven but also forgotten the inconsiderateness of the same, and did accept him to be in as good grace and favour as ever she did before.' 'Setting forth the great blessings we had received under her', he thought they should be thankful for the same; and therefore 'it was agreed that the Speaker in all our names should render her Majesty thanks for the same': which, in fact, he did in his closing speech.[3]

---

[1] Cf. the Spanish agent's remarks in *Spanish Cal. Eliz.* ii. 529, and the dispatch of Castelnau, February 15th in P.R.O. Baschet Transcripts, 3/27.

[2] *Spanish Cal. Eliz.* ii. 524; S.P. Dom. Eliz. 107/74.

[3] Cromwell's Diary.

The Queen's gesture was gracious, the sentiment magnani-
mous; and Sir Walter Mildmay, Chancellor of the Exchequer
and a Privy Councillor, was ready to moralize on the occasion.
'Sovereign princes', he said, 'placed by God, are to be honoured
with all humble and dutiful reverence, both in word and deed,
specially if they be good and virtuous, such as our most gracious
Sovereign is: a princess that hath governed this realm so many
years, so quietly, so justly, and so providently . . . Then see how
great an offence this was to reprove and charge so gracious a
Queen so unjustly: and that to be done not by any common
person abroad, but by a Member of this House; and not in any
private or secret place, but openly in this most honourable
assembly of the Parliament, being the highest Court and
Council of the realm. And thereby see also her most gracious
and good nature, that so mercifully and so easily can remit so
great an offence: a thing rarely found in princes of so great
estate, that commonly think themselves touched in honour if
they should pass over smaller injuries so lightly.'

He then commented on the gracious respect and favour
shown by her Majesty to the House in pardoning, for their
sakes, Wentworth's offence; 'and that so freely, as she would not
think of it at any time again (for those were her words)'. It was
their bounden duty to yield thanks, and also, by this example,
to learn how to behave themselves hereafter. 'True it is that
nothing can be well concluded in any Council but where there
is allowed, in debating of the causes brought in deliberation,
liberty and freedom of speech. Otherwise, if . . . men be either
interrupted or terrified, so as they cannot or dare not speak
their opinions freely . . . all the proceedings therein shall be
rather to satisfy the voice of a few than to determine that which
shall be just and reasonable. But herein we may not forget to
put a difference between liberty of speech and licentious speech.'
By the former, 'men deliver their opinions freely, but with this
caution: that all be spoken pertinently, modestly, reverently
and discreetly . . . And though freedom of speech hath always
been used in this great Council of the Parliament, and is a
thing most necessary to be preserved among us, yet the same
was never, nor ought to be extended so far as though a man in
this House may speak what and of whom he list: the contrary
whereof, both in our own days and in the days of our pre-

decessors, by the punishment of such inconsiderate and disorderly speakers, hath appeared.' He warned them not to take advantage of the Queen's clemency and drive her to necessary and just severity.

Thereupon, Wentworth was brought to the bar by the Serjeant, admonished by the Speaker, and after humble submission on his knees, acknowledging his fault and craving the Queen's pardon, 'was received again into the House and restored to his place, to the great contentment of all that were present'.[1]

[1] Northants Record Soc. MS. F. (M). C. 60, compared with B.M. Sloane MS. 326, fols. 40-3.

## CHAPTER III

# ARTHUR HALL AND PRIVILEGE

PETER WENTWORTH was not the only colourful person to get into trouble this Parliament. We have already met Arthur Hall Esquire of Grantham, the wayward Member who outraged the House of Commons by his sympathy with the Duke of Norfolk and Mary Queen of Scots in 1572. In 1576 he became involved in a notorious privilege case over the arrest of one of his servants, Edward Smalley, about which he published a pamphlet that was to land him in still greater trouble in 1581.[1] The narrative repays leisurely treatment. It illustrates one of the very many privilege cases, and Hall's pamphlet, besides giving a racy picture of Elizabethan life, furnishes intimate glimpses of the ways of the House of Commons, found nowhere else, not even in our most detailed Member's-diary.

The story begins in 1573 in the eating houses of the City; at Robert Phillipson's, 'who in Lothbury in London kept a table of twelve pence a meal for gentlemen', at the 'ordinary' table of John Crokes in Whitecross Street, where there was 'a bowling alley of the half-bowl', at 'one Wormes, who kept a table beside Fleet Bridge', and at Mistress Arundel's, a famous old tavern, with parliamentary associations: where Hall and his kind dined and supped, played cards and threw dice. One of the *habitués* was a certain Melchisedech Mallory, a decayed gentleman who perhaps lived by his wits. He and Hall got across one another: 'Etna smoked, daggers were a drawing'. This passing quarrel turned into a prolonged feud when a thoughtless remark was taken to be a suggestion that Mallory cheated at play, and was so reported to him. From then on, the two sparred at one another whenever they met, and on one occasion blood was drawn.

'*Fatum* is *inevitabile*, else Troy perhaps had stood.' In November 1574, after another threatening incident while playing at dice, Hall turned to his servant, Smalley, and said: 'Jesus! can

---

[1] *An Account of a Quarrel between Arthur Hall Esq. and Melchisedech Mallerie Gent.* (reprint of 1815). My narrative is drawn from this tract, except where indicated. Cf. WRIGHT, *Arthur Hall of Grantham*.

you not knock the boy's head and the wall together?' After play, he went walking in St. Paul's, and there Mallory came, passing twice or thrice 'with great looks and extraordinary rubbing him on the elbows', spurning as well at a friend's spaniel. When Mallory left, two of Hall's servants followed and there was an encounter in Ludgate, in which Smalley cut open Mallory's cheek.

The story is long. Suffice it to say that Mallory prosecuted Smalley and was awarded £100 damages by a London jury whom Hall accuses of manifest bias. Before much else could happen, Mallory died: 'he departed well', says the pamphlet, 'leaning to the old Father of Rome, a dad whom I have heard some say Mr. Hall doth not hate'. His executor and brothers pressed on with the case, obtaining a writ of execution for the debt or damages. Now the essence of such a writ was that once executed, a second could not be obtained. The creditor's sole legal rights then lay in the imprisoned body of the debtor as pledge for the debt, though if he escaped or was otherwise freed the officer responsible for his safe-keeping might become liable for the money. It made the extension of parliamentary privilege to such a prisoner a serious and dubious matter.

At this juncture, both sides were manœuvring for advantage. The Mallories, though not thinking of parliamentary privilege, wanted to avoid arresting Smalley: instead, they hoped to secure a return of *non est inventus* (he has not been found) to the writ, thus enabling them to recover the debt from Smalley's sureties — substantial persons. On the other hand, as the parliamentary session had just started and he was a Member's servant to whom the privilege of freedom from arrest applied, Smalley was anxious to be arrested: he would thus safeguard his sureties, in due course be freed by the privilege, and might either escape payment altogether or force the Mallories to compound for a fraction of the sum involved.

In this game of wits, Hall's schoolmaster, one Kirtleton, pretending to be a friend of Mallory's, went to the debtors' prison, the Counter, and asked the appropriate official if he had a process against Smalley; if so, there was the man, conveniently walking up and down in sight of them. The stratagem failed, since the warrant had not yet arrived; but the next day Smalley procured his own arrest. This done, Hall disclosed that a

question of privilege was involved, and an attempt was made by
the court to bring about agreement between the parties in the
hope of avoiding parliamentary intervention: a prospect
clearly feared by both justices and officials. It failed, partly
because Hall was determined to drive a hard bargain.

A little more patience might have saved a deal of subsequent
misfortune; but, after waiting four days, Hall precipitated
events by buttonholing the Speaker as he went into Parliament
on February 15th and telling his tale. He was instructed to
raise the question in the House, which he did at the beginning
of the sitting; but it was thought best that he should stay his
story 'till the company were full'. Shortly after, the matter was
again moved and the serjeant who had made the arrest was
ordered to attend the House the next day. After hearing this
officer's account, a committee of three was appointed to meet
that afternoon in the Speaker's chamber at the Temple. The
committee met twice, listened to the officials responsible for the
arrest, as well as to Hall, summoned one of the Mallories before
them, and tried, though in vain, to persuade him to settle for a
smaller sum. Apparently, such was the informality of these
occasions that the Speaker had with him three eminent Members — Robert Snagge being one on the first day — who were
not on the committee; while on the second day only one of the
three committee-men attended.

Having failed to bring the parties to agreement, the committee on February 20th made their report to the House. Hall
followed with a speech in which, among other points, he dealt
with the chief objection to granting privilege in a case such as
this: namely, that the creditor could not re-establish his legal
position by a second writ of execution. In the subsequent
debate there were divers arguments about what should be done.
Smalley was criticized for not revealing to the serjeant that his
master was a Member of Parliament; and it was objected that
the sheriffs of London, who were responsible for his safe custody,
would be liable for the debt if he were released. Sir James Croft,
the Comptroller, attacked Hall's speech, whereupon 'Mr.
Recorder, in very ancient precedents, wherein he is well seen —
having read much — stood fast for the liberties of the House'.
Among other precedents, he cited the cases of Speaker Thorpe
in 1453 and of Ferrers in 1543. Thorpe, he erroneously affirmed,

'was set at liberty and brought home to be Speaker': a convenient reversal of historical fact which he based, not on docu-
mentary but on oral evidence, having 'received it by Mr.
Carell, Mr. Carell from Mr. Mordaunt by tradition'. Men,
Fleetwood added, were 'at their peril to take heed with whom
they deal: whether they be of the Parliament House'.[1] 'Francis
Alford, Master Seintpole, Master Bainbridge, Master Newdigate soundly followed on', says Hall. Seintpole — Sampole, as
our diarist calls him — added to Fleetwood's fiction by declaring that in Henry VII's time 'the use was for the serjeant',
before making arrests, 'to send to know whether they were of
the House or attended upon any in the House'.

The Speaker evidently did not like the trend of the debate,
which was displaying the customary bias in favour of privilege.
He asked leave to give his opinion, and, this granted, advised
them to have a care and 'not to proceed to the discharging of an
execution against law'. Otherwise, the judges would overrule
them: an eventuality he would be loth to witness. He was in
fact anticipating an issue which was to emerge in the next
century: that of the relation between the Common Law and
Privilege of Parliament (*lex terrae* and *lex parliamenti*). It was to
have a long history before being finally settled in favour of
Parliament.[2] The Speaker's doctrine that the judges of other
and inferior courts could challenge the Commons' interpretation of parliamentary privilege was one fraught with peril, and
it was immediately refuted by a Member who declared that
they were not to be overruled by any in those cases, 'but others
to be directed by them'.

Having tried to adjourn the debate, but failed, the Speaker
then moved that Hall, as a party to the case, should withdraw.
This was carried by a majority. The debate seems to have gone
on. Our diarist records that there were many arguments against
granting privilege: among them, that the law should leave no
man without remedy. This would happen if the prisoner were
now set at liberty. The privilege should not extend to executions. 'One book-case [was] vouched where the judges had
affirmed that the setting at liberty of one in such a case was
taken erroneous by the judges.' On the other side, it was

[1] Cromwell's Diary. Cf. STUBBS, *Constitutional History*, iii. 510.
[2] Cf. CARL WITTKE, *Hist. of English Parliamentary Privilege* (Ohio, 1921).

shrewdly pointed out that to grant privilege in this instance would give them another precedent; 'and the liberty of the House was best known by precedents'.

When the motion was finally put, the 'Yea was the greater', but their opponents took it to a division. Eventually it was carried, 102 voting against: how many for, the Clerk omitted to enter. The Serjeant-at-Arms was ordered to go with his man to the Counter and fetch Smalley out.[1]

That afternoon Hall called on the Speaker at the Temple to reproach him for his hostile behaviour in the morning. They evidently had high words. As they were talking, Mr. Bowyer, the Serjeant-at-Arms, came in, perhaps to explain that the House had not given sufficient thought to the question of getting Smalley out of prison, since the normal method was to seek a writ of privilege from the Chancery. At any rate, the Speaker now told Hall that his man could not be delivered at once, and that he had better move the House for directions.

The following morning Hall did this. Thereupon a committee was appointed to meet at the Rolls Chapel (where the records were) to search for precedents, Recorder Fleetwood, appropriately enough, being one of them. When they reported the next day they explained that they had found a dozen precedents for the release of Members or their servants and to stay suits against them; that in most cases concerning servants, the master had taken an oath to the effect that at the time of arrest the man was his servant, attendant upon him; but that they could find no precedent 'for setting at large by the mace any person in arrest', nor for delivering by writ anyone imprisoned upon an execution — the situation of Smalley.[2] Ignoring this last, ominous item, the House decided that the Speaker should direct a warrant or certificate to the Lord Keeper for a writ of privilege and that Hall should go to his Lordship to take the oath. After dinner, Hall waited on Sir Nicholas Bacon at Suffolk Place, was duly sworn and very honourably used. This done, he reported to Mr. Speaker at the Temple, finding him at supper with Sandys and Norton, the Clerk Onslow, and another gentleman.

---

[1] Hall's Tract; Cromwell's Diary; *C.J.* i. 107.
[2] The item about the mace is in *C.J.* i. 107, but not in Cromwell's Diary. It is odd that they did not refer to Ferrers's case of 1543.

It was now that the extreme caution and formalism which fenced round the Chancery became apparent. Hall sent his servant with the Speaker's warrant to the office of Master Dister, a Chancery official. Dister announced that he had no appropriate precedent, but accompanied the servant to another official, Master Garth. To him 'this matter was French'; and so the pursuit moved on to Master Couper, 'who durst not deal in so extraordinary a cause'. Next to the Lord Keeper himself: he answered that 'he was not to receive messages from the House by anybody but by the Speaker'. And so back to the Speaker, who next day waited on Sir Nicholas after the House had risen, and at his request amended the warrant. Bacon now set his office in motion by letters to the Cursitors and to the Six Clerks, to which they replied — as Fleetwood and his colleagues had already discovered — that there were no precedents. It followed that there could be no writ of privilege.[1]

On February 27th the Speaker reported all this to the House, whereupon Hall criticized him for causing such delay. There was a passage of words between them. In the debate that followed, Newdigate 'wished the liberties to be preserved'; with which Knollys and Mildmay agreed, although they wanted recompense for the Mallories. Then came the two eminent lawyers, Popham and Norton, who 'could not brook that executions should be dispensed withal'; their fundamental principle being that a subject should not be deprived of his rights at law. To divert attention from principle to prejudice, Sir Henry Knyvet, Hall's chief friend, told the story of the original quarrel, of Mallory's abuse of Hall and gibes about his humiliation in the last session of Parliament — a subject taboo out of Parliament: it was no injustice, he claimed, to deprive such a man or his heirs of all recompense. This of course was to traverse another court's judgment against Smalley; and it is significant of the loose discipline of the time that the Speaker did not attempt to contain the debate within its proper province. Digges, Bainbridge, Alford and Seintpole 'stood firmly' with Knyvet. Christopher Hatton spoke, agreeing that Smalley should be released, but suggesting that six or eight be chosen, half by the House and half by Hall, who might award the Mallories compensation and discharge the sheriffs of London

---

[1] There is also a brief comment in Bodley, Tanner MS. 393, fol. 67.

from any legal peril into which they might fall if their prisoner were freed. To this Hall answered that 'he would first have his man at liberty and then he would do what he thought good'. He clearly believed that he was riding the wave and forgot the trough that might open before him.

Faced by the refusal of the Lord Keeper to issue a writ of privilege, yet intent on their liberties, the House decided to release Smalley 'by warrant of the mace and not by writ', ordering that the sheriffs of London should bring their prisoner to the House next day. Virtually the whole morning had been spent on the debate, a galaxy of talent employed; and only one bill had been read. It was prodigal use of time and energy; and more was to follow.[1]

The Speaker seems to have realized that in taking the question so early in the morning he had been unwise, and the next day, February 28th, he saw that quite a number of bills were read before the subject was reopened, towards the end of the sitting. He then announced that Smalley was without the door, accompanied by two serjeants of London. Another debate started, provoked by Robert Snagge. From his part in the 1572 debates, we can well imagine that he was no friend of Hall's. He had been with the Speaker when the initial committee held its first meeting about the case, and he now warned the House that it was being deceived. The committee's report, he asserted, had been untrue, and the House should investigate the tricks practised by Smalley and others. Though denied, the allegation had its effect. Alford and Newdigate remained stoutly on Hall's side, but Norton was insistent on saving the Mallory interest, while Recorder Fleetwood wanted further inquiry and was ready with a jocular precedent to justify reversing their decisions, if need arose. In the end, Smalley was released from the custody of the London serjeants, who were discharged of their prisoner: privilege was thus asserted. But he was committed to the charge of the Serjeant-at-Arms, and an influential committee was set up, including all the Privy-Councillor Members, to examine the matter and consider what recompense should be adjudged to the Mallories.[2]

Apparently, still more members were added later to the committee, and when they met, in the afternoon of March 2nd,

[1] Also cf. *C.J.* i. 108.      [2] Cf. ibid. p. 109; Cromwell's Diary.

Hall expressed surprise that in a cause to which he was a party these members should be named without his consent. He took exception to Thomas Norton — another of his prominent 1572 critics, clearly hostile to his interests. Norton was willing to withdraw, but Sir Walter Mildmay stayed him, curtly telling Hall that they were not to be ruled by him. It was an unpropitious start, in which Hall seems to have lost his temper. Hall then recounted his story, and Andrew Mallory his. The committee also had before them the officials concerned with the arrest: 'the Secondaries of the two Counters — Mr. Mosley and Mr. Christopher — some of the serjeants, Mosley's men, and others'. They also examined Smalley, who confessed to the intrigue with Kirtleton, the schoolmaster, admitted that he was willing enough to be arrested in order to save his sureties, and made an injudicious remark that seemed to involve his master in the deceit. It was a long meeting. The committee did not rise until about 7 p.m. and even so they had to defer till the next morning their decision on the sum to be awarded to the Mallories. Some of the committee were friendly to Hall: others were not. His friends told him rather too much about the disposition of their opponents; and he therefore followed Christopher Hatton to Court to make sure of his support, counting him and Knyvet as his chief defenders.

The next morning, when the committee met, they called in Hall and the Mallories to hear their decision. They had resolved to award £100 to the administrator of the Mallory estate, to be paid before the beginning of the next term; conditional on both parties dropping all suits against each other. Hall would have been wise to accept the award: though disappointing, in the circumstances it was not unfavourable. But his wrath got the better of him. He 'intemperately swore he would never perform the same' and proceeded to charge certain members of the committee with prejudice. Sir William Winter, one of those charged, retorted that his conscience was not to be ruled by another. And so, 'Hall almost mad for anger, divers of the committees disquieted', they departed, 'some to the Parliament, others to their own business'.

On March 6th the committee made its report to the House, apparently through the mouth of Thomas Wilson, the Master of Requests, once a friend. He proved very hostile, complaining

of Hall's criticisms and reporting that there appeared great
fraud and cunning in Smalley, whose words also suggested that
his master was the instigator. Winter, Snagge, and others, says
our pamphlet, 'shot their shafts into the same hole'; Sir Francis
Knollys was impartial; Mildmay, Hatton, Alford, and another
refuted Wilson and company. The matter was then adjourned
till the afternoon of the following day, when Hall, Mallory and
his counsel, and Smalley were to attend.

Early in that afternoon's proceedings, 'Hall being within and
the others attending without', Snagge 'called on the matter':
interesting light on how the course of business might be ordered.
Since his friends had not yet got back from dinner, Hall asked
for delay, in order to answer the 'invective speeches' recently
made against him, in as full an assembly as heard them. This
was tacitly conceded; but when, shortly after, Croft, Mildmay,
Sadler, and Hatton entered the Chamber, Snagge 'must needs
on with his chase'. The business was set going. The Speaker
suggested that they should start by discovering if the opposing
parties would agree to the committee's award. The Mallory
brothers, being called in, agreed, after a show of reluctance.
Hall likewise agreed, though in a more contentious spirit. The
House took order accordingly, appointing Fleetwood and
another lawyer-Member to see to its execution.

Then another storm blew up. Mr. Meredith of the Temple —
'a man', says Hall, 'whom I never heard speak before' — 'forthwith called out for the abusing of the House. His earnestness
was great, his thirst to punish abuse much'. Said he: both Hall
and his man Smalley 'had covinously, fraudulently, and cunningly dealt with that Council, and therefore he demanded
sharp penance for such misdemeanour'. Hall stood up to
answer, but those on either side of him plucked him down,
advising him to let others speak first, 'who were in hand to cast
liquour in Mr. Meredith's fire'. They meant well, but ruined
Hall's chances. Two Members rose: Mr. Gent of the Inner
Temple, 'to put dry water to increase the flame'; and Hall's constant champion, Francis Alford, ready 'with clear running
water'. A dispute arose as to who was up first. Gent insisted
that he was, and won. He was for punishing both servant and
master. The Comptroller, Sir James Croft, advised the House
to take no further action. His was a weighty voice and perhaps

would have prevailed, but he and the rest of the Privy Councillors, along with the hope of the side, Christopher Hatton,
went off to the Lords about a committee. As he left, Hatton
told Hall to get the debate adjourned until they returned. Sir
Henry Knyvet now spoke up forcefully for Hall; but then
everything went wrong because the Speaker — who certainly
was not favourably disposed towards him, nor had reason to be
— intervened to suggest that he be ordered to withdraw from
the Chamber. He thus lost any chance to speak or get the
debate adjourned until Hatton and Croft were present. His
enemies held the field. Sir William Winter was especially hard.
Alford rose to challenge the truth of one of his statements, and,
in spite of Snagge's attempts to interrupt, went on to a general
defence of Hall's and Smalley's conduct. Norton and many
others spoke against Alford: indeed, it looks as if Puritan dislike
of Hall and Alford was an unacknowledged strain in the debate.
They wanted the schoolmaster, Kirtleton, punished as well.
Seintpole, Digges, Dannet, and others spoke up for Hall; but
Robert Beale — one-time *émigré*, a Puritan who later won
notoriety in several roles, including that of the messenger who
carried Mary Queen of Scots' death warrant to Fotheringay —
'took of his conscience Hall was guilty of the fault'.

'Before they came to the question, it grew very late and dark,
being past seven of the clock.' The House had been sitting,
with an interval for dinner, since 8 a.m. There can only have
been a fraction in attendance, many of whom now wanted to
depart. The conditions were not those in which to look for
dispassionate and wise decisions. But the Speaker, who, having
no deputy, had been tied to his chair throughout all these hours,
was evidently heartily sick of the whole business and wanted
an end to it. He had the door kept closed to prevent anyone
leaving. Amid much disorder, with Members on their feet, two
moved that they should either close the matter with the money
agreement, or adjourn it until the House was full. They were
not heard. Instead, the Speaker propounded two questions:
whether Smalley should be sent to the Tower as guilty of contempt and abuse of the House, to which the answer was 'Yea';
whether the schoolmaster, Kirtleton, should be punished in the
same way. According to Hall, the answer to the second question was doubtful, and a division was demanded. 'Whether

lateness, lack, or will was the cause, I know not', says Hall, but
the 'Yeas' were declared a majority. 'I am sure', he added,
'the Clerk could not see to enter judgment.' However, as the
*Commons Journal* reveals, Onslow managed to enter the decisions
in his finished *Journal* with a precision and orderliness that
convey no hint of the confusion in which they were taken.[1]

As they came out of the House, disgusted with the proceedings
and wondering what to do, friends found Hall waiting at the
door. Told the news, he quoted two verses from Vergil and
then burst into bitter and angry comment: ten times the money
involved was nothing compared with the opprobrium he would
suffer from his enemies. To which his friends replied that 'a
prince's heart with a poor man's ability was an ill medley';
and 'continual kicking will make the back ache'. 'Plucking his
hat about his ears, mumbling the old wives' *Paternoster*', he
departed.

Among the resolutions of the Commons was one ordering the
Serjeant-at-Arms to bring Smalley and Kirtleton to the House
the next day to receive judgment. Scarcely had Hall got home
before the Serjeant's man arrived to pass on this order. He
was told that the culprits were not at home. Since Hall had
made himself responsible for restoring Smalley to the Serjeant's
custody, he too was bound to become involved. He commanded
his folk to deny that he was there if any came to inquire for
him.

The next day, in the afternoon, Hall's friends managed to
reopen the subject in the Commons, and Croft, Knyvet,
Hatton and others spoke for him. They seem to have secured
agreement that the imprisonment of his servants would be
brief. But this modicum of comfort Hall spurned. He stayed
at home, sulking, and kept his servants from obeying another
summons to attend the House the next day. As he had also
failed to enter into the necessary recognizance for securing the
monetary settlement with the Mallories, he had laid himself
open to the dangerous personal attack that was made on him
in the House. It was decided to give him one more warning;
and his good friends tried, but tried in vain, to persuade him
to obey.

In this situation, on March 10th, Recorder Fleetwood

[1] *C.J.* i. 111-12; Cromwell's Diary.

brought a bill into the House, 'wherein it should have been enacted that Hall should pay the £100, and to be turned out [of Parliament] for a wrangler' and excluded from 'ever being member of that assembly'. The first reading of this as 'The bill against Arthur Hall Esquire, Edward Smalley, and Matthew Kirtleton, his servants' is entered in the *Commons Journal*, but had it not been for Hall's pamphlet we should have been without an inkling of its extraordinary character and interest. The recourse to legislation in order to save the civil rights of a subject showed how wise some of the lawyers had been in resisting the extension of the privilege to servants imprisoned on a writ of execution. As for the proposed statutory exclusion of Hall from Parliament, that might have proved a dangerous precedent had the bill proceeded.

It did not proceed. No sooner had it been read than word was brought that Smalley was at the door of the House. ' "Yea", quoth Mr. Recorder, "I thought of some such matter, for I gave knowledge to Mistress Hall of this gear this morning. I doubted not but she would send her man." ' And so the wife saved her husband from his folly. Smalley was brought to the bar and committed to the Tower for a month, after which he was to remain there until sufficient assurance was made for payment of £100 to the Mallories. In addition he was to pay forty shillings, fees to the Serjeant-at-Arms. Curiously enough, no mention is made of Kirtleton, the schoolmaster. Though our sources all agree that he also was to be imprisoned, he evidently did not appear to receive judgment. The House seems to have been content to let the matter rest there, and Hall's rebellion did score a point; and incidentally saved the additional costs for a second prisoner.[1]

Along with Smalley, Hall had sent an explanatory letter to the House, which the Speaker first read himself and then read to the House. Perhaps this explains why they turned a blind eye to the schoolmaster's absence, though the utter submission for which the House looked on these occasions was still lacking. 'I am right sorry', wrote Hall, 'being a member of you, who have bent my poor good will toward the service of my country among you in all truth and plainness, that upon opinion conceived of me, otherwise than I have given cause in knowledge

[1] *C.J.* 1. 113.

of myself, [you] have proceeded against me as a stranger and
not with that favour as a member of such a body might in good
equity have looked for; which hath forced me, sore to my great
discontentation, to withdraw myself till a time of better favour;
assuring your honours and worships all, that if my cause had
been heard and judged in a full court, in the presence of the
chief of the committees, who were absent, I should have abidden
your uttermost sentence, even to the loss of all that I had . . .
Of absenting myself, I pray you consider no otherwise than as
of one who is much grieved of your offence conceived of him,
and as one that cannot endure the continual hard speeches
brought to mine ears, much sounding to my discredit . . . But
in all, I submit myself to your honours' wisdoms, as one who
is most desirous of your good opinions and favours, and wish
you good success in all honourable proceedings.'

Into the frets and worries and delays that this business still
imposed on Hall, we must not enter. He dismissed his schoolmaster at once, whereat his son, Cecil Hall, 'was no whit discontented'. Though the Comptroller, the Treasurer, and the
Chancellor of the Exchequer, all important and busy men,
allowed themselves to be involved in trying to expedite a
settlement — showing that singular patience which so often
strikes one in Elizabethan ministers of state — it was May 9th
before the release of Smalley could be secured. And then there
were the fees and charges of the imprisonment to pay, as well
as the £100, which was raised 'with hard shift enough', probably as a loan at high interest. On his release, Hall discharged
him. 'Because he hath sung in so worthy a gaol, his master
thought him not meet to chant in so mean a cage as the best
house he is like to have; so that now he may, being summer,
learn a new note in the green fields.'

'Here have you the end of this great cause', says the pamphlet.
As we shall see, it was not the end. Hall wrote and published
his account of the quarrel — in itself sufficient to get him into
serious trouble — and appended to it a second pamphlet,
shocking to the self-esteem of an Elizabethan House of Commons. The further instalment of the story belongs to the
Parliament of 1581.

CHAPTER IV

# CHAPTER IV

## THE SUBSIDY, RELIGION, AND OTHER TOPICS

MONEY was the principal reason for this session, and on February 10th, in the quiet aftermath of the Wentworth affair, Sir Walter Mildmay, Chancellor of the Exchequer, made the opening speech, from which came the appointment of what might be called a committee of supply. This statesman's speeches were collected by contemporaries, as model orations; and they merit their reputation. He had a clear, orderly mind, and took pains about their structure.

Mildmay, like Peter Wentworth, was a brother-in-law of Sir Francis Walsingham. He, too, was a Puritan, living in that county of Puritans, Northamptonshire, at Apethorpe, not far from Peterborough and Lord Burghley's estates. Inheriting wealth, he added to it, and was a generous benefactor. Among other notable actions he founded Emmanuel College, Cambridge. 'Sir Walter', Queen Elizabeth is said to have remarked, apropos of this College, 'I hear you have erected a Puritan foundation', to which Mildmay replied: 'No, Madam; far be it from me to countenance anything contrary to your established laws, but I have set an acorn, which, when it becomes an oak, God alone knows what will be the fruit thereof.'[1] Like many another Elizabethan story it is *ben trovato*. Mildmay was about fifty-six years of age in 1576: a Member of increasing significance in the House of Commons, and well placed in that cultured, zealous assembly.

On this occasion he spoke on three themes: 'how the Queen found the realm'; 'how she hath restored and conserved it'; 'how we stand now'. They reflect the historical perspective in which Elizabethan Protestants saw their own times, and are inspired by that sense of purpose and faith which were essential elements in the greatness of the age. 'No man can be ignorant that our most gracious Queen, at her entry, found this noble realm, by reason of the evil government preceding, miserably

[1] *D.N.B.* sub Mildmay, Walter.

GUALTERUS MILDMAY. *Eq. Aur.* Coll: Emanuel.ʲ Fundʳ
A.º Dñi 1584
Hanc Effigiem Revᵈᵒ Viro Johᵉˢ Balderſton. S.T.P et iſtius
Coll: Magiſtre, a Tabula in Suis Ædibus
aſſervata factam. Summa cum Humil: & Observantia D.D.D. I. Faber A.º 1714

overwhelmed with Popery, dangerously afflicted with war, and grievously oppressed with debt.' Having, under Henry VIII and Edward VI, been 'utterly delivered from the usurped tyranny of Rome', the kingdom 'was nevertheless, by the iniquity of the later time, brought back again under the former captivity, to the great thraldom both of body and soul'. 'A wretched time and wretched ministers . . . brought hither a strange nation [Spain] to press our necks again into the yoke . . . From them and by their occasion came the war that we entered into with France and Scotland, not upon any quarrel of our own.'

In contrast, their own most gracious Sovereign had delivered them from the tyranny and restored the most holy religion of the gospel, 'not slacking any time therein, but, even at the first, doing that which was for the honour of God, to the unspeakable joy of all her good subjects'. In so doing she had preferred the glory of God before her own quietness, adventuring the malice of the mighty princes of the world, her neighbours, 'enemies of our religion'. She made peace with France and Scotland, the one a mighty nation, the other, though not so potent, yet more dangerous. 'The peace with Scotland, which in time past was found always very tickle, is now become so firm as in no age there hath been so long and so good peace between them and us.' 'Two notable journeys with her forces' had contributed to this: the one to Leith, delivering Scotland from the French, and the recent one to Edinburgh, putting out the fire of civil war. These had brought unto her Majesty 'great and immortal honour and renown'. They had been costly. Costly also had been the suppression of the Northern Rebellion, 'practised by the Pope, the most principal and malicious enemy of this State'.

In spite of this expenditure, the Queen 'hath most carefully and providently delivered this kingdom from a great and weighty debt . . . begun four years at the least before the death of King Henry VIII and not cleared until within these two years, and all that while running upon interest: a cancer able to eat up not only private men and their patrimonies . . . but also princes and their estates . . . The truth whereof may be testified by the citizens of London, whose bonds . . . for assurance of payment . . . are now all discharged.' Not only is the realm

acquitted of this burden and the merchants freed, 'but also
her Majesty's credit thereby, both at home and abroad, [is]
greater than the credit of any other prince . . . She hath kept
promise with all men, wherein other princes have often failed.'
They stood now 'in peace, and all our neighbours in war';
'in quietness at home and safe enough from troubles abroad';
'in wealth and in all prosperity'; 'and, that which is the greatest,
we enjoy the freedom of our consciences, delivered from the
bondage of Rome'. Nevertheless, 'as wise mariners in calm
weather', it behoved them to 'prepare their tackle and provide to withstand a tempest that may happen . . . The tail of
those storms which are so bitter and so boisterous in other
countries may reach us also, before they be ended'. The adversaries of our religion hate us, for 'this realm is a merciful
sanctuary for such poor Christians as fly hither for succour'.
'Albeit her Majesty is not to yield an account how she
spendeth her treasure, yet for your satisfactions I will let you
understand such things as are very true.' Here he commented
on the favourable taxation or assessment of subsidies, 'whereby
far less cometh to her Majesty's coffers than by law is granted
a matter now drawn to be so usual as is hard to be reformed'.
He enumerated various special causes of expenditure which the
last aid was insufficient to cover, thus needing great supplementary sums from the Queen's own revenues. She lives, 'as
you see, in most temperate manner, without excess either in
building or other superfluous things of pleasure'. Nor has she
those helps which were used in the times of her father, her
brother, or her sister, such as the debasement of the coinage,
'which brought infinite sums . . . but wrought great damage';
the sale of land, no longer possible; and borrowing of money
upon interest, which 'is never more to be done if by any means
it may be avoided'. He wound up the speech with a 'perora-
tion' appealing to the House of Commons to come to the
Queen's aid . . . The usual subsidy and two fifteenths and tenths were
granted, thus indicating that the theory of parliamentary taxation as an extraordinary source of revenue was beginning to
wear a little thin. There was no attempt to make supply sub-
serve grievances, nor even to frustrate the government's desire

B.M. Sloane MS. 326, fols. 1-8; C.J. i. 104.

for a speedy end to the session. It was indeed proving a quiet
and pliant Parliament.

Quiet and pliant; but religion was not altogether forgotten.
There is an item from the House of Lords to be recorded before
we continue with the Commons. It will be remembered that
in the Parliament of 1571 the Queen vetoed a bill to enforce
attendance at church by surer penalties and to introduce compulsory attendance at Communion; and that in 1572 the House
of Lords vainly tried to persuade her to allow them to reintro-
duce it in that Parliament. In 1576 it reappeared in the Upper
House in the first week of the session. From its subsequent
fate, it seems that Elizabeth had not changed her attitude. The
bishops, backed by sympathizers among the peers, were presumably attempting an independent move. As Grindal had
just succeeded Parker in the see of Canterbury and it was he
who had taken the initiative in the previous session, we may
perhaps see his earnest, radical temperament in this third
attempt to make life more difficult for Catholics. The bill—
probably the same, or much the same, as the one vetoed in
1571—was committed to an imposing group, including Grindal, Burghley, Sussex, Bedford, and Leicester, on its second
reading. In committee the Queen's great ministers, if they did
not bring explicit orders from her, must, one suspects, have
reported that there was not a chance of securing her consent to
compulsory attendance at Communion. At any rate, a new bill
was drafted, to which the Clerk gave the restricted title, 'for
coming to church'. It was read once on March 3rd; and that
was the end of it. Probably the Queen had intervened: her
policy of opening no windows into men's souls was to be maintained.[1]

In the Commons, even the fate of Peter Wentworth, and
conditions otherwise unfavourable could not altogether silence
the Puritan voice. On February 29th, as our diarist, Thomas
Cromwell, reports, 'Mr. Pistor, with great zeal, declared to the
House the great prejudice [that] grew to the realm by the un-
learnedness of the ministry, abuses of excommunication, want
of discipline, dispensations, and tolerations for non-residency,
and such like'. He moved 'that an humble petition may be
made to the Queen's Majesty for reformation, and exhibited a

---

[1] *L.J.* i. 731-2, 740; LODGE, *Illustrations of British History* (1791), ii. 137.

supplication in writing for that purpose'. The motion was 'well prosecuted' by Robert Snagge, Edward Lewkenor, 'and others'; and in the end a committee was appointed, consisting of all the Privy Councillors in the House, along with sixteen others among whom were Pistor, Lewkenor, Snagge, Audley, Yelverton, Henry Knollys senior, and Lord Russell, the Earl of Bedford's eldest son. They were instructed to draft a petition; and, after submitting this to the House, the Privy-Councillor Members were to consult with their colleagues in the Upper House about presenting it to the Queen.[1]

It is a thousand pities that our diarist did not report the debate and that we are left to guess the significance of this move. That it was pre-arranged seems a reasonable assumption. Audley, as a member of the committee, was almost certainly among 'the others' who spoke in the debate; and he, Pistor, and Snagge were the three Members who had been most intimately associated with the egregious Puritan bill of 1572. As for Lewkenor, later in the reign he was imprisoned, along with Peter Wentworth and others, for organizing a campaign to presbyterianize the Church. As we have noticed, when Wentworth was examined about his speech at the beginning of this session, there was some suspicion that others were involved. Certainly it seems as if Pistor, Snagge, and Audley were acting in collaboration; and the odds are that their clerical friends of the Presbyterian party were in the background.

The caution and propriety of Pistor — an artless man — in proposing a petition and not a bill, and in confining himself to an attack on the administrative shortcomings of the Church, if not entirely the result of the recent deflation of Puritan hopes, may have been imposed by Wentworth's misfortune. At any rate, that incident surely operated in restraining the House from having Pistor's 'supplication in writing' read then and there, as would have happened in previous Parliaments. What the supplication contained we do not know, but we possess the text of the petition drafted by the committee. Though presumably less extravagant, its language remained that of Puritan zealots. Coming from a body on which Councillors sat, it is impressive.

After the opening phraseology of a petition, the preamble

[1] Cromwell's Diary; *C.J.* i. 109.

stated that 'whereas, by the lack of the true discipline of the Church' — authentic Puritan jargon — 'a great number of men are admitted to occupy the place of ministers in the Church of England, who are not only altogether unfurnished of such gifts as are by the word of God necessarily and inseparably required to be incident to their calling, but also are infamous in their lives and conversations; and also many of the ministry whom God hath endowed with ability to teach are by means of non-residence, pluralities, and such-like dispensations so withdrawn from their flocks that their gifts are almost altogether become unprofitable; whereby an infinite number of your Majesty's subjects, for want of the preaching of the word — the only ordinary means of salvation of souls and the only good means to teach your Majesty's subjects to know their true obedience to your Majesty and to the magistrates under you . . . have already run headlong into destruction, and many thousand of the residue yet remain in great peril . . .' The common blaspheming of the Lord's name, the great licentiousness of life, the abuse of excommunication, the great number of atheists, schismatics, and heretics daily springing up, and the hindrance and increase of obstinate Papists: all these were further consequences.

'Having regard, first and principally to the advancement of the glory of God, next to the long and most blessed continuance of your Majesty's reign and safety . . . and lastly respecting the peace of our consciences and the salvation of our souls, being at this present assembled by your Majesty's authority to open the griefs and to seek the salving of the sores of our country . . .; we are most humbly to beseech your Highness, seeing the same is of so great importance, if the Parliament at this present may not be so long continued as that by good and godly laws . . . provision may be made for supply and reformation of these great wants and grievous abuses, that yet by such other means as to your Majesty's most godly wisdom shall seem best, a perfect redress may be had of the same . . .' In doing this, they finally assured her, 'your Majesty shall be recommended to all posterity for such a pattern to be followed, that nothing may seem to be added to the perfection of your renown'.

The petition, after being read in the Commons on March 2nd, seems to have been presented to the Queen by six Privy Councillors, three from the Lords — including Burghley and Leicester — and three from the Lower House. It must have been a relief to Elizabeth, after so many painful efforts to teach her Commons that in matters of prerogative the correct constitutional procedure was to petition their sovereign, to find that they had apparently learnt their lesson, and that they had even left the remedy to her instead of demanding statutory action. In her answer — which Sir Walter Mildmay was charged to deliver to the House — she endeavoured to respond to their mood and make this a happy precedent.

'The Queen's Majesty', reported Mildmay, 'had of these things consideration before; in such sort as, though this motion had not been, the reformation thereof nevertheless should have followed. And yet she alloweth well that her subjects, being aggrieved therewith, have in such sort and discreet manner both opened their griefs and remitted them to be reformed by her Majesty. And, considering that reformation hereof is to be principally sought in the clergy, and namely in the bishops and ordinaries, her Majesty did in the beginning of her Convocation confer with some of the principals of them and such as she thought were best disposed to reform these errors in the Church; from whom, if she shall not find some direct dealings for the reformation, then she will, by her supreme authority with the advice of her Council, direct them herself to amend. Whereof her Majesty doubteth not but her people shall see that her Majesty will use that authority which she hath to the increase of the honour of God and to the reformation of the abuses in the Church.'

Elizabeth did take action on the petition. There can be little doubt that the outcome of her conference with the bishops was those articles touching the admission of fit persons to the ministry and the establishing of good order in the Church which were passed by Convocation during this session. They did not tackle all the Commons' grievances; and the Queen herself apparently refused to sanction two of the articles which were specifically Puritan in tone. Nor, if we can judge by later complaints, was much improvement effected in the quality of the clergy. Though the idealists — quite rightly — refused to recognize the fact, the problem was too stubborn. The Church was bound to reflect the shortcomings of society: perfection was unattainable.

The report of Elizabeth's answer to their petition was, as the Clerk noted, 'most thankfully received by the whole House with one accord'. Such was the surge of emotion that John Croke Esquire, a Buckinghamshire gentleman, Member for that county and father of two future judges, 'took occasion in most humble and dutiful wise to make a motion unto the House for another petition to be moved to the Lords for prosecution unto her Majesty for marriage'. But this echo from the past failed for the moment to evoke action: it was as the overflowing of one full heart.[2]

However, three days later, on Monday March 12th, when Peter Wentworth was released and when the House, stirred by another seductive message, decided that the Speaker should voice their thanks to the Queen in his closing oration, Croke tried again, this time suggesting that a petition for marriage be also included. The French ambassador — interested in the Alençon marriage project — reported the gist of his speech, in which, reviewing the last four Tudor reigns, Croke likened Mary to Amon, who slew and drove out the prophets and re-established idols: Elizabeth had done as Joshua, restored the prophets and good men, along with true and pure religion and the tranquillity of the kingdom. For this they ought all to praise God and pray ever for the Queen's happy prosperity. Nevertheless, it would be well, before they separated, to consider the future no less than the present quiet of the realm, and guard against the perils and cruel wars that might follow her death. There could be no better or surer way of providing for the succession than for them all to counsel her to marry some good and virtuous prince, like to herself, in the hope of a posterity, true successors and heirs of the kingdom.

This winsome speech, as it pleased the Queen when she heard of it and evoked her hearty thanks, so now it moved the Commons to action. They appointed a weighty committee, consisting of all the Councillors, other officials, and such stalwarts as Yelverton, Norton, and Alford, as well as the mover of the motion. They were to meet that afternoon to consider

[1] STRYPE, Grindal, pp. 288-91, 537-41.
[2] C.J. i. 113; Cromwell's Diary.

how they should brief the Speaker. And so, in the magical atmosphere of this curious session, another topic, which in the past had bred discord, was converted into a kind of romance between the Queen and her faithful Commons. We shall see the spell working in the closing scenes of the Parliament.[1]

On the main subjects that had troubled all previous Parliaments the Commons may have seemed strangely subdued, but they showed their mettle over a number of bills that came to them from the Lords. One was a bill for reforming excess in apparel: a measure attuned to that age, which accepted as its philosophy that people should dress according to their station in society, and that the State should enforce this by penal legislation. The problem was how to maintain the law against the wanton and extravagant ways of the individual.

> All new fashyons be plesaunt to me;
> I wyl have them, whether I thryve or thee.

The bill originated as a government measure to reform the great statute of apparel of 1533. It was introduced into the Lords, and there redrafted. Its effect was that the Queen from time to time might by proclamation appoint what kind of apparel every degree of person within the realm should wear, and impose penalties not exceeding those in the bill.[2]

On its second reading in the Commons it aroused much criticism: indeed, Burghley had shown poor political sense in starting a bill of this sort in the Upper House. However, since disorder in apparel was very great, the bill was committed to a strong committee, who were authorized to seek conference with the Lords. At the conference, Mildmay acted as spokesman: it is his account of the proceedings that has come down to us. What he said is of more than passing interest, for it reveals that jealousy of the executive which is engendered by a vigilant concern for liberty. Some, he told the Lords, misliked the whole bill utterly. Their principal reason was that whereas the subjects of this land had hitherto been bound to nothing that was not certainly established by authority of Parliament, if this act proceeded 'a proclamation from the Prince should

---

[1] P.R.O. Baschet Transcripts, bundle 27, Castelnau to the King, March 14th, 1575/6; Cromwell's Diary; *C.J.* i. 114.

[2] HARRISON's *Elizabethan England*, ed. Withington, p. 107; 24 Henry VIII, c. 13; *L.J.* i. 729-31.

take the force of law, which might prove a dangerous precedent in time to come. For though we live now in the time of a gracious Sovereign that will never offer us anything disagreeable from the nature and office of a good and merciful Princess, yet what this may work hereafter in more dangerous times, when the government shall not be so directed by justice and equity, is greatly to be foreseen, lest by this example the authority of proclamations may extend to greater matters than these are . . . It is seen by daily experience that of precedents great hold is taken, especially in the case of princes.'

He then turned to detailed criticism of the bill. Instead of open proclamation in every county, 'and often in sundry places of the shire', it made publication in one place sufficient and provided no interval of time before the penalty took effect; then the penalty — £10 a day compared with ten groats (3s. 4d.) under the statute of 1533, in addition to loss of the offending garment — was too heavy, the Henrician punishment being adequate; thirdly, they disliked giving authority to any officer, 'were he never so inferior', to arrest a suspected offender and take the garment from his back; and lastly, they thought seven years too long a trial for experimental legislation like this.

After conference among themselves, one of the Lords replied, dealing, however, with the detailed criticisms only. They considered the penalties of Henry VIII's statute inadequate, doubted if any good would come of the bill if the method of execution was changed, and thought a trial of seven years little enough. But provided the substance of the measure was retained, they were willing for the Commons to make what changes they liked.

The Commons went ahead. They drew up a new bill, passed it, and sent it to the Lords, along with the old bill as the custom was. It got no further than a first reading with their Lordships. Our narrator says that this was because they misliked the alterations. It might equally have been because they were left little time to pass it. Having taken nearly a month over the subject in their own House, the Commons returned the bill on the afternoon before Parliament rose.[1]

There was a similar conference about a Lords' bill concern-

[1] B.M. Sloane MS. 326, fols. 15 seqq.; *C.J.* i. 106-15; *L.J.* i. 749.

ing justices of the forests. It was conducted in a similarly
amicable way, with the two Chief Justices and the Attorney
General attendant, as well as five peers. But on this occasion,
when their representatives reported back and the Speaker
moved for a committee to amend the bill, 'the whole House,
a very few excepted, said they would hear no more of it.' And
so it stayed, without any further proceeding, because it
appeared the Common House did not think their objections
sufficiently answered by the Lords'. Judging by the case as
Mildmay presented it at the conference, the Commons acted
as excellent watch-dogs over the interests and liberties of the
people: which, of course, were also their own interests.[1]

The third occasion of difference between the two Houses
was much more serious and involved a notable quarrel. It
arose over a bill for the restitution in blood of John, Lord
Stourton, a peer whose father had been convicted of murder
in Mary's reign, and hanged — with a silken cord. Apparently,
felony did not affect the descent of the title, though tainting the
blood. At any rate, being now of age, this young man had been
summoned as a peer to the Parliament of 1576, and the Queen,
at his suit, had signed a bill — the one in question — restoring
him in blood. The Lords automatically and rapidly passed it,
for it came to them already ingrossed on parchment, with the
Queen's signature.[2]

The Lords might act as a rubber stamp to the Crown: not
so the Commons. The critics started up on the second reading.
Some were opposed to any favour for Stourton, deeming him
unworthy of it. This was indeed to challenge the royal signature and pit their opinion against the Queen's. The criticism
was silenced. But another line of attack, equally the product
of mistrust, caught on. It was argued that the bill did not contain adequate safeguards for those who had purchased lands
from the father and other ancestors. It was committed on its
third reading and the committee set about devising a proviso
to bar Lord Stourton from taking advantage of any error that
might be discovered in his ancestors' land transactions, leaving
him in this respect as one corrupted in blood — unable to bring

[1] Sloane MS. 326, fols. 9 seqq.
[2] L. O. PIKE, *Constitutional Hist. of House of Lords*, p. 149; *L.J.* i. 742-3. The narrative that follows is mainly from Sloane MS. 326, fols. 33 seqq.

a writ of error. They were the more insistent because, to their great annoyance, a few days earlier the Lords had rejected a bill of theirs, saving people generally from this very type of fraud.[1] Someone in the House gave Stourton secret warning of what was afoot. He therefore went to the committee-meeting and asked that he and his legal counsel might be heard; which was granted, without the usual authority from the House. The Committee thought that in the subsequent argument their views had been accepted; but Stourton went immediately to the Lords and prevailed on them to send a message to the Lower House. They asked that the bill be passed in its original state, arguing that without the Queen's assent no change could be made in a bill signed by her. They also seem to have suggested a conference. Thinking this manner of dealing very strange — to receive a message telling them what they should do — the Commons decided to pay no attention. But once more Stourton received warning, and the next day procured another and earnest message from the Upper House, coupled with a request for a conference.[2] The Commons were now really angry, regarding their liberties as in danger. They replied that as the bill was in their possession, it was for them to seek a conference, which they would do if they wanted one; and else not. They calmly dispatched the bill with its proviso and awaited results.

It was now the turn of the Lords to be irate. Time was running out; the session was to end in twenty-four hours. With the bill in their possession, they again demanded a conference. The delegation from the Commons, attending on the Lords before 8 a.m. on the last day of the session, was treated with studied rudeness. They were kept waiting a great while, and then a large number of peers, including the principal noblemen, came into 'the utter chamber', took their seats at a long table, and after conferring among themselves summoned the members from the Commons. Lord Burghley spoke, treating them like a set of offending schoolboys. The Lords, he said, greatly misliked their dealing: their addition of a proviso; their ignoring of messages; their rejection of a conference. 'They took themselves greatly

[1] This word is in the copy written by Mildmay's son-in-law (Northants Record Soc. MS. F.).
[1] The bill for errors in fines and recoveries (L.J. i. 740).
[2] Cf. C.J. i. 114-15. Cf. the entry in Cromwell's Diary, March

touched in honour and thought that the Common House did not use that reverence towards them as they ought to do.' 'The bill being signed by her Majesty, he said none might presume to alter or add anything to it without the assent of her Majesty, which they for their part durst not do.' He produced sundry provisoes of Henry VIII's reign, signed by the King, to prove his point. Moreover, in the opinion of the judges, who were in the Upper House, the new proviso was unnecessary. He ended by demanding to know their reasons for proceeding in this way.

It was a 'vehement' speech:[1] to which the Commons' spokesman — Sir Walter Mildmay — quietly replied that their commission merely permitted them to hear what their Lordships had to say. They would report to the House and bring an answer later.

That last morning of the session, when Mildmay brought back his report to the Commons, must have been a lively sitting. 'It moved them all greatly, and gave occasion of many arguments and speeches, all generally misliking this kind of dealing with them, and thinking their liberties much prejudiced in three points: one, that they might not alter or add to any bill signed by the Queen; another, that any conference should be looked for — the bill remaining with them — except themselves saw cause to require it; and the third, to yield a reason why they passed the bill in that sort.' These and other points were 'sufficiently debated'. Burghley had cited precedents: he was an amateur alongside Fleetwood and his fellows. Out they poured. Henry VIII's famous Statute of Proclamations was instanced as a bill 'preferred and subscribed by him' (the original bill, at Westminster, by the way, contains no such subscription): a proviso had been added by the Commons 'which took away the whole body of the act'. Other — more reliable — precedents were cited from Henry VIII's reign, Mary Tudor's, and even Elizabeth's. There was 'no precedent to the contrary', they confidently said. And so, with Mildmay briefed for his answer, the delegation was sent back to the Lords.[2]

Mildmay was courteous, considerate, but firm. 'They would

---

[1] This word is in the copy written by Mildmay's son-in-law (Northants Record Soc. MS. F. (M). P. 152).
[2] Cf. the entry in Cromwell's Diary, March 13th.

yield unto their Lordships all dutiful reverence so far as the same were not prejudicial to the liberties of their House, which it behoved them to leave to their posterity in the same freedom they received them.' He rehearsed and justified the procedure of the Commons and their ignoring of the Lords' messages. The Queen's signature to the bill they took to be only a recommendation of the cause, without which they could not treat of any bill of that nature. It did not bar either House from alteration. They had good reasons for adding their proviso, but would not declare them, 'for that were to yield an account of their doings', which would be prejudicial to their liberties.

Mildmay's speech ended, the Lords bade them retire to the nether end of the chamber while they conferred together. Then Burghley replied. This time he was tactful and friendly, though he again urged them to disclose their reasons for adding the proviso. Mildmay answered that their commission did not permit them to do that.

The Commons, to whom all this was duly reported, were satisfied, 'seeing that so great a storm was so well calmed and the liberties of the House preserved, which otherwise in time to come might have been prejudiced in those three points before remembered, which are indeed, if they be well considered, of great weight and importance'.

But the Lords would not agree to the proviso, nor would they agree to a similar proviso added to a similar bill for a commoner.[1] Both bills lapsed.

---

[1] For the restitution in blood of Anthony Mayney (*L.J.* i. 749).

## CHAPTER V

# END OF THE SESSION

IN the afternoon of Wednesday, March 14th, the two Houses sat to clear up business before the Queen arrived for the closing ceremony. Business done, in the Commons Sir Francis Knollys 'moved, according to an old order, that we might end in love and amity' and that 'thanks be rendered to our Speaker'. Then there was a motion to make a collection for the poor. These matters seen to, and the Queen and Lords in their robes being set in the Parliament Chamber, they went there, the Speaker having the bill of subsidy in his hands.

In his oration, Speaker Bell first discoursed on various kinds of government: anarchy, democracy, aristocracy, and monarchy, giving the last his commendation. 'He showed what a punishment it was to a nation to have a tyrannical king, and thereby what a blessing to have a virtuous, mild, and merciful princess; whereof we now had present taste of the benefit of the one, and understood of the misery of [the other from] our neighbours in France and Flanders.' This theme of pride and exultation in the present — a dominant *motif* with Elizabethans, and psychologically a powerful fillip to achievement — continued. 'He showed the great blessing we had received under her Majesty . . .: the restoring of religion, the delivery from foreign tyrannical jurisdiction, our quiet and peace . . . the relief of God's afflicted Church throughout Christendom.'

Turning to their activities that session, he declared that he had received commandment from the House 'to render thanks to her Highness, most humble thanks, for that it had pleased her to send so comfortable an answer to a petition . . . for reforming some abuses in matters of religion; which he desired to be performed as soon as conveniently might be'. 'We also rendered to her Majesty like thanks for the thankful acceptation of our services; and lastly for restoring to our House a member of the same [Wentworth], committed by us to the Tower for irreverent speeches of her Majesty, who slipped into the same by infirmity, not by malice, and upon his knees had desired the House that his thanks might be rendered.'

Next 'he showed that he had also a petition to make to her Majesty to incline herself to marriage: declaring the great commodities that grew by marriage; the commendation given thereto, as well by the word of God as also by divers philosophers; by common experience showed how willing every nobleman and gentleman was to continue their line; desired her Majesty to consider in what case we should be left if her Majesty should die without issue; to remember that she was mortal; how glad we would be to continue subject in that lineal descent under which we had long continued; desired her Majesty to consider that she was the last which could convey lineally; and therefore besought her Majesty, as shortly as conveniently might be, to incline herself to marriage'.

'Lastly, he presented the subsidy, desiring her Majesty, in the acceptance thereof, not to consider the value of the thing offered, but the grateful minds of the offerers; which was not so soon moved, as willingly with full consent yielded by all and every of the Members of the House.'[1]

When he had finished, the Queen made a novel and unique departure from practice by adjourning the rest of the proceedings till the next day. It was growing late; but perhaps she was also moved by the rare felicity of the occasion and the reappearance of concern about her marriage and the succession — moved to add an oration of her own to its memories, and wanted time to compose it.

At 3 p.m. the next day, the Lord Keeper delivered the reply to the Speaker, pursuing the latter's oration through its five topics. The Speaker's commendation of the Queen furnished an opportunity for that emotional response by which Elizabeth kept her people so intensely tuned to the present. 'Her Majesty', said Bacon, 'hath commanded me to say unto you that she wisheth of God, with all her heart, that all those royal virtues and princely parts, together with the great gifts of gracious government that you make mention of, were so perfectly planted in her as best might serve to the maintenance of God's glory (from whom her Highness confesseth all goodness to proceed), and best also might serve to the good governance of you, her good, loving, and obedient subjects; and withal prayeth you, with her and for her, to give God hearty thanks for

[1] Cromwell's Diary.

those virtues and graces that it hath pleased God to bless her withal.' 'From her Majesty's own mouth', he assured them 'that if all the virtues of all the princes in Europe were united within her Highness's breast, she would gladly employ the same to the best of her power about the good governance of you, that be so good and loving unto her: so great is her Highness's hearty good will and inward affection towards you.' 'I am to affirm unto you from her Majesty that she taketh your proceedings in this Parliament, both in the beginning and in the midst and in the ending, so graciously and in so thankful part that, if both art and nature did concur in me abundantly to make me eloquent (as neither of them do), yet I am sure I were not able to set forth this point according to her Highness's desire nor to the worthiness of it.' He told them that, as a manifestation of her satisfaction, she proposed to prorogue Parliament, not dissolve it: a statement which also leaves us in no doubt about the significance of this Parliament's exceptionally long life. The Queen, Bacon added, had commanded him to say 'that there is none of those benefits remembered by you but she wisheth them treble in number and quadruple in greatness and goodness. And further, her Highness thinketh that the oft faithful recognizing of benefits received is one of the greatest satisfactions that a subject can make to his Sovereign for them'. What art this woman displayed!

About the petition for marriage, the Queen, said Bacon, conceived that it proceeded from their inward affections and benevolent minds, the result, not of sudden whim but of seventeen years' experience of her reign; so assured, 'that it doth not only content you to have her Majesty to reign and govern over you, but also you do desire that some, proceeding of her Majesty's body, might by perpetual succession reign over your posterity also: a matter greatly to move her Highness, she saith, to incline to this your suit'. She was not unmindful of the benefits of marriage to the realm, nor of the perils through lack of it. Though of her own natural disposition she was not inclined to marriage, and, if a private person, would never marry, 'yet for your sakes and for the benefit of the realm' she is content to be disposed that way, provided conditions were favourable: some concerning herself, some her prospective husband, some the realm.

In commenting on the work of the session, Bacon — as our diarist's report of the speech shows — departed from his prepared text to refer to the Wentworth incident: 'and though one Member . . . had overslipped himself, yet upon his humble submission declared, she cannot but hope he will be a profitable member of his Commonweal'. He dwelt at considerable length on the need to enforce laws as well as make them, and his comments on the subsidy were planned in the same way. First, there was the Queen's gratitude for the money, couched in even more enthralling terms than usual. Proceeding from 'the earnest affections and hearty good wills of her good, loving and obedient subjects', her Majesty made greater account of it than of ten subsidies. She knew 'that before her time this manner of grant passed not but with a great persuasion and many difficulties', but now it was offered frankly, without any persuasion or difficulty at all, and with universality of consent. Having praised the grant, he turned to read a homily on its collection; but the Queen — in an unconventional act of inspired artistry — interrupted and stopped him, thinking it needless, as Bacon then went on to explain, 'to exhort men so willingly and lovingly disposed; and had rather hazard a part of the thing granted than to breed any suspicion in any of you, by long exhorting and persuading, that she is doubtful of your faithful and diligent dealing and proceeding in this matter'.[1]

The oration ended, the royal assent was given to bills, seven of which were vetoed.[2] And then the Parliament was prorogued. 'Hereupon,' says our diarist, 'the greatest company went forth': that is, of the Commons standing behind the bar, along, no doubt, with the interlopers who gate-crashed on these occasions and added to the discomfort and confusion in this inadequate space. They thought all was over, save the coming forth of the Queen through their midst. But it was not. Elizabeth rose to make a long oration of her own, carefully prepared — that is obvious — and replete with wisdom, obscurity, and literary artifice: a set Elizabethan piece. Maybe her voice did not carry well; maybe there was still confusion where our diarist, Thomas Cromwell, stood. He tells us, 'I could not

---

[1] The text is from C.C.C. Camb. MS. 543, fols. 25 seqq. Cromwell's Diary has an excellent summary.
[2] S.P. Dom. Eliz. 107/88, compared with list of acts in *Statutes of the Realm*.

hear the same, scant one word of twenty, no one perfect sentence.' If he had heard, one wonders how he would have reported so curiously involved and elusive a speech. The Earl of Shrewsbury's sons, also Members of the House of Commons, were more fortunate. They wrote to their father that the Queen herself 'made a very eloquent and grave oration, which was as well uttered and pronounced as it was possible for any creature to do'. Here, in its full and baffling perfection, is the speech:

'Do I see God's most sacred text of holy writ drawn to divers senses, be it never so perfectly taught; and shall I hope that my speech can pass forth through so many ears without mistake, where so many ripe and divers wits do oftener bend themselves to construe, than attain the perfect understanding? If any look for eloquence, I shall deceive their hope; if some think I can match their gift that spake before, they hold an open heresy. I cannot satisfy their longing thirst that watch for those delights, unless I should afford them what myself had never yet in my possession. If I should say the sweetest speech with the eloquentest tongue that ever was in man, I were not able to express that restless care which I have ever bent to govern for the greatest wealth. I should wrong mine intent and greatly bate the merit of my own endeavour.'

So far by way of prologue. She now reflected on those 'blessings' of her reign that the Speaker had eulogized. 'I cannot attribute those haps and good success to my device without detracting much from the divine providence; nor challenge to my private commendation what is only due to God's eternal glory. My sex permits it not; or, if it might be in this kind, yet find I no impeachment why to persons of more base estate the like proportion should not be allotted. One special favour, notwithstanding, I must needs confess I have just cause to vaunt of: that, whereas variety and love of change is ever so rife in servants towards their masters, children towards their parents, and in private friends one towards another, as though, for one year or two, they can content themselves to hold their course upright, yet after — by mistrust or doubt of worst — they are dissevered and in time wax weary of their wonted liking; yet still I find that assured zeal amongst my faithful subjects, to my special comfort, which was first declared to my great encouragement.

'Can a Prince, that of necessity must discontent a number to delight and please a few (because the greatest part is oft not the best inclined), continue so long time without great offence, much mislike, or common grudge? Or haps it oft that Prince's acts are conceived in so good part, and favourably interpreted? No, no, my Lords. How great my fortune is in this respect, I were ingrate if I should not acknowledge. And as for those rare and special benefits which many years have followed and accompanied me with happy reign, I attribute them to God alone, the Prince of rule, and account myself no better than his handmaid: rather brought up in a school to abide the ferula, than traded in a kingdom to support the sceptre.'

She next reminded them that she too had been an ideologist, deliberately choosing risks for the sake of religion when the conventional and easy way of marriage, alliances, and 'worldly wisdom' was open to her. Hers was the decision, hers the leadership; and under her direction God had prospered them. 'If policy had been preferred before truth, would I, trow you, even at the first beginning of my rule, have turned upside down so great affairs, or entered into tossing of the great waves and billows of the world: [I] that might, if I had sought mine ease, have harboured and cast anchor in a more seeming security? It cannot be denied but worldly wisdom rather bade me marry and knit myself in league and alliance with great princes, to purchase friends on every side by worldly means, and there repose the trust of mine assured strength where force could never want to give assistance.

'Was I to seek,[1] in that which to man's judgment outwardly must needs be thought the safest course? No, I can never grant myself to be so simple as not to see what all men's eyes discovered. But all those means of leagues, alliances, and foreign strengths I quite forsook, and gave myself to seek for truth, without respect, reposing my assured stay in God's most mighty grace, with full assurance. Thus I began, thus I did proceed, and thus I hope to end. These seventeen years God hath both prospered and protected you with good success under my direction. And I nothing doubt but the same main-

[1] i.e. Was I without skill.

taining hand will guide you still, and bring you to the ripeness
of perfection.

'Consider with yourselves the bitter storms and troubles of
your neighbours; the true cause whereof I will not attribute to
princes (God forbid I should), since those misfortunes may proceed as well from sins amongst the people. For want of plagues
declare[s] not always want of guilt, but rather prove[s] God's
mercy. I know, besides, that private persons may find sooner
fault than mend a prince's state; and, for my part, I grant
myself too guilty to increase the burden by mislike of any. Let
all men therefore bear their private faults: mine own have
weight enough for me to answer for. The best way, I suppose,
were both for you and me, by humble prayers, to require of
God that — not in weening, but in perfect weight; in being, not
in seeming — we may wish the best, and further it with our
ability. Not the finest wit, [or] the strongest judgment that can
rave most deeply and take up men's captious ears with pleasant
tales, hath greater care to guide you to the safest state, and be
gladder to establish you where men ought to think themselves
most sure and happy, than she that speaks these words.'

Still in reflective mood, she turned to the Speaker's remarks
about marriage and the succession, well aware of the dangers
her subjects feared, but conscious of present dangers that they
were inclined to overlook. 'Now, touching dangers chiefly
feared. First, to rehearse my meaning (lately unfolded to you
by my Lord Keeper) it shall not be needful. Though I must
needs confess mine own mislike — so much to strive against the
matter — as, if I were a milkmaid with a pail on my arm, whereby my private person might be little set by, I would not forsake
that poor and single state to match with the greatest monarch.
Not that I do condemn the double knot, or judge amiss of such
as, forced by necessity, cannot dispose themselves to another
life; but wish that none were drawn to change but such as
cannot keep honest limits. Yet, for your behalf, there is no
way so difficult, that may touch my private person, which I will
not well content myself to take; and, in this case, as willingly
to spoil myself quite of myself (as if I should put off my upper
garment when it wearies me) if the present state might not
thereby be encumbered.

'I know I am but mortal: which good lesson Mr. Speaker, in

his third division of a virtuous prince's properties, had reason
to remember. And so, therewhile, I prepare myself to welcome
death whensoever it shall please God to send it; as, if others
would endeavour to perform the like, it would not be so bitter
unto many as it hath been accounted. Mine own experience
teacheth me to be no fonder of those vain delights than reason
would; nor further to delight in things uncertain than may seem
convenient. But let good heed be taken that, in reaching too
far after future good, you peril not the present and begin to
quarrel, and fall by dispute together by the ears, before it be
decided who shall wear my crown. I will not deny but I might
be thought the indifferentest judge;[1] in this respect —— that I
shall not be, when these points are fulfilled: which none beside
myself can speak in all this company. Misdeem not my words,
as though I sought what heretofore hath been granted. I
intend it not: my words be too thin to carry so tough a matter.
Although, I trust God will not in such haste cut off my days,
but that, according to your own desert and my desire, I may
provide some good way for your full security.

'And thus, as one that yieldeth you more thanks (both for
your zeal unto myself and service in this Parliament) than my
tongue can utter, I recommend you unto the assured guard and
best keeping of the Almighty, who will preserve you safe, I
trust, in all felicity. And wish withal that each of you had
tasted some drops of Lethe's flood, to cancel and deface these
speeches out of your remembrance.'[2]

Unfortunately, the original draft of this speech has not survived, to show how its conceits and phrases were arrived at.
But, like many another author, Elizabeth looked on her work
and saw that it was good. She sent a copy to her godson, John
Harington, then a boy of fourteen or fifteen, with the following
note. 'Boy Jack, I have made a clerk write fair my poor words
for thine use, as it cannot be such striplings have entrance into
Parliament-assemblies as yet. Ponder them in thy hours of

---

[1] i.e. the most indifferent judge about the person to succeed her. Elizabeth
alludes to the fact that she, at any rate, would be dead, and therefore disinterested,
when her successor came to the throne.
[2] The text is from Sir John Harington's *Nugae Antiquae*, ed. Park (1804), i.
121-7. The transcriptions in this work are faulty. I have therefore preferred an
occasional reading from other texts, the best of which are B.M. Additional MS.
32379, fols. 22 seqq., and ibid. 33271, fols. 2 seqq. I have tried by punctuation to
help the understanding of these involved sentences.

leisure, and play with them till they enter thine understanding. So shalt thou hereafter, perchance, find some good fruits hereof when thy godmother is out of remembrance. And I do this because thy father was ready to serve and love us in trouble and thrall.' The last sentence was an allusion to the time of Mary Tudor. As for pondering and playing with her words till they enter the understanding, that, it is to be feared, must also be an injunction to the reader of this book.

[1] i.e. the most indifferent judge about the person to succeed her. Elizabeth alludes to the fact that she, at any rate, would be dead, and therefore disinterested, when her successor came to the throne.

[2] The text is from Sir John Harington's *Nugae Antiquae*, ed. Park (1804), i. 121-7. The transcriptions in this work are faulty. I have therefore preferred an occasional reading from other texts, the best of which are B.M. Additional MS. 39379, fols. 22 seqq., and ibid. 33271, fols. 2 seqq. I have tried by punctuation to help the understanding of these involved sentences.

# PART SEVEN

# THE PARLIAMENT OF 1581

## CHAPTER I

## INTRODUCTORY

IT was five years before this, the longest-lived of Elizabethan
Parliaments, held another session, its third and last. In the
meanwhile it had been prorogued no less than twenty-six
times.[1] Sometimes this was normal routine: nothing was then
implied save a repetition of the process. But, once prorogued to
a particular date, the assembly could not be brought together
earlier except by a dissolution and a new general election —
which took time; and some of the intervals between prorogations were so brief as to indicate that a crisis was at hand which
might necessitate a meeting. In 1578, for example, there were
prorogations from March to April to May. It was probably the
transient victory of Don John of Austria in the Netherlands,
and the pressure being put on Elizabeth to employ open intervention against him, that compelled her to keep Parliament on
quick call. So alarming was the outlook that Dr. Humphrey,
writing to Switzerland in August, gave utterance to his fears:
'These are the signs preceding the end of the world . . . Satan is
roaring like a lion, the world is going mad, Antichrist is resort-
ing to every extreme, that he may with wolf-like ferocity devour
the sheep of Christ.'[2]

Sooner than our divine, Elizabeth had taken a more sober
measure of the crisis, and parliamentary prorogations became
less feverish. But in August of the following year Alençon made
his grand assault on the maiden citadel of the Queen. Marriage
was the consuming topic of the autumn and early winter; and
Parliament was prorogued five times between October 20th,
1579, and February 29th, 1580. In the year 1580 prorogations
came thick and fast, for the marriage business merged into a
domestic and foreign crisis of extreme gravity.

*L.J.* ii. 19.    [2] *Zurich Letters,* i. 325.

The Holy War of Catholicism against Protestant England — the Enterprise as contemporaries termed it — seemed imminent; and the sapping of the stronghold from within — the creation of what, in comparable times, we have called a fifth column — had entered a new and disturbing phase. In 1579 a Papal force had actually landed in Ireland to stir up revolt there, and in September 1580 it had received reinforcements, including a sprinkling of Spaniards. Except that they had short shrift, the parallel with events in our own age is striking. The parallel continues in the alarm spread by the expansion of the leading Catholic power, Spain, through the overrunning of Portugal in 1580. This year also saw the start of the Jesuit mission to England led by two distinguished and contrasting men, Parsons and Campion. Already there had been a steady flow of secular priests as missioners from continental seminaries. But the Jesuits came, as it were, direct from England's capital enemy, the Pope; and he was already engaged in real warfare with Elizabeth in Ireland. One's pity and admiration can go out to these missionaries, or to most of them. But no one today should be incapable of seeing the English government's point of view; of perceiving that, in converting Englishmen back to Catholicism, the priests were in fact creating potential enemies of the Protestant State, on whose aid the Enterprise would count if and when it was launched. Certainly that eventuality was willed by the Papacy: of course, from spiritual motives. In its essential, or at any rate its secular, nature there is little to distinguish the situation from the ideological conflicts and strategy of our own days; and only the subsequent disentanglement of religion from international politics has obscured the issue.

To deal with this danger, and in doing so to supply the Crown with a further subsidy, were two of the major purposes for which Parliament met. It boded ill for the Queen's policy of tolerance. She had to bow to the facts of the time and the pressure of her advisers. But hitherto, as we have noted, she had resisted the extension of compulsory attendance at Church to compulsory attendance at Communion, deeming the latter an invasion of conscience. She had vetoed a bill with this provision in 1571, and attempts to revive it in 1572 and 1576 had been abortive, though its justification seemed to become more and more evident. Her resolute opposition presumably continued, for even in the threatening situation of 1581 the proposal foundered once more.

It may seem strange that a Sovereign, whom legend has portrayed as so irresolute and wayward — not without the aid of many petty incidents and stories, reinforced by lamentations from her ministers — clung so obstinately to a principle. She was equally unshakeable in her attitude to Puritanism. In December 1576 she had had a critical interview with Edmund Grindal, not yet a year in office as Archbishop Parker's successor. She was determined to suppress the Puritan conspiracy, the nature and danger of which she instinctively grasped when her earnest, liberal-minded Councillors were beguiled by its more admirable qualities. The conspiracy drew strength from two sources: the great number of preachers in its ranks, many of whom held no cure and were the more dangerous for that freedom; and the Prophesyings or Exercises, which infected the laity as well as the clergy and could not be kept safe by episcopal regulation. All who preached had to be licensed by a bishop. Elizabeth, at her interview, ordered Grindal to reduce their number drastically. She also ordered him to suppress all Prophesyings.

A Parker or a Burghley might have sighed as a Christian but obeyed as a subject: indeed, Parker had been told in 1574 to stop the Prophesyings and had issued an injunction, only to find his authority undermined by Privy Councillors. Grindal was different. The conscientious objector in him was reawakened. To place a Marian exile in the see of Canterbury was a mistake. In the quiet of his study he wrote the Queen a justly celebrated letter: so long, so didactic, it would be better termed a tract. He refused to obey. 'Bear with me, I beseech you, Madam, if I choose rather to offend your earthly majesty than to offend the heavenly majesty of God.' With appropriate scriptural and mundane arguments he maintained that the Gospel of Christ should be plentifully preached, and dismissed the substitute that Elizabeth favoured — the reading of homilies — as at best a *pis aller*. As for Prophesyings, they had scriptural warrant, and properly regulated were profitable and edifying. He could not with a clear conscience assent to their suppression, though the Queen deprive him of office in consequence.

This was bad enough; but he went on, in humble though fearless manner, to teach his Sovereign her duty. In 'questions of the laws of your realm, you do not decide the same in your Court, but send them to your judges to be determined'. Similarly, he told her, she should refer matters of religion to the bishops and divines of the realm, 'according to the example of all godly Christian emperors and princes of all ages'. She should not 'pronounce too resolutely and peremptorily' in the concerns of the Church. 'It is the antichristian voice of the Pope, *Sic volo, sic jubeo: stet pro ratione voluntas*': 'As I wish, so I command; take my will for reason'. 'Remember Madam, that you are a mortal creature . . . ; and although you are a mighty Prince, yet remember that He which dwelleth in Heaven is mightier.'[1]

For his temerity and persistence in it, Grindal was suspended from his administrative duties and for a time confined to his house. Elizabeth appears to have toyed with the idea of depriving him of office, but she was stayed from that scandal by the revulsion of her Councillors, if not by cooler thoughts. Blind and sick, still suspended and on the eve of enforced retirement, this pitiable victim of conscience died in 1583. The Queen did not allow his resistance to divert her from her purpose. In May 1577, ignoring the normal routine of sending such orders through the metropolitan, she wrote directly and peremptorily to the bishops, commanding them forthwith to suppress all Prophesyings in their diocese, restore uniformity in the conduct of church services, and remove all preachers and others of non-conforming views. 'We see', she wrote, 'that by the increase of these, through sufferance, great danger may ensue.'[2]

Twenty-two years had passed since the Elizabethan Acts of Supremacy and Uniformity had been formulated. The days of the Marian exile were becoming more and more remote. Turning over the pages of that truly remarkable correspondence which had ensued between the former *émigrés* and their Swiss hosts, change is sadly apparent. For years so abundant, the letters had now been reduced to a pathetic trickle which inexorable time was soon to efface. Heart and mind may yearn to linger over this rich and honourable intimacy of

---

[1] Strype, *Grindal*, pp. 558-74.    [2] Ibid. pp. 354, 574-6.

kindred spirits, quenched neither by distance nor nationality, and expressed in the *lingua franca* of learning. But in both countries the grave was claiming its participants. 'So many deaths of our most excellent men', wrote Laurence Humphrey to Gualter in 1578: 'Jewel, Parkhurst, Pilkington, and others'. Robert Horne, Bishop of Winchester — 'Your loving friend, and that of all the people of Zurich', as he subscribed himself to Gualter — was to die in the following year. Cox of Ely, another 'brother in Christ Jesus' — 'though in my seventy-fifth year, by the blessing of God . . . in good health', he had written in 1574 to Bullinger, a year before that great Reformer died — in turn died in 1581. Grindal died in 1583. The passing of these men broke one link after another in the deep-seated fraternity of radical memories between the episcopacy and many of their clergy. It is significant that the Queen made Whitgift, the prime foe of Puritans, a bishop in 1577 and chose him as Grindal's successor in 1583. Moreover, it was on the advice of some of her bishops that she had taken action to suppress Prophesyings.[1]

In spite of the Queen, these godly Exercises continued, and Puritanism, stoutly aided by the laity and drawing comfort and protection from its friends in high places, spread and deepened its roots. Our friend, Peter Wentworth, on the complaint of his bishop, was in trouble with the Council in 1579 because of the great resort of people from Northampton and elsewhere to his house at Lillingstone-Lovell, where the sacrament was administered in Puritan fashion.[2] Inevitably, the alarming development of the Catholic menace benefitted the Puritans, for, after all, none were more Protestant or patriotic than they. They were the counter-poison to Romanism. Nevertheless, when Parliament met the movement was under an official cloud: the blacker for the vigour with which its votaries had recently exclaimed against the marriage project with Alençon. John Stubbs, author of *The Discovery of a Gaping Gulf* — that offensive tract on the subject, which cost him his right hand — apart from being Thomas Cartwright's brother-in-law, was an active Puritan country gentleman, in touch with other patrons of the party: his tract may not have been a lone venture. The

---

[1] *Zurich Letters*, i. 309, 321, 325; STRYPE, *Grindal*, p. 404.
[2] DASENT, *Acts of Privy Council*, xi. 132-3, 218-19.

premier apostle of Puritanism, Cartwright, was still in exile abroad; the movement's activities were underground. Conditions were not propitious for a resounding parliamentary campaign; nor, on the other hand, were they so bad as to provoke one. There was, indeed, an agitation about reform of the Church in this Parliament: that we shall see. It was branded with the stigmata of Puritanism; and if only we could penetrate all secrets we might find more organization behind it than we dare suggest on present evidence. But its pattern is that of 1576 rather than earlier or later Parliaments.

By January 1581, the Parliament first elected in 1572 had been so long continued that many by-elections had taken place. Some had been to replace either sick members or others away on the Queen's service: dubious action which excited the attention of the House of Commons. Among newcomers was the paragon of cultivated young gentlemen, Philip Sidney, then in his twenty-seventh year. So far as we know, he was an ornament rather than a power in the House; but his sampling of Parliament was a striking sign of that siren-like attraction which membership was acquiring for men of spirit and breeding.

When the Commons assembled on the first day, January 16th, 1581, the company — as the Clerk noted — 'was not great'. A number played truant the whole session, having, one presumes, had more than they bargained for in this long-lived Parliament: they were fined. Some, after so many prorogations, could not believe the summons to be the real thing. As for the newcomers, since no Lord Steward had been appointed, they could not take the oath of supremacy and consequently were not yet entitled to sit.[1]

The small company was immediately faced with the problem that had confronted their predecessors in 1566. They were without a Speaker. Since the last session, Robert Bell had been made a judge, as Chief Baron of the Exchequer, but, alas, within a few months he and many others present at the Oxford assizes had caught jail fever and died: a tragic end for a notable parliamentarian. As informal leader of the House, Sir Francis Knollys called attention to their predicament and had the precedent of 1566 read by the Clerk. On that occasion

[1] *C.J.* i. 115-16, 136.

Privy Councillors had fashioned the procedure and the Commons had approached the Queen through the medium of the Upper House. It is a measure of the distance traversed in the interval that this precedent gave rise to a long debate and vigorous criticism. Some objected that it drew 'a special prerogative to those of the House which were of her Majesty's Council', and that the insertion of the House of Lords between them and the Queen was also a great peril. Many points were made, but at length it was agreed 'by the greater number of the few voices' to follow the lone precedent of 1566.[1]

Concern about punctilio showed itself again when Members objected to the omission of a proper summons to the Upper House to hear the commission bidding them elect a new Speaker. And on their return there were again some debating points when Sir Francis Knollys, following with surprising slavishness the precedent of 1566, wanted the Solicitor General, John Popham, to be brought from the Lords, with the obvious intention of making him Speaker. This had been done in 1566. It was now repeated. But before proceeding with the election — which went according to plan — there was an incident which, though trifling, seems in retrospect the first rumble of the approaching storm. Mr. Edward Lewkenor, the earnest Puritan associated later with Peter Wentworth, moved that, 'considering prayer was necessary to be used in all such actions', they might join in prayer to God to direct them with his Holy Spirit 'both in that and in the residue of the proceedings of this House'. He offered a prayer for the purpose, which was read by the Clerk; and afterwards the whole House said the Lord's Prayer.[2]

The next day, being at leisure — and, incidentally, being out of order, for the man in the chair was only Speaker-elect — they had a field day on the question of new Members elected in place of others, still alive though disabled by sickness or absent on the Queen's service. Thomas Norton, 'the great Parliament-man', who was to be as supreme in this his last Parliament as he had been in 1572, began the debate. He argued that sickness and service were good excuses for absence but not for by-elections. With his alert, radical instinct he anticipated an

[1] C.J. i. 116.
[2] Cromwell's Diary; D'Ewes, Journals, p. 281; C.J. i. 117.

issue that was to become controversial in 1586, contending that the initiative in such cases should lie with the House of Commons, not the Chancery: doctrine politically expedient for the future, but historically and constitutionally arrogant nonsense. Serjeant Flowerdew, Robert Snagge — strange company for this rebel — Seintpole, and our now highly respectable Recorder Fleetwood argued to the contrary, stigmatizing Norton's doctrine as discredit to the Lord Chancellor and scandal to 'the judicial proceedings of that court'. The Clerk noted that the latter view prevailed and the new members were received into the House. Doubtless he was right; but our diarist reported no agreement, thinking, probably, of the closing days of the session when the subject was reopened and the decision reversed.[1]

In the afternoon of January 20th the Queen came to the Parliament Chamber to approve of the Speaker's election. Among the assembled peers there was one conspicuous change. The learned, wise, and eloquent Sir Nicholas Bacon, distinguished in his own right and immortal in the fame of his son, Francis, had died in 1579. His place was now occupied by Sir Thomas Bromley, an old Parliament-man, once Recorder of London and afterwards Solicitor General. By what subtle refinement of reasoning the title of Lord Chancellor was adjudged to him whereas his greater predecessor had been merely Lord Keeper, no one seems to know. Perhaps — for Elizabeth had a regal sensitiveness about such matters — it was because Bromley came of gentle, and Bacon of yeoman, stock.

Hitherto the precedents of 1566 had been carefully followed. Now came a change. On the earlier occasion Richard Onslow had turned his disabling speech into an oration, since there were no privilege claims to be made for the Commons, and there was no need for a subsequent set speech. In contrast, Popham proceeded as if a new Parliament were being opened. Memories may have been dim, records defective, and logic inoperative; or possibly, the Queen desired a fresh opportunity of defining the limits of free speech. At any rate, after formally disabling himself and being formally enabled, he began a discourse — not 'of commonwealths, which he acknowledged himself unable to perform, having so little knowledge and

[1] D'Ewes. pp. 281-2; C.J. i. 117, 135; Cromwell's Diary.

experience', but of this commonwealth and its happy estate compared with foreign governments, 'most unhappy'. The ancient stock simile of the human body furnished him with the requisite padding. He concluded with 'the three ordinary petitions': for freedom from arrest for members, their servants, and their goods; 'for liberty of speech in the House'; and for his own access to the Queen and liberty to explain himself if he mistook his commission. To these he added a novelty: that 'generally . . . all words spoken by any member of the House might be expounded with favour, and the meaning of the parties [be] considered, not the words'.

Either our diarist was not impressed by the Lord Chancellor's reply, or it was brevity itself. He seems to have passed almost at once to the petitions. 'Concerning freedom of speech', he answered, 'her Majesty granteth it as liberally as it hath at any time heretofore [been] granted; notwithstanding, would have them to know that it is always tied within limits, namely, not to deal with her estate — which he showeth to be intended as well touching her prerogative as also in religion.' This declaration was evidently made with particular emphasis, for the Commons' Clerk referred to it in his *Journal*: 'My Lord Chancellor . . . did, amongst other things, give a special admonition unto this House not to deal with matters touching her Majesty's person or estate, or touching religion.' The petition for freedom from arrest was also granted with a caution: the Queen 'would not have any purposely become of the House or retain servants indebted, to defraud other creditors of their due debts'. Smalley's case in 1576 was possibly in her mind. The novel request about the interpretation of men's speeches received a favourable answer.[1]

Certainly, this Parliament, as the Clerk's entry shows, could have no illusions about the limits within which it was supposed to operate.

---

[1] Cromwell's Diary; *C.J.* i. 118.

## CHAPTER II

# THE BILL AGAINST CATHOLICS
## AND OTHER TOPICS

SERIOUS business started on January 21st: quietly enough, with an exhortation from the Speaker 'to use reverent and discreet speeches, to leave curiosities of form, to speak to the matter'; 'not to spend too much time in unnecessary motions or superfluous arguments'. It was his mistress's voice. Decorum was not forgotten: there was a charming motion about that. Thereupon, while late-comers filtered in, they read a bill. Discipline then broke.

In 1576 it had been Peter Wentworth who at a similar moment set the sobersides shaking. This time it was his brother Paul. He 'made a motion for a public fast, to the end that it might please God to bless us in our actions better than we had been heretofore, and for a sermon to be had every morning'. We do not possess the text of his speech, but the words in our diarist's report — 'better than we had been heretofore' — suggest a Pistor-like lamentation or an echo of brother Peter's diatribe on the profane and deplorable proceedings of past Parliaments. Whether or not he elaborated the point, Members doubtless took it.[1]

This apart, the motion was far from innocent and harmless, as we might suppose. Fasting was a conspicuous characteristic of Puritan practice; and the official attitude to it may be judged from the following admonition given to Bishop Chaderton by the Archbishop of York in the following May. 'My Lord, you are noted to yield too much to general fastings . . . There lurketh matter under that pretended piety. The devil is crafty; and the young ministers of these our times grow mad.' What is more, to prescribe a public act of worship was the exclusive right of the Supreme Governor of the Church and her ecclesiastical advisers. Coming directly after the royal injunction not to meddle in matters of religion, it seemed a blatant defiance of authority. When we reflect on Lewkenor's premeditated call to prayer three days before, we are tempted to suspect that once

[1] *C.J.* i. 118; Cromwell's Diary; D'EWES, *Journals*, p. 282.

more a group of Puritans had concerted their strategy, intending to launch an attack on the shortcomings, if not on the structure of the Church, in the aura of daily revivalist excitement. Indeed, from an obscure passage in a later speech by Sir Christopher Hatton we might even infer that Wentworth in his motion had linked the fast with such a programme.[1]

The godly Knollys, though ready to fast with the best of them, was shocked. As leader of the House he rose at once to oppose the motion. Our diarist, Thomas Cromwell, followed, speaking for it. Next came Alford; and — need we add ?— he was against it. Four subsequent speakers were in favour: Mr. Cooke — possibly a grandson of Sir Anthony; Mr. Secretary Wilson; Serjeant Flowerdew; and Thomas Norton. Wilson's support illustrates that independence and lack of cohesion among Privy Councillors which is typical of high Elizabethan days, a secret of their greatness, and a clue to the harmonious evolution of parliamentary power. As for Norton, he unblushingly 'showed precedents that there had been fasts in London by order only from the Council'; whence — if we may supply his corollary — it followed that *a fortiori* the greatest Council, Parliament, could do the same. These details come from the rough notes of the Clerk, Fulk Onslow, jotted down in the House, a few entries from which have luckily been preserved.

The motion 'was long argued': '*pro* and *con*'. As the *Journal* shows, this delectable topic left them no time that morning to read a second bill. Fast, the majority of members were evidently determined to do. The opposition therefore tried to ride off on an amendment, that it 'be private, everybody to himself'. On this issue — public or private — the House divided: 115 voted for the former, 100 for the latter. 'The better side had the greater number', added Onslow in his rough notes (not in his *Journal*). How appropriate that even the Clerk put his soul into the business! Conscious that they had been greatly daring, the House turned diplomatic and agreed that their Councillor-Members should nominate the preachers for the fast, 'to the end they might be such as would keep convenient proportion of time and meddle with no matter of innovation or unquietness'.[2]

---

[1] Peck, *Desiderata Curiosa* (1779), i. 102; *C.J.* i. 119a.

[2] D'Ewes, pp. 282-3. The rough notes can be detected by comparison with the *Commons Journal*. They cease before the end of January. Also cf. Cromwell's Diary; *C.J.* i. 118.

Next morning the Speaker was absent. He did not turn up until after 11 a.m., and then, having read the usual prayer, omitting the Litany for the shortness of time, adjourned the House. He had been at the Court, summoned to attend on her Majesty. And the following day, when the assembly was full, they heard about it.

The Speaker expressed his sorrow for the error they had committed and showed her Majesty's great misliking. He had feared this would happen. He advised them to apologize, and for the future to confine themselves to 'matters proper and pertinent for this House to deal in', suggesting that, as 'of old time', all bills be submitted first to the scrutiny of a standing committee of four, and no motions be made except for privilege or good order. What a drubbing he must have received: 'such', to quote his own words, 'as himself could not bear'.

Vice-Chamberlain Hatton then delivered a message from the Queen. He showed 'her great admiration of the rashness of this House in committing such an apparent contempt against her Majesty's express commandment, very lately before delivered unto the whole House by the Lord Chancellor . . . ; blaming first the whole House, and then Mr. Speaker'. 'No public fast could be appointed but by her, and therefore [their action] impeached her jurisdiction.' She herself 'liked well of fasting, prayer, and sermons', and used them; but, as St. Paul enjoined, 'Good things must also be well done.' From reproof Hatton turned to set forth 'very eloquently and amply . . . her Majesty's most honourable and good acceptation of the zeal, duty, and fidelity of this whole House towards religion, the safety of her Highness's person, and the state of this Commonwealth (in respect whereof her Majesty hath so long continued this Parliament without dissolution)'. To their great joy and comfort he declared further 'that her Majesty, nevertheless, of her inestimable and princely good love and disposition . . . construeth the said offence and contempt to be a rash, unadvised, and inconsiderate error . . . proceeding of zeal and not of the wilful or malicious intent of this House or of any member of the same; imputing the cause thereof partly to her own lenity towards a brother of that man which now made this motion': a thrust at Peter Wentworth. 'After many excellent discourses and dilations' on the Queen's concern for the welfare of religion

and the state, he announced that she had already deeply consulted on these matters and prepared fit courses for them, ready
to be delivered to the House in the proper way. He thought it
very meet that the whole House or someone on its behalf
should make humble submission, and ended with a rebuke to
the Speaker, telling him that her Majesty liked his opposition
to Wentworth's motion, but misliked his venturing to put it to
the question, 'being no bill'.

The Comptroller, Sir James Croft, followed, to the same
effect, but — added our Clerk in the secrecy of his rough notes
— 'urged and enforced the fault of the House with much more
violence'. Though the tide had turned, there was not lacking
one courageous man. Nicholas St. Leger, 'with a great deal of
discretion and moderation' — appreciation that comes from the
Clerk — extenuated their fault. He spoke of their deep affection for the Queen and the sincerity of their intention; then of
the imperfections and sins to which states as well as men were
subject, needing prayer and humiliation. This merged into an
attack on the slackness of bishops; concluding 'that he trusted
that both her Majesty and all her subjects would be ready to
express their true repentence to God in humbling themselves in
sackcloth and ashes'. Seintpole followed: he was on the side of
authority. Then Mildmay, urging submission: a judicious
speech, one infers. Seckford, Master of Requests, joined the
official chorus; and Serjeant Flowerdew recanted. After these
rose George Carleton, the dyed-in-the-wool Puritan, quite un-
abashed, ready to speak his conscience: or so it seems Speaker
and House anticipated, for they interrupted him and the
Speaker put the question.

'With whole consent' it was resolved that the Vice-Chamberlain should tender to the Queen 'the most humble submission
of this whole House, with their like most humble suit unto her
Majesty to remit and pardon their said error and contempt'.
This carried, 'Mr. Carleton offered again to speak, saying with
some repetition that what he had to move was for the liberty of
the House'. But Speaker and House 'did stay him': or, as our
diarist reports, 'Mr. Speaker [did] rise and would not tarry.'[1]

If Paul Wentworth's motion was really intended as the opening move in a concerted Puritan campaign, then it was a tactical

[1] *C.J.* i. 118-19; Cromwell's Diary; D'EWES, p. 284.

blunder with consequences similar to his brother's in 1576. Members' nerves were shattered before the crucial issues over religion were raised, and when these appeared the House moved with propriety as it had done in the previous session. In contrast, Elizabeth's prompt counter-offensive proved astute and successful.

The following day, January 25th, Sir Christopher Hatton reported on his mission. In place of storm there was sunshine. The Queen accepted their submission 'very lovingly and graciously', and was pleased 'freely and clearly' to remit their offence and contempt. To avoid misunderstanding of her action, she wished not only the House but all her subjects to know that it was not the matter — 'fasting and prayer being godly and virtuous exercises' — that she misliked, but the manner: 'tending to innovation, presuming to indict a form of public fast without order and without her Majesty's privity, intruding upon her Highness's authority ecclesiastical'. She hoped this would be sufficient admonition to them to employ their endeavours more advisedly, 'according to their special vocations in this service'.[1]

In the congenial atmosphere thus engendered, Sir Walter Mildmay rose to make the set government speech for supply: a speech carefully prepared, ranging over general policy as well as finance, and in its felicity of phrase and emotional appeal a great oration. It was divided into three sections: 'of the present state we be in; of the dangers that we may justly be in doubt of; what provision ought to be made in time to prevent or resist them'.

'That our most gracious Queen, even at her first entry, did loosen us from the yoke of Rome and did restore unto this realm the most pure and holy religion of the Gospel . . . is known to all the world and felt of us to our singular comforts . . . From hence, as from the root, hath sprung that implacable malice of the Pope and his confederates against her . . . They hold this as a firm and settled opinion that England is the only sovereign monarchy that most doth maintain and countenance religion . . . This being so, what hath not the Pope essayed to annoy the Queen and her state, thereby, as he thinketh, to remove this great obstacle that standeth between him and the

---

[1] *C.J.* i. 119; Cromwell's Diary.

overflowing of the world again with Popery?' For proof Mild-may instanced events from the Northern Rebellion to the recent invasion of Ireland; 'the Pope turning thus the venom of his curses and the pens of his malicious parasites into men of war and weapons to win that by force which otherwise he could not do'.

'Though all these are said to be done by the Pope and in his name, yet who seeth not that they be maintained underhand by some other princes, his confederates? . . . The Pope of himself . . . is far unable to make war upon any prince of that estate which her Majesty is of', having lost 'those infinite revenues which he was wont to have out of England, Scotland, Germany, Switzerland, Denmark and others, and now of late out of France and the Low Countries . . . The Queen, nevertheless, by the almighty power of God standeth fast maugre the Pope and all his friends.' Here Mildmay instanced 'the Italians and Spaniards, pulled out by the ears at Smerwick in Ireland, and cut in pieces by the notable service of a noble captain and valiant soldiers' . . . 'This seemeth to be our present state: a blessed, peaceable, and happy time.'

But, 'seeing our enemies sleep not, it behoveth us also not to be careless'. The storm is but partly over, the main tempest like to fall upon us; and 'this realm shall find at their hands all the miseries and extremities that they can bring upon it . . . If they can, they will procure the sparks of the flames that have been so terrible in other countries to fly over into England and to kindle as great a fire here'.

In the mean season, the Pope, by secret practices, leaves nothing unproved, 'emboldening many undutiful subjects to stand fast in their disobedience to her Majesty and her laws . . . The obstinate and stiff-necked Papist is so far from being reformed as he hath gotten stomach to go backwards and to show his disobedience, not only in arrogant words but also in contemptuous deeds. To confirm them herein, and to increase their numbers, you see how the Pope hath and doth comfort their hollow hearts with absolutions, dispensations, reconcilia-tions, and such other things of Rome. You see how lately he hath sent hither a sort of hypocrites, naming themselves Jesuits, a rabble of vagrant friars newly sprung up and coming through the world to trouble the Church of God; whose principal errand

is, by creeping into the houses and familiarities of men of behaviour and reputation, not only to corrupt the realm with
false doctrine, but also, under that pretence, to stir sedition.'
In consequence, not only former recusants, but many, very
many who previously conformed, now utterly refuse to be of
our Church.

Turning to remedies, Mildmay commented on the contrast
between the persecuting Church of Mary Tudor's reign and the
clemency of her Majesty's merciful reign. 'But when by long
proof we find that this favourable and gentle manner of dealing
... hath done no good ... it is time for us to look more
narrowly and straitly to them, lest ... they prove dangerous
members ... in the entrails of our Commonwealth.' Severer
laws were needed to constrain them to yield at least open obedience in causes of religion, so that, 'if they will needs submit
themselves to the benediction of the Pope, they may feel how
little his curses can hurt us and how little his blessings can save
them from that punishment which we are able to lay upon
them'.

The next requirement was the provision of forces sufficient to
answer any violence that may be offered, here or abroad. 'God
hath placed this kingdom in an island environed with the sea,
as with a natural and strong wall, whereby we are not subject
to those sudden invasions ... which other frontier countries be
... What the Queen's navy is, how many notable ships, and
how far beyond the navy of any other Prince, is known to all
men.' This involved great charges. Land forces were also
necessary, but her Majesty does not need, 'as other Princes are
fain to do, to entertain mercenary soldiers of foreign countries,
hardly gotten, costly and dangerously kept, and in the end little
or no service done by them; but may bring sufficient forces of
her own natural subjects ... that carry with them willing,
valiant, and faithful minds, such as few nations may easily
compare with.' This too required treasure, the nerve of war;
and Mildmay went on to explain that the taxes, granted five
years ago, had not even covered half the extraordinary charges
incurred since then.

His patriotic eloquence then soared to new heights. 'The
love and duty that we owe to our most gracious Queen, by
whose ministry God hath done so great things for us — even

such as be wonderful in the eyes of the world — ought to make us more careful for her preservation and security than for our own: a princess known by long experience to be a principal patron of the Gospel, virtuous, wise, faithful, just; unspotted in word or deed, merciful, temperate, a maintainer of peace and justice amongst her people without respect of persons; a Queen besides of this realm, our native country, renowned through the world, which our enemies gape to overrun, if by force or sleight they could do it. For such a Queen and such a country, and for the defence of the honour and surety of them both, nothing ought to be so dear unto us that with most willing hearts we should not spend and adventure freely.'

'Let us think upon these matters as the weight of them deserveth', he concluded, and provide for them in time both by laws and by provision.[1]

When Mildmay had finished, Norton rose, 'pursued the same admonition', and moved for a committee 'to consult of bills convenient to be framed'. He was assuming the leading role among non-official Members. Also he was setting the stage for one of the main bills of the session, to come not from the government — as would certainly have happened in earlier years — but from a committee of the House. He was proposing to steal the legislative initiative for the House: another significant moment in this great theme of Elizabethan and early Stuart parliamentary history.

A grand committee was appointed, consisting of all Privy Councillors and fifty-seven others. Philip Sidney was one, Peter Wentworth and Lewkenor others: not, however, Paul Wentworth or George Carleton. They met that afternoon in the Exchequer Chamber. Our Clerk was there and wrote an entry in his rough notes. Once more, it seems, Norton seized the leadership. He 'spake very well' to the matters contained in Mildmay's speech that morning; 'and did thereupon exhibit certain articles to the like purpose which were by the committees considered, and some others added unto them'. He and four lawyers, including Fleetwood and Yelverton, were ordered to digest into article form the points agreed upon and exhibit them at the committee's next meeting. At subsequent

---

[1] B.M. Sloane MS. 326, fols. 19-29. Cromwell gives an epitome of the speech in his diary.

meetings it was Norton alone who was entrusted with the drafting.[1]

Two bills emerged from this committee: the subsidy, and what they referred to as 'the bill for religion'. The latter ultimately became the 'Act to retain the Queen's Majesty's subjects in their due obedience' — the notorious law which ushered in the period of severest persecution of the Catholics. Behind the scenes in its passage lies a remarkable story of royal intervention; and for that reason we must follow it with a degree of detail which in the end will bring reward.

The committee was ready with its report on February 7th, and on the following day its bill, entitled 'For obedience to the Queen's Majesty against the see of Rome' — a far sterner measure than the one finally passed — was read the first time.[2] Sir Christopher Hatton then informed the House that the Lords had before them a bill tending to many of the things contained in theirs. He suggested that they seek a conference; and this was agreed to by both Houses.[3]

The bill to which Hatton alluded was our old friend, 'For the coming to church, hearing of divine service, and receiving of the Communion', amended and extended — if an undated State Paper represents its provisions — to fit the deepening crisis. In its main clauses it was a rather severer version of the 1571 bill which had been vetoed by the Queen: failure to attend church once a quarter incurred a penalty of £12; failure to receive Holy Communion twice a year involved fines ranging from £20 for the first offence to £100 for the fourth. The bishops, one supposes, had been at it again.[4]

Except for the compulsory attendance at Communion, which had not been included in the Commons' bill — perhaps because the Councillors on the committee knew that Elizabeth would not consent to it; perhaps because Puritans such as Wentworth, holding their own Communion services, were no longer enamoured of it — the Lords' bill was a very pale affair indeed compared with its rival. It would have been fatal to let the

[1] D'Ewes, pp. 288-9; C.J. i. 119-20.
[2] Its contents are given in Cromwell's Diary. From this we are able to identify S.P. Dom. Eliz. 83/29 (misdated) as 'articles' of this bill. Other versions are ibid. 147/34 (with annotations by Burghley), and 147/33.
[3] C.J. i. 123.
[4] S.P. Dom. Eliz. 147/46; L.J. ii. 29.

Upper House proceed along such mild lines, if Councillors thought as the Commons did, and were already finding the Queen far too merciful for their liking. Any hope of screwing up their mistress to the Draconic provisions of the bill in the Lower House lay in presenting her with a solid front of Lords and Commons. This may have been the principal reason for Hatton's motion about a conference.

The representatives of both Houses — eighteen peers (six of them bishops) and the whole of the grand committee from the Commons — met several times. A new, a longer and amended bill emerged; but the main provisions and penalties remained much the same.[1] In other words, Lords and Commons — including the Privy Councillors of both Houses — were agreed in wanting an extremely drastic penal code against Catholics. It is a crucial point in our story, and is corroborated — at least as regards the temporal Lords — by a later comment from Thomas Norton.[2]

The new bill was read in the Commons a first time on February 18th. It was still at that stage when on February 27th, after an interval which in itself almost suggests that something was amiss, there came a message from the Lords appointing a new meeting between the committees of both Houses. This was indeed extraordinary, for with the bill in their possession, the right of initiative lay with the Commons. They reinforced their already large committee, as though to meet an assault.

On March 4th, as the result of a fresh batch of meetings, Sir Francis Knollys, on behalf of the representatives of the Commons, brought into the House a third bill. It was read once, and then, with a vote on the motion which implies opposition, was pressed to an immediate second reading. 'After many speeches' — alas! unrecorded — it was sent to be ingrossed. It passed at the next sitting, sailed through the Lords without any apparent fuss in three consecutive days, and in due course received the royal assent.[3]

What had happened? What caused the representatives of both Houses to scrap their agreed bill and replace it with a new, and, as we shall see, a very much milder measure? The only

---

[1] The text is in S.P. Dom. Eliz. 148/10, endorsed by Burghley as 'The second bill...' Cf. Cromwell's Diary, February 18th.
[2] *Archaeologia*, xxxvi. 111-12.
[3] *C.J.* i. 128, 130, 131; *L.J.* ii. 44-8.

explanation that seems to fit the background of detail and make sense is that the Queen had intervened to scale down the severities. She had been told about the preliminary, Commons' bill: that we know.[1] She must have been shown the provisions of the second bill. The halt of nine days after its first reading may have been due to paralysis at Court while Councillors tried to overcome her misgivings. When she had come to a decision, she appears to have transmitted her wishes to the House of Lords: both the expedient and the more fitting way of attaining her purpose. Such interference by the Crown may seem to us despotic; but while the royal veto remained a live institution, it served the same practical purpose as a conference between both Houses, indicating the limits to which one of the essential parties was prepared to go in a bill that no one wanted to lose. The Sovereign held the trump card. After Elizabeth had spoken, Parliament might grumble but had to submit. The 'many speeches' noted in the *Commons Journal* probably reflect the chagrin of the House and the fighting retreat of its more outspoken Members.

And now to discover what changes resulted from this intervention. The bill as finally enacted falls broadly into two sections, the first concerned with the work of the Catholic missionaries, the second stiffening the penalties for ordinary recusancy or refusal to attend church. As historians have pointed out, it drew a statesmanlike distinction between being and becoming a Catholic: or, to express this more pungently in the language of today, it directed its greater severities against recruitment for the fifth column.

By its main provision, whoever withdrew the Queen's subjects from their natural obedience, or converted them *for that intent* to the Romish religion, were to be adjudged traitors, as were those who willingly allowed themselves to be thus withdrawn or converted. Those significant words, *for that intent*, made the approach political and secular: as a modern scholar expressed it, 'the law refrains from plainly defining conversion to Catholicism as treason, it was rather conversion accompanied by withdrawal of allegiance which was condemned'.[2]

---

[1] S.P. Dom. Eliz. 83/29 is headed, 'Brief notes for her Majesty', and contains at the end two questions on which her pleasure was to be known.

[2] *Statutes of Realm*, IV. i. 657 seqq.; A. O. MEYER, *England & the Catholic Church under Elizabeth*, p. 148.

In the two earlier bills, our three important words did not exist. The bills were framed as an extension of the statute of 1571 against the Papal Bull of deposition, which — quite reasonably in view of the nature of the Bull — had made it treason to reconcile or be reconciled to Rome by virtue of such instruments. This statute and its penalties were now applied to Jesuits and seminary priests and their converts. It was thus treason to reconcile or be reconciled to Rome by virtue of the missionaries' priesthood.[1] Lords and Commons had been concerned, not with principle but with the stark perils of ideological warfare. Alarmed and irate Protestants, they were facing a dilemma which in a milder way is with us today. To them conversion to Catholicism was in itself synonymous with treason.

Thus in its main provision the bill as finally enacted changed a principle. It did not change the penalty. Elsewhere this was done. The first two bills dealt with the saying and hearing of Mass by making the former felony (involving the death penalty) and for the latter imposing a fine of 200 marks and (in the second bill) imprisonment for six months at the first offence, and the pains of praemunire (imprisonment during pleasure and forfeiture of lands and goods) at the second offence. In striking contrast the statute, based on the third bill, reduced felony to a fine of 200 marks, while the fine for hearing Mass was scaled down to 100 marks: there was no increase for further offences. These were indeed changes of substance: mercy it would, no doubt, be misleading to call them.

Perhaps the best-known clause in the final statute is the one imposing a fine of £20 a month for non-attendance at church. Though the modern critic is apt to forget that there was many a slip twixt Tudor law-making and law-enforcing, it was certainly for most recusants a ruinous penalty when enforced. But compared with the two earlier bills it was as whips to scorpions. Both of these drew a distinction between Catholic recusants and others — that is, Protestant sectaries, for whom Puritans entertained no sympathy. Catholic recusants were to incur the staggering fines of £20 for the first month, £40 for the second, £100 for the third, and the pains of praemunire for the fourth. Non-Catholic recusants, who were dealt with at the

[1] S.P. Dom. Eliz. 83/29; 148/10.

end, almost as an afterthought, were subject to a scale of £10, £20, £40, and nothing higher.

There were many other provisions in these two parliamentary bills: thirty-eight in all in the second. It would be tedious to describe them, but there was a group which had the significant purpose of excluding Catholics from positions of influence in society; and here again we cannot fail to note the parallel with our own times. Lawyers guilty of recusancy and refusing thereupon to take the oath of supremacy were deprived of the right to practise or hold any office; to save the youth of the country from contamination, all schoolmasters and tutors were obliged not only to take the oath but also to subscribe to the Articles of Religion as limited in the act of 1571 (that is, the doctrinal articles — a Puritan touch, this!); and the oath of supremacy was also imposed on all law-students and anyone connected with the ecclesiastical or civil courts.[1] That this group of clauses was dropped after the intervention of the Queen is in some ways even more impressive than the remarkable censorship of the rest of Parliament's proposals.

Assuming that the Queen was responsible for these striking changes — and no other explanation seems feasible — what light they cast on her hostility to extreme doctrinaire policy! Better than anyone she kept her head in the fanatical atmosphere of the time. Of course, there must have been individuals about her who advised moderation. They hardly detract from the personal quality of the decision, especially as Burghley was probably not among them. The attitude of this great statesman is a conundrum. Like other eminent fellow-Councillors, he wrote his periodic passages in the book of lamentations against the clemency of his mistress. Though during this session he seems to have been absent — presumably with gout — from many meetings of the House of Lords,[2] we know that both the early severe bills passed through his hands, as did the third and last bill. His many corrections in the draft of the third bill point to his being on the joint-committee of both Houses and in charge of the bill. He may have played the same role on the occasion of the second bill, and if so, he must either have

---

[1] S.P. Dom. Eliz. 148/10.
[2] Cf. the attendances in the *Lords Journal*, though too much confidence should not be put in this source.

agreed in general with its provisions, or — which is hardly likely, and certainly Norton does not hint at lay discord — have found the committee's zeal beyond his control. Moreover, if he disliked the parliamentary proposals he must have been out of line with other Privy Councillors; and yet there are indications that they were pursuing a concerted policy.

Failing any direct evidence, it looks as if we might assume that Burghley was in favour of a measure planned to eradicate Catholicism from England by making life intolerable even for its peaceful and loyal adherents. Once the Queen had finally decided against this policy, doubtless he became the instrument of her wishes, and his able mind was at her disposal. The situation was possibly analogous to that implied in the advice which he wrote to her later on the Catholic problem: 'Compel them you would not; kill them you would not; . . . trust them you should not.'[1] Here he was exercising his statecraft within limits imposed by his mistress. It is interesting to note that the main clause of the third bill in 1581 went through two preliminary stages before the solution embodied in those celebrated words, *for that intent,* was finally evolved.[2] Whose mind — Burghley's or the Queen's — hit on that inspired qualification, we shall probably never know.

Some eight or nine years later, Francis Bacon observed that Elizabeth grounded her proceedings in religion on two principles: 'that consciences are not to be forced'; and that 'causes of conscience, when they exceed their bounds and grow to be matter of faction, lose their nature'. 'Her Majesty, not liking to make windows into men's hearts and secret thoughts, except the abundance of them did overflow into overt and express acts or affirmations, tempered her law so as it restraineth only manifest disobedience, in impugning and impeaching advisedly and maliciously her Majesty's supreme power, and maintaining and extolling a foreign jurisdiction.'[3]

The Queen's action in 1581, as in previous Parliaments, bears out Bacon's observation. Its essentially personal character is

---

[1] 'Lord Treasurer Burleigh's Advice to Q. Elizabeth . . .', in *Harleian Miscellany* (1746 edn.), vii. 59.

[2] Cf. S.P. Dom. Eliz. 148/5 with 147/32. The latter (wrongly endorsed as 'the bill of slander') is the crucial redrafting of the main clause, along with another.

[3] SPEDDING, *Life & Letters of Bacon,* i. 97-8. Note Spedding's comment on the authorship.

its most distinctive feature. By an exercise of royal authority she resisted the great advisory bodies of the realm: Council, Lords and Commons. We have only to consider what would have happened if she had been prepared to give her assent to that second bill, to realize how much the English liberal tradition owes to her sanity.

## CHAPTER III

# THE SEDITION BILL: RELIGION

HITHERTO moderation has not been a feature of the Elizabethan House of Commons. If there has been hunting of the Queen's enemies and detractors, they have always been well in advance of the field. But in this Parliament there was a striking and rather droll reversal of roles over a measure intended as a second line of defence against the Catholic menace. The main bill, whose story has just been told, dealt with 'due obedience' to the Queen and her ecclesiastical establishment; this one with the dangers from propaganda. It was 'An act against seditious words and rumours uttered against the Queen's most excellent Majesty'. The same double line of defence had been found necessary in the similar but reversed conditions of Mary Tudor's reign. Indeed, the new bill was devised and explicitly worded as an extension of an act of 1554-55, now declared to be insufficient in its punishments.[1]

Presumably a government measure, it was introduced into the House of Lords, either because the presence of Lord Burghley, the chief official architect of legislation, attracted it there, or because Councillors anticipated a critical reception in the Commons. It began its career early, had a rapid passage, and was with the Commons on January 30th.[2]

The Marian statute, on which it was based, had made the penalty for slandering the Sovereign loss of both ears and imprisonment for three months, with the option of a fine in lieu of the ears. In the new bill this option was withdrawn and the imprisonment increased to last during the Queen's pleasure. For repeating (as distinct from inventing) any slander, the Marian penalty had been loss of one ear and one month's imprisonment, again with the option of a fine in place of the ear. In the new bill, the option disappeared, the term of

---

[1] 23 Eliz. c. 2 (*Statutes of Realm*, IV. i. 659-61); 1 & 2 Philip & Mary, c. 3 (ibid. pp. 240-1).

[2] *L.J.* ii. 22-7. The duplication of the first and second readings may be due to cancelling readings before the Speaker's election, or may imply a committee and a new bill.

imprisonment became three years. The amended pattern, containing no option and a startling increase in the length of imprisonment, should be noted. It is crucial to our story. But to continue. For a repetition of either offence the old statute imposed life imprisonment and forfeiture of all goods and chattels. The new bill made it felony, involving death. To write or print any such slander had formerly involved loss of the right hand. Now it became felony. The bill incorporated a new crime: anyone who 'shall by setting or erecting of any figure or figures or by casting of nativities or by any prophesying, calculation, or other unlawful act . . . seek to know . . . how long her Majesty shall live . . . or who shall reign . . . after her Highness's decease', became liable to a charge of felony. By modern standards the bill was savage.[1]

That an anti-Catholic bill passed by the Lords should prove too strong for the digestion of the Commons, seems incredible; and we need not doubt that if the measure had been specifically limited to Catholics, it would have raised no qualms in the Lower House. What sounded the alarm there was that it seemed likely to be even more dangerous to their Puritan friends. Indeed, it was under this very statute of 1554-55, now to be made so terribly severe, that their brave hero, John Stubbs, had recently suffered for his pamphlet *The Gaping Gulf*; and in the previous session a Member had wanted to use it against Peter Wentworth. One wonders if government and Lords intended to catch Puritans as well as Catholics. Were they unaware of the two strings to their whip?

The Commons certainly perceived the danger. With their Puritan friends, clerical and lay, displaying an increasing urge to outrival the Old-Testament prophets in outspokenness, they had visions of an earless *élite* of godly men, languishing for years in prison. Consequently, it became their object to restore the option of a fine for an ear, scale down the terms of imprisonment, and inject a frankly anti-Catholic virus into this infant that boasted so obscene a parentage. As we shall see, they ended up by drafting a new bill, which recast the framework of the Lords' bill and ejected all reference to the Marian statute — except in a clause repealing it! It is hard to resist the conclusion that they were paying conscious tribute to the redoubtable John

[1] The text of this Lords' bill is in S.P. Dom. Eliz. 147/20.

Stubbs, now signing himself *Scaeva* — left-handed. A reproach
to the Queen? She evidently thought so.

The assault began on the second reading, when Thomas
Norton came forward with an addition which made it a seditious rumour, and therefore punishable by this bill, to affirm
that the doctrine established by law in the Church of England
was heretical or schismatical. In this way the measure would
become a powerful supplement to the other great anti-Catholic
bill, still in its early, severe form. If Norton and the majority of
the House of Commons had had their way — and supposing
(which of course is fantasy) that the legal machinery had been
able to function efficiently and rigorously — they would have
imposed orthodoxy in their ideological State as ruthlessly as the
totalitarian régimes of our contemporary world. Employing
the gallows instead of the stake, the secular courts in place of the
ecclesiastical, they would certainly have been more thorough in
their persecution than the medieval Mary Tudor. Norton had
the fanatic's confidence in his opinions. At a supper party
shortly afterwards, when he was taxed with being one of the
Members whom the Queen had excluded from her thanks at the
close of the session, because of this addition to the bill, he replied: 'I wrote it, but the House put it to. And thereof I repent
me not, for as it is her Majesty's greatest honour to have
restored true religion, so there cannot be a more dishonourable
slander to her than to say that the religion her Majesty main-
taineth is false, or that the Romish religion, being contrary
thereunto, is true.'[1]

Norton's addition was read to the House, and bill and addition were sent to a grand committee, on which such unquenchable Puritans as Carleton and Bainbridge found themselves.
The addition was approved and amendments were made.
What these latter were, we cannot say precisely, although they
were certainly along the lines already indicated. In several
places, for example, the committee inserted the qualifying
words, 'intending the slander and dishonour of the Queen's
Majesty', their object being to save a future John Stubbs, since
the loyal intentions of Puritans were beyond dispute. Elsewhere they took out a vague phrase for fear it might stretch too
far.

[1] *Archaeologia*, xxxvi. 109.

The Lords, perhaps under official tuition, were inclined to stand no nonsense. They disliked both these particular amendments. Nor did they like the addition. When the bill came back to them, they demanded a conference to understand why the Commons had made their alterations; and doubtless it went badly. After a little by-play, because the Clerk below had forgotten to write the formal endorsement on Norton's addition — an incident which gave them the chance of conveying a broad hint to suppress it — they proceeded to deal roughly with the amendments.

They might have foreseen the result. The Commons became stubborn in turn. When the bill was returned, with amendments to their amendments, they decided to send it back as one with which they were unable to deal. Our diarist explains the reasoning. The Lords having disallowed certain amendments, the Commons could not undo what they had already done. It was conceded that the other House might add to an amendment but they could not directly impugn it. As for the Norton addition, the Lords had so altered it that 'the very substance of the sense' was changed; and, by what must surely have been calculated subtlety, some of the amendments here involved consequential changes in the Commons' amendments. Members, in their debate, differed about the limits allowed to the other House in dealing with an addition to a bill.

Back the bill went to the Lords, where it was found that two could play at this formalistic game. The Lord Chancellor refused to accept it, saying that their Lordships 'were not to take knowledge of the opinion of this House touching the state of the said bill'. In consequence, the bill remained dead in the Lower House.[1]

It was one of those absurd situations in which dignity without tact so often lands human beings. It could not be allowed to endure. The next day the Council put up the eloquent and persuasive Sir Christopher Hatton — who incidentally cuts a very different figure in Parliament from the Dancing Chancellor of legend — to make a seductive speech in the Commons, 'setting forth the great benefits and blessings of God upon this realm in the godly, most loving, and careful government and ministry of her Majesty; and withal, the great, earnest, most

---

[1] *C.J.* i. 121-33; Cromwell's Diary, February 20th, March 11th.

faithful and dutiful zeal and obedience of this House unto her Highness, no less in every particular Member of the same than . . . in any other subject of this realm whatsoever, noble or other'. What with his battery of superlatives and by laying the entire blame on the House of Lords — not to mention all the rest, 'by him most excellently, amply, and effectually, and no less aptly declared' — he easily obtained a large committee to draft a new bill.[1]

This bill — substantially our statute — was in the main a triumph for the Commons. They phrased it without reference to the Marian statute, except to repeal that obnoxious law in one of the clauses; and they inserted the option of paying a fine instead of losing ears. For imprisonment during the Queen's pleasure they substituted imprisonment for six months; and they reduced the three-years penalty to three months. True, a second offence remained felony, as did writing or printing a slander; but they got a qualifying phrase — 'with a malicious intent' — into all these offences, thus hoping to save their Puritan friends.

One major sacrifice was made: Norton's addition. And here it looks as if they found themselves confronted, not only with the disapproval of the Lords — which may in turn have had a higher inspiration — but with what amounted to a royal fiat. There is sufficient evidence to leave one in little doubt that Elizabeth would have vetoed the bill and rested content with the existing Marian statute rather than consent to Norton's insidious and merciless clause. Her Councillors were probably none too sure about her assent in any case.

The bill rapidly passed the Commons, though as the Clerk's entry — 'sundry motions and arguments and some amendments' — suggests, Puritan extremists were still on the alert at its third reading and may have been indulging in a final grumble about the concessions. It was at this stage that they made a last demonstration of distrust by inserting the words, 'at the election of the offender', thus making absolutely certain that the option of a fine for an ear should be at the discretion of any outspoken friends caught by the act, and not of the justices trying them.[2]

[1] C.J. i. 134.
[2] The insertion can be seen in the ingrossed act at Westminster.

The session had only a day or two to run. What with the Queen's lukewarmness and the Commons' obstinacy, the Lords were afraid of losing the measure. They handled it as though it were delicate china. They wanted amendments, but dared not do anything without first asking for a conference of both Houses and then putting specific questions to the Lower House. They were concerned about the repeal of the statute of 1554-55, and asked if the Commons would allow it to stand unrepealed, except as altered in the new bill. Their reason for this was that the Marian law made provision against slandering noblemen and the lords of the clergy. Earlier in the session they had initiated and passed a bill on this subject, which gave statutory authority to the Star Chamber to try such offences and to levy fines at its discretion and impose other penalties. It was not likely that Puritan Members of the House of Commons, whose clerical and other friends were exhausting their vocabulary in violent attacks on the bishops, would take kindly to such a bill. Nor did they. The measure was subjected to much criticism at its second reading, and then allowed to die in committee.[1] They were equally obdurate on this second occasion. They refused to qualify their repeal of the Marian statute; and the Lords were compelled to give way. To another suggested amendment the Commons agreed, but only after eliminating a dangerously vague word.[2]

And so the sedition bill, or bill against slanders, passed its final stage on the last day of the session. How well its story brings into focus the partners in an Elizabethan Parliament. The Queen behind the scene, with her opposition to extreme measures, is not the least typical.

Absorbed in the two major bills against Catholics, both of which engaged their religious passions, and intimidated, not only by the Queen's emphatic injunction against meddling with religion, but also by her swift reaction to Wentworth's motion for a fast, it was towards the end of the session that the zealots recovered their wind sufficiently to venture once more on the forbidden topic.

On March 3rd, as the Clerk records in his *Journal*, there were 'sundry motions and arguments' concerning the reforms in

[1] Cromwell's Diary, January 31st, February 3rd; *C.J.* i. 121.
[2] *C.J.* i. 135.

matters of religion about which the House had petitioned the
Queen in 1576. It is evident that much time and talk were
devoted to the subject. What was said we do not know, except
that some of the Privy Councillors intervened and, to allay
concern, explained that the Vice-Chamberlain (Hatton), the
two secretaries (Walsingham and Wilson), and the Chancellor
of the Exchequer (Mildmay) had already, and presumably in
anticipation of trouble, spoken to the bishops on the subject.
In the end, the House decided that these four Councillors should
again approach the bishops, on this occasion in the name of the
House, and move them to continue pressing the Queen on the
subject of reform. They were to inform them at the same time
of 'the earnest desire of this House' for redress of other grievances mentioned in the course of that day's debate.

As recorded in the *Journal* it was a most orderly proceeding,
skilfully restrained by the ability and popularity of Hatton as a
parliamentarian and the sympathetic influence of his three
colleagues as Puritans; directed, moreover, into channels which
— if discussion of religious grievances was to be tolerated at all
— could not fail to be acceptable to the Queen. To make
doubly sure that no offence should be taken, after the resolution
was carried 'then, upon a motion made by Mr. Speaker, it was
further agreed that all the said speeches, motions, and arguments should by the whole House be deemed in every man to
proceed of good and godly zeal, without any evil intent or
meaning at all; and so . . . to be construed and reported accordingly, and not otherwise or in any other manner'.[1]

*Qui s'excuse, s'accuse.* We know enough about Pistor and
Carleton, Paul and Peter Wentworth, Robin Snagge and the
rest to be sceptical about this whited *Journal* entry. The conclusion of the debate might be — it obviously was — a triumph
for the tact of popular and trusted Councillors, and a testimony
to the strange potion of mixed affliction and affection which
the Queen administered to her devoted Commons. But the
process of arriving at it: was that so innocent? Fortunately, we
can make a shrewd guess, though we must anticipate the end of
the story in order to obtain the evidence that probably fits in
here.

When the session was over, Sir Walter Mildmay delivered to

[1] *C.J.* i. 130.

his fellow-Puritan, the Secretary Sir Francis Walsingham, a
series of reform 'articles' 'for him to treat thereof with her
Majesty, that they might be enacted at the next Parliament,
holden whensoever'.[1] Though Parliament was dispersed and
the Queen could hope for a lull of several years in their embarrassing agitation, she did not take advantage of the respite or
dilly-dally, but passed the 'articles' to the Archbishop of York,
who consulted five other bishops, including the dour, unbend-
ing Whitgift. They appended their comments.

These 'articles' repay a little attention. They were in three
sections: 'concerning ministers'; 'concerning excommunication'; 'concerning dispensations'. The ten articles of the first
section began with the demand for an enactment that none be
admitted minister of the word and sacraments except in a
benefice with cure of souls, vacant in the diocese of the bishop
admitting the candidate. The bishops had little difficulty in
showing how impracticable such a policy would be in the Anglican Church. They went on: 'this article is grounded upon a
false principle of T[homas] C[artwright] against ministers having no pastoral cure'. Though Cartwright was not mentioned
in their hostile comment on the next two articles, he might
equally well have been, for the proposals aimed at an approximation to that central feature of Presbyterianism, popular
election or approval of ministers. It must be conceded that the
realistic approach of the bishops to these and other reforms
was devastating, for the attempt to import Presbyterian features
into the episcopal Anglican system was like trying to mix oil
and water. The fourth article is peculiarly interesting. Whitgift had turned Cartwright out of his Cambridge fellowship for
failing to take holy orders. This article proposed to dispense
with that necessity. Again the bishops' answer was shattering,
and they added — how justifiably! — 'It is a piece of T.C. his
platform.' The bishops were not one hundred per cent hostile
to this section of the paper; but little of it survived their criticism. The section on excommunication they may have left to
their ecclesiastical lawyers. The commentators spread themselves, their learning, and their conservatism on criticizing it in

[1] Northants Record Soc. MS. F. (M). P. 148. This is one of many Mildmay
papers owned by his son-in-law, Wm. Fitzwilliam. I interpret its heading to imply
the dating I have adopted. A fuller version of the 'articles' is in B.M. Additional
MS. 29546, fols. 124-5.

a rather unimaginative way. On dispensations the bishops were again realistic, but not unhelpful.[1]

We are concerned with these documents, not for their ecclesiastical but their parliamentary interest. The 'articles' may be described as distilling into precise proposals the Puritan reforms envisaged in the Commons' petition of 1576. We learn from the endorsement of one of the documents that they were 'exhibited by some of the Lower House';[2] and it looks as if they constituted the brief to which the Puritan leaders spoke. They are not likely to have been drafted by the Members alone. Either they came from a radical party in the Lower House of Convocation, or they were evolved at secret meetings of Puritan clergy and their friends among the Commons. Clearly there was a prepared campaign, and once more we are confronted with the organizing proclivities of these people. We ask, did a Puritan plan go off at half-cock? If Paul Wentworth's fast had not misfired, if the Queen had not issued so clear a veto on the topic, would there have been an attempt to legislate along the lines of these 'articles', not 'at the next Parliament, holden whensoever' — as the Mildmay document proposed — but at this Parliament of 1581?

To return, however, to the narrative. The four Privy Councillors carried out the commission given them by the Commons, and Sir Walter Mildmay reported the result on March 7th. At this stage in the proceedings it would seem that neither they nor the House had committed themselves to such a specific programme as the 'articles': which was very wise, for they would surely have got nowhere with those tendentious proposals. Mildmay reported that they had 'conferred with some of my Lords the Bishops . . . for some things very requisite to be reformed in the Church: as, the great number of unlearned and unable ministers; the great abuse of excommunication for every matter of small moment; the commutation of penance; and the great multitude of dispensations and pluralities; and other things very hurtful to the Church'. In the name of the House they had desired their Lordships to join with them in petition to her Majesty for reformation of these abuses. They had found

---

[1] B.M. Lansdowne MS. 30, fols. 203-10. A copy with corrections by Whitgift and endorsed by him is in Inner Temple Petyt MS. 538/54, fols. 247 seqq.
[2] Lansdowne MS. 30, fols. 203-10.

'some of the bishops' — the limitation may suggest a lack of co-operation from Whitgift, among others — ready to confess to the abuses and very willing to join in moving her Majesty.

Afterwards, they and these bishops joined in humble suit to the Queen, and received her most gracious answer: 'That as her Highness had, the last session of Parliament, of her own good consideration and before any petition or suit thereof made by this House, committed the charge and consideration thereof unto some of her Highness's clergy, who had not performed the same according to her Highness's commandment; so now her Majesty would eftsoons commit the same unto such others of them as with all convenient speed, without remissness and slackness, should see the same accomplished accordingly, in such sort as the same shall neither be delayed or undone.' Evidently sharing the characteristic and growing Puritan dislike of bishops Mildmay added, 'that the only cause why no due reformation hath been already had in the said petitions, was only by the negligence and slackness of some others, and not of her Majesty nor of this House; alleging withal that some of the said bishops had yet done something in those matters delivered by her Majesty to their charge — as in a more advised care of allowing and making of ministers; but yet, in effect, little or nothing to the purpose'.

He concluded by moving the House to rest satisfied with the Queen's most gracious answer, and to resolve upon some form of yielding thanks to her. The House then turned to a little business and read a couple of bills before they reverted to this time-consuming subject. There was evidently a good deal of talk: 'sundry motions and arguments'. Intent on action rather than promises, some wanted the whole House to go to the Queen, others were for a delegation; but the admirable Mildmay persuaded them to be content with commissioning their Speaker, in his closing oration, to give the Queen their humble and dutiful thanks, and also to put her 'in remembrance for the execution and accomplishment' of her promise at her good pleasure. As we shall see, the Speaker did this.[1]

Whether it was the House or merely its Puritan leaders who briefed Mildmay with the series of 'articles' that he afterwards gave to Walsingham (whence they reached the Queen), we

---

[1] *C.J.* i. 131-2; Cromwell's Diary, March 7th.

cannot be sure. It is a curious episode. Elizabeth's reign is full of paradoxes. It may seem strange that a Sovereign who proved herself so resolute an opponent of Puritanism chose these two confirmed Puritans for her ministers. But, as this session of Parliament demonstrated, they were invaluable in the House of Commons; and so indeed they were in Elizabethan society. To do as Elizabeth did, harness the dynamic of revolution to her service without succumbing to its doctrinaire philosophy — combine the merits of the liberal and the fanatic — was a feat of personality and statesmanship rare in a Sovereign or even in a less exalted leader. Her Mildmays and Walsinghams were a tribute to genius.

There are several incidental points of interest in this story. The Queen really did take action in fulfilment of her promise: which suggests that the mere absence of evidence on other occasions should not be taken for proof of inaction. The arresting details were told in a letter dated May 2nd from Archbishop Sandys of York to the energetic Bishop of Chester, William Chaderton. 'The Parliament men of the Nether House', he wrote, 'found themselves greatly offended with the bishops of this realm, as negligent in their office and abusing the ecclesiastical jurisdiction . . . It pleased her Majesty to send for me to open the matter unto me and to require me to make answer; and if I liked of it, to call unto me three or four bishops to assist me in this action.' He chose five bishops, including Whitgift. Presumably the occasion was after Walsingham had given the Queen the Puritan 'articles'. 'We set down', continued Sandys, 'that which we thought good and could gladly yield unto'; and again we may presume that the resultant document was the one we possess, containing 'articles' and answers. 'I delivered the same book to her Majesty', who kept it to herself, 'saying she would consider of it. Mr. Vice-Chamberlain, with others, pressed me for answer. Whereupon I repaired to her Majesty and prayed answer. The answer was, that her Highness was sufficient of herself to deal with the clergy in matters ecclesiastical; and that the Parliament House should not meddle therein; neither could her Majesty yield unto the alteration of any ecclesiastical law. I gave them this answer, which was much misliked of. Yet we bishops concluded upon some reformations and acquainted her Majesty with the same. Her Highness liked thereof; commanded the bishops of the province of Canterbury [the Archbishop being suspended from duties] to monish their fellow-bishops of the same, and that I should impart this thing to the bishops of my province; requiring them to be dutiful in their offices and service in punishing of sin, and that our negligence should be no more complained of. The execution of sharp discipline', added Sandys, 'will stop the mouths of their cries against us.'[1]

It was one thing to give orders: that the Queen could do. For their execution she was dependent on others; and reforms were often impracticable, evils always stubborn, her bishops — as this letter from Sandys might suggest — no crusaders.

Another interesting point is Mildmay's open criticism of the bishops and refusal to let blame fall on the Queen, though he must have been fully aware of her antipathy to parliamentary interference. At his supper party after the end of the session, talking of this episode, Thomas Norton displayed the same prejudices. In his account of that occasion he records the conversation. 'The whole House', said Norton, holding themselves assured of Mildmay's and the other three Councillors' faithfulness, 'and acknowledging her Majesty's graciousness, did impute the default to the bishops.' Hence their resolve to renew the petition through the Speaker, who was answered graciously by the Queen. This showed that there was no default in her Majesty: it was with the bishops. One Member of Parliament, he added, had quoted Cicero: 'If those could be trusted who ought to be most trustworthy, we should not have to strive.'

At this attack on the bishops, one of the company — the Cambridge tutor of his host's son — protested. 'I warrant you', said he, 'they made no delay nor did anything but by the Queen's direction and as the Queen appointed.' Angrily Norton retorted that 'the Queen was most honourable and did not use to dissemble with her subjects: to make them openly a show of granting her people's petition, and underhand to over-throw it by contrary commandment to bishops'. The tutor persisted in blaming the Queen, while Norton grew hotter and hotter in her defence and in denunciation of the bishops. He told how in the conference between representatives of both

---

[1] PECK, *Desiderata Curiosa*, i. 102.

Houses over 'the bill of religion' — the great act against
Catholics — when 'both the temporal Lords and Commons of
that committee' were 'dealing zealously in religion', the bishops
were chiefly concerned about their jurisdiction. 'One great
bishop said, that rather than he would yield that private schoolmasters should acknowledge their conformity in religion before
Justices of Peace in open sessions' — there was a clause about
this in both the first and second bills — 'he would say Nay to the
whole bill of religion: which saying', added Norton, 'was not
comparable to the most godly zeal of her Majesty, nor of the
Lords then present.'

The dispute went on, and Norton told the tutor 'that he was
a fool: which, and more to like effect', he added by way of
explanation, 'I spake of him and not of the bishops, saving that
I said that whosoever so told him, the more beasts and fools'.
Playing a scurvy trick on a fellow-guest at his master's table, the
tutor denounced Norton to the Council for slandering the
bishops. Hence this illuminating narrative in self-defence.[1]

Norton does not seem to have suffered for his anti-episcopal
outburst, though, as the letter from Sandys shows, there was
more to be said for the Cambridge tutor's thesis than he would
concede. But his extreme views and unrestrained tongue landed
him in trouble at the end of the year, when Alençon was paying
his second visit to the Queen, and Elizabeth was playing out the
last and most fantastic scene in that strange romantic drama.
'Mr. Norton, the great Parliament man,' wrote Roger Manners
from Court, 'is committed for his overmuch and undutiful
speaking touching this cause.'[2] A few weeks later — such were
the congruities of this bewildering age — we find Sir Francis
Walsingham, the Queen's Principal Secretary, ordering the
Lieutenant of the Tower to provide Norton with pen, ink and
paper, in order to take advantage of his enforced leisure and
get from him a long memorandum — 'A Book of Mr. Norton's
Devices' — on 'the reformation of the present corruption in
religion'. The Lieutenant was to tell him that, as requital for
his pains, Walsingham would look after his wife during his
absence from her.

'When all is said and done', wrote Norton from the Tower,
'this is true: that God sent us our Queen in His blessing. It is

---

[1] *Archaeologia*, xxxvi. 109-15.    [2] *H.M.C. Rutland MSS.* i. 130.

God that preserveth and blesseth her. It is the only religion of God that knitteth true subjects unto her . . . Woe is [it] to be wretch, that in offending her have wounded the profession of that religion.'[1]

Norton's friends on the Privy Council appear to have procured his release from the Tower immediately Elizabeth got rid of Alençon at the beginning of February. He was then kept under restraint in his own lodging in the Guildhall until early April, when Burghley and Hatton managed finally to appease the Queen.[2]

He died on March 10th, 1584, before another Parliament was called. When his son, Robert Norton, translated Camden's *Annals of Queen Elizabeth* (1635), he inserted a note of the event and a panegyric at the appropriate place:[3] 'To the promoting of religion, the safety of his Prince, and good of his country . . . he applied his uttermost studies and endeavours, his best credit in Court and City, and his sundry excellent speeches in Parliament, wherein he expressed himself in such sort to be a true and zealous *Philopater* that he attained the noted name of *Master Norton the Parliament man*, and hath left, even to this day, a pleasing impression of his wisdom and virtue in the memories of many good men.' How enviable an epitaph!

---

[1] Yelverton MS. (at Elvetham), xxvi. fols. 41b, 33b. I owe these quotations to Miss Bibby's papers. Norton's Book of Devices is in S.P. Dom. Eliz. 177/59 (misdated).

[2] Cf. WRIGHT, *Q. Elizabeth & Her Times*, ii. 167-8 and footnote; S. P. Dom. Eliz 152/72, 153/5.

[3] Pp. 254-5.

CHAPTER IV

# END OF THE SESSION

BEFORE we come to the close of this session a minor miscellany may enrich its story. And first, there is a postscript to add to the lamentable tale of Arthur Hall of Grantham, told in our account of the previous session.

Between the two meetings of this Parliament Hall had written and printed his tract about the quarrel with Melchisedech Mallory, along with a second tract, *An Admonition by the Father of F. A. to him being a Burgesse of the Parliament for his better Behaviour therein.*[1] The first was bad enough, with its detailed account of the proceedings in his servant, Smalley's privilege case, and its bitter remarks about Speaker Bell and other opponents; but the second contained pungent comments on current practice in the House of Commons, and a historical study of the constitution describing the Lower House as a new person in the trinity of King, Lords, and Commons. To the precedent-quoting, wishful-thinking House of Commons of Elizabethan times, whose fantastic notions about the antiquity and powers of Parliament were the prop of their adolescent egoism, it was lese-majesty. Though only one of the counts against Hall, it was the one that stung deepest: witness the long (and dull) manuscript tract among the papers of Mildmay's son-in-law refuting, point by point, this attack on 'the antiquity of our third voices'.[2]

Appropriately enough it was Thomas Norton — who might be suspected of waging a vendetta, if the antipathetic temperaments of the two men did not offer adequate explanation — who first called the attention of the Commons to the offending book. Secretary Wilson rose to say that the author had already been before the Council for publishing it; Sir Walter Mildmay dilated upon its 'dangerous and lewd contents'. The House was aroused to instant action. They sent their Serjeant-at-Arms, with two knightly Members for countenance, to apprehend the culprit,

[1] Cf. WRIGHT, *Arthur Hall.*
[2] Northants Record Soc. MS. F. (M). P. 112.

who was not in the House and whose elusiveness in 1576 they remembered. They also set up a committee to examine the printer of the book.

At the next sitting the committee reported on their proceedings with the printer, and Hall himself was brought to the bar, where, according to our diarist, he displayed his wonted pigheadedness and 'would not by any means be induced to confess that he had offended or given cause of offence'. After spending most of the morning on the business, the House again referred it to a committee. Eight days later the major part of another morning went in receiving the committee's report, re-examining both the printer and Hall himself, deciding on the punishment to be imposed, and recalling Hall to sentence him. Interspersed were 'sundry motions and arguments'. Sir Christopher Hatton — a Councillor not unfriendly to Hall — was disturbed at the waste of energy. In making the committee's report he had urged them to come to a decision and to spend the time 'as much as might be in matters of greatest moment, wherein much less hath been done this session than in any other these many years in like quantity of time'. It was too rosy a picture of the past.

As for Arthur Hall, his behaviour on this, his latest appearance at the bar, was not calculated to win compassion. The Clerk remarks that the 'reverence done by him' was not 'in such humble and lowly wise as the state of one in that place to be charged and accused requireth', and that the Speaker admonished him for it. The sentence he received was severe. He was committed to the Tower for six months or for so long thereafter until he willingly made retraction of his book to the satisfaction of the House or of those commissioned to accept it. In addition he was fined 500 marks to the Queen's use. And most interesting of all — for it stands in our parliamentary precedent books as the first exercise of this power by the House of Commons — he was expelled from membership of that Parliament, the Speaker being authorized to issue a warrant for a new election in his constituency. Finally, it was resolved, 'That the said book and slanderous libel should and shall be holden, deemed, taken and adjudged to be utterly false and erroneous; and that the same shall be publicly testified . . .' Deviationist history castigated by authority: another curious example of the likeness of those days to ours! After Hall had been brought in again to hear the judgment pronounced, and then remitted to the Tower in the Serjeant's custody, it was agreed, on the Speaker's motion, to have the whole course of the proceedings clearly written out by the Clerk, read to the House, and entered in the *Journal*.

This was duly performed on March 18th, the last day of the session: though the Clerk appended the wordy formal account to his already very full entry of the proceedings on February 14th, thus creating an astoundingly long and repetitious item in the *Journal* for that day. Since no submission had come from the culprit and the session was ending, seven Councillor-Members, or any three of them, were commissioned to receive it; without which, made in writing to their liking, Hall was not to be released after the expiry of six months. Moreover, these Councillors were to report on their action to the next session of Parliament. This last provision is of considerable interest. Today we speak of 'Parliament': one continuum. Medievally and for the sixteenth century the historian rightly speaks of 'Parliaments': each distinct and separate. Here in this resolution was the modern idea in its birth-throes.[1]

Hall made his retraction to the Councillors on April 2nd: a fortnight after the close of the session. The pen was submissive; the heart was not, and between the lines this is apparent. There was a paragraph of submission to the Queen, in which, alas, he toed the 'party' line on history. It might rank, if not for rotundity of phrase at any rate for being as near idolatry, with the great eighteenth-century lawyer, Blackstone's encomium of the British Constitution: 'There cannot be any better order by wit of man devised for the making, abrogating, or changing of laws . . . than is already provided for, and of ancient time hath been practised in this realm, by calling and assembling the three Estates of the realm.'[2]

Apparently Hall neither paid his fine nor served out his six months in the Tower. The Queen pardoned him: perhaps soon after his submission. His patron, Burghley, may have secured this; but Elizabeth, one imagines, acted with a readiness and

[1] *C.J.* i. 122-3, 125-7, 132, 136; Cromwell's Diary, February 4th, 6th, 14th, March 18th.
[2] WRIGHT, op. cit. pp. 190-1.

approval that reflected her dislike for heresy-hunters, and for the hotheads of the House of Commons in particular.

A wise man, after such experience, would have been glad to retire from the parliamentary stage; but Hall secured his own re-election for Grantham in 1584. Though the Parliament started on November 23rd, he had not taken his seat by December 13th, terrified, it seems, by a report that some Members were determined to inquire whether the sentence of 1581 against him had been performed, and if not, why not. 'Her Majesty's pardon and gracious deliverance of me', he wrote to Burghley, 'will be allowed for no satisfaction.' 'What authority one House of Parliament hath to execute such a judgment against any subject, I refer to your Honour's grave and wise knowledge. If they have neither law nor precedent therefor, my fortune is hard.' We can perhaps better answer his question than Burghley. For his expulsion they had no precedent; though a constructive argument, if a weak one, might have been devised. For the fine and imprisonment, their precedents were no older than living memory. Hall was right. The House of Commons was a new person in the trinity.[1]

The two main bills of the session had dealt with Catholics. The problem of Protestant sectaries arose in a bill that appeared before the Commons on February 15th, proscribing the Family of Love, a strange, mystical sect originating in Holland. Both orthodox and Puritan loathed them as much as they loathed Anabaptists, with whom, indeed, they were sometimes confused. Their loyalty was suspect, and the Queen had felt constrained to issue a proclamation against them the previous October. When Parliament met, the Privy Council prompted Convocation to discuss the matter, and, as we learn from Thomas Norton, 'divers preachers' brought the bill to the Commons, 'commended . . . from the Convocation'. The measure may be described as a government-inspired bill sponsored by Convocation.[2]

It denounced the Family's doctrine as 'not only heresy, but also tending to sedition and disturbance of the State'. The penalties were whipping for the first offence; branding with the

---

[1] WRIGHT, op. cit. pp. 193-4.
[2] STEELE, *Tudor & Stuart Proclamations*, i. 81; STRYPE, *Grindal*, p. 383; *Archaeologia*, xxxvi. 113-14.

letters H.N. — the initials of its Dutch founder and prophet — for the second; felony for the third. Committed on the second reading, a new bill was drawn, but apparently no member of the committee liked it. Consequently, in its turn it ran into rough weather at the second reading. It was 'long argued whether pains of death might be inflicted to an heretic'; and, apparently, most of the morning went on the debate, with agreement to continue the discussion next day. Religion was like drink to this assembly of Commons, and we can appreciate why Sir Christopher Hatton kept an anxious eye on the clock and the calendar. The measure was re-committed, and a new, a third bill was given two readings five days later. It, too, was committed. But by now exhaustion had set in. The bill did not re-emerge: it was let sleep. So much for a government-inspired bill, backed by Convocation and commended by the Speaker.[1]

Norton and the Cambridge tutor had a bout over it at their supper-party. The tutor said that the bishops had turned against the measure because 'the Lower House had made heresy felony, and so laid a temporal pain to a spiritual offence'. Norton retorted: Why cannot Parliament decree 'that an heretic may as well be hanged as burned'? There are obscurities in the story, but one suspects that in addition to secularizing the bill the Commons had increased its severity, thus alienating its official friends and leaving it at last abandoned, if not, indeed, prohibited.[2]

There was another bill which helps to bring into clearer focus the views of some prominent Members. Its purport was that the children of foreigners, born in England since the first year of the Queen's reign, should in all respects be deemed as aliens. Surely an unofficial bill, it pandered to the popular dislike of foreigners, understandably acute in years of crisis and sensitive patriotism. At its second reading, as our diarist Thomas Cromwell tells us, it 'was much impugned, first as being against charity, against the law of nature', and 'an imposition of punishment' where there was no offence; 'very perilous to all, a

---

[1] *Archaeologia*, xxxvi. 114; Cromwell's Diary, February 15th, 22nd, 27th; *C.J.* i. 127-30.

[2] *Archaeologia*, xxxvi. 114. In Cromwell's description of the bill at its first reading, a third offence is felony; but perhaps the description really applies to a later re-drafting.

thing that might be objected to our children after two or three descents and call every man's inheritance in question; finally, that under pretence of providing for the Queen's custom, it would do much harm'.

Coming early in the session, a few comments on the debate have survived in the Clerk's rough notes. We discover with interest that our diarist, Cromwell, started the debate by opposing the bill. Norton, characteristically, was for it, and, equally true to character, moved an anti-Catholic addition: 'that Englishmen taking oath to the Pope or foreign potentates beyond sea ... shall have no benefit as Englishmen'. The incorrigible Norton! 'Act, insist, speak, read, write, in season and out': how well the anonymous satirist had delineated him nearly twenty years before! Richard Broughton, man of affairs to the Earl of Essex, spoke against the bill; Sir Francis Knollys, his narrow zeal uppermost, was for it; our eminent lawyer, Dalton, against it. The bill was committed, and re-emerged as a new bill, now providing that foreigners' children born in England 'should no longer enjoy their birthright than they shall be dwelling in England and continue their sole obedience to the Queen of England'. There was much discussion at the third reading: 'great imperfections' were discovered, and it was committed and amended before being given a fourth and final reading. In the Lords it did not get beyond a second reading. It was 'not liked of by the Lords', Cromwell noted. Nor, one suspects, would it have escaped the Queen's veto if the Lords had not suppressed it for her.[1]

These vignettes — all of subordinate episodes — strengthen our major portrayal of an independent, wayward body of men. One might linger over others. For example, the House was reprimanded by the Lords — in connection with a measure for the maintenance of the Borders — for venturing to replace a bill from the Higher House by a new one of their own, without first seeking a conference: an action, their Lordships declared, contrary to duty and precedent. Earlier in the session, Thomas Norton had sought and obtained from the Commons a general order about two-House conferences, permitting their representatives to defend the proceedings of the Lower House at such

---

[1] D'EWES, *Journals*, pp. 284-5; Cromwell's Diary, January 25th, February 4th, 7th, 17th; *C.J.* i. 119, 122-3, 127; *L.J.* ii. 38.

meetings, but on no account to yield anything new without first consulting the whole House.[1]

It is against such a general background that we must interpret an obscure entry in the *Commons Journal* about an attack made on the Speaker at the end of the sitting on March 16th. Mr. Anthony Cope, Member for Banbury and an unadulterated Puritan, 'standing up and offering to speak to the House, said . . . that Mr. Speaker, in some such matters as he hath favoured . . . hath, without licence of this House, spoken to the bill; and in some other cases, which he did not favour . . . he would prejudice the speeches of the Members of this House with the question'. Undoubtedly, Cope had in mind the silencing of George Carleton during the episode of the fast. Probably the Speaker had also spoilt extremist Puritan plans in connection with the petition for Church reforms. Unfortunately, it can be but surmise.[2]

Two days later, about 5 p.m. on Saturday, March 18th, the Queen came to end the session. The Speaker began his oration by saying that in the making of laws three things were specially to be considered: 'First, that they should be to the honour of God and to the advancement of His true religion; next, to the safety of her Majesty's person and state; and last, to the public benefit of the subjects of the realm. Every of which parts he handled severally.'

In the first, he noted two things as requisite: 'one, the diligent and sincere preaching of the word . . . which he termed to be the watering and refreshing of the souls and consciences of men, as gardens were refreshed with sweet showers to make them bring forth plenty of good fruits; and the other . . . the extirpation of heresies and reformation of manners, as in gardens weeds are rooted out, lest the good plants be choked up or hindered. In the second, he remembered the great benefits and blessings that we receive of Almighty God through the ministry of our most gracious Queen, that so many years together hath maintained us in so great peace and wealth; together with her singular virtues, justice and mercy, seen and deeply felt of all her people . . . And in the third part, he noted how necessary it was to provide laws tending not only to the maintenance and increase of the wealth of the subjects of the land — being the

[1] *C.J.* i. 133-4, 123.    [2] Ibid. p. 134.

strength and glory of the Queen — but also to the refreshing and correcting of those ill members, which, by indirect means and of private respect to themselves, would any wise procure the detriment of the Commonwealth.'

After asking the Queen to give her assent to the bills they had passed, 'he remembered a petition made by the Common House the last session of Parliament . . . for redress to be had of certain enormities in the Church . . . Whereunto her Majesty made them a most gracious answer that she had [given] and would give order therein . . . He remembered likewise that because those things, for lack of time, were not fully reformed, the House had eftsoons this session presumed to put her Majesty in mind thereof again: whereunto also, as to the former, they received a gracious answer, that those matters belonging to her as incident to that supreme authority which she hath over the clergy and state ecclesiastical, she would give such direction therein as all the disorders should be reformed, so far as should be necessary. For the which answer also he rendered the like most humble thanks, beseeching her Majesty, in the name of the whole Commons, that it might please her to command that to be done without delay which the necessity of the things did require.'

On behalf of the whole state of the Commons of her realm, he besought the Queen to 'have a vigilant and provident care of the safety of her own most royal person, against the malicious attempts of some mighty foreign enemies abroad and the traitorous practices of most unnatural, disobedient subjects both abroad and at home, envying the blessed, most happy, quiet government of this realm under her Highness, upon the thread of whose life only, next under God, depended the life and whole state and stay of every her good and dutiful subjects.'[1]

Replying, the Lord Chancellor 'very excellently and briefly' touched on the points of the oration. 'Concerning the law made against disobedient subjects', the Queen meant, he said, 'to see it put in execution'. Concerning the second law, against seditious words, 'she nothing doubteth her safety, though no law were made; . . . yet, considering their request, she will consent thereto, and rendereth thanks for the care of the House

---

[1] There are three reports of this speech: Northants Record Soc. MS. F. (M). P. 148; *C.J.* i. 137; Cromwell's Diary. My version is derived from the first two.

therein'. But, 'within those general thanks' she did not comprehend some members of the Lower House who 'have this session
dealt more rashly in some things than was fit for them to do' —
or, as Cromwell reports it, 'who forgot themselves'. As we
know from the conversation at Norton's supper-party, this exclusion of some members from the Queen's thanks was taken
to heart. It was evidently meant to include Norton and his
principal supporters for their behaviour over the bill against
seditious words; it was probably directed also at intemperate
speeches on religion and certainly at Paul Wentworth's action
about a fast: generally, it suggests that there was more indis-
cipline this session than our limited evidence reveals.

The Chancellor continued: Concerning the Speaker's petition
about religion, her Majesty 'saith it needed not any such
reiteration. The House might have been satisfied with her
answer before made. It should be found she would deal effectually with her bishops therein; and if that served not, should
use her supreme authority granted to her Highness by Parliament in those causes.' He finished by conveying in the usual
felicitous words the Queen's thanks for the subsidy.[1] Thereupon, the titles of the bills were read and the royal assent given,
the Queen vetoing only one bill, and that an unimportant
measure concerning hops.

Parliament was prorogued until April 24th next — little over
a month. Thereafter, by a whole series of prorogations, often
from month to month, it was kept on call, lest some critical
event demanded a meeting. It was finally dissolved on April
19th, 1583, having lived for eleven years but functioned during
a mere twenty to twenty-one weeks, split into three sessions.[2]
It expired of old age. As a familiar if perverse friend, which had
got used to her ways and she to its, Elizabeth probably regretted
the passing. She was now old enough to be sensitive to change
and decay.

[1] Cromwell's Diary; *C.J.* i. 137.          [2] *L.J.* ii. 55-60.

# CONCLUSION

THE end of Elizabeth's long Parliament is a convenient place to halt our story. Before the next Parliament met, in the autumn of 1584, Whitgift had been made Archbishop of Canterbury and the scene set for the decisive battle with Puritanism; the problem of Mary Queen of Scots had entered on its last and tragic chapter; abroad, William the Silent had been assassinated and the day of open intervention in the Netherlands was near. The Parliament of 1584-85 is inseparably linked with its successor of 1586-87, and that belongs to the war period. Looking back, the great themes of the first half of the reign had played themselves out or were changing their character. The Anglican Church Settlement had come of age and shed its 'interimistical' appearance, while the successors of the Marian exiles were revolutionaries. Time had erased the question of the Queen's marriage: she was in her forty-eighth year when the 1581 Parliament ended. The succession remained unsettled and men were still haunted by the awful mark of interrogation it wrote across the future. It might again become a live issue. But time and luck had so far vindicated Elizabeth, and she was no longer isolated in her policy. Obscurities had deepened, perils multiplied, and there were now thoughtful people inclined to share her pragmatical approach, while others were ready to trust a leader whose instinct found irrefutable testimony in a quarter-of-a-century's success.

A major theme in our story has been religion. Rightly so. It inspired the agitations about the Queen's marriage, the succession to the throne, and Mary Queen of Scots, as well as the penal legislation against Catholics. We in our generation, though more secularly minded, are better able to understand Elizabethan times than our Victorian predecessors of the nineteenth century, to whom Catholicism and Protestantism were merely two variants of the Christian faith, and religious toleration the rational, humane axiom of political life. Ours is a revolutionary age: so was the Elizabethan. In the first half of the reign, and indeed until Mary Queen of Scots was executed, their revolution seemed in constant jeopardy. At any time the

417

powers of darkness might reconquer the land and plunge it back into the experience of Mary Tudor's reign. We have seen Members of Parliament, in speech after speech, express their thankfulness for the emancipation of November 17th, 1558 — 'the birthday of the Gospel', as it became known to Englishmen through many generations:

> Fixt in our hearts thy fame shall live;
> And maugre all the Popish spite,
> To honour thee our youth shall strive,
> And yearly celebrate this night.

These verses, written in 1679 to celebrate Queen Elizabeth's Accession Day, echo, a century and more later, the emotion that glowed in Sir Walter Mildmay's supply-speeches and inspired the orations of Elizabethan Speakers.[1]

It is not surprising that devotees of the new order wished to guarantee its permanence by eliminating the hostile forces within the community. For them the essence of the State was its creed; and since the threats to its safety came from the rival creed, their desire was to make religion a test of political loyalty, probe the conscience of suspects, and purge society, especially its influential official, legal, clerical, and teaching sections.

In such an atmosphere, those who aimed at clarifying the revolution by advancing a further stage acquired an influence disproportionate to what they might have exerted in times of less stress. Religious purists who wished to erase every mark of the beast from the Church, to propound the unadulterated simplicity of the Gospel, and to impose the Truth on everyone — enthusiasts whose number was greater than most historians have supposed — stood out as ardent patriots amidst dangers that exalted that spirit. They assumed the role of leaders and were supported by others whose zeal was perhaps more political than sectarian. Certainly, one fact emerges from our narrative with undeniable clarity: Elizabethan England, as mirrored in the House of Commons, was overwhelmingly Puritan in its sympathies.

With equal clarity it appears that the one effective restraint

---

[1] E. K. WILSON, *England's Eliza*. p. 73; C. H. FIRTH, 'The Ballad History of the . . . Later Tudors', *Trans. Royal Hist. Soc.* 3rd ser. iii. 117-18.

on this revolutionary urge was the Queen. How far the Sovereign ruled as well as reigned is one of the subtlest and most difficult problems facing the historian of this period. We know that all major decisions of policy — and innumerable minor decisions — were the personal responsibility of the Queen. We also know enough about Elizabeth I's character to realize that she was rarely perfunctory and was nobody's rubber-stamp; that mind and will entered into her decisions, and without this process of intellectual enlightenment or assurance it was difficult to obtain a decision from her. But such a generalized picture would still leave room for a predominant adviser, whose arguments as a rule prevailed with her: it would leave room for a '*Regnum Cecilianum*' — 'Cecil's Commonwealth'.

In our parliamentary history the person of the Queen is seen isolated in a unique and most significant way. On the Succession Question in 1566 she stood alone, against her Council (including Cecil) and her Parliament (including the Lords). In 1572 she withstood even more impassioned and concerted pressure and saved the life of Mary Queen of Scots: as Cecil bitterly remarked, the fault was not in 'us that are accounted inward counsellors', but in 'the highest'. On a lower plane of excitement, but apparently also against all official advice, in 1571 she vetoed the bill imposing attendance at Communion; and in 1581 procedural and other evidence leaves little or no doubt that it was her insistence that forced Lords and Commons to tone down their Draconic bill against Catholics. Had it not been for her, the broad way of English life would have been narrowed and an experiment made with what we today term the ideological State. The instances are too numerous, the whole story too consistent, to leave any doubt about the personal nature of Elizabeth I's rule.

Her constant intervention in the proceedings of Parliament is a striking feature of our tale. Any idea that the Sovereign, after opening Parliament, went into a kind of retirement, to emerge, armed with the veto, at the closing ceremony, will not fit Elizabethan times. The Queen, though indeed retired in her palace while Lords and Commons were at work, obviously kept a watchful eye on proceedings, ready to intervene at any moment with command, message, or indication that some bill or other was not to her liking and would need to be modified to secure her assent. The existence of a live veto was a practical reason for this procedure; but if we could only know the Parliaments of Henry VIII's reign in sufficient detail we might not find it surprising, nor perhaps will it seem as strange to the medievalist as to the modernist. If the Queen's interventions were beginning to arouse criticism among the Commons, it was probably the latter who, in this as in all similar matters, were thinking unhistorically.

As we can now see, the pattern of the reign was set in its first Parliament. Though there is a speculative element in our interpretation of the Religious Settlement, the evidence on which it is based goes far to establish its main lines, and further support comes from the convincing way in which it fits into subsequent events. The Vestiarian Controversy, otherwise rather puzzling, follows naturally, as do the reform agitations in Convocation and Parliament, before the Calvinists launched their Presbyterian programme. One might almost say that had some such thesis not been arguable from the evidence, it would have had to be invented to explain these later happenings. At first glance, two features may seem strange, as indeed they are remarkable, about the Parliament of 1559: that a young woman of twenty-five should have fought so obstinately for her point of view; and that the House of Commons should have been so overwhelmingly radical. Yet, as we look back from the end of our story, both are credible.

From 1559 to 1581 the conflicts and divergencies between the Queen and the House of Commons were for the most part concerned with religion or with issues involving religion. There was not a session free from collision of some sort. In the prevailing intellectual climate of the time, which wrapped the monarchy in an aura of divinity, no other subject could have evoked significant resistance. God alone surpassed His earthly image, the Prince. A higher loyalty was called into play. 'Those causes . . . be God's. The rest are all but terrene; yea, trifles in comparison', as Tristram Pistor said in 1571. On the continent this conflict of loyalties led to civil war. In Elizabethan England it found vent in Parliament, preparing the way to constitutional monarchy and parliamentary sovereignty.

The might-have-beens of history often repay reflection. If Elizabeth had married and produced children, the pattern of the reign would certainly have been changed. The Catholic menace from without, and therefore from within, would have been less serious, perhaps even negligible; the crusading or revolutionary spirit would probably soon have dissipated. Certainly those crucial parliamentary sessions of 1563 and 1566, when, taking advantage both of the youth and sex of their Queen, the Commons learnt the ineradicable lesson of defying their Sovereign, would have been completely different. Completely different would have been the problem of Mary Queen of Scots, and with it the remarkable Parliament of 1572. The reign might have been much more like that of Henry VIII, and in consequence the evolution of parliamentary government in this country — especially with no Stuart dynasty — appreciably delayed. The symbol of the Virgin Queen is more than a curiosity: it is a transcendent clue to the age.

An antiphony of Queen and Commons: so our narrative might be described. A strange, unique harmony; but essential to the phenomenal development of the House of Commons. Essential, also, was the concerted preparation behind so many of the agitations. The evidence may be speculative, yet it is constant and surely convincing. Planning came from the Marian *émigrés*, an art learnt in exile and prolonged and refined by the organizing genius of Calvinism: a 'conspiracy', as the Bishop of London so aptly described it in 1573. The Puritan divines who operated through their gentlemen-friends and patrons in the Lower House taught their generation, and through them their Stuart successors, the rudiments of parliamentary politics. The Parliament of 1559 was an astonishing initial experiment. When we reach the Parliaments of 1584-85 and 1586-87 we shall see the striking culmination of all this. The mastery of parliamentary tactics acquired by the unofficial leaders of the Commons, no less in dealing with individual bills than with the great campaigns of 1566 and 1572; their far-reaching definitions of privilege; the extreme sensitiveness of the House whenever it thought its liberties touched — by the Queen, by the Lords, or by others; the vigour of debate, straining the narrow limits of the official time-table: all these our story has made sufficiently clear.

In assessing where we stand in 1581 no better witness could be invoked than an anonymous Member who, on the eve of that session, wrote a letter of advice to a Privy-Councillor friend, also a Member of the House.[1] The background to his comments belongs to another age than that which inspired Sir Thomas More in 1523. It is even remote from November 1558. Stuart Parliaments are not far distant.

The writer begins with the reflection that by proroguing the Parliament the best way had been taken 'to have a Parliament least offensive'. 'For', wrote he, 'every dissolution driveth the next assembly to a new choice of men, who, besides the great charge to her Majesty in new fees, and trouble about new swearing and other matters of ceremony that prolong time, are commonly most adventurous and can be gladdest of long Parliaments to learn and see fashions'; whereas 'the old continuers have, among other things, learned more advisedness'.

From this introductory remark, he went on to offer advice about filling the vacant Speakership. He was opposed to following precedents from previous reigns and choosing a Privy Councillor. It would deprive the royal service of a Councillor's voice in debate and presence on committees. It might provoke a challenge in the name of liberty at the nomination, and so start off the session in a dangerous humour. Both lines of argument are striking. They could hardly have been made at a much earlier date; and the criticisms which Sir Francis Knollys did in fact provoke over the procedure at this election indicate that the writer was not misjudging his fellow-Members. He went on to name two lawyers for the office, discussing the merits of his nominees. One of them, John Popham, was selected, which may perhaps denote that our Member was a person of some weight.

Next, he suggested various devices for keeping the session short: and here, indeed, he touched the sophisticated level of adult politics. The number of private bills would have to be limited. But it must be done subtly. There must be no royal

---

[1] B.M. Harleian MS. 253, fols. 32 seqq. The MS. is a copy, among the papers of Ralph Starkey, the early seventeenth-century antiquary. It is headed, 'A Discourse . . . written by Mr. Francis Tate of the Middle Temple . . .' However, Francis Tate was not born till 1560 (cf. *D.N.B.*); so far as we know, he was not a Member of this Parliament; and, in any case, he cannot have been the person of experience and authority revealed in the letter. Perhaps Starkey got his text from Tate's antiquarian collections: hence the erroneous ascription. Other quotations from the document will be found in my *Elizabethan House of Commons*, pp. 355-6, 358, 383-4, 402, 419.

command through Speaker, or Councillor, or any other 'for choice, or admitting, or rejecting of bills'; 'for so would by and by be raised by some humorous body some question of the liberty of the House and of restraining their free consultation — perhaps offensive to her Majesty, and assuredly with long speeches to the troublesome prolonging of the session'. 'Note, sir,' — he added in parenthesis a little later on — 'that my often speaking against the course of commanding is not that I think her Majesty's subjects mislike her commandments, but because I suppose her people do love her more than they fear her, and it serveth to avoid long question of the liberty.'

Dealing with 'motions', which made for disputation — and how right he was! — he suggested that the best way to be eased of them was immediately to instruct the mover to confer with a second person and bring his motion in writing. If anyone else desires to speak on it, then join him to the other two: the more members you put on a committee, 'the longer it will be ere the matter come in again, specially if you will appoint lawyers in term time'. And to appoint the same man on many committees 'maketh the best thing neglected, and great delay in all'. As for 'matters of long argument', 'let them not be moved in the beginning or midst of the forenoon, but near toward the rising of the House': a piece of wise counsel which our narrative would bear out. He thought that in this sort of problem lay 'the great difficulty of the Speaker's whole service', whose business was to restrain 'and yet to avoid opinion of overruling or straitening the liberties of the House. Here must be the discreet interposing of committees, and such good means'.

In the Parliament of 1576 conferences with the House of Lords had caused much friction and wasted much time. Our writer devoted a paragraph to limiting these. And then he came to a crucial matter: the Queen's relations with Parliament. 'And, sir, hard messages make speeches, questions, petitions, and great delays.' The people's disposition 'to love her Majesty, being so good a one, doth so far exceed the fear of her, being a woman and so merciful, that her lovingest means doth make them most obsequious'. Leaving that hazardous hint to expand itself, he went on to suggest that his Councillor-friend, when trouble was brewing, should now and then 'secretly' summon some of the minor Members of the House and flatter them by seeking their advice, at the same time binding to himself as many as he could of the more influential Members 'by truly reporting them and defending their honest reputation with her Majesty'.

With an apology and a request to be construed 'tenderly', he went on to note that among Privy Councillors some 'be more gracious, I mean more acceptable in the House than some other[s]'. That Sir Walter Mildmay was one of the 'more gracious' we can be sure, as that Sir James Croft was one of the 'others'. Consequently, he continued, circumspection should be used in the business committed to them; and to employ too many Councillors in any one commission may now and then harm the Queen's service. A significant comment, with its flavour of early Stuart days.

'Lastly, sir, I conclude: the perfectest way to have the Parliament short and not offensive', and to have anything done that the Queen requires, 'is to cherish the tenderness and good affection between her Majesty and the House'. In such a remark there is scarcely room for 'Tudor Despotism'. Early in the letter our Member had urged 'full liberty' for the House; 'who', he added, 'in their greatest liberty will be most frankly obsequious'. While his paradox will hardly contain all our story, it enshrines a truth.

# INDEX

DATE DUE